Managing Contacts with ACT!® 2005

Covers ACT! 2005 and ACT! 2005 Premium for Workgroups

THOMSON
COURSE TECHNOLOGY
Professional ■ Trade ■ Reference

Managing Contacts with ACT!® 2005

Covers ACT! 2005 and ACT! 2005 Premium for Workgroups

Edward Kachinske and Timothy Kachinske
Foreword by Greg Head, General Manager of ACT!

SVP, Thomson Course Technology PTR: Andy Shafran

Publisher: Stacy L. Hiquet

Senior Marketing Manager: Sarah O'Donnell

Marketing Manager: Heather Hurley

Manager of Editorial Services: Heather Talbot

Senior Editor: Mark Garvey

Associate Marketing Managers: Kristin Eisenzopf and Sarah Dubois

Project Editor/Copy Editor: Estelle Manticas

Technical Reviewer: Sanford Silver

Thomson Course Technology PTR Market Coordinator: Amanda Weaver

Interior Layout Tech: William Hartman

Cover Designer: Mike Tanamachi

Indexer: Sharon Shock

Proofreader: Laura R. Gabler

ISBN: 1-59200-338-9

Library of Congress Catalog Card Number: 2004108260

Printed in the United States of America

04 05 06 07 08 BH 10 9 8 7 6 5 4 3 2 1

THOMSON

COURSE TECHNOLOGY

Professional ■ Trade ■ Reference

Thomson Course Technology PTR, a division of Thomson Course Technology
25 Thomson Place ■ Boston, MA 02210 ■ http://www.courseptr.com

For Judith

–TK

For Dana

–EK

Foreword

Long before CRM became a hot buzzword, and during a time when ACT! was really the only major contact and customer management software available, I became a diehard ACT! fanatic.

Now, after more than 18 years on the market and with more than 4 million users worldwide, ACT! is the best-selling contact- and customer-management solution. The world is full of ACT! fanatics.

In 1989, I joined Contact Software International (the original creator of ACT!) as a sales rep and traveled the country demonstrating ACT!. After a short while, I became the first product manager for ACT!. Then, in 1993, ACT! was sold to Symantec. Years later, in 2000, Pat Sullivan (the founder of Contact Software and original co-creator of ACT!) bought ACT! back, and I returned to ACT! to be the General Manager for the ACT! division, working again for Pat.

In 2001, we started developing what is now known as ACT! 2005. The new ACT! 2005 is a complete re-write and represents the largest development investment ever made in the ACT! line of products. ACT! 2005 is the first major application written entirely on the .NET platform.

We've added more than 250 major new features to ACT! 2005. In addition to those features, you'll find that we've also added thousands of minor navigation and feature enhancements. Just about every part of the ACT! interface has been overhauled to incorporate feature requests and recommendations we've received from customers over the years.

The stability of ACT! has been dramatically increased with the introduction of a Microsoft SQL Server backend database, and it's now possible to have more than 50 users and more than 100,0000 contacts in a single ACT! database. The addition of a company entity makes it possible to track both accounts and contacts. We've added a new opportunity view, and the ability to track multiple products per opportunity with customizable opportunity user fields makes the new version of ACT! an even better tool for salespeople. Synchronization, activities, groups, administration, and other popular aspects of the program have also seen major improvements in this version.

In this book, Edward and Tim Kachinske do a great job explaining ACT!'s functionality in a straightforward and easy-to-reference format. *Managing Contacts with ACT! 2005* is an essential resource for anyone looking to get the most out of ACT! 2005.

Greg Head
General Manager, ACT!
Senior Vice President, Best Software

Acknowledgments

There are many people to thank for the behind-the-scenes efforts that made this book possible.

It has truly been a pleasure working with the Premier Press and Course ILT staff. Thanks to Stacy Hiquet, Andy Shafran, and Mike Springer for believing in this project and for lending it such tremendous support.

Kudos to our great project editor, Estelle Manticas, for putting up with us and providing excellent feedback.

Special thanks to our technical editor, Sanford Silver. Sanford is a Senior Support Analyst for the ACT! product; he served as an invaluable wealth of knowledge throughout the writing process. Sanford knows more about the ACT! SDK than either of us will ever forget.

Many people on the ACT! team helped us as we learned the new version of ACT!. They are: Bob Anderson, Joe Bergera, Brad Burks, Brian Cagney, Poppy Casper, George Egan, Kyle Frankel, Donna Hacker, Greg Head, Bryon Jones, Beth Kohler, Chuck LaRosa, Dan Lever, Melissa Lorch (Quack!), Richard McMakin, Doug Meyer, Richard Nordstrom, Clifford Roberts, Lindsay Sullivan, Debra Williams, and Michaela Zwinakis.

Much of the text of this book was adapted into ACT!'s official course manuals, also published by Course Technology. Ted Cooper, the Director of Partner Programs for Best Software's Small Business Division, was instrumental in getting this deal off the ground. Thanks, Ted! We appreciate your persistence with the project.

ACT! 2005 was a complete product rewrite, and many parts of the user interface changed with each beta update. Thanks to Paul Selby, we were always working with the latest beta build. Every few weeks, Paul uploaded a new version of the software for us, and without his help, we would have outdated screenshots and incorrect instructions in this book.

We will be forever indebted to Paul Burke and Rick Cannon for laying the groundwork that made this book and so many other things possible. Hopefully we didn't violate too many of your ten rules in this book, but if we did, get your rubber stamp ready!

About the Author

Edward and **Tim Kachinske** are longtime ACT! fanatics and recognized leaders in the ACT! and sales automation industries. They are the principal partners in Innovative Solutions, a platinum-level ACT! consulting and training company based in the DC/Baltimore area. Both Edward and Tim are ACT! Certified Consultants and ACT! Premier Trainers.

Just after selling ACT! to Interact Commerce Corporation in May 2000, Symantec (the former owner of ACT!) turned to Innovative Solutions to train their sales staff and set up ACT! synchronization for their corporate licensing sales group.

In 2002 and 2003, Innovative Solutions was ranked in the top one percent of ACT! resellers by Best Software, the makers of ACT!. ACT! selected Edward to teach a train-the-trainer class at the 2001 Annual ACT! Certified Consultant's conference. In 2002, Best Software chose Innovative Solutions to co-host the Mid-Atlantic ACT! 6.0 product-launch event. In 1999, Edward co-authored the textbook used in the ACT! Certified Consultant training class. Edward sits on both the ACT! and ACT! for Web Partner Advisory Councils.

Together, Edward and Tim have written a total of 32 ACT! course manuals covering versions 3, 4, 2000, 6, and 2005. Their ACT! 6.0 course manuals were ranked the best selling ACT! add-on product in any category by the ACT! Add-On Store. They are co-authors of the official ACT! 2005 course manuals, also published by Course ILT.

Edward and Tim are co-Editors-in-Chief of *ACT! Advanced eNews*, a quarterly newsletter published by Best Software. The PDF newsletter covers key topics for ACT! power-users and workgroup administrators. Tim writes the monthly advice column, "Ask Tim," for both *ACT! Advanced eNews* and *ACT! Extra*, the official ACT! print newsletter.

Edward freaks out when the ground under him isn't paved, but Tim is quite content to spend the whole day fishing without so much as a nibble. Tim is the Fishing Editor of *American Scouting Digest*, the largest circulation-independent scouting magazine.

Contents at a Glance

Contents

Chapter 20 Database Creation and Design 253

Introduction

Rarely do we come across someone who will admit to reading a computer book from beginning to end. Chances are good that you won't take this book to the beach, so when we set out to write this book, we designed it to be a reference manual, not a novel. You won't find long paragraphs of information in this book. You won't find multiple explanations of the same topic. And you won't ever have to sift through a mountain of words to get to what you're looking for.

This book is divided into chapters, and each chapter is divided into sections. Within each section, you'll find a task. Each page in this book covers a single task, and the tasks make up the bulk of the book. The task begins with a small introductory paragraph, followed by simple, step-by-step instructions for accomplishing the task.

What Is ACT!?

ACT! is a contact manager—a database, letter writer, e-mail tool, activity scheduler, notepad, report writer, Internet research tool, and more. All of this functionality is combined into one product, with one goal in mind: When you make contact with someone, you will be able to initiate that contact from within ACT!.

When you need to record information for a contact, you can do so using ACT!'s Fields or Notes features. When you write a contact a letter, you can initiate the letter from within ACT! and the letter will be sent into Microsoft Word. When you want to send an e-mail to a group of contacts, you can perform that mass e-mail merge in ACT! and each e-mail will be sent through ACT!'s built-in e-mail client, Outlook, Outlook Express, or one of the supported e-mail systems. When you schedule an activity with a contact, you can schedule that activity on the ACT! calendar.

ACT! will make it easier to develop your business relationships. Whenever you use ACT! to contact someone, a history of the event will be created in your contact's record. At the end of the day, you'll have a list of every communication you (and your colleagues, if you're using a networked version) have had with your vendors, customers, partners, and friends.

ACT! created the contact management category of software, and it has held the dominant position in the market for the last 18 years. With more than 75 percent market share in the small office contact management category, ACT! has over four million registered users. (And that's just the people who paid for the software!)

The History of ACT!

Back in the mid-1980s, when floppy disks were larger than your present-day laptop, Pat Sullivan and Mike Muhney developed the first version of ACT!. Pat and Mike were salespeople, and they recognized that none of the programs on the market were really geared toward salespeople—that was, until ACT! was introduced in 1986.

ACT! actually got its start as a series of macros in Lotus Symphony. ACT! originally stood for *Activity Control Technology*, but the marketing folks at ACT! didn't push the full name. Just before ACT! 2.0 for DOS was released, the name was changed to *Automated Contact Tracking*. Today, ACT! doesn't stand for anything. It's just ACT!.

Pat and Mike built up their company, Contact Software International, and just before ACT! 2.0 for Windows was released, they sold ACT! to Symantec. Symantec developed ACT! Versions 2.0, 3.0, 4.0, and 2000 (5.0).

After his non-compete contract with Symantec expired, Pat opened the doors at a new software company, SalesLogix. SalesLogix, a sales database system geared toward mid-market customers, was in many ways similar to ACT!. For customers whose databases had outgrown ACT!, SalesLogix was a great fit.

By 1999, SalesLogix was the CRM leader in the mid-market category. In fact, SalesLogix was doing so well that Pat bought ACT! back from Symantec for $100 million. The new company, Interact Commerce Corporation, started development of Mercury, the code name for what became ACT! 2005.

Today, ACT! is part of Best Software, the makers of MAS 90, Peachtree, Timeslips, ACCPAC, Timberline, and about 30 other products.

Contacting Best Software

Best Software, the makers of ACT!, offer fee-based technical support plans. Although they offer a per-call option, it is almost always a better value to purchase one of the ACT! Advantage unlimited support plans. In addition to the fee-based support options, most questions can be answered by searching ACT!'s free Knowledge Base.

If you need to get in touch with someone about ACT!, try these useful phone numbers and Web sites:

- ACT! Technical Support: 800-992-4564
- ACT! Customer Service: 877-386-8083
- Single Box Sales: 877-501-4496

- Corporate Licensing Sales: 888-855-5222
- Support Web Site: support.act.com
- Free Knowledge Base: http://www.act.com/search

ACT! Advanced eNews

Best Software publishes a free quarterly publication for advanced users and workgroup administrators. If you're an ACT! fanatic, you should definitely sign up for it.(And we're not just saying that because we're the editors!)

To get your free subscription to the *ACT! Advanced eNews*, go to http://www.act.com/advancedenews.

Chapter 1
New Features

ACT! 2005 is the most advanced, most feature-filled, and most impressive upgrade in the history of the ACT! line of products. The new product is a complete re-write that leverages the Microsoft SQL Server and .NET technologies.

When ACT! 6.0 was released, the product boasted seven major new features and a handful of small user interface improvements. ACT! 2005, however, includes more than 200 major new features. In fact, just about every component of the product has been overhauled to include expanded functionality and greater stability.

In this chapter, you'll learn about the major new features of ACT! 2005 that make the upgrade so compelling. This list just contains major new features, but as you begin to use the product, you'll notice that many more user interface enhancements have been made to the product as well.

One of the biggest changes in ACT! is the division of the product into two separate products: ACT! 2005 Standard Edition and ACT! 2005 Premium Edition. In this chapter, the parenthetical (Premium) indicates that the feature is only available in the Premium Edition.

Stability

The Microsoft SQL Server backend database for ACT! 2005 Premium (and MSDE backend for ACT! 2005 Standard) has made the product much more stable in a large group or large database environment. In previous versions of ACT!, it was difficult—if not impossible—to have more than 30,000 contacts in a database. In ACT! 2005, you can have upwards of 100,000 contacts. (Of course, you must have sufficient hardware to support such a large database.)

- **SQL backend.** The Microsoft SQL Server backend database provides a much more stable database environment. (Premium)
- **MSDE backend.** Microsoft SQL Desktop Edition (MSDE) backend provides extra stability for single users and workgroups of ten or fewer users.
- **.NET platform.** ACT! 2005 was written completely on the .NET platform.
- **Capacity for more users.** Scalable database allows 100 users or more.
- **Capacity for more contacts.** With sufficient hardware, it's possible to have databases of 100,000 contacts or more.
- **Open over VPN.** You can now open an ACT! database over VPN without corrupting your database. (A broadband Internet connection is required.)

Security

ACT! 2005 now includes five user access levels and record-level security; this is great news for workgroup users. You can now set up teams within your database and restrict contact access to specific users or teams. With previous versions of ACT!, the quasi-dBase database backend allowed users to open your database files in Microsoft Excel, making it possible for non-login users to gain access to the ACT! database. With the new SQL backend, this is no longer possible.

- **Private data**. Notes, histories, activities, and opportunities can now be made private for any user in the database.
- **Limit contact access**. You can now limit contact access to specific users or teams of users. If you limit access to a specific contact, only users with appropriate access will be able to see the contact when they log into the database. (Premium)
- **Manager security level**. This new security level gives the user access to all data in the database, but the user does not have appropriate rights to manage users or perform database maintenance. The manager users will be able to access all public data in the database. (If another user has limited the access of a contact to a specific set of users or teams, then all managers will see the contact and related data—even if the manager has not been specifically granted access to that contact by the original user.)
- **Restricted security level.** Restricted users have full read/write access to all contacts for whom the user is the record manager. Restricted users can add new contacts to the database, but the restricted user cannot delete any data.
- **Shared file system**. You now have the ability to store files inside the database system. These shared files (documents, templates, layouts, and so on) will synchronize to remote users.
- **Handheld security**. The administrator of the database can now specify whether or not specific users can synchronize their data with a handheld device.
- **Automatic updates**. If a new build of ACT! becomes available, the program will notify you automatically. Updates to the SQL backend are delivered through the ACT! update.

Contact Management

Many general enhancements have been made to the data input and general navigation features of ACT! 2005. The duplicate matching and consolidating features have been greatly expanded, and many small contact management features—such as the ability to select multiple items from a drop-down field—have been added to the program.

- **Multi-select dropdowns.** In Act! 2005, you can select multiple items from a drop-down list.
- **Export list views to Excel.** In the Opportunities and Contact List view, export all of the items in the list view to Excel with one click of the mouse.
- **Update salutations.** You now have the ability to update the salutation for the current contact, the current lookup, or the entire database.
- **Scan for duplicates.** On the fly, and without locking the database, you can now specify the duplicate matching fields and perform a scan for duplicates.
- **Accurate edit date.** In previous versions, inserting a note for a contact would not update the Edit Date field. In ACT! 2005, any change made to the contact will accurately update the Edit Date field.
- **Consolidate duplicates.** Copy or move field, note, history, sales, and other information from one contact to another with the wizard-driven Duplicate Consolidation feature.
- **Copy/swap/replace field values.** The copy, swap, and replace fields functionality has been redesigned to make it easier to mass update field data for the contacts in your current lookup.
- **Sort.** When sorting contacts in Edit | Sort, you now have the option to sort in either ascending or descending order by any of the three sorting fields.
- **Tab improvements.** Tabs are now listed at the top part of the bottom pane in the Contact view. This allows you to have more custom tabs with a smaller computer monitor. Also, the Notes/History tab has been separated into two tabs—one for notes and the other containing histories.

Word Processor

The ACT! Word Processor has been completely revamped to include expanded HTML table and image functionality. If you've been using the ACT! Word Processor to create your e-mail templates, you'll love the new functionality.

- **Support for tables.** The new support for tables allows you to create better-looking e-mail templates.
- **Improved spell check.** The new spell check engine has been reworked. In previous versions, many correctly spelled words, like contractions, were incorrectly flagged. (The spell check actually works now!)
- **Save formats.** You can now save ACT! Word Processor documents in Microsoft Word or HTML format.
- **Improved envelope and label templates.** The new envelope and label designer allows you to be much more precise with the field placeholder spacing. You can now get an extra line of text on an Avery 5160 label.
- **Consistent e-mail and letter templates.** ACT! 2005 has abolished the Graphical Mail Template (.gmt) file format. Now, e-mail and letter templates share the same format.
- **Pre-created letter templates.** ACT! now ships with a set of pre-created letters that you can customize to create your own library of templates.

Lookups and Queries

With the new SQL backend database, lookups on large databases can be performed much more quickly in the new version of Act! The Keyword Search feature has been redesigned to provide a completely graphical interface. Also, many of the lookup quirks from previous versions of ACT! (such as the inability to narrow a lookup by e-mail address) have been addressed.

- **Save a lookup as a group or company.** After performing a lookup, you can create a dynamic group or company based on the lookup. So, for example, if you lookup everyone in Alabama and then save the lookup as a group, then any Alabama contact added to the database will automatically become a member of this lookup-based group.
- **Create a query-based synchronization set.** This feature is quite useful if you want a remote user to only be able to see a certain set of data.
- **Greater than/less than.** Whenever you perform a lookup on a date or numeric field, you'll have the ability to search for values greater than or less than a specific number or date.

- **Lookup by contact name**. There's now a "Contact" option on the Lookup menu that lets you search for a contact by his or her full name.
- **Search any field**. In the Lookup | Other Fields area, you'll be able to search on any field in the database. In previous versions, some system fields – like the Create Date and Edit Date—were only searchable in the Lookup | By Example area.
- **Lookup By Example**. The Lookup By Example screen has been redesigned. In previous versions, it looked identical to the new contact screen, but now it's more obvious that you're performing a lookup after clicking Lookup | By Example.
- **Sticky lookups**. ACT! now remembers the last five lookups you performed on a specific field.
- **Right-click lookups**. Right-click inside any field in the Contact view and click to perform a lookup on that field.
- **Exclude private**. In the Lookup dialog box, you have the option of excluding private records from a lookup. This is especially useful if you use the database for both personal and business data.
- **Lookup any**. Many fields—like the address and city fields—now give the option to search for any address or any city.

Groups

Groups in ACT! 2005 are much more powerful. The main new group feature is the ability to create self-updating dynamic groups. Other additional functionality, like the ability to add 15 levels of subgroups, has also been added.

- **Dynamic (self-updating) groups**. Query-based membership rules now automatically add and remove contacts. In previous versions, you could get some of this functionality by manually running group membership rules, but the rules were not dynamic and the group rules would not remove a contact from a group.
- **15 levels of subgroups**. In previous versions, you could only have one level of subgroups. Now, any group can have 15 levels.
- **Save a lookup**. You can save a lookup as a dynamically-updating group.
- **Group List view**. In the Group List view, you can view critical data for your groups and subgroups in a spreadsheet-like format.
- **Associate with multiple groups**. Activities, notes, histories, and opportunities can now be associated with multiple groups.

Companies

ACT! 2005 now includes a company entity. If you've been using the Groups feature in a previous version of ACT! to manage companies, you can easily convert companies to groups in the new version.

- **Companies as a database entity**. ACT! now has a company-level record. You can track contacts and information at the company or account level.
- **Auto-updating key fields**. You can update key company fields—such as the address fields—and automatically push the data down to individual contacts in the company.
- **Automatically create companies**. As you add new contacts to the database, you can set the program to automatically create company records. Alternatively, you can manually link contacts with company records.
- **Query-based companies**. Set up a query-based membership rule to automatically update the list of contacts associated with a company.
- **Divisions**. Within each company record, add up to 15 divisions.
- **Convert groups to companies**. If you've been using Groups to track companies or accounts, you can convert your existing groups to company records.

Calendars

The ACT! 2005 calendar has been streamlined and redesigned. If you've used the calendar in Microsoft Outlook, you'll notice that many of the new features in the ACT! calendar—such as the ability to check availability and send meeting invitations—are similar to those found in Outlook.

- **New look and feel**. The entire calendar interface has been redesigned to give it a more modern, streamlined look.
- **Expandability**. In previous versions of ACT!, the program was notorious for slowing down considerably when many activities were added to the system. This version, because of the SQL backend database, is able to handle many more activities without slowing down the system.
- **Calendar security**. You now have the ability to specify the specific users in the database who are allowed to schedule, reschedule, or delete activities on your calendar.

- **Improved Outlook activity integration.** Activities sent from ACT! to Outlook are no longer read-only. You can update your ACT! activities in Outlook and vice-versa. Updates occur automatically in the background.
- **Manage resources.** You can now link resources—such as conference rooms, projectors, or computer equipment—with activities in the database. Conflict checking is built into this feature, so you'll never double-book your conference room. (Premium)
- **Filter private activities.** You can now select to show or hide private activities in any of the calendar views.
- **Work week and today calendar views.** These additional views make it easier to show specific information on your calendar.
- **Quick print.** Right-click on any calendar and select Quick Print to print the calendar.
- **New schedule menu.** This new menu consolidates all of the scheduling features in one centralized spot.
- **Locations.** You can now schedule an activity for a specific location. If you use this feature, you'll be able to configure a report at the end of the year to show all of your activity sorted by location.

Activities

In ACT! 2005, you now have many more options when adding an activity to your calendar. You now have the ability to add custom activity types and priority levels, and if you're not sure about another user's availability, you can check it right within the Schedule Activity dialog box.

- **Custom activity types.** Out of the box, ACT! includes three extra activity types: vacations, support tickets, and personal activities. If you have other activity types you'd like to track, your administrator can add them to the database.
- **Custom history types.** Custom history types are created for each type of activity.
- **Custom priority types.** In the past, ACT! has only allowed high-, medium-, and low-priority activities. The new version allows you to customize the types of priorities for the activities you schedule.

- **Activity triggers**. Since Version 3, you've been able to add triggers to fields in the database, but you can now have triggers for activities as well. Triggers are events or programs that are executed after an activity is cleared.
- **Check availability**. Check the availability of your users or resources before scheduling an activity. (Premium)
- **Meeting invitations.** When scheduling activities for other users in the database, you can send an invitation that the user will be able to accept or decline.
- **RTF activity details.** Add Rich Text Format (RTF) formatting—such as bolded text—to any activity's details.
- **Longer Regarding field**. In previous versions of ACT!, the Regarding field for any activity was limited to 254 characters. Now, you can keep typing in this field until your fingers get tired.
- **End Time/End Date fields.** When you schedule an activity in the database, you can now specify a start time, end time, start date, and end date. This makes it much easier to schedule activities—such as conferences—that span multiple days.
- **Global events**. Scheduling a global event puts this timeless activity on everyone's calendar.
- **Schedule activities from annual events**. In the Lookup | Annual Events area, you can automatically schedule an activity for all resulting contacts.

Activity Series

Previous versions of ACT! included an activity series feature, but once the activities were scheduled on the calendar, they lacked any sort of linking. Now, when you reschedule one of the activities that is part of a series, ACT! will prompt you to reschedule all other activities in the series.

- **Linked activities.** Activities scheduled as the result of an activity series are now linked with each other. So, when one is rescheduled or deleted, the user has the option to automatically update all activities in the series.
- **Schedule with specific users.** In any activity series, you can now schedule specific activities with different users in the database.
- **Enhanced interface.** The new activity series interface makes it easier to schedule an activity series with contacts in the database.

E-mail Merging

If you've ever tried to send an e-mail to many contacts using ACT!'s mass e-mailing features, you'll be impressed with ACT! 2005's blazingly fast e-mail functionality. It's now possible to send thousands of mass template-based e-mails in just a couple of minutes. Built-in e-mail validation also helps you isolate contacts without a valid e-mail address.

- **Performance**. E-mail merging is slightly faster in the new version of Act!. It's now possible to send a mass e-mail to a thousand contacts in a minute or two. Network users will especially notice the speed increase.
- **E-mail validation**. If you attempt to send an e-mail merge to a group of contacts that have some incomplete e-mail data, you'll have the option of omitting the missing e-mail addresses from the merge. ACT! will also give you the option to create a lookup of contacts that did not receive the e-mail.
- **E-mail templates**. You can now use regular document templates as mass e-mail templates.
- **Company e-mail merge**. In the Mail Merge Wizard, you now have the option to send the mass e-mail to all contacts in a specific company.

E-mail

The E-mail interface in ACT! has been updated to include useful features such as an advanced keyword search and the ability to send template-based e-mails.

- **Multiple e-mail fields**. Maintain multiple e-mail address fields for each contact in your database.
- **Advanced search**. In the ACT! interface, you can now perform keyword searches through your e-mails.
- **Create from template**. You now have the option to create a new template-based e-mail from within the ACT! E-mail interface.
- **Outlook 2003 compatibility**. A hotfix made ACT! 6.0 work with Outlook 2003 for most users, but Outlook 2003 integration was not officially supported in ACT! 6.0. If you call ACT! technical support with an Outlook 2003 issue, they'll help you now.

Secondary Contacts

Remember those 2nd Contact and 3rd Contact fields in previous versions of ACT!? They've been replaced with the Secondary Contacts tab. This tab lets you add an unlimited number of secondary contacts (assistants, business partners, employees, and so on) for any main contact. If you start dealing regularly with a secondary contact, you'll have the option to promote that contact to main contact status.

- **Unlimited secondary contacts**. You can now add an unlimited number of secondary contacts.
- **Promote existing secondary contacts**. In the Database Conversion Wizard, you'll be able to use your existing secondary contact fields (from an ACT! 3-6 database) to ACT!'s new secondary contact format.

Document Management

If you have key documents—such as proposals, quotes, or letters—that you'd like associated with a contact, you can now link the documents in the Documents tab. This tab replaces ACT! 6.0's Library tab and allows for storage of an unlimited number of documents per contact.

- **Documents tab**. The new Documents tab replaces the Library tab in ACT! 6.0. You can't edit documents within the Documents tab the way you could in the Library tab, but you can now add an unlimited number of documents to the tab.
- **Increased stability**. The Documents tab is much more stable than the ACT! 6.0 Library tab.
- **Synchronize documents**. If the documents are kept within your supplemental files folder, then the documents will synchronize to remote users.
- **Network support**. In ACT! 6, if you shared your Netlinks folder on a network drive to share Internet Services attachments, then the Library tab ceased to work. Now, the Documents tab will function in a fully-networked environment.
- **Support for all file types**. Unlike ACT! 6.0's Library tab, the Documents tab in ACT! 2005 lets you attach any file type to a contact.

Opportunity Management

As a business owner or sales manager, you know it's always critical to have a good understanding of your sales pipeline. The sales functionality in previous versions of ACT! was pretty weak, but this new version includes a robust, complete opportunity management system.

- **Opportunity List view.** The new Opportunity List view lets you slice and dice all of your sales data in one centralized place.
- **Extensive filtering capabilities.** In the Opportunity List view, you can filter the list of opportunities to show just the data you want. If you need to bring up a list of all contacts in the database managed by a specific sales rep and due to close this week with an estimated worth of more than $500, you can now easily do this in the Opportunity List view.
- **Export opportunity list to Excel.** With a single click of the mouse, you can now export all of the data (subject to the filter you've set) in the Opportunity List view to Microsoft Excel.
- **Shared product list.** Maintain a centralized (controlled by the administrator of the database) list of products, part numbers, and MSRPs.
- **Multiple sales processes.** If you sell multiple types of products, and if each product line requires a different sales process, you can now maintain these processes in ACT!. Each sales process has its own individual sales stages.
- **Enhanced reporting.** More than 20 new sales reports have been added to the product to help you better slice and dice your data. Included in the new reports is an Opportunity Summary report that includes all history entries that have been associated with the opportunity.
- **Opportunity lookups.** Search for specific opportunities based on specific opportunity fields—such as the product, estimated cost, close date, or any of the customizable user fields.
- **Create lookup.** You can now create a lookup of all contacts with an open opportunity showing in the Opportunity List view. This feature is similar to the one in the Contact List view in previous versions.
- **Add/narrow opportunity lookups.** You can now add to or narrow any opportunity lookup.
- **Calculated totals.** At the bottom of the Opportunities view, view totals for the opportunities (subject to the filter you've set).

Opportunity Dialog Box

When you're entering a new opportunity into the database, you'll notice that you can now track a lot more information on each sale. Support for multiple products, customizable user fields, built-in quoting, and support for a centralized product list are just a few of the new features you'll find in the Opportunity dialog box.

- **Multiple products**. In previous versions of ACT!, any opportunity could only contain a single product. In ACT! 2005, you can add an unlimited number of products to any opportunity.
- **Custom user fields**. If you need to track additional information about your sales, you now have up to eight additional customizable user fields. If, for example, you are a home builder and need to track square footage of a potential sale, you could devote one of the user fields to track this information.
- **Built-in quoting**. With a single click, create a quote for any opportunity in the database. Quotes are written in to Microsoft Word with an embedded Excel spreadsheet.
- **Automatic pricing**. As you select one or more products for an opportunity, ACT! automatically populates the amount field for the product based on the MSRP for the product in the central list. At your discretion, you can discount by a percentage or a specific amount for any product. (Or, if you're lucky, you could charge extra!)
- **Decimal support**. If you've used the Opportunity feature in previous versions of ACT!, you might have noticed that ACT! didn't support decimals in the Unit field. This issue has been fixed in ACT! 2005 and is now especially useful for users who are selling a service. If you need to sell 4.5 hours of consulting time, you can now do so with ACT!.
- **Auto-updating probability**. You can now link the sales stage with the probability field within the Opportunity dialog box. You could, for example, set ACT! to automatically change all of the opportunities at a final/closing sales stage to have a probability of 90 percent.
- **Private opportunities**. You can now make opportunities private. Other users won't be able to see opportunities you've set as private.
- **Create history option**. You can flag fields within the Opportunities area to generate a history whenever the value in a field is changed. By default, histories are created whenever the estimated Close Date, Status, and Sales Stage fields are changed. Also, the History entry (in the contact's History tab) will indicate both the previous and the new field values.

- **Create follow-ups.** When entering a new opportunity, you have the option to schedule follow-ups for the contact associated with the opportunity.
- **Associate with groups/companies.** You can now associate any single opportunity with multiple groups or companies.
- **Additional results.** Now, you can change the status of any opportunity to: Closed Won, Closed Lost, Open, or Inactive.
- **Resizable dialog box.** You can now resize the Opportunity dialog box to see all of your information without scrolling.

Interface Customization

The graphical user interface in ACT! 2005 has been streamlined to give it a more modern look. But the program isn't just a pretty face! Best Software has added lots of additional options for customizing the interface.

- **Ability to deploy.** You can now mass-deploy menu and toolbar customization for all of your users.
- **Long and short menus.** In the menu and toolbar customization area, you now have the option to show either long or short menus on your menu bar. Short menus only show items that you frequently use.
- **Show shortcut keys.** You now have the option to show keyboard shortcut key tooltips when hovering your mouse over a toolbar item.
- **View bar.** You can now add, remove, and delete items from the View bar on the left side of the ACT! interface.

Synchronization

Good news! Synchronization has been completely overhauled, and the process is now very robust.

- **Redesigned sync architecture.** The new sync architecture maintains a direct relationship between the main database and remote database.
- **IP synchronization.** For users on the same network or VPN, you can establish a direct IP connection with the server for synchronization.
- **HTTP synchronization.** If you don't have a VPN set up, you can set up your synchronization server to listen for incoming sync requests from any Web user. (For security reasons, only requests sent by databases created from your master database will be completed.)
- **Consolidated sync panel.** All synchronization setup features have been consolidated into one area.

- **No more sync packets.** If you've synchronized ACT! databases in previous versions, you'll be happy to know that you won't have to worry about whether or not your remote users correctly apply synchronization updates in ACT! 2005.
- **Automatic background synchronization.** This new feature lets you set a specific time for ACT! to automatically sync with the master database.
- **Query-based sync.** Specify the contacts that each sync user should receive by creating a query. Let's say that you set up a synchronization query to send all contacts who have a Record Manager of "John Smith" to John Smith's remote database. If you add a new contact to the database, and if you make John Smith the Record Manager, John will automatically get the contact the next time he synchronizes.
- **Optional subscription list.** You can specify a user's synchronization set by creating a query, but you can also specify to send specific other contacts to any remote users.
- **Simple territory realignment.** Territory realignment has always been a major pain with ACT!, but the new version makes it almost effortless. If you change a user's synchronization query, the user will automatically get a new set of contacts and any non-matching contacts will be automatically removed from the database. (They'll remain in the master database, and you'll be able to reassign them to another user.)
- **Database expiration.** If your remote users aren't synchronizing every X number of days, then you can set the remote databases to expire and become unsynchronizable with the main database.
- **Shared file system synchronizes.** The supplemental file system of documents, layouts, reports, queries, and so on will synchronize with your remote users.
- **New Synchronization log.** The Synchronization log for all users is now located in the Synchronization Panel instead of the sync user's Notes/History tab.
- **Sync lookups.** You can now pinpoint the data sent through a synchronization by user and time frame. Wondering what a specific user synchronized up to you last week? Two weeks ago? With the new sync lookup capabilities, it's easy to find out.
- **Sync service.** You can run the ACT! synchronization as a service on your server. Without having an actively-logged in user on the server console, ACT! will listen for and process remote sync requests.

Field Structure

ACT! 2005 offers support for many new field types, including check mark fields, picture fields, and memo fields. Other improvements, like the ability to customize opportunity fields and share common drop-down items, have also been added.

- **Customize company and opportunity fields**. In addition to contact and group fields, you can now add custom fields for companies and opportunities. You're limited to adding eight opportunity fields, but you can add as many company fields as you like.
- **Yes/no fields**. These fields show up as check mark fields on the layout.
- **Address fields**. Because addresses have their own field type in ACT! 2005, you have the ability to perform a lookup on all address fields in the database at once.
- **Picture fields**. After adding a picture field to the layout, click anywhere inside the picture field to browse and select a graphic file. Once you've selected a picture to display in the picture field, it will always display for that contact's record.
- **Memo fields**. Memo fields are similar to character fields, but you can add text of unlimited length into a memo field. Hard returns are also allowed in memo fields.
- **Common drop-downs**. You can configure a drop-down list in the Define Fields area and share the field among multiple fields.
- **Generate history**. For any field that has the Generate History attribute, the history created when the value inside the field changes will now include both the Before and After values.
- **Modify Trigger**. Previous versions have had field entry and field exit triggers, but ACT! 2005 adds a new trigger type. The Modify Trigger will launch a program or script only when data is entered into a field.
- **Field properties**. In the Define Fields area, you'll be able to view additional information for a field, such as the date the field was created and whether or not the field is a system field.
- **Support for middle names**. Click the button to the right of the Contact field, and you'll have the option to specify your contact's first and last name. In ACT! 2005, you can also specify the contact's middle name.

Layout Design

If you've used previous versions of the ACT! layout designer, you'll love how easy it is to create a good looking layout with equally spaced and aligned fields in this version. Because layouts can synchronize to remote users, you'll be able to share your layout masterpiece with others!

- **Layouts synchronize.** If you make a change to a layout, you can set ACT! to synchronize the changes down to your remote users.
- **Create new fields.** You can now create new fields without leaving the Layout Designer.
- **Hide system tabs.** If you're not using one of the system tabs, you can now remove it in the Layout Editor. This is especially useful for ACT! users who aren't selling a product and want to remove the Opportunities tab.
- **Property grid.** The new Property Grid shows all of the attributes for the currently-highlighted object.
- **Easier interface.** The new Layout Designer makes it a lot easier to perform simple tasks, such as align all of your fields.
- **Equal spacing.** After selecting multiple items on a layout, you can now automatically adjust the items so they're equally spaced.

Internet Services

In previous versions of ACT!, the Internet Services view has always opened a Web browser within the ACT! interface. Now, Internet Services integrates directly with Internet Explorer.

- **Internet Services.** This feature now opens in Internet Explorer, instead of the built-in Internet browser that previous versions used.
- **Driving directions.** In ACT! 5, you could get Yahoo! driving directions from within ACT!. The functionality was taken out in ACT! 6, but it's back in ACT! 2005 with the built-in links to MapQuest.

Reports

A few new features have been added to the Reports interface in ACT! 2005, but the main general functionality is the same as it has been in previous versions of ACT!. The interface has been redesigned, however, to give it the same look and feel found in the Layout Editor.

- **Redesigned interface.** The entire Report Designer has been redone to provide a smoother, less buggy user experience.
- **Output formats.** Reports can now be set to output to either HTML or PDF formats.
- **Support for subreports.** You can now embed subreports into any report.
- **Automatic spacing.** You can now highlight multiple fields in the Report Designer and automatically equally space them horizontally or vertically.
- **Add any data to a report.** You can now incorporate activity, note, history, and opportunity data into any single report. When running the report, each type of data can be filtered.
- **Support for additional field types.** ACT!'s new field types—such as the picture fields and memo fields—can now be included in reports.
- **Auto hiding toolbox.** The toolbox (the tool palette in previous versions) can be set to automatically hide to give you more room when designing a report.
- **Properties window.** The new Properties window will show and allow editing of any object in a report or subreport.

Database Maintenance

In previous versions of ACT!, it was very important to perform periodic maintenance of your database. The new SQL database that ACT! uses does not require as much hands-on maintenance.

- **No Compress and Reindex.** Because the new SQL backend database format is self-indexing, the Compress and Reindex feature is not something that you need to do on a regular basis with this database.
- **Check up and repair.** ACT! now ships with a Check Up option that will scan your database for corruption and fix problems that exist.

- **Database information**. In the Help | About area, you can now view statistical information about your database, such as the size (in megabytes) of each data table. This is important if you are using the Standard Edition with a large database because MSDE (the backend database engine for ACT! 2005 Standard Edition) has a 2-gigabyte maximum size. The Premium version (with a Microsoft SQL Server backend) does not have this limitation.

Other New Features

ACT! 2005 includes a few more helpful new features to make your life easier.

- **Streamlined look and feel**. All of the icons, menus, and toolbars have been completely overhauled to give the product a sleek, more modern look.
- **Automatic updates**. Should a new build of ACT! become available, the program will notify you automatically. (An Internet connection is required.)
- **Quick Print**. Throughout the program, you can use the Quick Print feature (usually found on the File or right-click menus) to perform a quick print screen.

Chapter 2
Installation and Conversion

Installing ACT! 2005

A successful ACT! installation is a prerequisite for a successful ACT! experience. In this chapter, you will learn how to successfully install the ACT! product. You'll learn about serialization issues, and you'll learn the process of updating to the latest ACT! build. There are two versions of ACT! 2005: a standard edition and a premium edition. Each product has a similar feature set, but standard and premium users can't share a database.

Task A Installing ACT! on a Workstation

If you are using a previous version of ACT!, you can run that version and ACT! 2005 at the same time. ACT! 2005 has its own separate file structure, so it can coexist with other versions on the same machine. The installation process is fairly straightforward, as long as you have appropriate installation rights for your computer.

To install ACT! 2005 on a workstation:

1. Insert the ACT! 2005 installation CD.
2. If the setup program does not automatically appear, open Windows Explorer and double-click the setup.exe file on the ACT! installation CD.
3. Choose the option to install ACT!. The Installation Wizard will appear.
4. Follow the on-screen instructions to install the product. Unless you have good reason to change any of the settings, accept all of the default settings in the installation.

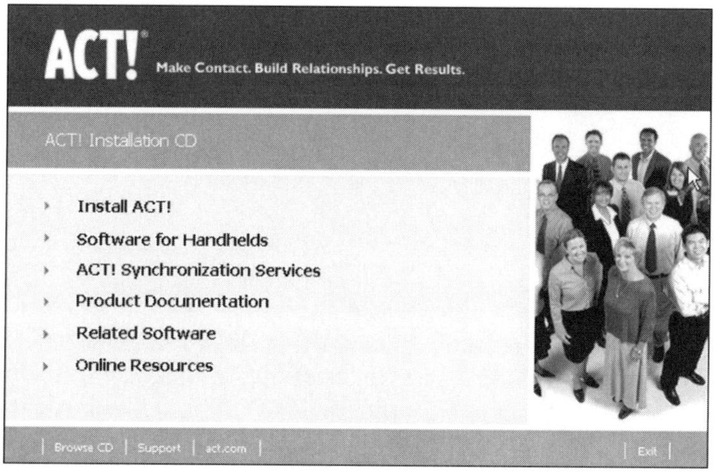

The ACT! Installation menu

Activation required

After installing ACT! 2005 on any computer, you must register and activate the product to use it past the 30-day grace period. Activating the product lets the folks at ACT! know that you've installed the product and it prevents users from using illegal serial numbers for installation.

Install for all users

One of the steps in the installation process will ask if you want to install the product for all users using your computer, or for just the currently logged-in user. Unless your system administrator advises otherwise, always choose the option to install for all users. Now in ACT! 2005, the installer automatically selects to install for all users.

Task B Updating Your Installation

From time to time, Best Software releases updates for ACT! 6.0. You'll want to ensure that all of your users have the latest update applied to their ACT! installations. There are two ways to update your ACT! installation: You can update right from within the ACT! application or you can download and run the update patch from http://www.act.com.

To install ACT! 2005 on a workstation:

1. In ACT!, click Help | ACT! Update. If an update patch for ACT! is available, a balloon will appear in the bottom-right corner of your screen.
2. Click the Download option in this balloon to download and apply the update patch.
3. Follow the on-screen instructions to apply the update patch.

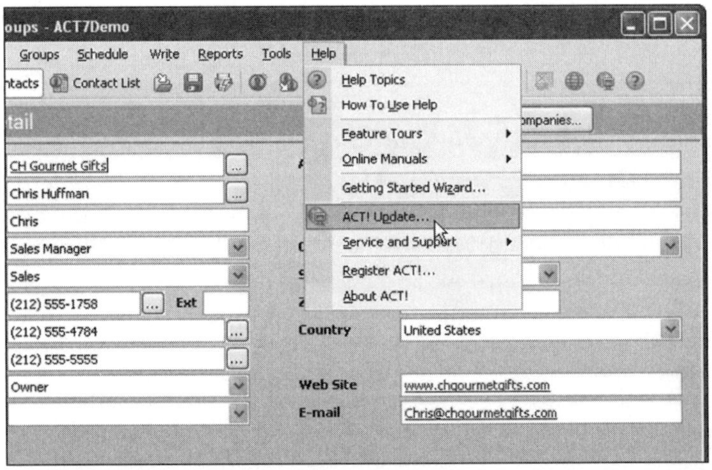

ACT! Update finds any available product updates.

Close other programs first

You should shut down all programs before updating ACT! to the latest build—especially add-on products that work with ACT!.

Connection problems?

Some cable modems and firewalls prevent ACT! from downloading updates from within the ACT! Update Wizard. If you get an error saying that ACT! can't establish a connection to the Internet, you'll have to download and apply the update patch available on http://www.act.com.

Task C Installing the ACT! Instance of Microsoft SQL Server 2000

If you have more than ten users, you'll need to install the ACT! 2005 Premium product on your server and workstations. The Premium product uses Microsoft SQL Server 2000 (instead of MSDE) as the backend database. You'll need to install the ACT! instance of Microsoft SQL Server 2000 on your server before installing ACT! on the server. The SQL Server 2000 installation is on a separate CD.

To install the ACT! instance of SQL Server:

1. Insert the ACT! 2005 installation CD #2.
2. If the setup program does not automatically appear, then open Windows Explorer and double-click the setup.exe file on the ACT! installation CD. The Installation Wizard will appear.
3. Follow the on-screen instructions to install the product. Unless you have good reason to change any of the settings, accept all of the default settings in the installation.

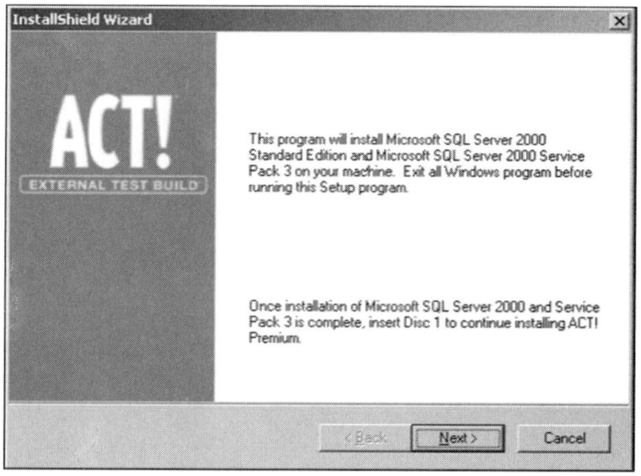

The ACT! SQL instance installation

Existing SQL users

Even if you already have Microsoft SQL Server installed on your server, you'll need to install the ACT! instance of SQL. The ACT! instance of SQL can coexist on the same machine as another SQL installation.

SQL updates

Updates and service packs to the ACT! instance of Microsoft SQL Server 2000 are delivered only through the ACT! update process.

Registration and Activation

Unlike previous versions, ACT! 2005 requires that you register and activate the product. Registering the product sends your contact information to ACT!, and product activation registers your serial number with ACT! in order to prevent unauthorized trading of serial numbers.

Task A Registering and Activating Your Copy of ACT!

When you first launch ACT! on each workstation, you'll be prompted to register and activate the product. In the registration process, you'll be prompted to enter your basic contact information and fill out a brief survey. The survey is optional, but you must enter your contact information to register the copy of ACT!.

Can I get around the registration process?

No. You must register and activate your copy of ACT! to use it past the 30-day grace period. Even corporate license users must register and activate each product at each workstation.

To register your copy of ACT!:

1. Open ACT!. If you have not yet registered ACT!, the Registration Wizard will automatically appear.
2. Select the option to register ACT! and click Next.
3. Enter your serial number. Click Next.
4. Enter your contact information in the fields provided. Click Next.
5. If you wish, you can complete the user survey. If you do not wish to complete the survey, then simply click Next through the survey screens.
6. Click Finish to register and activate ACT!.

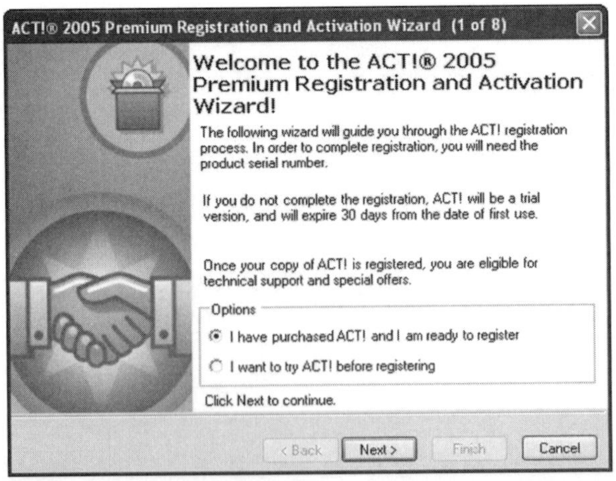

The Registration and Activation Wizard

Data Conversion

ACT! 2005 now has a SQL backend database. There are many advantages to having a more robust backend for the software, but because the database structure has changed, you'll have to convert any existing databases to ACT! 2005 format.

Task A Converting an Existing ACT! Database

In the Database Conversion Wizard, ACT! will ask a series of questions that will help it convert your existing data to ACT! 2005 format. It's important that you answer each question in the Wizard carefully, or your data might not convert properly.

To convert an old ACT! database to 2005 format:

1. Back up all of your existing data.
2. In ACT!, click File | Open Database.
3. In the Files of type drop-down, select the ACT! 3 – 6 Database (*.DBF) option.
4. Browse to the ACT! 3-6 database and double-click it.
5. Click OK to confirm that you want to convert the database. The Database Conversion Wizard will appear.
6. The first screen of the Wizard is a confirmation. Click Next.
7. If you have customized any of the fields in your ACT! 3-6 database, then choose the Custom Conversion option. If not, choose the Standard Conversion. Click Next.
8. If you chose the Custom Conversion option, then follow the on-screen instructions to specify a data map for ACT! to use in the conversion process.
9. Specify a database name. When converting an ACT! 3-6 database, ACT! 2005 will actually create a new database. All of your old information will be imported into this new database. Click Next.
10. You'll have the option to convert ACT!'s supplemental files. Click Finish to complete the process.

There's no going back!

Once you convert a database to ACT! 2005 format, you cannot revert it back to a previous version of the software. Because of this, you may want to convert a sample copy of your database to ACT! 2005 format before converting your production database.

The original ACT! 3-6 database remains unchanged after the conversion process, but the new ACT! 2005 database can't revert back to ACT! 6.0 format.

Pre-ACT! 3.0 database conversions

If your computer was cryogenically frozen in the 1980s, and your database is still in ACT! 1.x or 2.x format, you'll need to convert it to ACT! 3-6 format before converting it to ACT! 2005 format. You can use the ACT! 6.0 free trial to do this.

Task B Converting Ancillary ACT! 3-6 Files

Just about all of ACT!'s file types have changed in ACT! 2005. Letter templates, e-mail templates, e-mails, reports, labels, envelopes, and ACT! Word Processor documents all have new file formats. If you've used ACT! in a previous version, it's easy to convert these supplemental files to the new ACT! 2005 format. The Conversion Wizard will attempt to convert the files for you, but if you have additional files in other folders on your system, you can convert any ACT! file from within the ACT! interface.

To convert ancillary ACT! files:

1. In ACT!, click Tools | Convert ACT! 3.0 – 6.0 Items.
2. In the resulting dialog box, select the file type you'd like to convert.
3. Click the Browse button and select the folder that contains the files you'd like to convert.
4. In the list on the left, you'll see the available files in the folder.
5. Highlight the files you'd like to convert and click the > button to add them to the list of files to be converted.
6. Click Next. ACT! will convert the files. When the process is complete, click Finish to exit the Wizard.

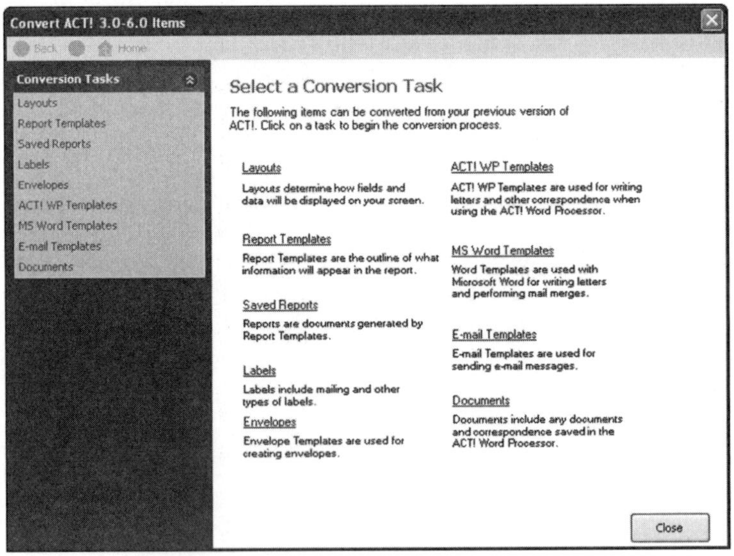

The Convert ACT! 3.0-6.0 Items Wizard

Remember the horror stories?

The last time ACT! did a major re-write to its code base was with Version 3.0. The conversion from ACT! 2 to 3 was not particularly smooth. Many file types—like templates and reports—did not convert at all. If you're a veteran ACT! user, you'll be glad to know that all database fields and ancillary files will convert from ACT! 3-6 format to ACT! 2005 format.

Opening a Database

In previous versions of ACT!, you could open a database by simply locating the .DBF file of the database and double-clicking it. ACT! 2005, however, uses Microsoft SQL as its backend, and the database files are housed differently in the new version. Each database is now connected to either MSDE or Microsoft SQL Server.

Task A Opening a Database on a Local Computer

When each ACT! database is created, a pointer to the ACT! database—a .PAD file—is created. No matter where your actual database files are located, the .PAD file can be copied anywhere on your computer. Double-clicking this .PAD will open the database.

To open a database on your local computer:

1. Open ACT!.
2. Click File | Open Database.
3. Browse to the .PAD file for your database. Double-click it.
4. If prompted, enter your username and password for the database.

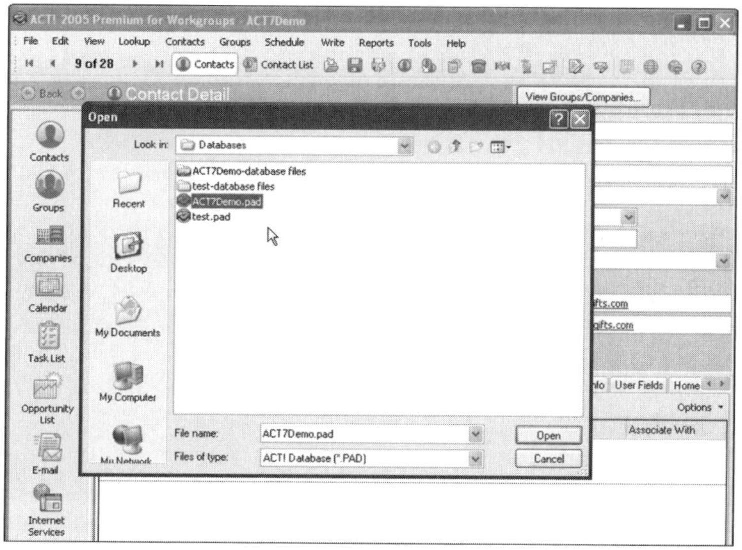

Opening a database on the local computer

Transferring a database?

If you need to move a database from one computer to another, you cannot simply copy the database files. You should back up the database on the original computer and restore it onto the new computer. Performing a backup and restore will connect the database properly with the ACT! SQL instance running on your computer. (See Chapter 19, "Database Maintenance and Administrator Tools," for information on backing up a database.)

Editing the .PAD file

You can edit the .PAD file in Notepad. Make sure you know what you're doing before trying this, though. If you change the .PAD file to point to a spot where no database exists, you may run into problems opening your database.

Task B Sharing a Database

Once you have created an ACT! database on a workstation or server, you can share that database with other network users. After setting an ACT! database to be shared with other users, simply copy the .PAD file for your database to a spot on the network accessible to other users. (See the previous task for more information on the .PAD file.)

To share a database:

1. On the server or workstation that will house the ACT! database, open the database.
2. Click Tools | Database Maintenance | Share Database.
3. Copy the .PAD file for this database to a common network drive.
4. On another networked computer, click File | Open Database from within ACT! and browse to the .PAD file to open the shared database.

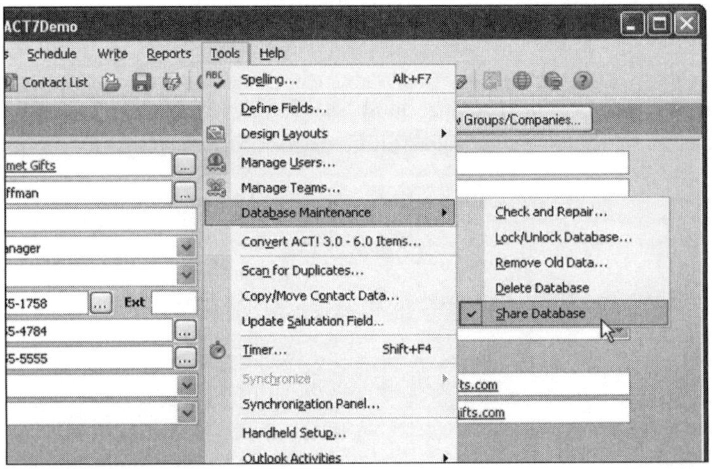

Sharing a database with other users

Sharing supplemental files

When you select to share an ACT! database, all of the supplemental files associated with the database will be shared with other network users in addition to the database files.

Sharing from a workstation

If you share a database on a Windows 2000 or XP machine, only ten concurrent users will be able to log into that database at any given time. Sharing a database from a server operating system does not have this restriction.

Chapter 3
Working with Contacts

The My Record

When you log into an ACT! database, the record that immediately appears is called your My Record. You'll want to make sure that this My Record contains accurate information about yourself. Each login user in a database has his or her own My Record.

Task A Find and Correct the My Record

Whenever you write a document in ACT!, the name and title information will be pulled from your My Record to sign the document, so it's important that your My Record information is complete and correct.

To find and correct the My Record:

1. Click Lookup | My Record. Your My Record will appear.
2. Complete all necessary fields with your personal information.

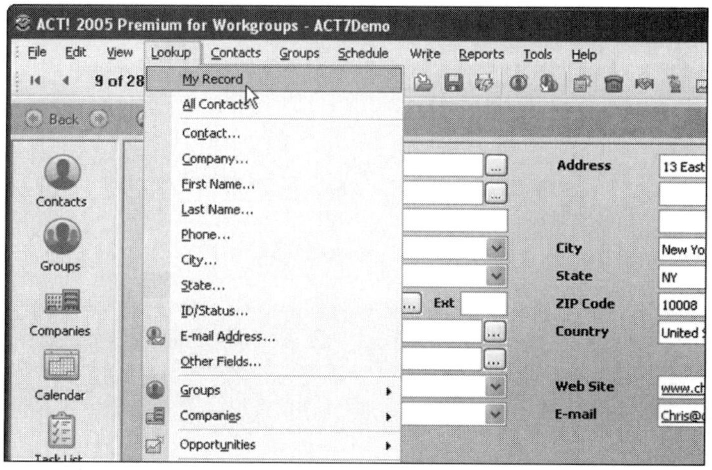

Performing a lookup of the My Record

My Records in the Contact List view

The first column in the Contact List view will display a special icon if the contact is a My Record for a login user in your database.

Creating and Deleting Contacts

A database is only as good as the data you've entered. In this section, you'll learn how to add new contacts to the database and enter information about these contacts.

Task A Creating a New Contact

Adding contacts is easy in ACT! 2005. Depending on the speed of your hardware and the total number of notes, histories, activities, and opportunities, you can add somewhere between 60,000 and 200,000 contacts in any ACT! database. Whenever you add a new contact to the database, ACT! will check to make sure the contact isn't a duplicate. If ACT! determines that you're entering a duplicate, it will prompt you to confirm the duplication.

To create a new contact:

1. In the Contacts or Contact List view, click Contacts | New Contact. A new contact will appear.
2. Enter all necessary field information for this new contact.

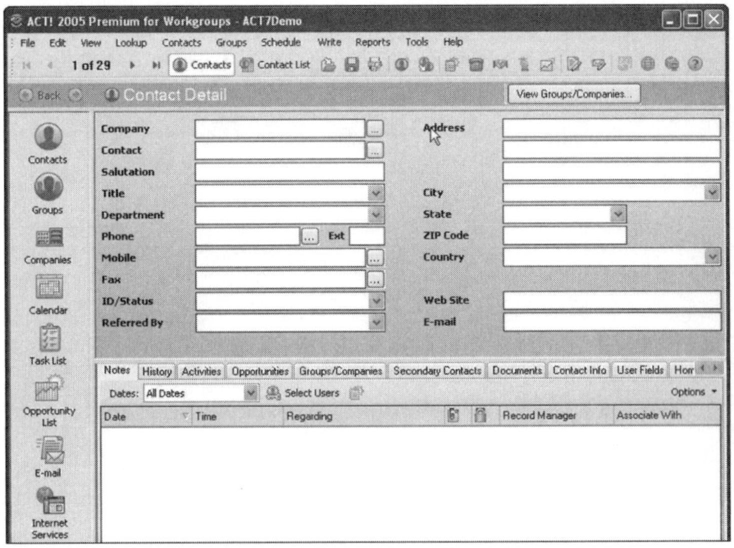

A newly-created blank contact

Adding lots of contacts?

Rather than retype information that already exists in another database, you can import existing contacts into ACT!.

Keyboard shortcuts

Press the Insert key to insert a new contact.

Press the Ctrl and Delete keys at the same time to delete a contact.

Task B Duplicating an Existing Contact

Why repeat work you've already done? Every once in a while, you'll find yourself adding contacts from the same company as an existing contact in the database. Rather than re-type the new contact's address, you can duplicate the existing contact. Once you've duplicated the contact, just enter your new contact's name and the other field information will come over from your original contact.

To duplicate an existing contact:

1. In the Contacts view, go to the contact record you'd like to duplicate.
2. Click Contacts | Duplicate Contact. The Duplicate Contact dialog box will appear.
3. Select whether you'd like to duplicate data from all fields or just from primary fields. A duplicate contact will appear. Even if you selected to duplicate data from all fields, ACT! will not duplicate contact-specific data, such as the contact's name, e-mail address, and phone extension.

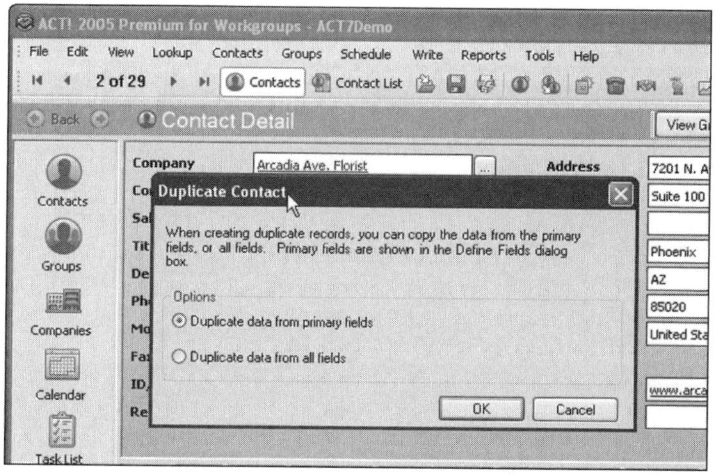

Duplicating a contact

ACT!'s default primary fields

- Company
- Address 1
- Address 2
- Address 3
- City
- State
- Zip
- Country
- Phone
- Fax

Task C Deleting a Single Contact

Deleting an unwanted contact is just as simple as adding a new one. Be careful when deleting contacts, though. There's no simple way to undo a deletion.

To delete a contact:

1. Go to the contact record you'd like to delete.
2. Click Contacts | Delete Contact. ACT! will remind you that deleting contacts cannot be undone. (ACT! 2005 does not have an undelete feature.)
3. Click the Delete Contact button.
4. Click Yes to confirm the deletion. The contact will be permanently removed from the database.

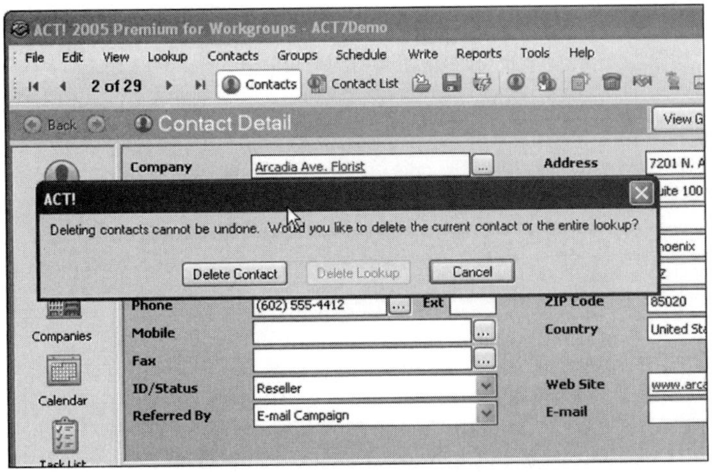

Confirming a contact deletion

Be careful when deleting!

If you perform a lookup and then click Contacts | Delete contact, you will be presented with two options:

1. to delete the current contact, and
2. to delete all contacts in the current lookup.

If you click the Delete Lookup button, every contact in your current lookup will be permanently removed from the database. It's a good idea to make a backup of your database before deleting any contacts. See the next task for more information on deleting multiple contacts.

Task D Deleting Multiple Contacts

You may find a need to remove multiple contacts from your database, and rather than delete each contact individually, you'll save time by creating a lookup of contacts and deleting this lookup.

To delete a contact:

1. Perform a lookup in ACT!. For example, you could lookup all contacts in your database in Texas.
2. Click Contacts | Delete Contact. ACT! will remind you that deleting contacts cannot be undone.
3. Click the Delete Lookup option to delete all contacts in the current lookup. (If you used the example in Step 1, all contacts in Texas will be permanently deleted from the database.)
4. Click Yes to permanently delete the lookup of contacts from your database.

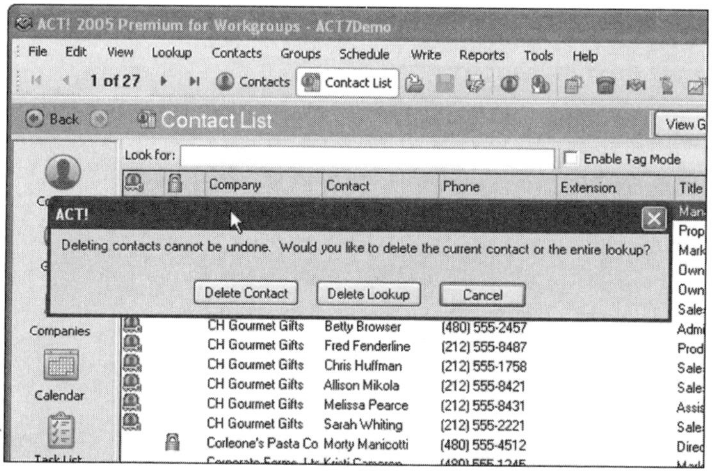

Confirming the deletion of multiple contacts

Oops! How can I undo that deletion?

ACT! 2005 does not have an undelete feature, but if you accidentally delete a group of contacts, you can restore them if you have a current backup. Just restore the backup on your system, lookup the contacts that you want to restore, and export the lookup to your current database. All notes, histories, activities, and opportunities for the exported contacts will also be restored. When restoring the backup, be sure to use the Restore as feature. Using the Restore feature will overwrite your current database.

Secondary Contacts

In previous versions of ACT!, you could only add secondary contacts to a database by adding additional contact fields for a main contact. In most layouts, these fields were housed in the Alt Contacts tab. In ACT! 2005, secondary contacts are their own database entity. You can add an unlimited number of secondary contacts for each main contact, and each secondary contact can have its own field values.

Task A Adding a Secondary Contact

You can view, add, and edit secondary contacts in the Secondary Contacts tab in the Contacts view.

To add a new secondary contact:

1. In the Contacts view, go to the Secondary Contacts tab.
2. In the upper-left corner of the Secondary Contacts tab, click the New Secondary Contact button. The New Contact dialog box will appear.
3. Add any relevant data for your contact.
4. Click OK to add the secondary contact.

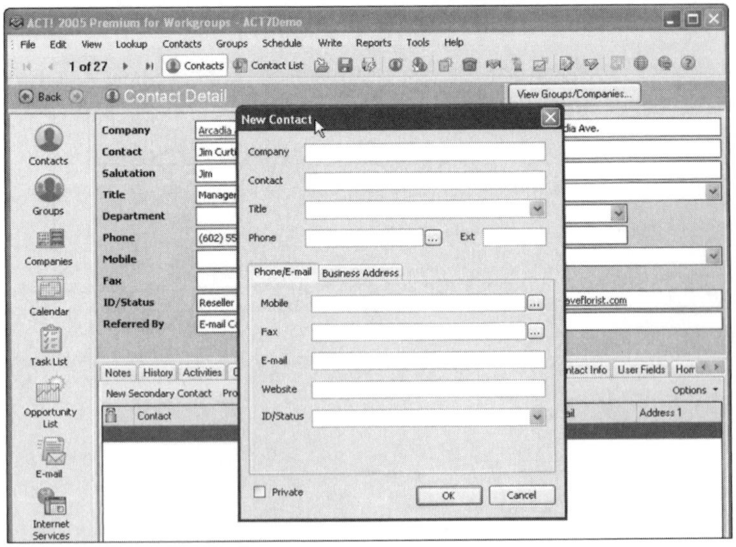

Creating a new secondary contact

Customize the Secondary Contacts tab columns

You can customize the columns that are displayed for each of your secondary contacts by clicking the Options button in the upper-right corner of the tab. From the drop-down, select the Customize Columns option. In the resulting Customize Columns dialog box, you can add, remove, and reorder the fields displayed in the Secondary Contacts tab.

Task B Editing and Deleting Secondary Contacts

You can view any field data for a secondary contact in the Secondary Contacts tab. To edit a secondary contact, just double-click it from the list. To remove a secondary contact, right-click it and select the Delete Secondary Contact option.

To edit or delete a secondary contact:

1. In the Contacts view, go to the Secondary Contacts tab.
2. To edit an existing secondary contact, double-click the contact from the list in the tab.
3. To delete a secondary contact, right-click the contact and choose the Delete Secondary Contact option.

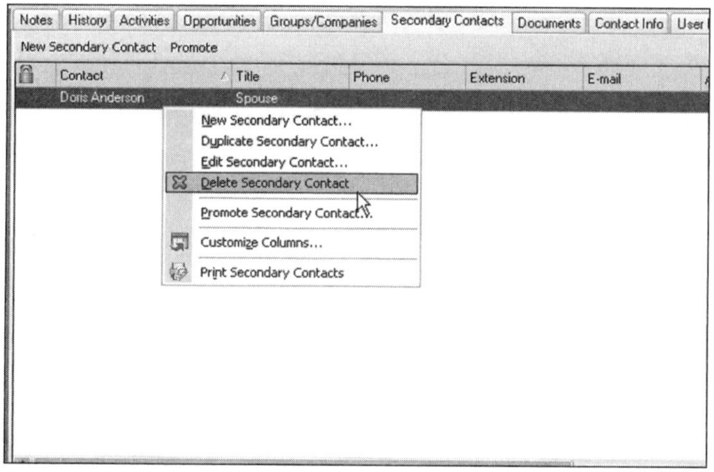

Deleting a secondary contact

Duplicate a secondary contact

If you need to add a new secondary contact, and if the secondary contact shares many of the same fields (such as the address, fax number, and so on), then duplicating the secondary contact can save you a few keystrokes. Just right-click on your existing contact and select the Duplicate Secondary Contact option.

Promoting multiple contacts

In the Secondary Contacts tab, Ctrl + Click multiple contacts to highlight them. Then click the Promote button to promote all of them at once.

Converting existing secondary contacts

If you are converting a database from a previous version of ACT!, the Conversion Wizard will allow you to map existing fields (like the alternate contact fields) into the secondary contact area in ACT! 2005.

Task C Promoting a Secondary Contact

If you often work with a secondary contact, you might want to promote the secondary contact to main contact status. Many items—such as activities, opportunities, notes, and histories—can only be associated with main contacts.

To promote a secondary contact to main contact status:

1. In the Secondary Contacts tab of the Contacts view, locate the contact that you would like to promote.
2. Highlight the secondary contact and click the Promote button in the upper-left corner of the Secondary Contacts tab.
3. If you'd like to duplicate data from the parent contact's primary fields, then select the Duplicate data from primary fields option. Otherwise, select the Duplicate data from all fields option and click OK. The secondary contact will appear in your database as a main contact 4.

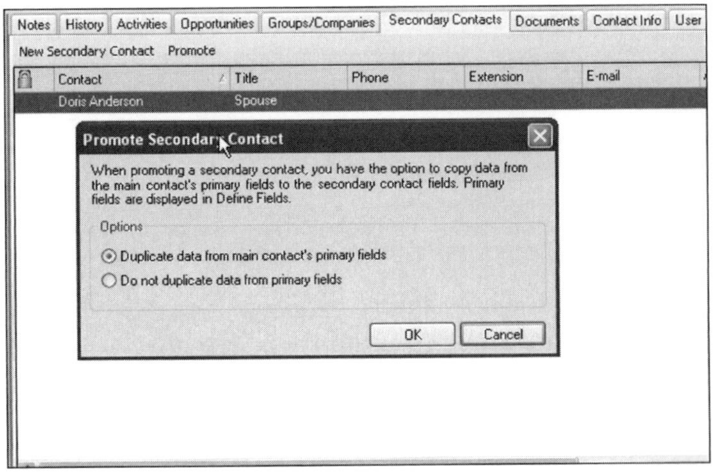

Promoting a secondary contact

Understanding Names and Salutations

In ACT!, you can lookup contacts by their first and last names. But there's no editable first or last name field in an ACT! database—only a single contact field. When you enter a contact's name into an ACT! database, the program looks at the first word in the contact field. If the first word is one of ACT!'s recognized prefixes (such as Mr. or Mrs.), ACT! won't count the word as the first name. The next word—assuming it's not a recognized prefix—will be flagged as the contact's first name. The same logic is used to recognize the last names in the Contact field.

Task A Specifying a First, Middle, and Last Name

If you were to enter Mr. John Smith, Jr. into your database, ACT! would:

1. Look at the first word, Mr. Mr. is one of ACT!'s recognized prefixes. Because of this, ACT! will go to the next word, John. John isn't a recognized prefix, so ACT! would designate John as the first name.
2. Then, ACT! would look at the last word in the contact field. In this example, it's Jr. Jr. is one of ACT!'s recognized suffixes, so the program would skip to the previous word, Smith. Smith isn't a recognized suffix, so ACT! would designate the last name for this contact as Smith.

To specify a contact's first, middle, and last name:

1. Add a new contact to your database.
2. Type the contact's name into the Contact field.
3. Click the button to the right of the Contact field. The Contact Name dialog box appears.
4. Specify your contact's correct first name, middle name, and last name.
5. Click OK. ACT! has now correctly recorded the contact's name.
6. When your cursor leaves the Contact field, ACT! will automatically populate the Salutation field with either the contact's first or last name, depending on the preference you've set.

The Salutation field

By default, ACT! will auto-populate the salutation field with the contact's first name. The salutation is the text that traditionally follows the word *Dear* in business letters.

Task B Setting Name Preferences

When you enter a contact into a database, ACT! figures out your contact's first and last names based on what you've entered into the contact field. ACT! uses its stored list of recognized name prefixes and suffixes to make this determination. If you regularly add contacts with non-standard name prefixes or suffixes, you should add these prefixes and suffixes to your preferences. Otherwise, ACT! may flag the prefixes or suffixes as first or last names.

To set contact name preferences:

1. Click Tools | Preferences. The Preferences dialog box will appear.
2. In the General tab, click the Name Preferences button.
3. Set your default first name prefixes, last name prefixes, and last name suffixes. ACT! uses these settings to determine a contact's correct first and last name.
4. If you'd like ACT! to automatically prompt you to specify a contact's first and last names when you've entered a name containing three or more words, check the Automatic Prompt option at the bottom of the dialog box.
5. Click OK to save your changes.

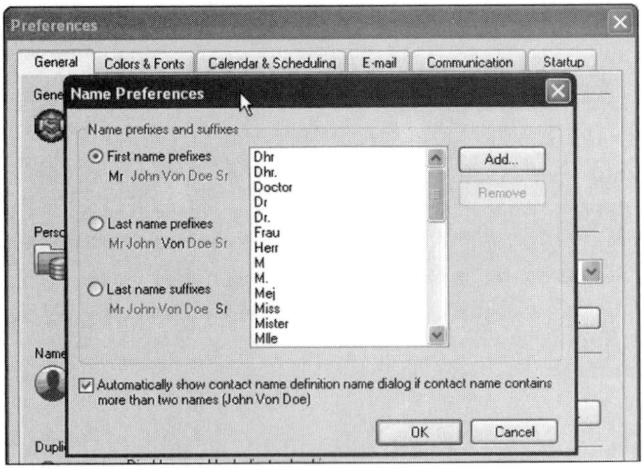

Specifying contact name preferences

Salutation changes

When you change the default name options, you might want to have ACT! update your salutations. To do this, perform a lookup of contacts and click Tools | Update Salutation Field. Select the Current Lookup option and click OK.

Task C Updating Salutations

Each time you enter a new contact into ACT!, the program will automatically populate the contents of the salutation field. The name that is entered in the salutation field for new contacts is dependent on your current name preferences. (See the previous task for information on name preferences.) Salutations are not automatically updated when you change these name preferences, but ACT! 2005 lets you retroactively update the salutation for a single contact or a lookup of contacts. Of course, you can also manually edit the text in the salutation field.

To update salutations:

1. Update your name preferences. ACT! will use the name preferences to determine the new value for the salutation field.
2. If you plan to update the salutation field for multiple contacts, perform a lookup of these contacts.
3. Click Tools | Update Salutation Field.
4. When the Update Salutation Field dialog box appears, select whether you'd like to update salutations for the current contact, the current lookup, or all contacts in the database.
5. Click OK.

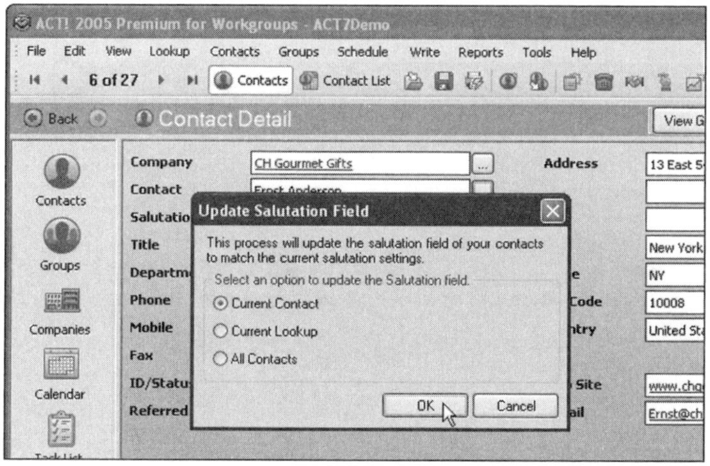

Mass updating the Salutation field

Do you have a backup?

Before mass updating your salutation field, it's probably a good idea to have a backup of your database. You won't be able to easily undo the changes made after updating salutations without reverting to a backup.

Entering Notes

Once you've entered a contact into ACT!, you might find it useful to be able to add notes for that contact. You can add a virtually unlimited number of notes for any ACT! contact, and each note can be as long as you require. In previous versions of ACT!, notes and history entries were housed in the same tab. ACT! 2005 now houses notes in its own tab, and notes can now include text formatting (specific text types, font sizes, colors, and so on).

Task A Inserting a Note for a Contact

Notes can contain just about any kind of information you wish to store for a contact. Perhaps you want to enter driving directions for a contact? Maybe you just want to make a note about your contact's likes or dislikes. Entering a note in the Notes tab is an ideal place to store random information that doesn't fit in any of your contact fields.

F9 to insert a note

Pressing F9 on your keyboard will insert a note for the current contact. If you prefer to use the menus, then you could also click Contacts | Insert Note.

To insert a note for a single contact:

1. In the Contacts view, go to the contact for whom you'd like to add a note.
2. Click the Notes tab.
3. Click the Insert Note button in the upper part of the Notes tab. A new note will be created.
4. Type the text of your note.

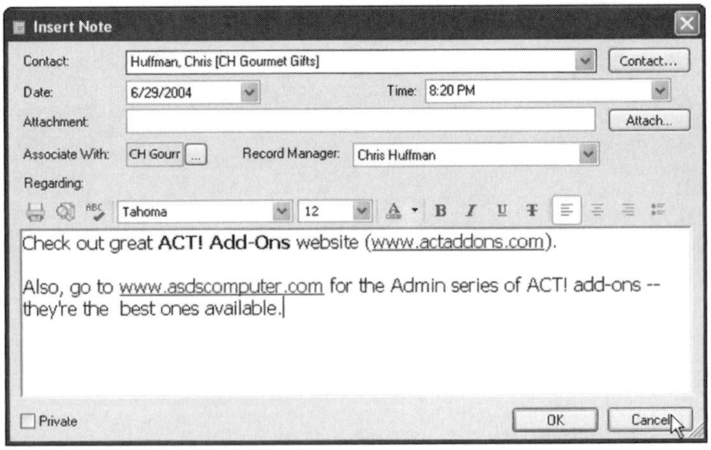

Inserting a note for a contact

Task B Entering a Note for Multiple Contacts

Inserting a single note for a contact has always been an easy thing to do in ACT!. In ACT! 2005, however, you can easily add the note for multiple contacts in one simple step. If you plan to add a note for multiple contacts, it's a good idea to perform a lookup of these contacts before proceeding.

To enter a note for multiple contacts:

1. Perform a lookup of the contacts for whom you'd like to enter a note.
2. Click Contacts | Insert Note. The Insert Note dialog box appears.
3. Click the Contact button in the upper-right corner.
4. In the resulting dialog box, select the Current Lookup option from the drop-down box in the upper-left corner.
5. Click the >> button to add all of the contacts in the current lookup to the list of contacts for whom you're inserting a note.
6. Click OK.
7. Type the text of your note.
8. Click OK. The note will be inserted in each contact's Notes tab.

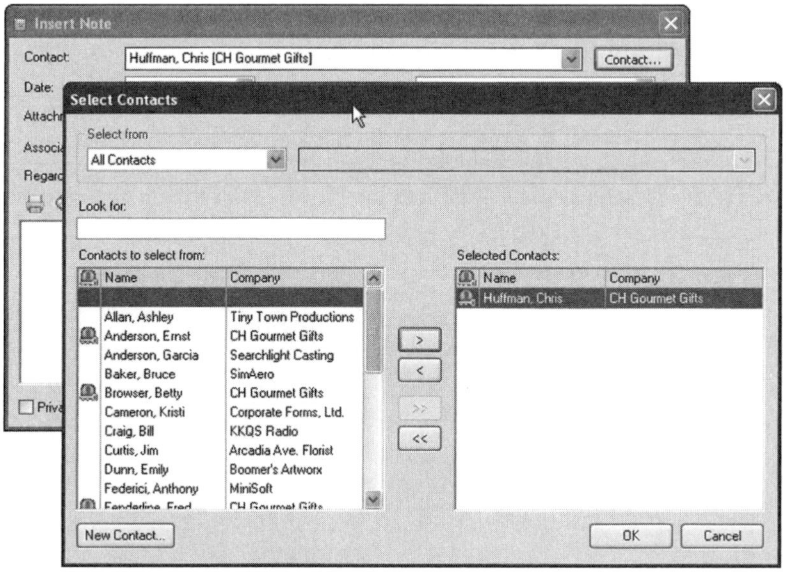

Associating a note with multiple contacts

Looking up notes

If you enter a specific note for multiple contacts, then you can easily bring up a list of these contacts by performing a keyword search for the text in the note. Click Lookup | Keyword Search. Type (or copy) the note text in the Search for field. In the Look in area, make sure that only the Notes option is checked. Click Find Now to perform the lookup.

Attaching Files to a Contact

You can attach any file on your hard drive or network to a contact in your ACT! database. Attached files can be viewed in the History tab alongside histories of events. Perhaps you have an Excel spreadsheet that you'd like to associate with your contact? Maybe you have a Word document or PowerPoint presentation? If you attach the file to a contact record in ACT!, you'll be able to double-click the attachment in the History tab to launch the file. This feature is great for organizing your documents and keeping relevant information at your fingertips.

Task A Attaching a File to a Contact Record

Attaching a file doesn't actually physically attach the file to your ACT! database. It merely provides a hyperlink to a spot on your local computer or network where your file has been saved. If you move a file that has been attached to an ACT! contact record, then ACT! won't be able to find its new location. If you're using a multi-user database, you won't be able to see files that your co-workers have attached to their individual hard drives. If you would like the attached files to synchronize, you should include them in the supplemental files system.

To attach a file to a contact record:

1. In the Contacts view, go to the contact for whom you'd like to attach a file.
2. Click Contacts | Attach File.
3. Browse and double-click the file you'd like to attach.
4. The file attachment will appear in the History tab for your current contact.

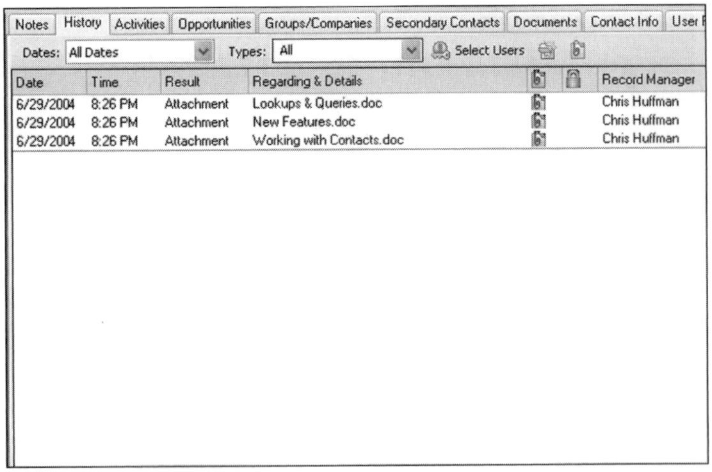

Attached files in the History tab

Documents tab

If you're attaching documents, spreadsheets, PDF files, or other similar files, you might consider attaching them to the database in the Documents tab. For more information, see Chapter 12.

Task B Viewing an Attached File

You can see a list of attached files for each contact in the History tab. You can also launch any attached file right from within the History tab.

To view an attached file:

1. Locate an attached file in the History tab.
2. In the History tab, locate the attachments column. You'll notice an icon in the header for this column that looks like a piece of paper with a paperclip on it.
3. Double-click the icon in the attachments column for the attached file you'd like to launch.
4. ACT! will launch the attached file in its appropriate program.

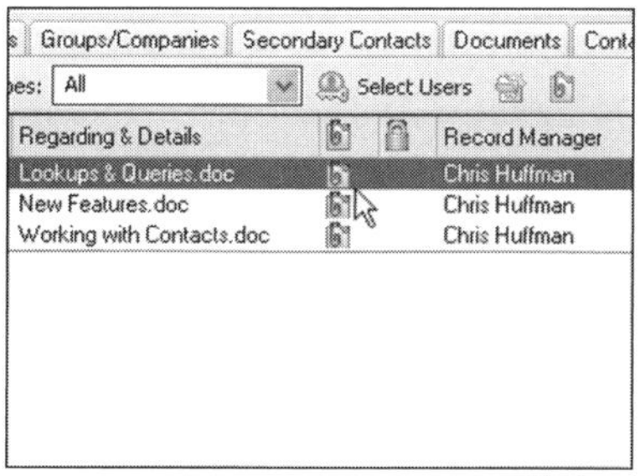

Clicking the attachment icon launches a document.

Sharing documents in a multi-user environment

If you're sharing an ACT! database with other users, and if you want other users to be able to double-click and launch files you've attached to contacts, your attached files must be stored on a shared network drive. If, for example, you were to attach a file on your local desktop, then other users will receive an error if they attempted to launch the file from the History tab on their computers.

Scanning for Duplicates

ACT! can check your database for duplicate contacts. When you perform a scan for duplicates in ACT!, the program will lookup all of the contacts in the database that have the same value in each of the duplicate matching fields you've specified. You can then use the duplicate merging feature (see the next task) to consolidate the contact data.

Task A Finding Duplicate Contacts

Each time you perform a scan for duplicates, try changing the duplicate matching field. Searching for duplicates using the Company, Contact, and Phone fields will produce one set of duplicate contacts. Change the fields to First Name, Last Name, and Phone number, and you'll get a different set of duplicates. Repeat the process using different sets of fields until you've found all duplicates in the database.

To perform a scan for duplicates:

1. Click Tools | Scan for Duplicates. The Scan for Duplicate Contacts dialog box appears.
2. Specify up to three fields for ACT! to use when looking for duplicate contacts. If two or more contacts have the same value in all of the fields specified, then the contacts will be flagged as duplicates.
3. Click OK. ACT! will perform a lookup of duplicate contacts.

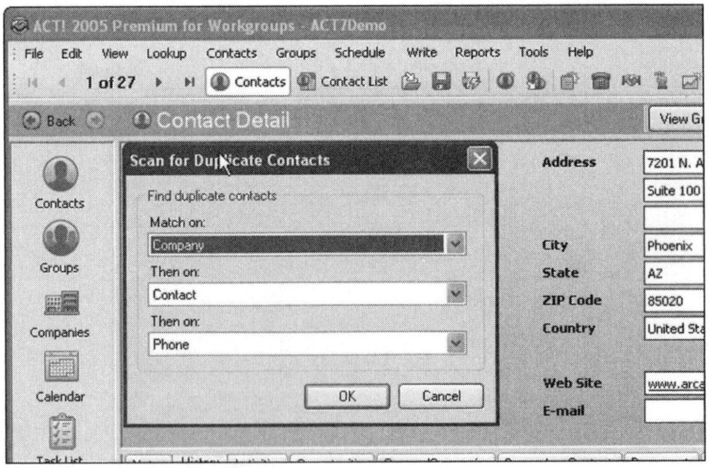

Specifying the duplicate matching fields

A useful strategy for dealing with duplicates

If you have many duplicates in your database, it may help you to create a duplicate contacts group:

1. Run a scan for duplicates and add your current lookup (all of the duplicates) to the duplicates group.
2. Then, change your duplicate matching fields and run the scan for duplicates again. Add all of these contacts to your duplicates.
3. Repeat the process with different sets of duplicate matching fields until you've created a complete group of duplicates.

Task B Combining Duplicate Contacts

Dealing with duplicate contacts is never easy, but ACT! 2005 offers a new feature to help you merge field data, notes, history entries, sales opportunities, and documents for multiple contacts. When merging contact data, it might be easier to locate the duplicate contacts if you perform a lookup of them before proceeding.

To merge two duplicate contacts:

1. Click Tools | Copy/Move Contact Data.
2. In the Copy/Move Contact Data dialog box, locate the first duplicate contact. Highlight it from the list.
3. Locate the other duplicate contact. Hold down the Ctrl key and click the second contact. This will highlight both the second contact and the first one you clicked in Step 2. Click Next.
4. Specify a source and target contact. Click Next.
5. Specify the data to contact from the source to the target field. Click Next.
6. Select whether to move additional items (such as notes, histories, and opportunities) from the source to the target contact. Click Next.
7. Select whether or not to delete the source contact from the database. Click Next.
8. Click Finish.

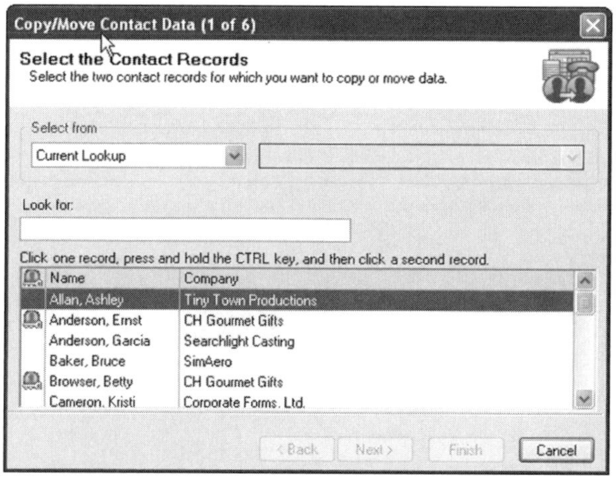

Merging duplicate contacts

More than two duplicates?

If you have more than two duplicates of the same contact, you'll have to go through the Copy/Move Contact Data Wizard multiple times to merge all contacts together.

Mass Updating Fields

Your biggest client has just moved, and you're now faced with the job of changing the address for the hundreds of contacts at this company in your database. Using ACT!'s mass field replacing feature, changing fields for multiple contacts is really quite simple.

Task A Mass Replacing a Field Value

If you haven't made a backup of your database, now would be a good time to do so. Accidentally mass updating fields for the wrong group of contacts will cause irreparable harm to your database, and there's no easy way to undo a mass field update.

To mass replace a field value:

1. Perform a lookup of the contacts you'd like to mass update.
2. Click Edit | Replace Field. The Replace Data dialog box appears.
3. On the left, select a field to mass replace.
4. On the right, type a new value for this field.
5. Click OK.
6. Click Yes to confirm that you'd like to mass update contacts in the current lookup. The new value will be mass updated for all contacts in the current lookup.

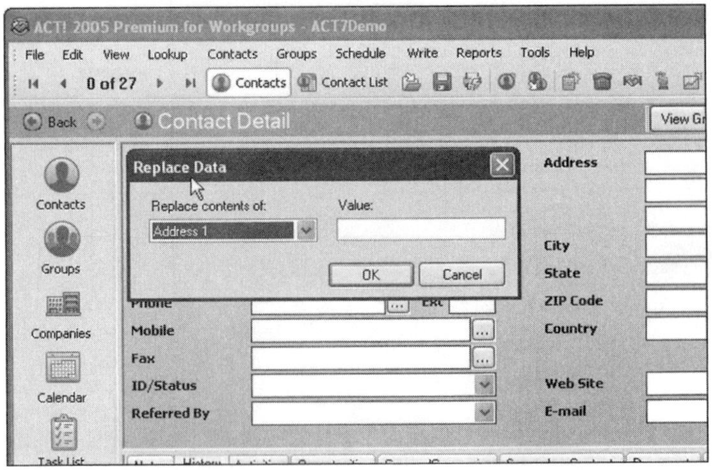

Mass replacing data for all contacts in the current lookup

Removing data

To remove all data from a field for the current lookup, click Edit | Replace. Select a field from the drop-down, but do not enter a new value in the field on the right. Click OK.

Task B Swapping Field Values

If you ever want to swap the values in two fields for all of the contacts in your current lookup, the process is very similar to the Mass Replace feature in the previous task.

To swap the contents of two fields:

1. Perform a lookup of the contacts whose data you'd like to swap.
2. Click Edit | Swap Field.
3. Select the two fields whose data you'd like to swap.
4. Click OK.
5. Click Yes to confirm that you'd like to swap the contents of these two fields.

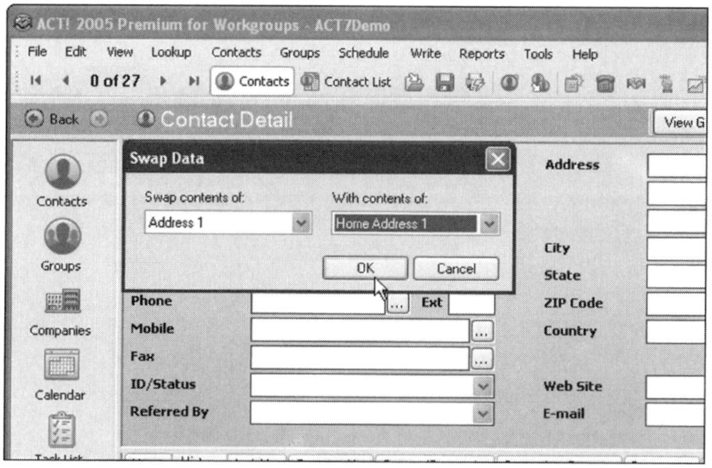

Mass swapping data for all contacts in the current lookup

Back up your data

Always perform a backup before trying to swap, replace, or copy fields. If you don't, you could end up with a database that's missing valuable data.

Task C Copying Fields

You can copy the contents of one field into another field using the Copy Field feature on the Edit menu. When you use this feature, all data in the target field will be overwritten with data from the source field. Just like the Mass Replace and Swap features, the Mass Field Copy feature will alter contacts in the current lookup.

To copy the contents of one field to another:

1. Perform a lookup of the contacts for whom you'd like to copy field values.
2. Click Edit | Copy Field. The Copy Data dialog box appears.
3. Select a source and target field. Click OK.
4. Click Yes to confirm that you'd like to copy the contents of the source field into the target field.

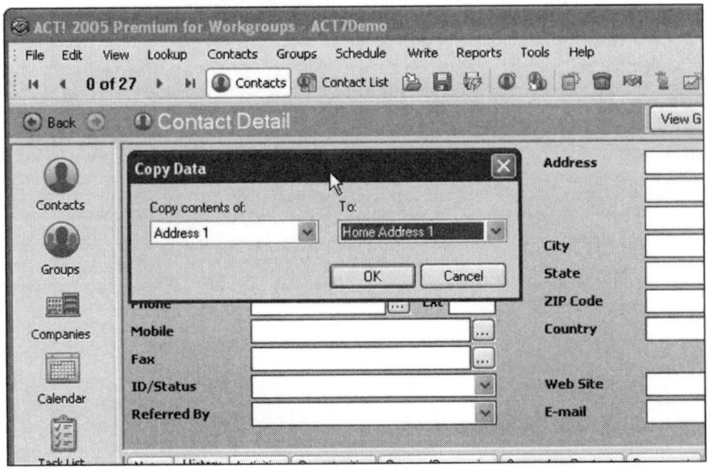

Mass copying data for all contacts in the current lookup

Chapter 4
Companies and Divisions

Adding/Removing Companies

In addition to the contact entity, ACT! 2005 now offers an additional record type: the company record. Company records can be viewed in the Company and Company List views, and you can add as many companies to the database as you require. Best of all, contact records can be linked to companies, so ACT! can now work as a company-centric database system.

Task A Adding a New Company

Adding a new company to the database entails the same general process you use to add a new contact. You should probably go to the Companies view before adding a new company to the database—in the Companies view you can check to see if the company already exists before adding a potential duplicate.

To add a new company to the database:

1. Click Groups | Companies | New Company. A blank company record will appear in the Companies view.
2. Enter a name or your company name in the Company field. If necessary, populate the other company fields with information.

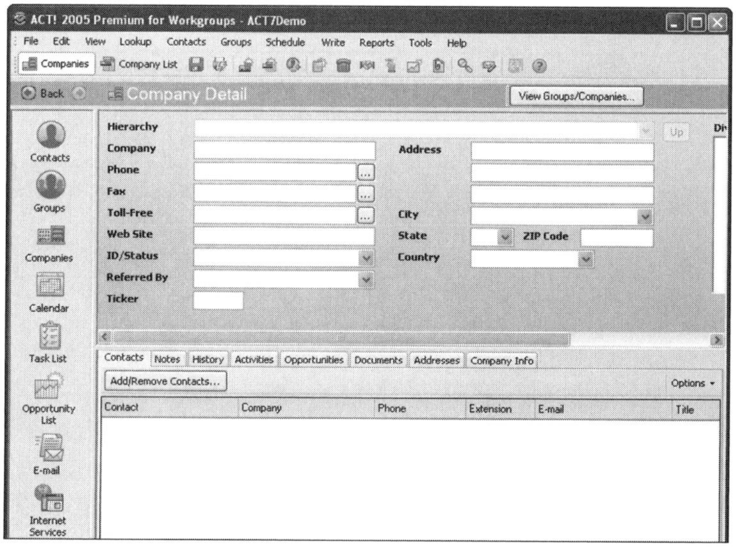

A newly-created blank company record

Insert to add a new company

To add a new company to the database, go to either the Companies or Company List view and click the Insert button on your keyboard.

Whoops!

There's no Undo feature to bring back mistakenly deleted companies, so be sure to have a backup of your database before deleting.

Right-click to delete

In the Company List view, right-click any company or division and select the Delete option to permanently remove the company or division from the database.

Task B Deleting a Company

You may occasionally need to delete company records from the database; you can do this in either the Companies view or Company List view. Deleting a company record will not delete any of the divisions within the company, and deleting a company will not delete any contact records associated with the company.

To delete a company record:

1. In the Companies view, go to the company (or division) you'd like to delete. Do this by double-clicking the company/division in the Company List view or by performing a lookup to find the company.
2. Click Groups | Companies | Delete.
3. Click Yes to confirm the deletion.

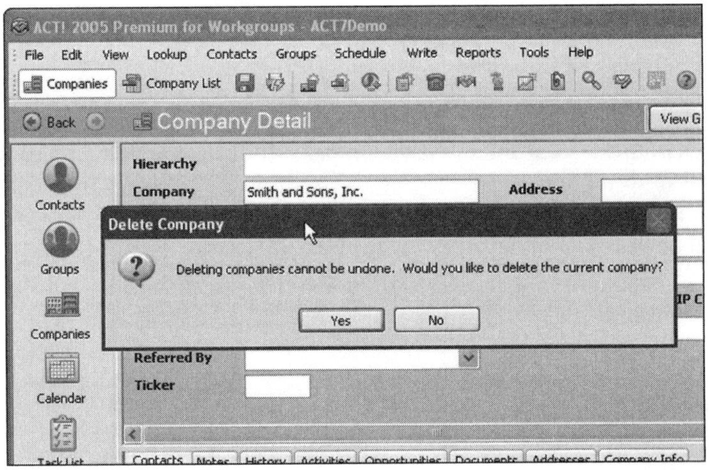

Confirming a company deletion

Managing Companies

With the new company record feature, you can use ACT! 2005 as a company-centric database. You can link contacts with company records, and some key information—such as the address fields—can be dynamically linked between the company and contact records.

Task A Associating Contacts with Companies

The first step in using ACT! 2005 as a company-centric database is to link your contact records with company records. Before linking contacts to a company, you must have first set up the company record.

To associate a contact with a company:

1. In the Contacts view, click Contacts | New Contact to add a new contact to the database.
2. Click the button to the right of the Company field for this new contact.
3. Select a company or division, and then click OK. ACT! will link this contact record to the company you selected.

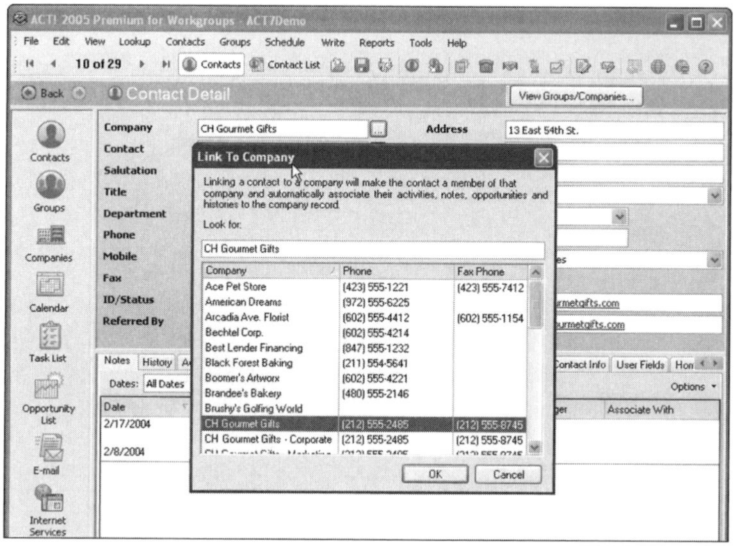

Linking contacts with a company record

Company hyperlinks

Anytime a contact is linked to a company, you'll notice that the text in the company field becomes highlighted and blue, just like the text in the e-mail address field. If you click anywhere on the blue underlined company text, ACT! will take you directly to the main company record.

Task B Auto-Updating Company/Contact Address Data

If a company moves its offices, you'll probably need to go through all of the contacts at the company and update their address fields. If you have linked your contacts with a main company record, ACT! will automatically update the contacts' address fields when the main company fields are updated.

Not all fields auto-update

Some company-specific fields—such as the Referred by field—do not auto-update. Only the Address 1, Address 2, Address 3, City, State, Zip, Country, and Web Site fields auto-update.

To auto-update company/contact addresses:

1. Make sure that you have one or more contacts associated with your main company record. (See the previous task for information on linking contact and company records.)
2. Update the main address information in your company record. When you move off the company record, ACT! will ask if you would like to update contacts linked to this company with the changes you made.
3. Click Yes, and ACT! will update the address in each contact record linked to the company.

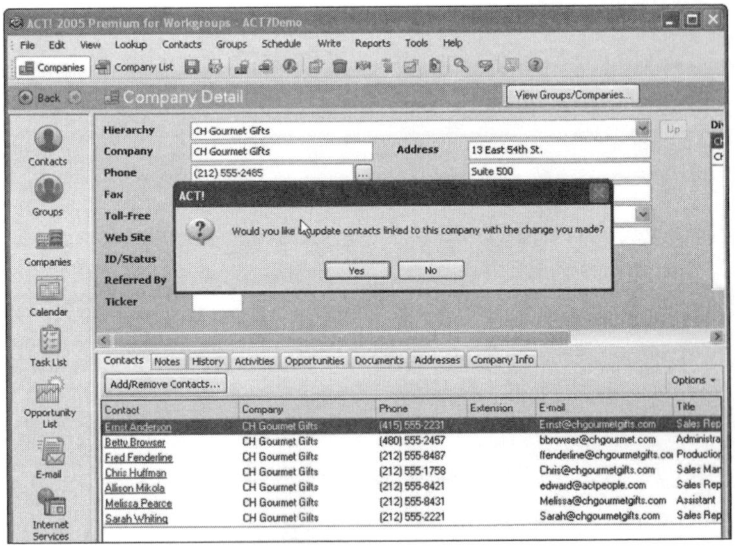

Automatically updating contact and group addresses

Managing Divisions

Within each company record, you can have 15 sublevels of divisions. Companies and divisions are essentially the same type of records in ACT! 2005. If you can do something to a company record—such as link a contact with the company record—you'll be able to do the same with a division record.

Task A Adding a New Division

Before adding a new division, you'll need to make sure the main company record already exists in the database.

To add a new division:

1. In the Company view or Company List view, locate the company for which you'd like to add a division. If you're in the Company List view, highlight the company.
2. Click Groups | Companies | New Division. A new division record will appear. You'll notice that the new divisions look almost identical to the new company records. The only difference is that divisions are placed under companies in the company hierarchy.
3. In the Company field for the division, enter the name of the division.

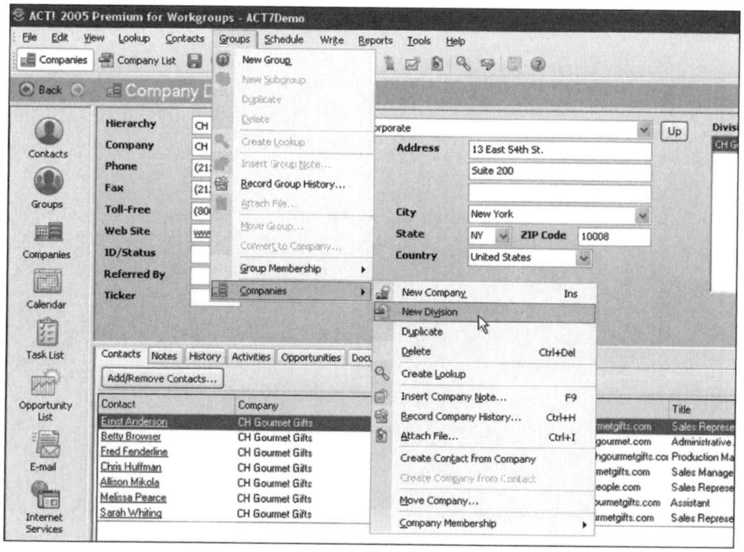

Creating a new division

Two ways to delete a division

1. Go to the division record in the Companies view and click Groups | Companies | Delete.
2. In the Company List view, right-click the division you'd like to delete and select the Delete option.

Showing divisions in the Company List view

To show divisions in the Company List view, check the Include divisions option at the top of the screen. You'll notice that divisions appear in alphabetical order mixed in with company records. Divisions in the Company List view do not appear under their parent companies.

Chapter 5
Lookups and Queries

Simple Lookups

Your data becomes a lot more valuable when you can find it! You can search for almost anything that has been entered into an ACT! database. ACT! calls these searches lookups, and this chapter will guide you through some of the lookup capabilities of ACT! 2005. We'll start with simple lookups.

Task A Looking Up All Contacts

In the Contacts and Contact List views, ACT! will always display your current lookup, or the results of your last search. The record counter in the upper-left part of the Contacts and Contact List views will show the total number of contacts in your current lookup. If you need to work with all of the contacts in your database, you might need to perform a lookup of all contacts in the database.

To lookup all contacts in the database:

1. Click Lookup | All Contacts.
2. Your current lookup will contain all contacts in the database.

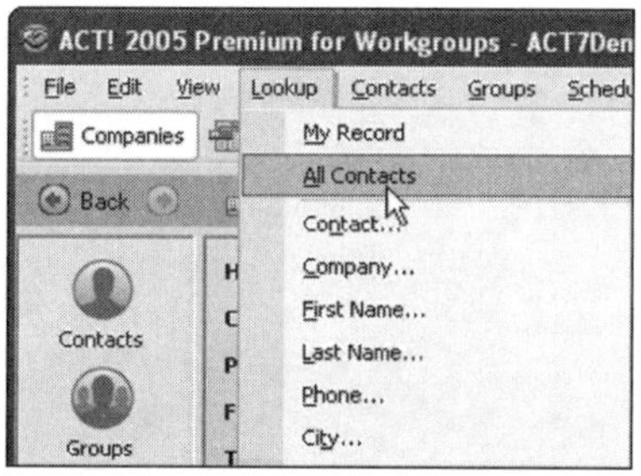

Performing a lookup of all available contacts

Scroll through contacts in the current lookup

You can navigate through all of the contacts in your current lookup by clicking the Previous and Next buttons on the record counter. You can use the Page Up and Page Down buttons on the keyboard to move through contacts in the current lookup.

Limited Access

If you're using ACT! 2005 Premium Edition, then a lookup of all contacts will not include contacts that are private to other users or teams.

Task B Looking Up Basic Fields

Most of your lookups will probably be simple lookups. You'll want to find a contact based on his or her name, company name, city, state, zip code, and so on. You can lookup by any of these basic fields directly from the Lookup menu.

Calling all keyboard people!

If you'd rather use the keyboard to perform a lookup, then press ALT + L. Then press the underlined letter of the option on the menu bar you'd like to use. For example, to lookup by company, press ALT + L, and then press C.

Looking up by contact name

In previous versions of ACT!, finding someone by name was only possible by searching for a specific first name or last name. ACT! 2005 now lets you search by the entire contact name. Just click Lookup | Contact and type the full name of the contact you'd like to find.

To perform a lookup on a basic field:

1. Click Lookup on the menu.
2. Select the basic field you'd like to use for your lookup. (Basic fields are Contact, Company, First Name, Last Name, Phone, City, State, and ID/Status.)
3. The Lookup Contacts dialog box appears. In the Search for area, type the field value you'd like to find. (So, if you were searching for all of the people with a last name of Huffman, you'd enter Huffman in the Search for area.)
4. Click OK to find all of the contacts that match your search terms.

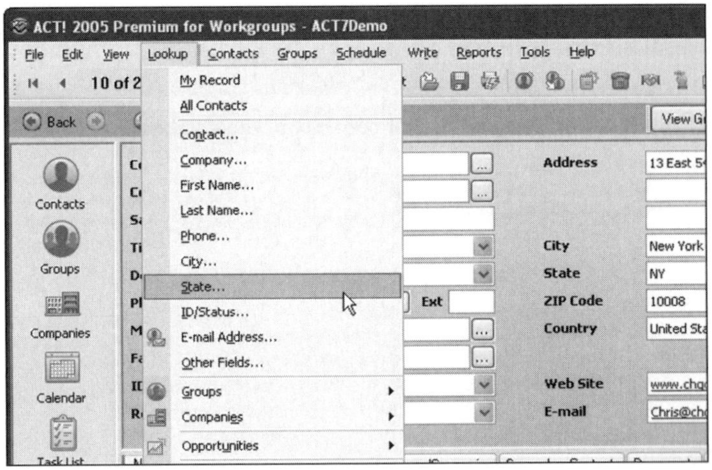

Performing a lookup on the State field

Task C Looking Up Other Fields

If you need to lookup on a field that isn't listed on the Lookup menu, then you can search almost all fields in your database using the Other Lookups search. Some fields—like the Edit Date and Create Date—are not searchable in this area, but any custom fields you've added to the database are searchable in the Other Fields lookup.

To lookup on other fields:

1. Click Lookup | Other Fields.
2. The Lookup Contacts dialog box appears. Click on the Lookup drop-down to see a list of fields in your database.
3. Select the field on which you'd like to search.
4. In the Search for area, type the field value you'd like to lookup.
5. Click OK to perform the lookup.

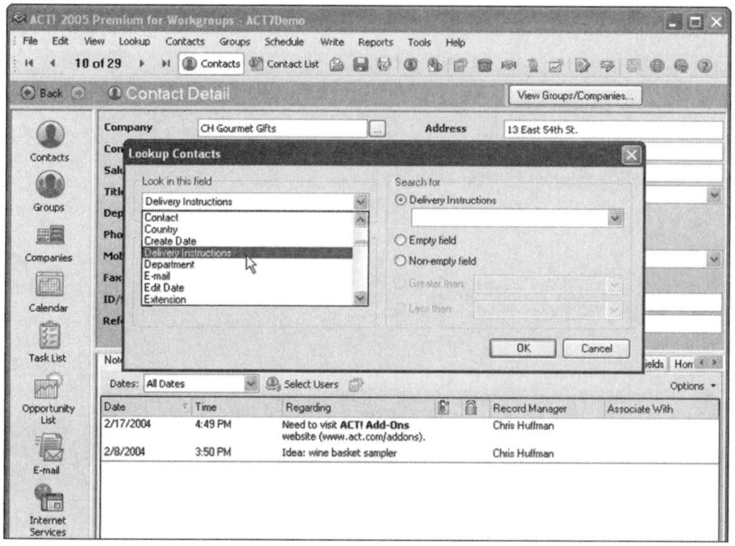

Performing a lookup on a custom field

Click inside a field before performing an Other Fields lookup

If you click inside a field in the Contact view before performing an Other Fields lookup, ACT! will automatically bring up a lookup dialog box for the field you clicked.

You can now search on any field

In previous versions of ACT!, some fields—like the Edit Date and Create Date—were not searchable using the Lookup | Other Fields feature. ACT! 2005 lets you search through any field in the database when performing an Other Fields lookup.

Task D Performing Greater Than/Less Than Lookups

If you're performing a lookup on a number, currency, or date field, ACT! will display the option to search for contacts that have a field value that is either greater than or less than the value that you specify.

Advanced Queries

You can perform greater than or less than searches in the Advanced Query area, too. Click Lookup | Advanced | Advanced Query.

To perform a greater than/less than lookup:

1. Click Lookup | Other Fields.
2. In the field list in the upper-left corner of the Lookup Contacts dialog box, select either a number, currency, or date field.
3. On the right side of the Lookup Contacts dialog box, select the Greater than option.
4. Type a value in the Greater than field. For example, if you were searching for values greater than 500, you'd type **500** in the Greater than field.
5. Click OK to perform the lookup.

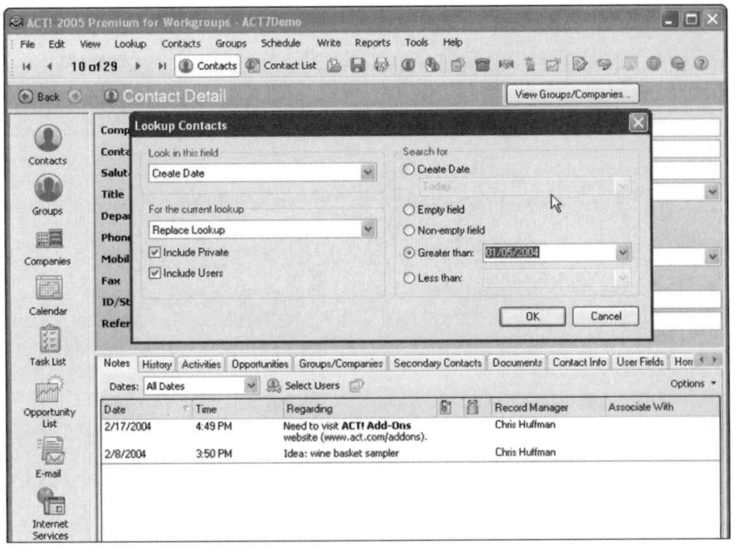

Performing a greater than date search

Task E Performing Right-Click Lookups

ACT! 2005 includes a great new feature that makes it easy to perform lookups on fields that aren't listed on the Lookup menu. Just right-click in any field on your contact, company, or group layout to perform a lookup on that field.

To perform a right-click lookup on any field:

1. Right-click somewhere inside a field in the Contact, Company, or Groups view.
2. Select the Lookup [FieldName] option. (If you right-click the E-mail field, you'll choose the Lookup E-mail option.)
3. The Lookup Contacts dialog box will appear, ready to perform a lookup on the field you right-clicked.

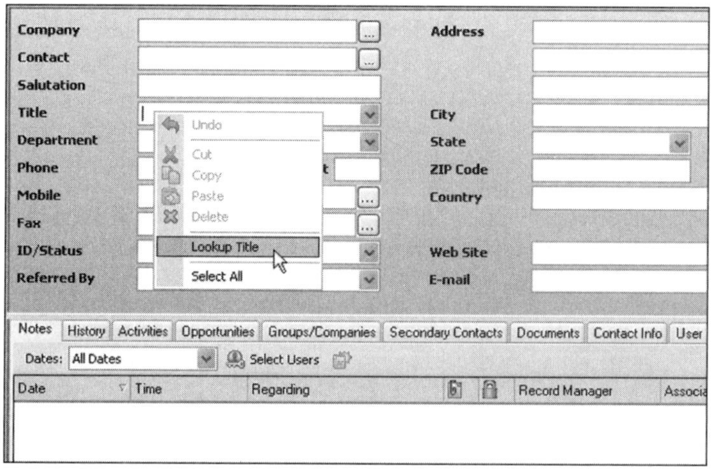

Right-clicking on any field brings up a lookup option.

Be careful where you click your mouse!

Right-clicking on an actual field will bring up the option to perform a quick lookup on that field. Right-clicking anywhere else around the field—including the field label—will not bring up any lookup options.

Looking Up Empty/Non-Empty Fields

You can search for data in any field in ACT!, but from time to time you may find it just as useful to find fields that contain no data. ACT! gives you the built-in ability to search for contacts that have either something or nothing in a field.

Task A Looking Up Empty Fields

Looking up empty fields is especially useful when you're cleaning up incomplete data. For example, if you know that you don't have many e-mail addresses in your database, you might want to lookup all contacts that have an empty e-mail address field. Doing so will give you a lookup of the contacts that need to be updated.

Finding empty/non-empty contacts in a keyword search

You can find empty or non-empty contacts in a keyword search by using the Contains Data and Does Not Contain Data operators.

To find all contacts with an empty field value:

1. Click Lookup | E-mail Address. The Lookup Contacts dialog box will appear.
2. Instead of looking for a specific e-mail address, click the Empty fields option in the Search for area.
3. Click OK to perform the lookup.

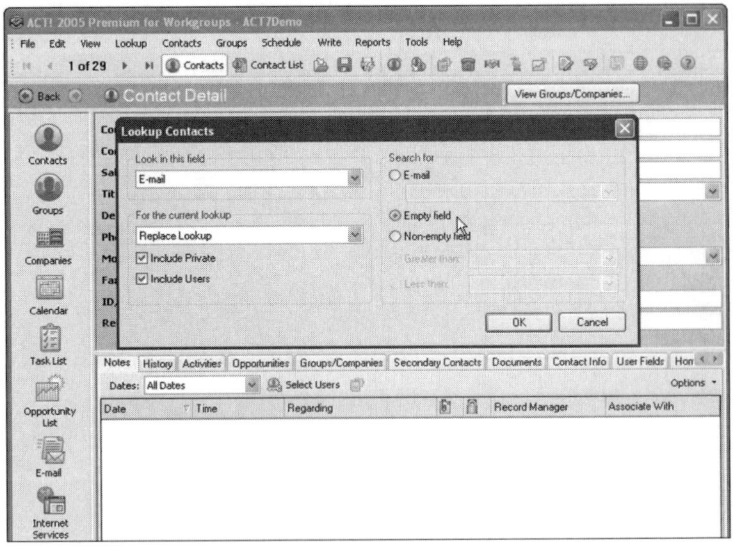

Searching for contacts that have an empty field value

Task B Looking Up Non-Empty Fields

You may find yourself in a situation where you'd like to find contacts that have information in a specific field. Before you do a mail merge, for example, you may want to lookup the contacts in your database that have an address. ACT! makes it easy to isolate these contacts that have a non-empty field value.

To find all contacts with a value in a field:

1. Click Lookup | Other Fields.
2. In the Lookup drop-down, select a field from the list.
3. In the Search for area, select the Non-empty field option.
4. Click OK to perform the lookup.

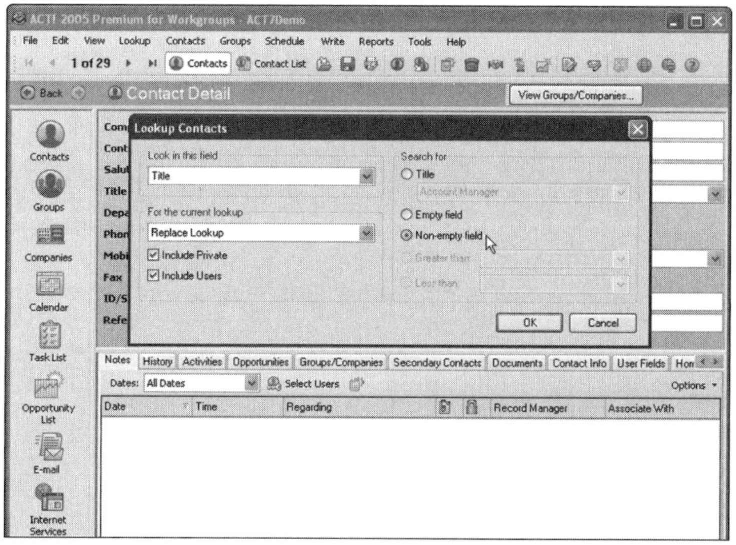

Searching for contacts that have a non-empty field value

Finding empty/non-empty contacts in the Contact List view

In the Contact List view, click any column header to sort the current lookup by the column. All of the contacts with empty field values will appear at the top of the alphabetical list.

Replacing, Adding, and Narrowing Lookups

When you perform a lookup in ACT!, you'll have the option of either replacing, adding, or narrowing the lookup. Using these options, you can use a series of simple lookups to produce a current lookup of contacts that would otherwise only be possible by creating an advanced query.

Task A Replacing a Lookup

Let's say you have everyone in Texas looked up. You perform a new lookup of all contacts in Connecticut and choose to replace the lookup. ACT! will ignore your previous lookup and will search through all contacts in the database. Your new current lookup will become a list of everyone in Connecticut. Replacing the existing lookup is the default lookup option.

To replace a lookup:

1. Perform a basic lookup. To do this, click Lookup on the menu and select a field from the list. The Lookup Contacts dialog box will appear. Type a value in the Search for area.
2. In the Lookup Contacts dialog box, select the Replace Lookup option if it isn't already selected.
3. Your previous lookup will be discarded and the lookup you just performed will become your current lookup.

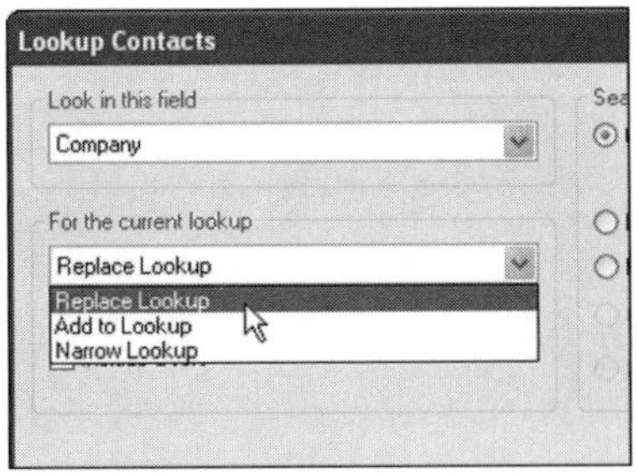

Replacing a basic lookup

Why is the current lookup so important?

The current lookup in ACT! is a lot like a temporary group. In fact, almost all features of the program that can be applied to multiple contacts can be applied to the current lookup.

A few examples of things you can do to all of the contacts in your current lookup:

- Send a mass letter to the current lookup
- Send a mass e-mail to the current lookup
- Schedule an activity or activity series
- Add the current lookup contacts to a group
- Run a report that includes only information for contacts in the current lookup
- Export the contacts in the current lookup

Task B Adding to a Lookup

When you perform a lookup and choose to add to the lookup, ACT! will search through your entire database, and the result of this lookup will be added to your previous lookup to become a new, expanded current lookup. For example, let's say you had all of the people in New York looked up. You then perform another lookup (using the Add to Lookup option) for all of the people in California. The resulting current lookup would contain all of the contacts in both New York and California.

To add to a lookup:

1. Perform a basic lookup. (For example, you might lookup all contacts in the state of New York.)
2. Perform another basic lookup. (For example, you might lookup all contacts in the state of California.)
3. In the Lookup Contacts dialog box, select the Add to Lookup option.
4. Your previous lookup (everyone in New York) will be added to this lookup (everyone in California) to create a current lookup of everyone in New York and California.

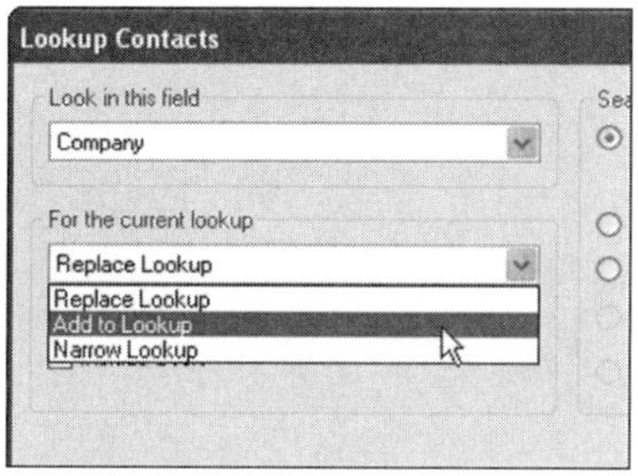

Adding to an existing lookup

You can now add and narrow system fields

In previous versions of ACT!, it wasn't possible to add to and narrow some system fields, such as the E-mail Address or Create Date fields. ACT! 2005 now lets you add/narrow using any field in the database.

A practical example

You're ready to do a mass e-mail to your current lookup in ACT!. Before actually sending the mass e-mail, it's probably a good idea to narrow the lookup to just those contacts with a non-empty field value in the E-mail Address field.

Task C Narrowing a Lookup

When using the narrow lookup option, you'll be able to search just in your current lookup for contacts that have a specific value in a field. Let's say you need to send a letter to all of the contacts in your database who are CEOs and work in New York. You could perform a lookup of all New York contacts, and then you could narrow that lookup to just the contacts who have a title of CEO. The end result will be a current lookup of all CEOs in New York.

To narrow a lookup:

1. Perform a basic lookup. (For example, you could perform a lookup of all contacts in New York State.)
2. Perform another basic lookup. (For example, you might lookup all contacts with the word *CEO* in the Title field.)
3. In the Lookup Contacts dialog box, choose the Narrow Lookup option.
4. ACT! will search through your previous lookup (contacts in New York) for just those with a title of CEO.

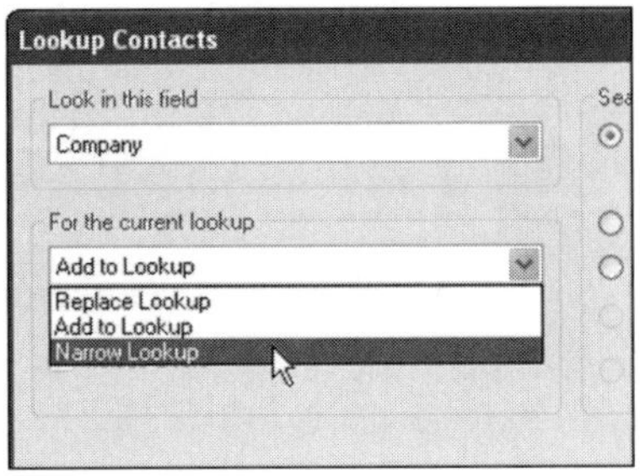

Narrowing a lookup

Company Lookups

ACT! 2005 now includes companies as an entity in the database. You can now include an unlimited number of companies in your database, and you'll need to be able to search on the company fields. Any text entered into the company areas of ACT! is searchable with the new company lookup options.

Task A Looking Up on Company Fields

From the Lookup menu, you'll have the option to search on any of the company fields in your database. Or, you can select to perform a lookup of all companies in the database. The results of these company lookups will appear in the Company List view.

To perform a lookup on company fields:

1. Click Lookup | Companies.
2. Select a field from the list.
3. If the field you'd like to use for your search is not listed, then select the Other Fields option and select the field from the list that appears.
4. In the Search for area, type the field value you'd like to find.
5. Click OK.

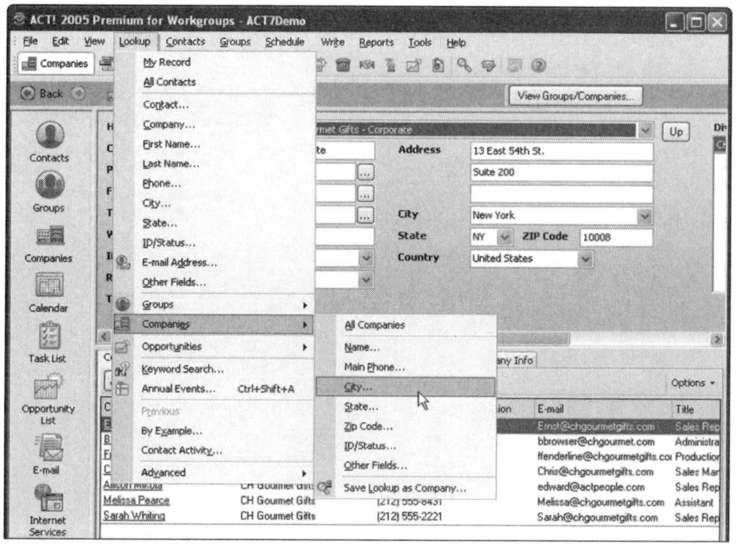

Performing a lookup on company fields

Looking up contacts associated with a group

To find all of the contacts in your database that are associated with a specific company, click the View Groups/Companies button in the upper-right corner of the ACT! interface.

Task B Saving a Lookup as a Company

If you perform a lookup of all contacts at a specific company, you can easily associate all of these contacts with a company in the database.

To save a lookup as a company:

1. Perform a lookup of all of the contacts in your database at a company.
2. Click Lookup | Companies | Save Lookup as Company.
3. Type the name of the new company in the Company field. Anytime a contact is created that matches the query, it will automatically be linked to the company.

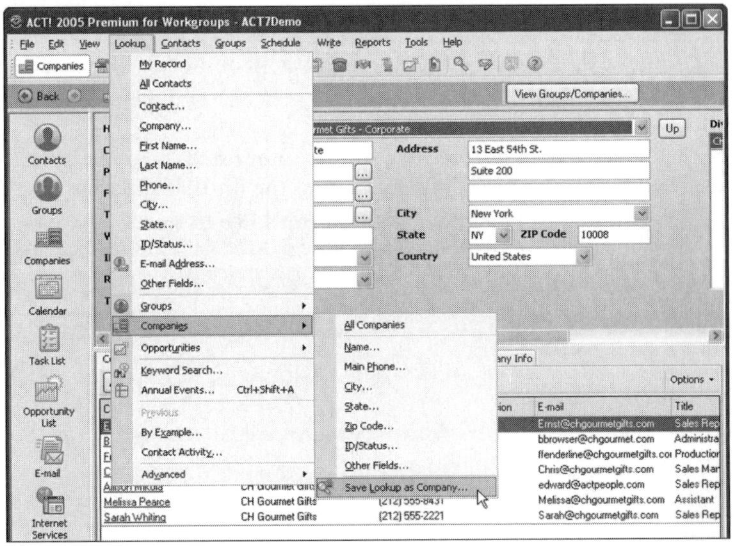

Saving a lookup as a query-based company

Dynamic companies

If you save a lookup as a company, the resulting company becomes a dynamic company. Any new contact added to the database matching the lookup will be automatically added to the company.

So, for example, let's say you perform a lookup of all the contacts at IBM and save that lookup as a company. If a colleague adds five new contacts with IBM in the Company field, then those contacts will be automatically associated with the IBM company record.

Group Lookups

The expanded group capabilities in ACT! 2005 have intensified the need for robust search capabilities for groups. You can now have thousands of groups (each with up to 15 levels of subgroups) in your database. This section will guide you through finding specific groups.

Task A Looking Up All Group Members

In previous versions of ACT!, you'd click the Group popup in the bottom-left corner of the ACT! interface to perform a quick lookup of all group members. In ACT! 2005, the feature has been moved to the top part of the ACT! interface.

To lookup all contacts that are members of a group:

1. Click the View Groups/Companies button in the upper-right corner of the ACT! interface.
2. In the View drop-down, select the Groups option.
3. Select a group or subgroup from the list.
4. Click OK. ACT! will lookup all of the group or subgroup members.

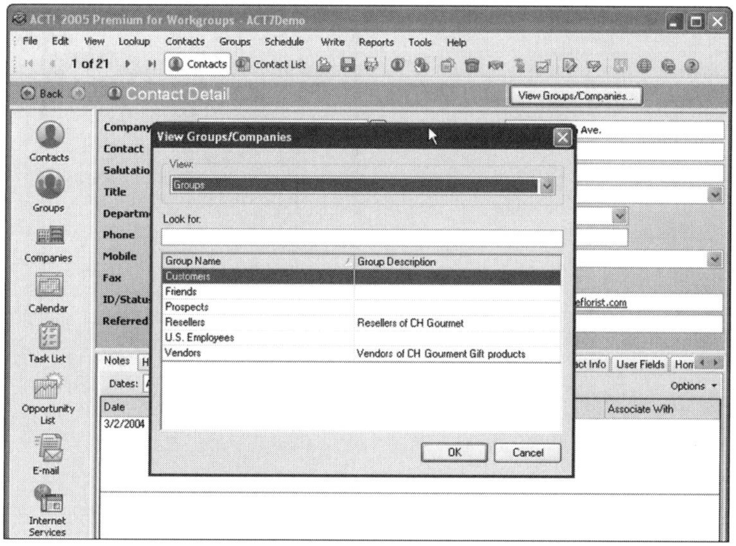

Performing a lookup of contacts in a group

Lookup in the Group List view

In the Group List view, right-click any group or subgroup and select the Create Lookup option to perform a quick lookup of all group members.

Task B Finding a Group by Name

If you have a thousand groups in your database, chances are good that you won't want to browse through all of them to find a specific group. Following these quick steps, you'll be able to find a specific group by searching on the group name field.

To find a group by name:

1. Click Lookup | Groups | Name.
2. Type the name of the group you'd like to find.
3. Click OK. ACT! will display a list of groups that match your lookup.

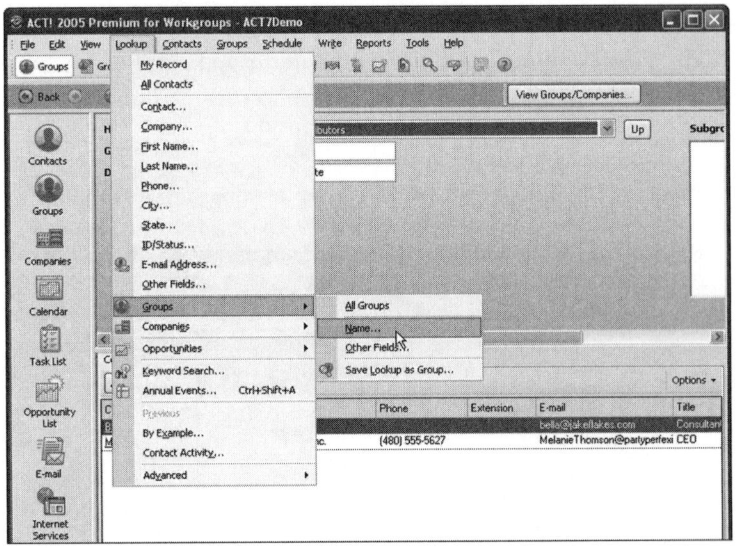

Performing a lookup on group fields

Show or hide subgroups

In the Group List view, click the Include Subgroups option to show or hide the subgroups.

Task C Looking Up Groups by Other Fields

You might have noticed a number of fields in the Groups view. If you want to find all of the groups that have a specific value in any of these groups' fields, just follow these simple steps.

To search on group fields:

1. Click Lookup | Groups | Other Fields.
2. Select a field from the list of group fields on the left side of the Lookup Groups dialog box.
3. Type a value in the Search for area on the right.
4. Click OK to find groups that match the lookup.

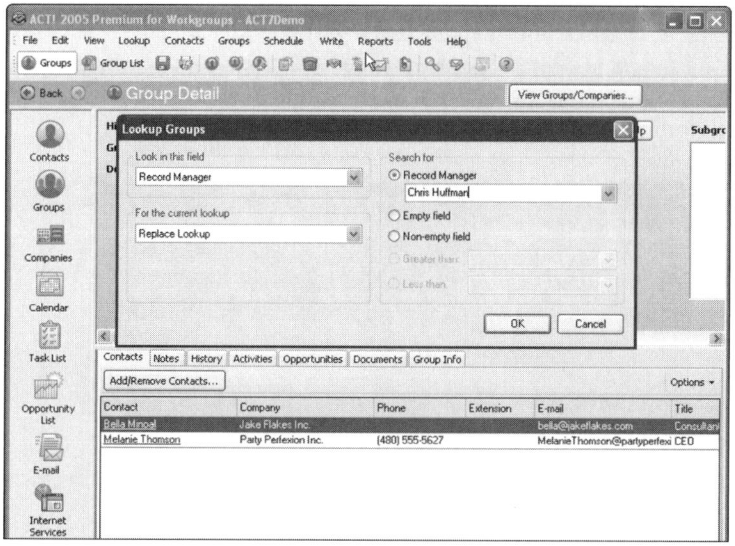

Performing a group lookup on the group Record Manager field

Looking up group fields

Performing a lookup on the group fields will not return a list of contacts. If you lookup by any of the group fields, ACT! will search for all of the groups that match the criteria.

Task D Saving a Lookup as a Group

In ACT! 2005, you can easily add all of the contacts in your current lookup to a new group. When you save a lookup as a group, ACT! will create a dynamic group. In other words, if you lookup all contacts in Texas and save that lookup as a group called Texas, any new Texans entered into the database will automatically get added to the group. If anyone moves out of Texas, they'll automatically be removed from the group.

Dynamic groups

If you save a lookup as a group, then the resulting group will have dynamic membership. Anytime a new contact that matches the lookup is added to the database, it will be automatically added to the group.

To save a lookup as a group:

1. Perform a lookup of the contacts you'd like to save as a group.
2. Click Lookup | Groups | Save Lookup as Group. The Groups view will appear.
3. In the Group field, type the name of your group. ACT! will add the contacts that match your lookup to the group.
4. As soon as you leave the Groups view, ACT! will save the new dynamic group. You may need to click View | Refresh to begin working with the group immediately.

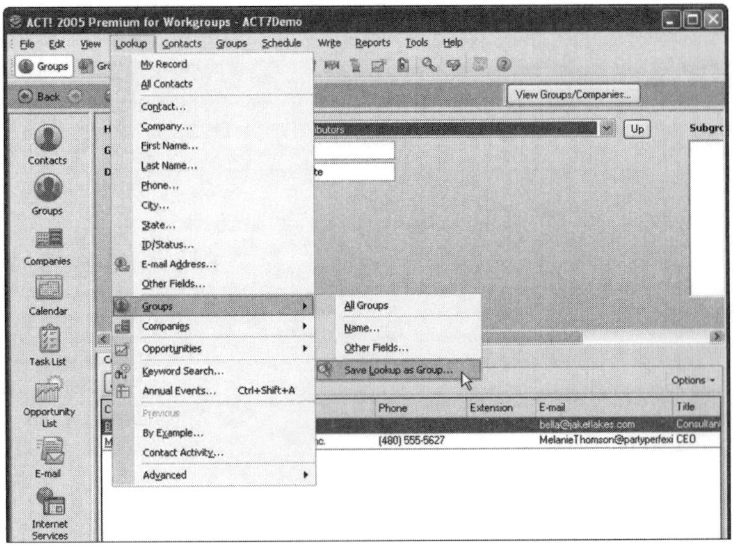

Saving a lookup as a group

Opportunity Lookups

The opportunity management features in ACT! 2005 have been completely redesigned. You now have the ability to track a lot more information on each potential sale, and with the addition of user fields, custom sales processes, and other features, ACT! now also includes expanded lookup functionality to help you find a specific set of opportunities.

Task A Looking Up All Opportunities

If you need to see a list of all open opportunities, you can perform a lookup of all open opportunities. Doing this is similar to the process of performing a lookup of all contacts in the database. The resulting list of opportunities will appear in the Opportunity List view.

To lookup all open opportunities:

1. Click Lookup on the menu.
2. Select the Opportunities option.
3. Click All Opportunities.
4. A list of all opportunities (subject to the filter you've set) will appear in the Opportunity List view.

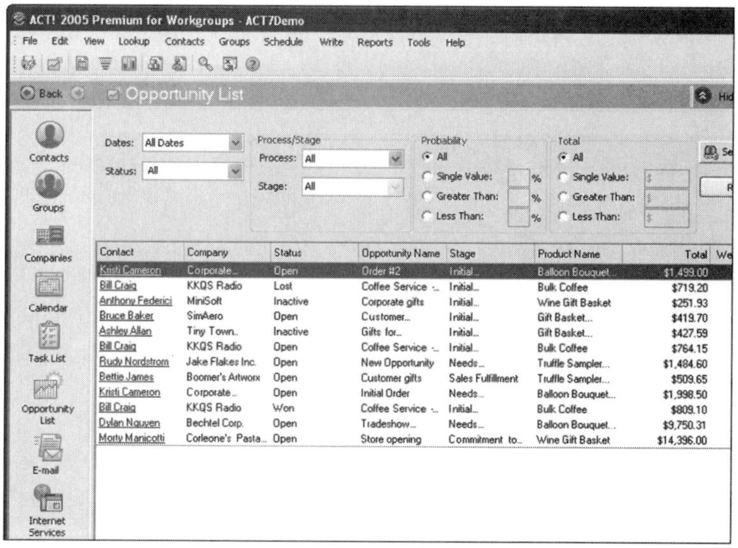

Viewing a lookup of opportunities in the Opportunity List view

Searching for all opportunities doesn't necessarily show all opportunities

If you perform a lookup of all open opportunities, the resulting list of opportunities is still subject to the filter you've set in the Opportunity List view. See Chapter 9, "Opportunity Management," for more information on filtering the Opportunity List view.

Task B Looking Up a Specific Opportunity by Name

ACT! 2005 now lets you give a specific name to each opportunity entered into ACT!. If you need to find an opportunity with a specific name, you can now search by opportunity name with just a few clicks.

To lookup an opportunity by name:

1. Click Lookup | Opportunities | Name.
2. The Lookup Opportunities dialog box will appear. In the Search for area, type the name of the opportunity you'd like to find.
3. Click OK.
4. A list of all opportunities matching the name you specified will appear in the Opportunity List view.

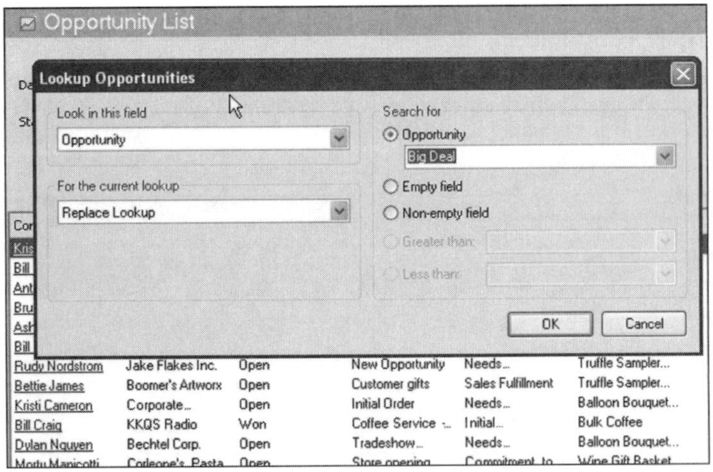

Performing a lookup by opportunity name

When you don't know the full name...

If you don't know the full name of the opportunity you'd like to find, you might need to perform an advanced query using the CONTAINS operator. The advanced query feature is also useful if you need to search through multiple opportunity fields at once.

The advanced query feature in ACT! 2005 now supports opportunity fields. Advanced queries are covered in a later task in this chapter.

Task C Looking Up Opportunities by Other Fields

As you enter a new opportunity into ACT!'s opportunity list, take a look at all of the fields of data in the Opportunity dialog box. When you're entering a new opportunity, you can enter a product, type, status, total, record manager, and more. ACT! also includes eight customizable user fields. It's easy to perform lookups on any of the fields for an opportunity.

To lookup an opportunity by other fields:

1. Click Lookup on the menu and select Opportunities.
2. Choose a field from the available list or select the Other Fields option. The Lookup Opportunities dialog box will appear.
3. From the list on the left, select an opportunity field.
4. Enter a search value in the space on the right side of the Lookup Opportunities dialog box.
5. Click OK.

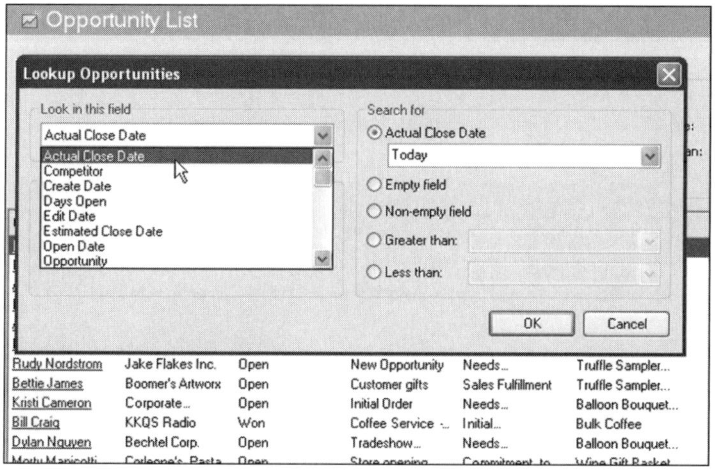

Performing an opportunity lookup by any opportunity field

Private opportunities

Whenever you perform an opportunity lookup, ACT! will not search through contacts that have been made private by other users. You will, however, see any opportunities that you have made private. To make an opportunity private, click the Private option in the bottom-left corner of the Opportunity dialog box.

Task D Using the Filter to Lookup Opportunities

If you're looking for a specific set of opportunities, you may need to filter your Opportunity List view. In the Opportunity List view, you can filter by date range, status, sales stage, probability, amount, or user.

To filter the Opportunity List view:

1. Click the Opportunity List button on the View bar. The filter options will appear in the upper part of the Opportunity List view. If you don't see them, click the Show Filters option in the upper-right part of the ACT! interface.
2. Change any of the filter items to show specific opportunities in the list.
3. To reset the filter and show all opportunities, click the Reset button in the filter area.

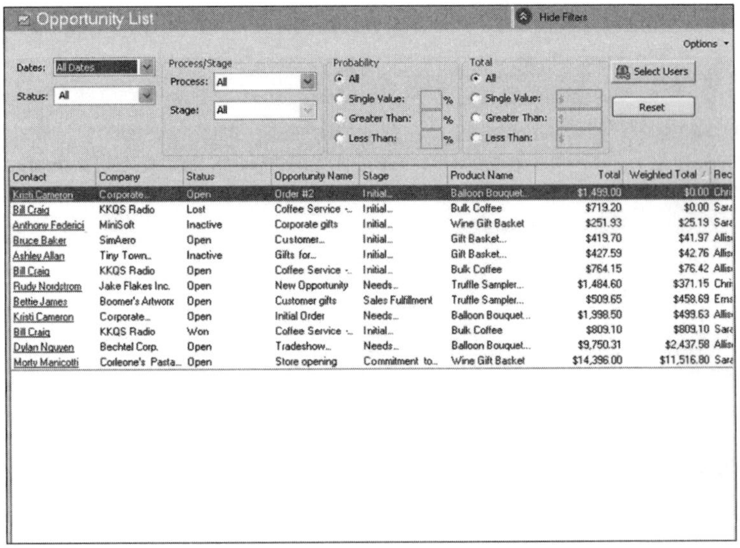

In the upper part of the Opportunity List view, filter to show just specific activities

Export to Excel

Once you've set a filter to show a specific set of opportunities, click the Export to Excel button on the toolbar to export the list to Excel. The resulting spreadsheet will automatically set up Pivot Tables to help you better analyze the data.

Annual Events Lookups

Annual events fields are a type of date field that can be added to any ACT! 2005 database. Once you've added an annual events field to the database, you can perform a special lookup on the field. You'll be able to search for annual events that will occur in the current week, the current month, or in a specific date range.

Task A Looking Up Annual Events

If you want to see a list of all of the subscription renewals that are due this month, all the birthdays that happen this week, or all the anniversaries that happen today, you could perform an annual events lookup.

To perform an annual events lookup:

1. Click Lookup | Annual Events. The Annual Events Search dialog box appears.
2. In the Search for drop-down, select the annual events field(s) you'd like to include in your search.
3. In the Time Range area, select a time range for your lookup. You can search for annual events that happen sometime in the current week, in the current month, or in a specified date range.
4. Click Find Now. The matching contacts will appear in the lower part of the Annual Events Search window.
5. If you'd like to create a lookup of the resulting contacts, click the Create Lookup button.
6. If you'd like to schedule a to-do (like a reminder to send a card) for the resulting contacts, click the Schedule To-do button.

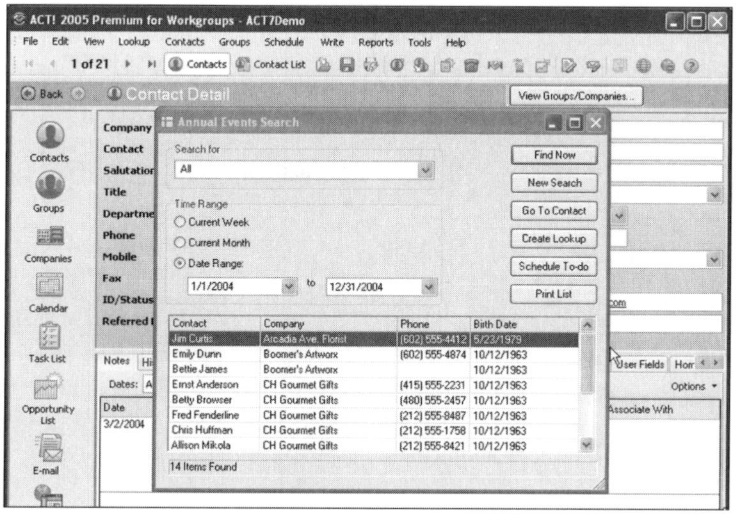

Searching for annual events that fall within a date range

Potential uses for annual events fields:

- Subscription renewals
- Contract expirations
- Anniversaries
- Birthdays

Annual events fields

All databases created in ACT! 6.0 or 2005 have one annual events field by default: the Birth Date field. Databases upgraded from previous versions will not contain an annual events field unless you add one in Edit | Define Fields. You must have manager or administrator access to the database to edit fields.

Contact Activity Lookups

Have you ever wondered how many contacts in your database had a call attempted last month? How many contacts have been sent an e-mail in the last year? How many contacts were modified in any way this quarter? You can locate these modified/unmodified contacts with the Contact Activity lookup feature.

Task A Looking Up Modified Contacts

With the new Contact Activity lookup feature in ACT! 2005, you'll be able to locate contacts based on what you've done with that contact in a given time range.

ACT! add-ons

There are literally hundreds of add-on products available that enhance ACT!'s core functionality. To view a list of add-on products, go to http://www.actaddons.com or http://www.actsolutions.com.

To perform a contact activity lookup:

1. Click Lookup | Contact Activity.
2. In the top area, select whether you'd like to search for the contacts that were changed or were not changed in the time range you specify.
3. In the Since Date section, select a date.
4. In the Search In area, select the areas of the database on which you'd like to search. For example, if you select Contact fields, you'll find all the contacts that had a field modified (or not modified) since the date range you specified.
5. For more options, select history and activity types from the Histories and Activities drop-downs.

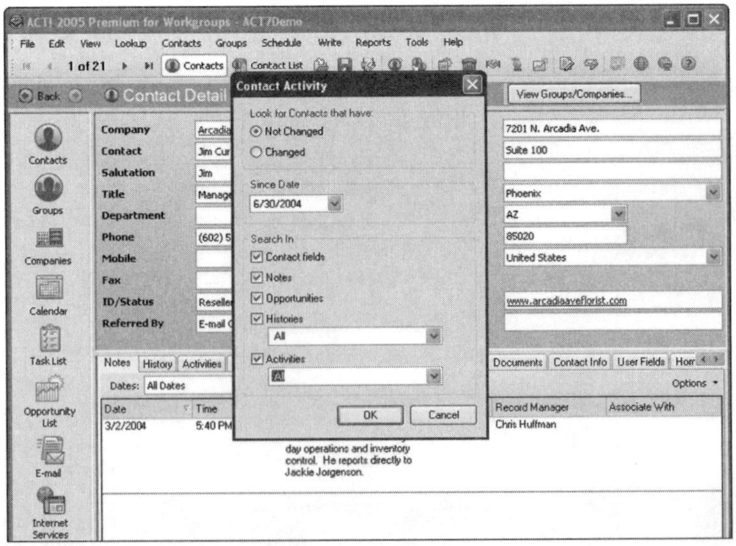

Searching for contacts that have not been modified since a specific date

Keyword Searches

When all else fails, you can use a keyword search to find each instance of a word or phrase throughout your database. A good rule of thumb to remember when performing a keyword search is this: With the Keyword Search feature, there isn't an area of the database that isn't searchable.

Task A Searching for a Specific Keyword

You can search for anything in an ACT! database with the Keyword Search feature. With a keyword search, you'll have the option of searching all fields, notes, activities, sales/opportunities, and more.

To perform a keyword search:

1. Click Lookup | Keyword Search.
2. In the Search for field, type the keyword you'd like to find.
3. Select the areas of the database you'd like to search. (You can search through contacts, groups, and companies. You can also look in the activities, opportunities, histories, notes, and fields areas of the database.)
4. Select whether to search through all records, the current record, or the current lookup.
5. Click Find Now.
6. The results of the keyword search will appear in the lower part of the Keyword Search dialog box.
7. Click Create Lookup to view the results of the keyword search in the Contact view.

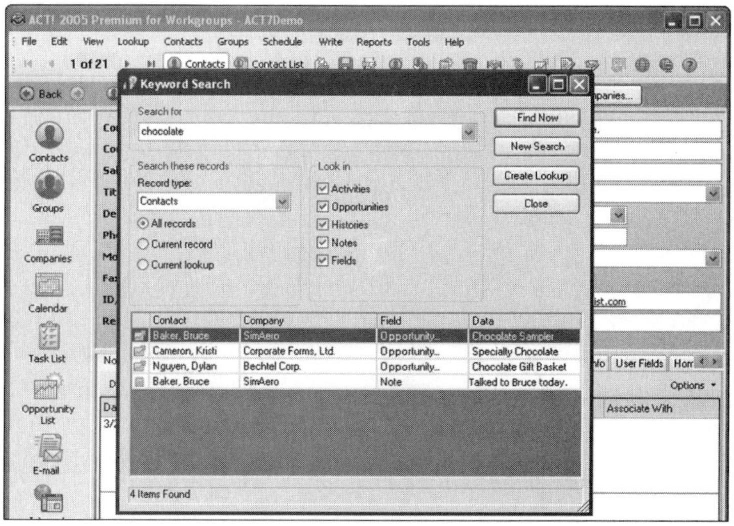

Performing a keyword search across all data in the database

Why use the keyword search?

There are two main reasons for performing a keyword search in ACT!:

1. You may want to find all of the contacts in the database that have something to do with a certain keyword. Maybe you want to find all of the contacts in the database that like to play golf?
2. You're looking to find a specific contact that you haven't been able to find using conventional searches. Perhaps you talked with someone yesterday, and you can't remember his name but you remember entering a note about his daughter's hockey game. You could keyword search the database for the word *hockey* to find your contact.

Lookups By Example

Using the Lookup By Example feature in ACT!, you can search on multiple fields in one step. The Lookup By Example screen slightly resembles the screen that you see when entering a new contact. But instead of having you enter new data for a contact, the Lookup By Example screen prompts you to show an example of the contact you'd like to find.

Task A Searching for a Field Value

You can use the Lookup By Example feature to search for all contacts with a specific value in a field. When you initiate a Lookup By Example, just enter a field value in any field. ACT! will find all of the contacts that match the example you've provided.

To use the Lookup By Example feature to search on a field:

1. Click Lookup | By Example. The Lookup By Example screen will appear.
2. Type a value in any field and click Search.
3. The Run Query Options dialog box appears. Select to replace the lookup.
4. Click OK.
5. The Run Query Options dialog box will appear. Choose replace the lookup and click OK. (Information on replacing, adding, and narrowing lookups is covered in an earlier task in this chapter.) ACT! will perform the search. If multiple matching contacts are found, the results will display in the Contact List view. If only one matching contact is found, the contact will appear in the Contact view.

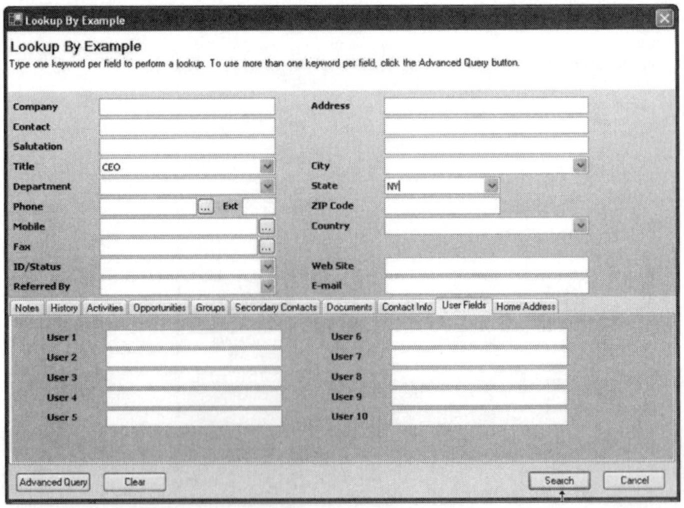

Performing a Lookup By Example

Task B Searching for Multiple Field Values

One of advantages of using the Lookup By Example feature to find contacts is that with Lookup By Example, you can search on multiple fields in one step. If you need to find all of the CEOs in New York, you can use a Lookup By Example to perform both lookups together in one step.

To search multiple fields with a Lookup By Example:

1. Click Lookup | By Example. The Lookup By Example screen will appear.
2. Type a value in a field. For example, you could type the word **CEO** in the Title field.
3. Type a value in another field. For example, you could type **NY** in the State field.
4. Click Search.
5. The Run Query Options dialog box will appear. Select to replace the lookup.
6. Click OK. ACT! will perform the search, and the New York CEOs will appear in the Contact List view.

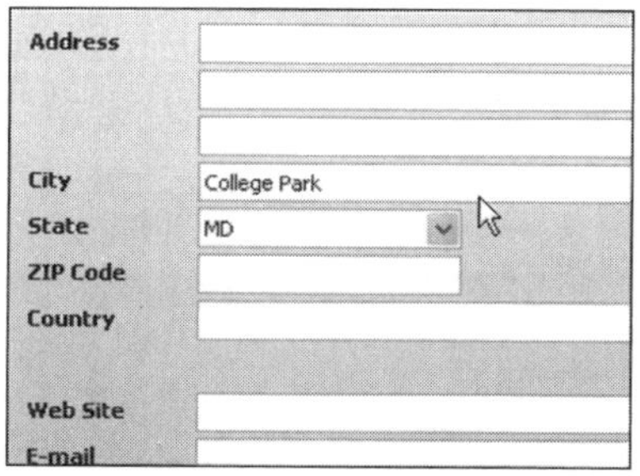

Searching on multiple fields in the Lookup By Example view

Lookup By Example queries are AND searches

If you enter values into more than one field in the Lookup By Example screen, ACT! searches for contacts that have the same value in both fields.

If you'd like to perform a lookup of contacts that have either of the two values, you can convert the Lookup By Example to an advanced query to perform an OR search.

See the next task for information on converting a Lookup By Example to an advanced query.

Task C Converting a Lookup By Example to an Advanced Query

For access to more advanced searching capabilities, you can convert a Lookup By Example to an Advanced Query. In the Advanced Query area, you can use Boolean operators to create as advanced a query as you require. ACT!'s advanced queries are now written with a graphical interface, so there's no need to learn a special query language.

.qry files

ACT! queries can be saved as .qry files. By default, they're kept in the Query folder within your database supplemental files folder.

To convert a Lookup By Example to an Advanced Query:

1. Click Lookup | By Example and enter information into all of the fields you'd like to use in your advanced query.
2. Click the Advanced Query button in the bottom left corner of the Lookup By Example screen. The Advanced Query editor will appear. ACT! will have converted your Lookup By Example into the graphical Advanced Query interface.
3. Make any necessary changes to the query.
4. Click the Preview button to preview the results of the query.
5. Click OK.
6. Select whether you'd like to Replace, Add, or Narrow the current lookup. The results of your advanced query will appear in the Contact List view.

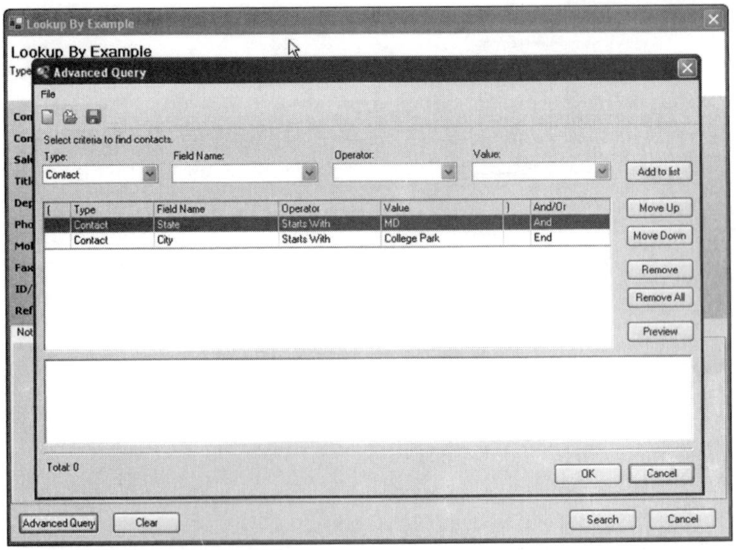

Performing an advanced query

Advanced Queries

Most of your searches in ACT! will be simple lookups, but every once in a while you may need to find contacts based on a complex query. For example, if you're looking for all contacts in a certain territory who haven't been contacted in six months and have purchased more than $5000 in the past year, you could perform an advanced query to isolate just those contacts—all in one step.

Task A Performing an Advanced Query

The Advanced Query functionality has been completely redesigned in ACT! 2005. The new interface is menu-driven and doesn't require that you learn any sort of advanced query language.

To perform an advanced query:

1. Click Lookup | Advanced | Advanced Query.
2. The Advanced Query dialog box appears. In the Type drop-down, select the type of field you'd like to add to the advanced query. (You can search through contact fields and opportunity fields in the advanced query feature.)
3. In the Field Name drop-down, select a field you'd like to search on.
4. Choose an operator from the list of available operators.
5. Type a value in the Value field.
6. Click the Add to List button to add the query string to the list.
7. Repeat Steps 2-6 until you have added all of the query strings necessary for your advanced query.
8. If necessary, change the value in the And/Or column for the query strings you've added to the advanced query.
9. Click the Preview button to preview the results of the query.
10. Click OK to view the resulting contacts in the Contact List view.

Query operators

Most basic searches in ACT! use the Starts With query operator. If you click Lookup | Last Name and type the first few letters of someone's last name, ACT! will search for all of the contacts that have a last name that begins with the letters you typed. In the advanced query area, you can use these query operators:

- Contains
- Contains Data
- Does Not Contain Data
- Ends With
- Greater Than
- Less Than
- Equal To
- Not Equal To
- Starts With
- Within Last [days]
- Within Next [days]
- On or Before
- On or After

Task B Saving an Advanced Query

If you spend a lot of time creating an advanced query, or if you plan on running the query often, it's probably a good idea to save the query. Queries are saved as .qry files in your database supplemental files folder. For instant access to the query, you could even add the query as a Custom Command in Tools | Customize | Menus & Toolbars. Custom Commands can be added to any menu or toolbar.

When executing an advanced query in ACT!, you'll be prompted to save the query. Queries are saved as .qry files and can be shared across multiple ACT! users. It's a good idea to save your advanced queries if you've spent a lot of time creating them.

Queries from previous versions of ACT!

If you have created queries in previous versions of ACT!, they won't convert to ACT! 2005 format. Queries are the only data type that will not come over in the Conversion Wizard.

To save an advanced query:

1. Click Lookup | Advanced | Advanced Query.
2. Set up your advanced query. (Information about adding an advanced query is covered in a previous task in this chapter.)
3. Click File | Save As.
4. Specify a filename and location for your query file. Queries are saved as .qry files.
5. Click Save.

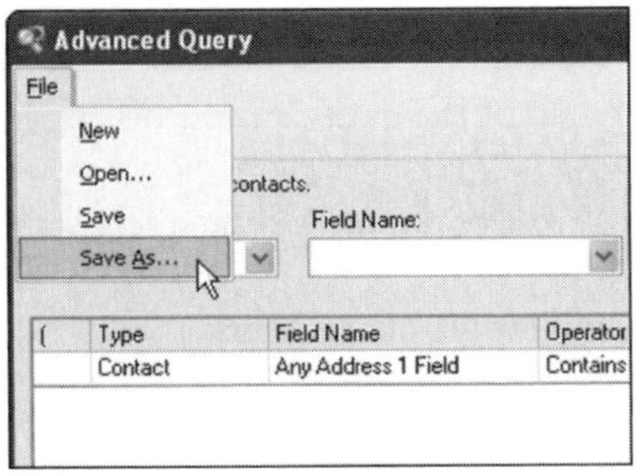

Saving an advanced query

Task C Editing an Existing Query

If you've saved a query somewhere on your hard drive or network, you can edit the query at any time and update it as needed.

To edit an existing query:

1. Click Lookup | Advanced | Advanced Query.
2. Click File | Open.
3. Browse to the folder that contains your query and select the saved query file.
4. Click Open. ACT! will open the saved advanced query.
5. Make any changes to the query.
6. To save your changes, click File | Save.

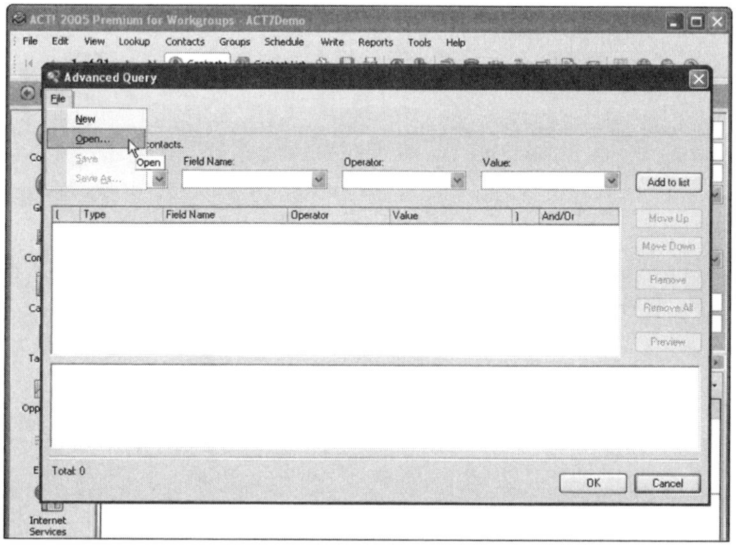

Opening a saved query

Chapter 6
Contact List View

Contact List View Basics

The Contact List view in ACT! 2005 performs the same function that it did in earlier versions of ACT!. It gives you a spreadsheet-like view of your contact data. In ACT! 2005, the Edit Mode feature has been removed, but some problems with previous versions—like the inability to sort by system fields—have been addressed.

Task A Launching the Contact List View

New users of ACT! will quickly notice that the Contact List view, by default, is no longer listed on the View bar on the left side of the ACT! interface. The feature is still a key part of the product, though. To launch the Contact List view, you'll now click the Contacts button on the View bar and then click the Contact List button on the toolbar.

To launch the Contact List view and show all contacts:

1. Click the Contact List button on the View bar. The Contact List view will appear.
2. Click Lookup | All Contacts. All contacts in the database will show in the Contact List view.

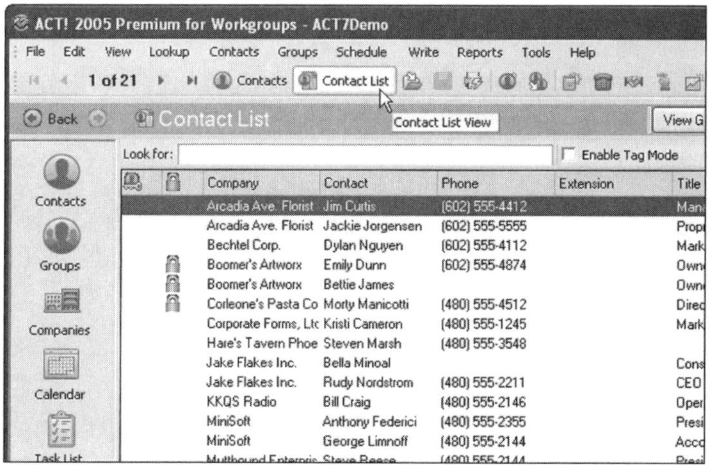

Viewing multiple contacts at once in the Contact List view

Add the Contact List view

If you'd like to see the Contact List view listed as one of the icons on the View bar on the left side of the ACT! interface, then right-click anywhere in the View bar and select either the Expanded menu or Classic menu.

Where's the Edit Mode?

If you haven't been able to find the Edit Mode in ACT! 2005, you're not going crazy! The feature was removed from ACT! 2005. This is the only major feature that was removed from the program.

F8 for the Contact List view

Click F8 from anywhere in ACT! to bring up the Contact List view.

Always the current lookup

The Contact List view always shows just the contacts in your current lookup. If you perform a lookup of all contacts in a specific state, you'll just see those contacts in the Contact List view. If you click Lookup | All Contacts, you'll be able to see all contacts in the database.

Task B Sorting Contacts

You can sort the contacts in your Contact List view by any field in the database. In previous versions of ACT!, you couldn't sort by e-mail address or by any system field. In ACT! 2005, however, you can sort by any field.

To sort the contacts in your Contact List view:

1. In the Contact List view, click a column header. The column header is the gray bar at the top of each column of data. The contacts in the Contact List view will be sorted by the field whose column header you just clicked.
2. You'll notice that a small arrow shows in the column header next to the field name. This arrow indicates whether your list is sorted in ascending or descending order. To change the sort order, click the column header again.

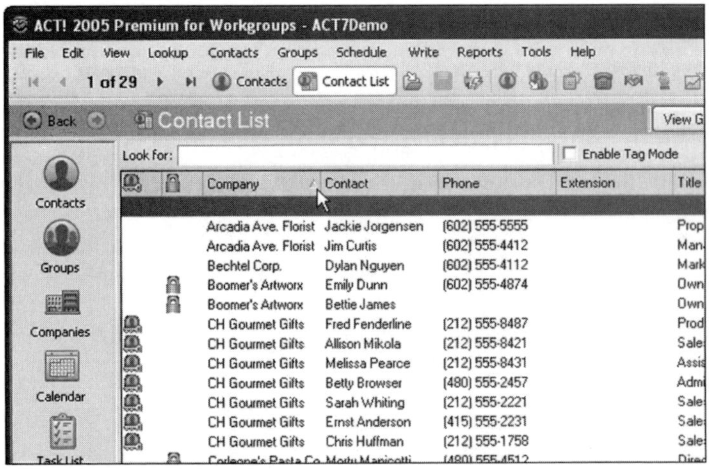

Sorting the current lookup in the Contact List view

Task C Searching for Contacts in the Contact List View

The Contact List view will always show the contacts in your current lookup. If you're looking for a specific contact, you could perform a lookup to find that contact. However, you can also use the Quick Find feature within the Contact List view to go to a particular contact's record within the current lookup.

To find a contact in the Contact List view:

1. Sort the Contact List view by any field by clicking the column header for that field.
2. In the upper-left corner of the Contact List view, type a word into the Look for field.
3. ACT! will take you directly to the contacts that have the word in the field that you clicked in Step 1.

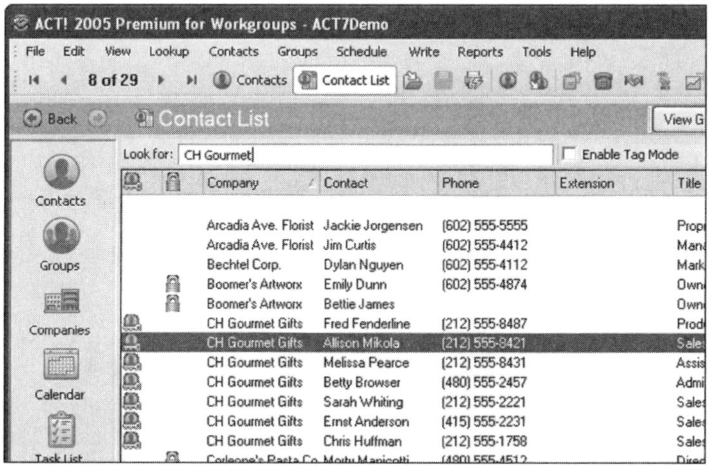

Performing a quick search for contacts in the Contact List view

Speed increase

You'll notice that the Contact List view is a lot faster in ACT! 2005 than it has been in previous versions. Also, ACT! 2005 doesn't slow down when the E-mail Address field is added to the Contact List view. (This was a problem with previous versions of the software.)

Refining and Creating Lookups in the Contact List View

It's nice to be able to view your contact data in a spreadsheet-like view, but the real power of the Contact List view comes with its lookup refining capabilities. In the Contact List view, you can lookup sets of tagged contacts and omit unneeded contacts from a lookup. This functionality is very useful when you need to refine a lookup before sending a mass letter or e-mail.

Task A Looking Up Tagged Contacts

At the end of the year, most people send out a holiday card (and those who don't probably should). But how do you create a list of card recipients? In the Contact List view, you could tag contacts for inclusion in your holiday card mailer and then perform a lookup of the tagged contacts. Once you've created a lookup of these contacts, it's easy to save the lookup as a group (refer to Chapter 5) or print mailing labels for your lookup (see Chapter 10, "Letters, Envelopes, and Labels").

Why is the current lookup so important?

The current lookup in ACT! serves as a temporary group in the database. Just about anything that can be done to multiple contacts in the database can be done to the contacts in your current lookup. You can send a mass e-mail or letter to the contacts in your current lookup. You can save your current lookup as a dynamic group. You can even schedule an activity for all contacts in the current lookup. As you start to perform these tasks for multiple contacts, having the ability to refine the current lookup will be invaluable.

To create a lookup of tagged contacts:

1. In the Contact List view, click the Enable Tag Mode option (you'll find it next to the Look for field above the field column headers).
2. Click each contact that you'd like to include in your lookup. As you click contact records, they'll become highlighted.
3. Click the Lookup Selected button. Your current lookup will become a list of the selected contacts.

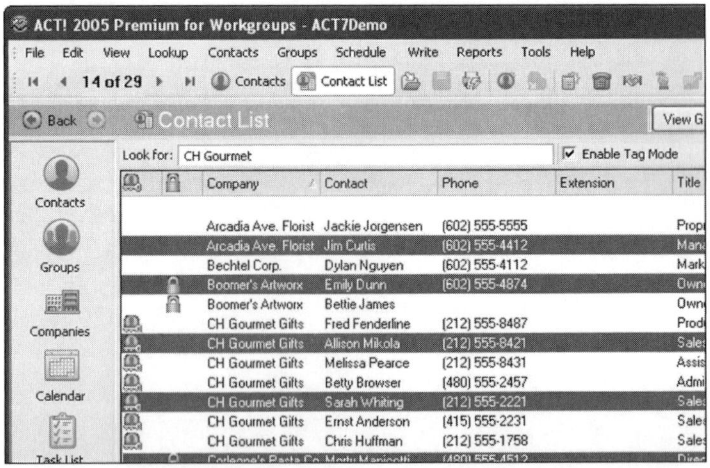

Tagging multiple contacts in the Contact List view.

Task B Omitting Tagged Contacts

If you're about to send a mass e-mail or letter to the contacts in your current lookup, you can use the Contact List view to omit specific contacts from the lookup.

To omit tagged contacts from the current lookup:

1. In the Contact List view, click the Enable Tag Mode option.
2. Click each contact that you'd like to omit from the current lookup. As you click the contacts, ACT! will highlight them.
3. Click the Omit Selected button to omit the highlighted contacts from the current lookup.

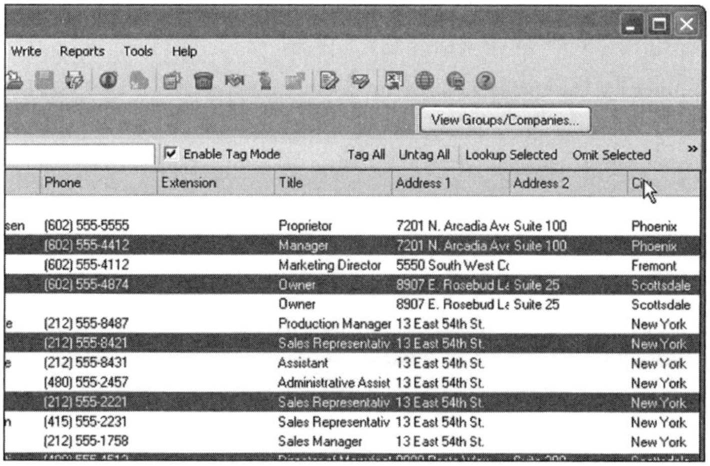

Omitting contacts from the current lookup

Shift + Click

To select multiple consecutive contacts, enable the Tag Mode in the Contact List view. Then, click a contact to highlight it. Hold down the Shift key and click another contact. ACT! will tag all contacts between the two that you clicked.

Omit does not delete

If you right-click somewhere in the Contact List view, you'll have the option of omitting the contact from the lookup or deleting the contact. Be careful when choosing the Delete option.

Omit will remove the contact from the lookup, but the contact will not be permanently removed from the database.

Delete will permanently remove the contact from the database. There's no easy way to undelete a contact.

Customizing the Contact List View

The real power of the Contact List view lies in its customizability. You can re-sort the columns, change the length of columns, add columns to the list, and remove the columns when you don't need them anymore. These features let you build a Contact List view that shows just the specific information you require.

Task A Adding Columns

By default, ACT! shows the main contact fields in the Contact List view. If you've added extra fields to your database, or if you use any of the fields that aren't shown on the Contact List view, you may want to add these additional fields to the Contact List.

Reset the list

To reset the Contact List view columns to the factory default, click the Options button in the upper-right corner of the Contact List view and select the Customize Columns option. Then, click the Reset button and click OK.

To add columns to the Contact List view:

1. In the upper-right corner of the Contact List view, locate the Options drop-down. Click this option's drop-down and select the Customize Columns option. The Customize Columns dialog box will appear.
2. On the left side of the dialog box, you'll see a list of fields that are in the database but aren't currently showing in the Contact List view. Highlight any field and click the > button to add it to the list.
3. Click OK.

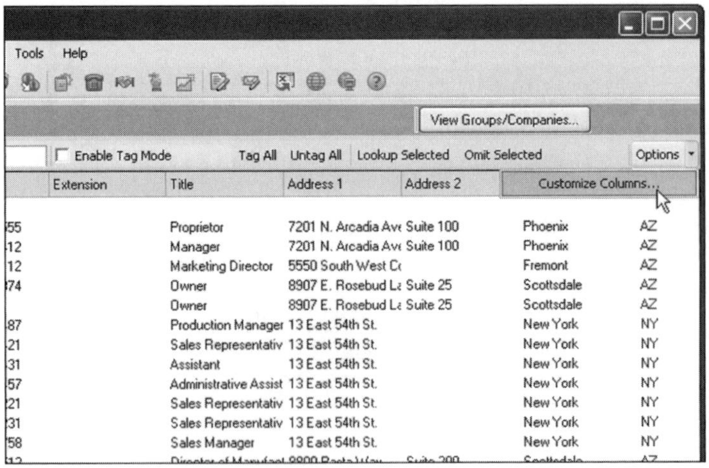

Customizing the column display options

Task B Removing Columns

Some time after adding columns to the Contact List view, you'll likely want to remove them. Removing columns entails the same general process as adding new columns.

To remove a column from the Contact List view:

1. In the Contact List view, click the Options button in the upper-right corner. Select the Customize Columns option.
2. From the list on the right, highlight the column that you'd like to remove.
3. Click the < button to remove the column.
4. Click OK.

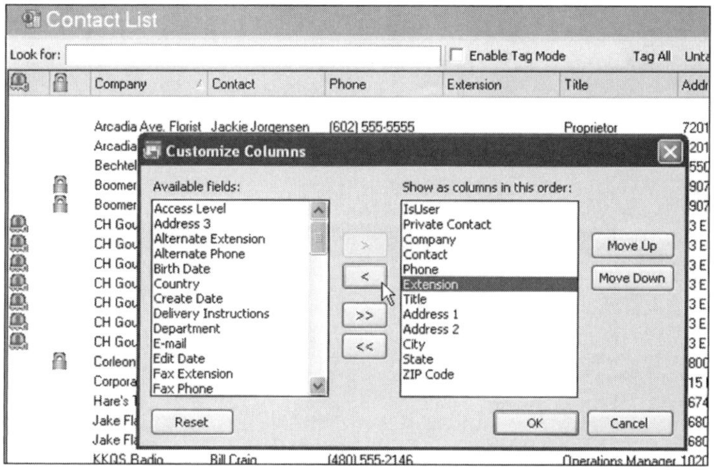

Removing a column from the Contact List view

Removing a column does not delete data

Removing a column from the Contact List view will temporarily hide the data in the Contact List view, but doing this will not permanently delete any data. Your field will still be available in the Contact view, and you can always add the column back onto the Contact List view.

An easier way

In the Contact List view, you can click and drag any field's column header to a new spot.

Task C Rearranging Columns

After adding a number of fields to the Contact List view, you may need to rearrange the fields. You can do this in the Customize Columns dialog box, or you can simply drag a field's column header to a new spot in the Contact List view.

To rearrange columns in the Contact List view:

1. In the Contact List view, click the Options button in the upper-right corner. Select the Customize Columns option.
2. From the list on the right, highlight the column that you'd like to rearrange.
3. Click the Move Up and Move Down buttons to change the order of the column.
4. Click OK.

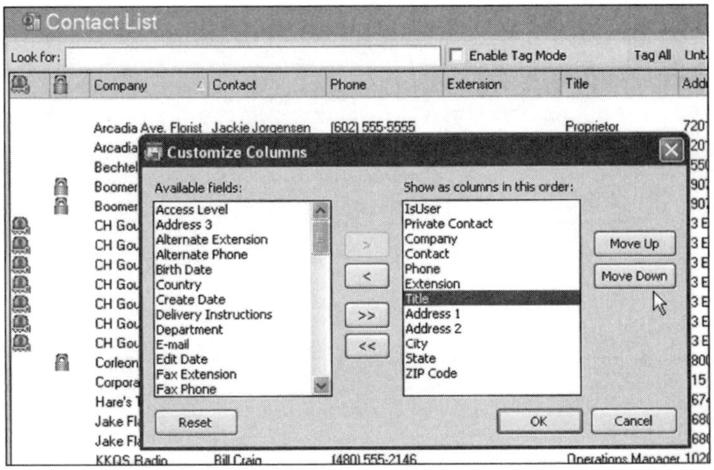

Changing the order of columns in the Contact List view

Microsoft Excel Integration

If you've performed a lookup to refine the contacts that show in the Contact List view, and if you've customized the columns that show for each contact, you might want to export the on-screen data in the Contact List view to Microsoft Excel. In ACT! 2005, you can do this with a single click.

Task A Exporting the Contact List View to Excel

After you click the Export to Excel button in the Contact List view, ACT! will export all of the information currently showing in the Contact List view to an Excel spreadsheet.

To export the Contact List view to Excel:

1. Click View | Contact List to launch the Contact List view.
2. Perform a lookup of the contacts that you'd like to export to Excel.
3. If needed, customize the columns that show in the Contact List view (see the previous task in this chapter).
4. Click the Export to Excel icon on the toolbar (or click Tools | Export to Excel).

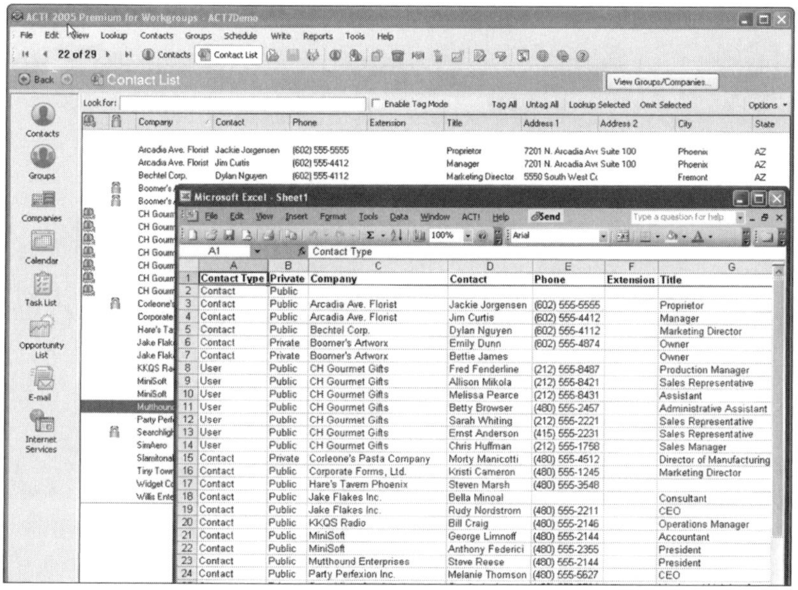

Exporting the Contact List view contents to Microsoft Excel

Sending a mailing?

If you use an outside mail service to send letters or postcards to your customers, you can use the Excel integration as an easy way to send your contacts' address information to the mail house. Just customize the columns that show in the Contact List view, perform a lookup of the mailer recipients, and click the Excel button to create a spreadsheet that you can send to the mail service.

Restricted and Browse users

Restricted and Browse users cannot export data to Excel. You must be at least a Standard user to use this feature.

Chapter 7
Using Groups

Creating Groups

From time to time, you'll want to associate certain otherwise unrelated contacts with one another. ACT!'s Groups feature enables you to do this. With groups, you can make temporary or permanent associations of contacts. You can easily perform a lookup of a group or send a mass mailing to the members of a group.

Task A Creating a Group

In ACT! 2005, you can add a virtually unlimited number of groups to the database, and, if you're a longtime ACT! user, you'll notice that performing basic tasks—such as lookups—on groups is a lot faster in the new version. You can now create a new group from any view using the new Groups menu.

To create a new group:

1. Click Groups | New Group. A new group record will appear in the Groups view.
2. In the Group field, enter a name for your new group. If necessary, enter data into the other group fields.

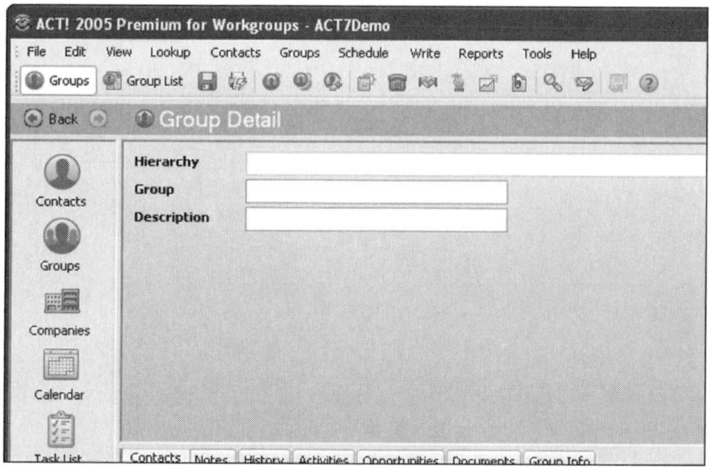

A newly created group in the Groups view

Private groups

If you don't want other users (including the database administrator) to be able to see your new group, go to the Group Info tab in the Groups view and click the Private option. Now, only you will be able to see your private groups.

15 levels of subgroups

In ACT! 2005, you can now have 15 levels of subgroups. (Previous versions only allowed one level.)

Subgroup clarification

If a contact is a member of a subgroup, that contact does not automatically become a member of the parent group.

Task B Creating a Subgroup

Creating a new subgroup entails the same general process as creating a new group, but you can only create new subgroups in the Groups view or Group List view.

To create a new subgroup:

1. In the Groups view, go to the group for which you'd like to add a subgroup. Alternatively, you could highlight the group in the Group List view.
2. Click Groups | New Subgroup. The new subgroup will appear in the Groups view.
3. Enter the name of the subgroup in the Group field.

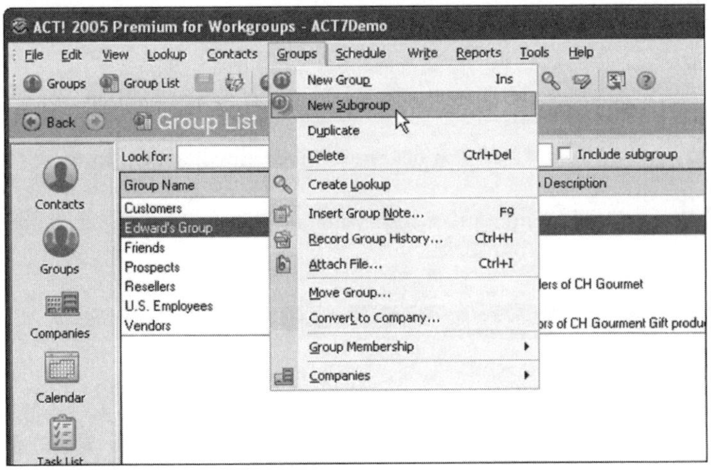

Creating a new subgroup

Task C Deleting Groups or Subgroups

Deleting a group does not delete the contacts in the group. Deleting the group only deletes the association of otherwise unrelated contacts. There's no easy way to undelete a group deletion, so it's a good idea to back up your database before removing groups.

To delete a group or subgroup:

1. In the Groups view, go to the group or subgroup you'd like to remove from the database.
2. Click Groups | Delete.
3. Click Yes to confirm the group deletion.

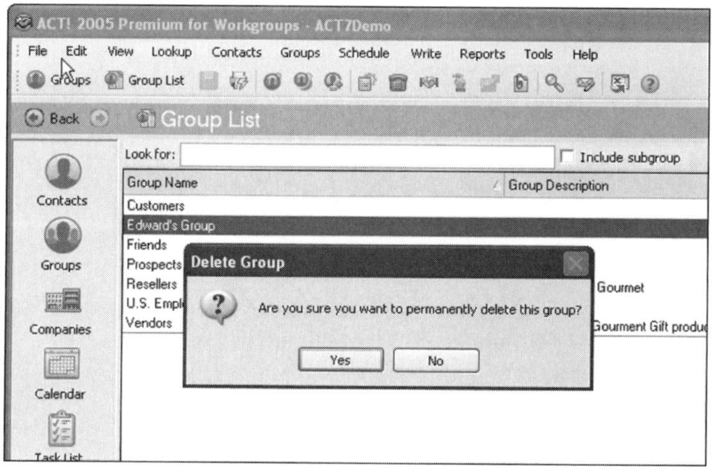

Confirming a group deletion

Deleting a main group

When you delete a parent group, the subgroups are not deleted. If you want to get rid of the subgroups as well as the parent group, you'll have to delete all of them individually. When you delete a parent group, any subgroups left behind are automatically promoted up a level.

Task D Renaming an Existing Group

You can change the name of any existing group by changing the value in the Group field in the Groups view.

To rename an existing group:

1. In the Groups view, go to the group whose name you'd like to change.
2. Change the value in the Groups field. ACT! will rename the group.

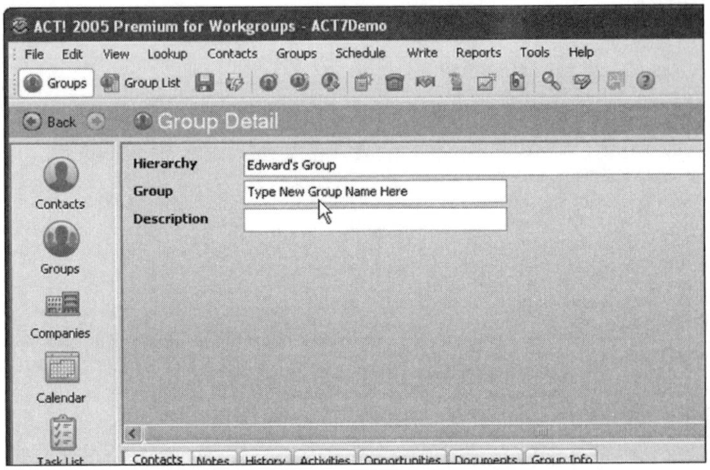

Renaming an existing group

Duplicate an existing group

To duplicate an existing group, highlight the group in the Groups List view and click Groups | Duplicate.

Task E Converting Groups to Companies

Previous versions of ACT! did not have a company entity, and so many users used the Groups view to track companies or accounts. To accommodate this legacy data, ACT! 2005 allows you to convert group records to company records.

To convert a group to a company:

1. Click Groups | Convert to Company.
2. The Convert Groups to Companies Wizard will appear. Click Next when the introduction screen appears.
3. From the list on the left, select the group or groups you'd like to convert to companies and click the > button to add them to the list to be converted. Click Next.
4. Select a field map for ACT! to use when sending data from the group fields to company fields. Click Next. ACT! will display a screen confirming the records to be converted.
5. Click Next. ACT! will convert the selected items.
6. Click Finish to exit the Wizard.

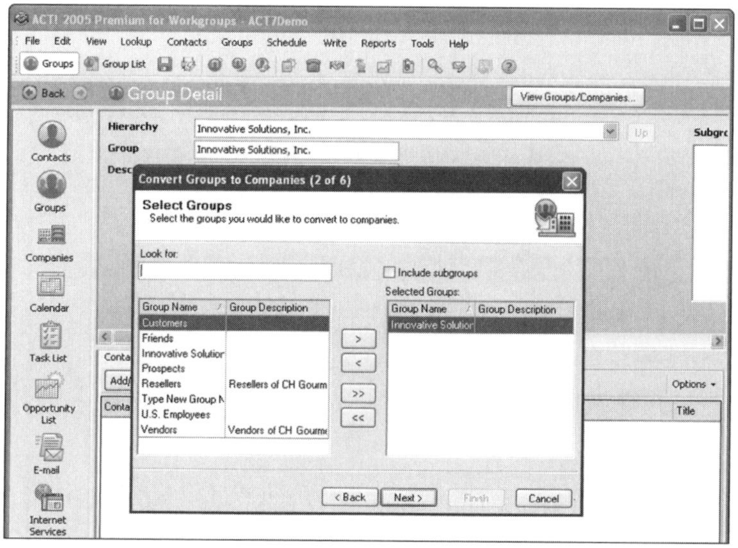

Converting existing groups to company records

No Undo

If you accidentally convert groups to company records, you won't be able to easily undo the changes. It's a good idea to make a back up of the database before proceeding.

Changing Group Membership

In ACT! 2005, you can add both static and dynamic members to a group. Static members are added individually and remain in the database until you manually remove them. Dynamic members are added and removed automatically.

Task A Adding Static Members to a Group

You can add an unlimited number of static members to any group. Static members will always be included in the group membership, and they do not rely on any rules or queries to update membership status.

Add the current lookup

When adding multiple static members to a group, you can add the contacts in the current lookup by selecting the Current Lookup option from the Select from drop-down at the top of the Contacts dialog box.

To add static members to a group:

1. In the Groups view, go to the group record whose membership you'd like to change. Alternatively, you could highlight the group in the Groups List view.
2. Click Groups | Group Membership Add/Remove Contacts.
3. Click the Contacts button to add new static members to the group.
4. From the list on the left, select the contact(s) you'd like to add to the group and click the > button to add them to the membership list on the right.
5. Click OK twice to return to the main ACT! interface.

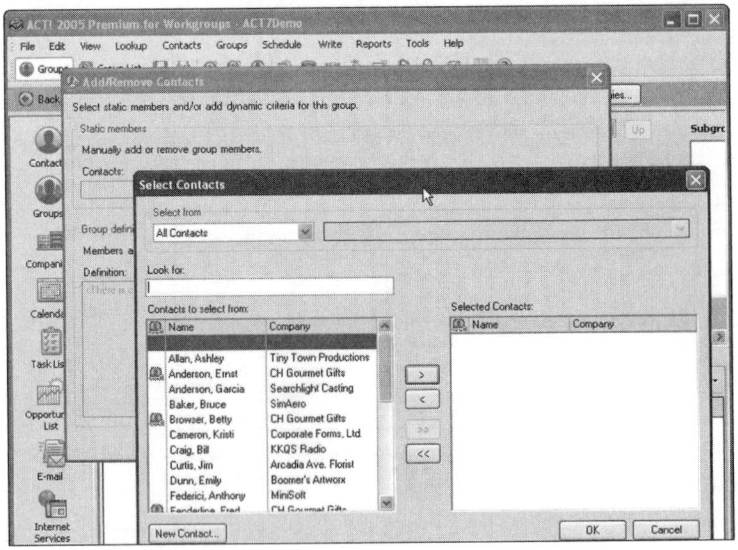

Adding contacts to a group

Task B Adding Selected Contacts to a Group

In the Contact List view, you can tag multiple contacts and add them automatically to a group. In previous versions of ACT!, you could do this by adding a current lookup of contacts to a group, but the new process is much faster.

To add selected static members to a group:

1. In the Contact List view, click the Enable Tag Mode option.
2. Tag the contacts that you would like to add to a group.
3. Click Groups | Group Membership | Add Selected to Group.
4. When the Add Contacts to Group / Company dialog box appears, highlight a group or subgroup and click OK.

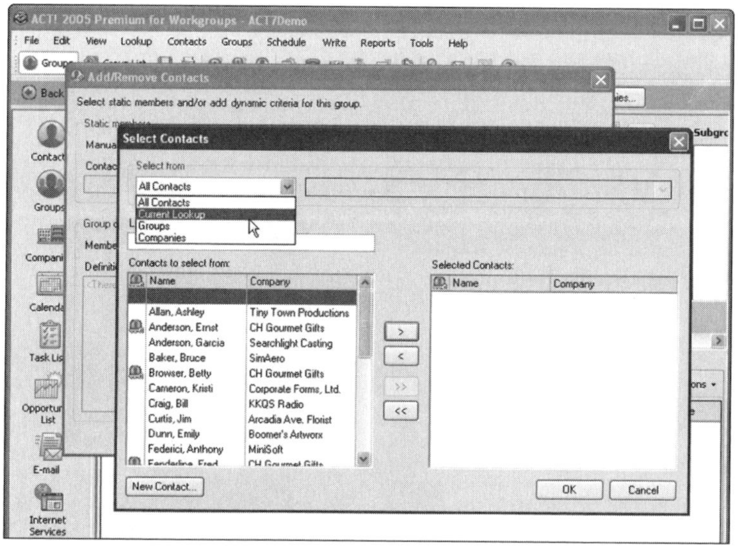

Adding the current lookup to a group

ACT! add-ons

For a complete listing of programs that work with and enhance ACT!, point your Web browser to http://www.actaddons.com.

Task C Removing Contacts from a Group

From time to time, you may want to remove contacts from a group. Removing static members to a group entails the same general process you took to add them. If you need to remove a contact from a group that has been added to the group by virtue of the dynamic group rules, you won't be able to specifically remove the contact without either changing the field values for the contact or changing the query that ACT! uses to add contacts to the group.

To remove static members from a group:

1. In the Groups view, go to the group record whose group membership you'd like to change. Alternatively, you could highlight the group in the Groups List view.
2. Click Groups | Group Membership | Add/Remove Contacts.
3. Click the Contacts button to change the static group membership.
4. From the list on the right, highlight the contact(s) you'd like to remove from the group membership list.
5. Click the < button to remove the selected contacts.
6. Click OK twice to return to the main ACT! interface.

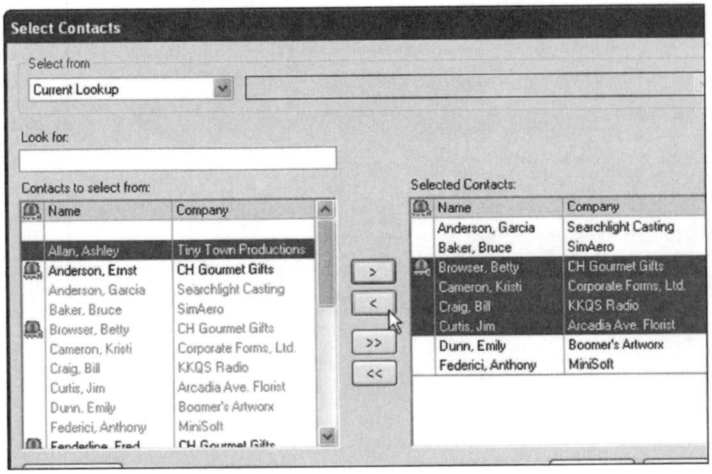

Removing multiple contacts from a group

Removing dynamic group members

If you need to remove contacts that were added to a group through a dynamic group rule, you'll have to update the group rule to do so. You can view the query that ACT! uses to assign dynamic group membership by clicking Groups | Group Membership | Add/Remove Contacts.

Task D Changing Dynamic Group Membership

In previous versions of ACT!, you could assign group rules to semi-automatically update group membership information. In ACT! 2005, the group rules are dynamic. Once you assign a query-based rule to a group, members are automatically added or removed from the group.

To set dynamic group membership:

1. In the Groups view, go to the group record whose group membership you'd like to change. Alternatively, you could highlight the group in the Groups List view.
2. Click Groups | Group Membership | Add/Remove Contacts.
3. In the Group definition area, click the Edit Criteria button to edit the query-based rule that ACT! uses to assign contacts dynamically to the group.
4. Make any necessary changes to the query and click OK.
5. Click OK to save the changes.

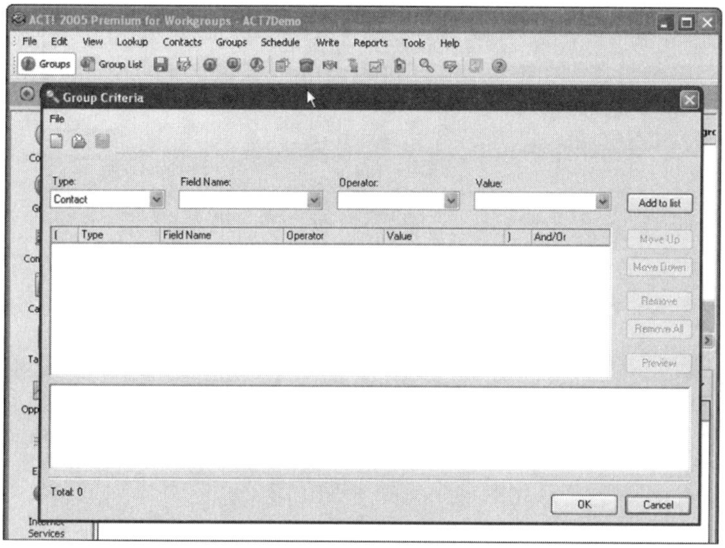

Setting the dynamic group definition

ACT! add-ons

For a comprehensive list of add-on products that work with ACT! 2005 go to http://www.actaddons.com or http://www.actsolutions.com.

Task E Saving the Current Lookup to a Group

When you save a lookup as a group, all contacts in the current lookup will become members of the group. The group membership that is added to the group is dynamic. In other words, if you lookup everyone in Texas and add this lookup to your group, then everyone in the database currently in Texas becomes a member of the group. If you add more Texans to the database, they'll automatically become members of the group. If you change the state for any existing group members, they'll be removed from the group automatically.

To save the current lookup as a group:

1. Perform a lookup. (This could be a simple lookup or an advanced query.)
2. Click Lookup | Groups | Save Lookup as Group. A new blank group will appear in the Groups view.
3. Enter information into the Group field to give the group a name.

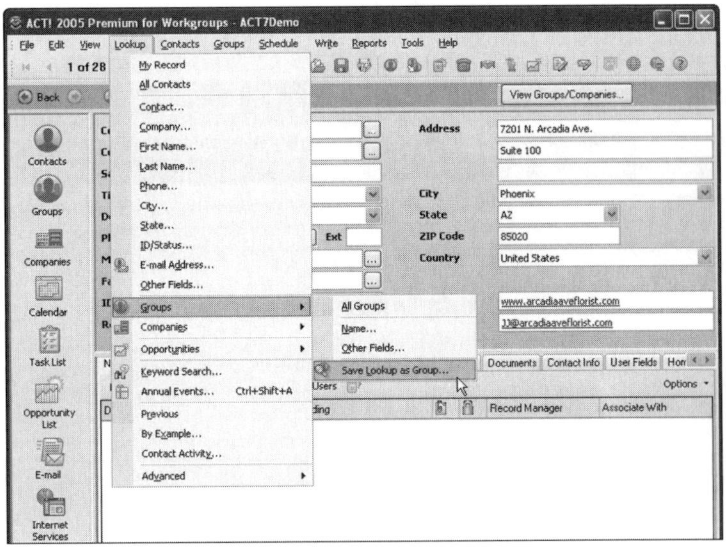

Saving a lookup as a group

Working with Groups

Once you have created populated groups, you can view group membership information in various parts of the ACT! interface. You can also quickly lookup all contacts that are members of the group or subgroup.

Task A Looking Up Group Members

You may find it useful to perform a lookup of all contacts that are members of a specific group or subgroup. In previous versions of ACT!, the group lookup was located in the bottom-right corner of the interface. In ACT! 2005, they've moved the group lookup button to the upper-right corner.

To lookup group members:

1. In the upper-right corner of the ACT! interface, click the View Groups/Companies button. The View Groups/Companies dialog box will appear.
2. Highlight a group or subgroup and click OK. ACT! will perform an instant lookup of all group/subgroup members.

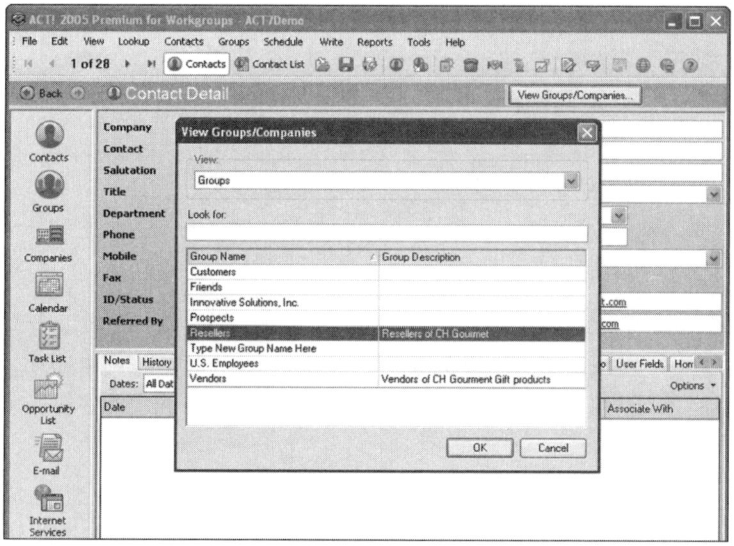

Looking up contacts in a group

Can't find subgroups?

In the View Groups/Companies, you may not see the subgroups in your database. From the View drop-down, select the Groups and Subgroups option to show subgroups for an instant lookup.

Task B View Group Membership for a Contact

You can view group membership for any contact by opening the Groups/Companies tab in the Contacts view. You can also easily add the current contact to a group or subgroup in this tab.

Add a contact to a group

In the Groups/Companies tab, you can click the Add Contact to Group button to add the current contact to a group or subgroup in your database.

Change the group fields

In the Groups/Companies tab, you can modify the list of fields that display in the tab. Click the Options button in the upper-right corner of the tab, and select the Customize Columns button.

To view group membership for a contact:

1. In the Contacts view, click the Groups/Companies tab.
2. In the Show membership for drop-down, choose the Groups and Subgroups option. (This option displays by default.) If the current contact is a member of any group or subgroup, the group or subgroup will be listed in the tab.

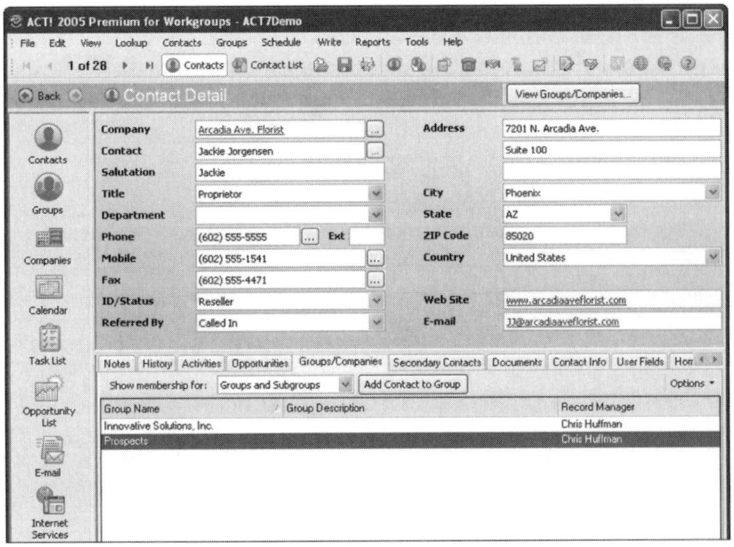

Viewing group membership in the Contacts view

Associating Items with a Group

You're probably used to associating notes, history entries, activities, and opportunities with contacts in the database. Each time you lookup a contact and click the Insert Note button in the Note tab, ACT! automatically associates the note with the current contact. Every activity that you schedule in the database is associated with a contact in the database. Each new opportunity has a record manager. Just as you can associate all of these database items with contacts, you can also associate them with groups.

Task A Associating Notes and History Entries

In ACT!, you can associate any note or history with a group in the database. Then, at the end of the day, you can easily view all of the associated notes and histories for a group within the Notes and History tabs in the Groups view.

To associate notes and history entries with a group:

1. In the Notes tab, click the Insert Note button. (Or, if you're adding a history entry, click the Record History button in the History tab.) The Insert Note (or Record History) dialog box will appear.
2. Type the text of your note (or history) item.
3. Click the button to the right of the Associate with field. The Associate with Group/Company dialog box appears.
4. From the list of groups and subgroups on the left, highlight a group and click the > button.
5. Click OK twice to add your note and associate it with a group.

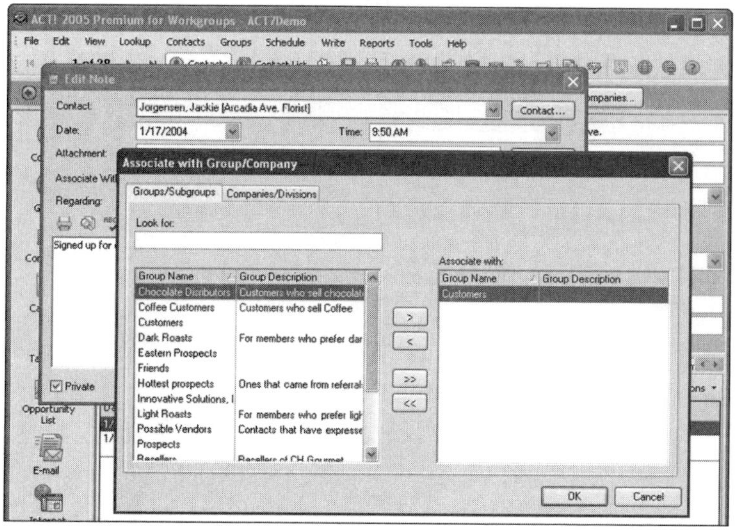

Associating a note with a group

Associating notes with a company

You can also associate notes with a company record in the Associate with Group/Company dialog box. Any notes or history items associated with a company record will appear in the Notes or History tab within the Companies view.

Task B Associating Activities with a Group

Just as you can associate notes and history items with groups in a database, you can also associate any activity with a group. At the end of the day, you'll be able to easily generate a list of activities that have been associated with the group. This is especially useful when you need to group a list of otherwise unrelated activities that center around a specific event—such as in a marketing campaign. If you want to know how many sales calls your company has made in response to an ad in the newspaper, just have your sales reps associate the activities with a common group.

Print a list of associated activities

In the Groups view, click the Activities tab. Select the Group option from the Show for drop-down. ACT! will display a list of all activities associated with the group. Click File | Quick Print Current Window to print a list of the activities in the tab.

To associate activities with a group:

1. Click Schedule | Call, Meeting, or To-do to schedule an activity.
2. Enter any relevant details for the activity.
3. Click the button to the right of the Associate with field. The Associate with Group/Company dialog box will appear.
4. From the list of groups and subgroups on the left, highlight a group and click the > button.
5. Click OK to return to the Schedule Activity dialog box.
6. Click OK to schedule the activity.

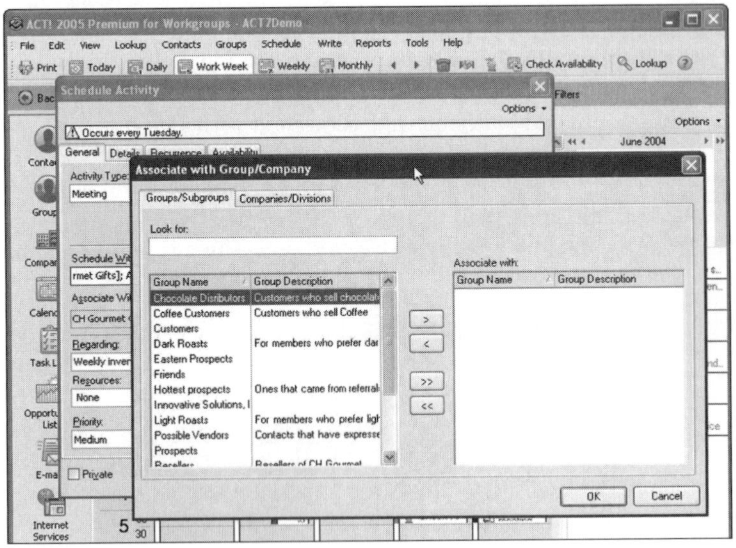

Associating an activity with a group

Task C Associating Opportunities with a Group

You can associate any opportunity with a group in the database. This gives you the ability to group opportunities much as you group contacts. Need the ability to pull up a list of all opportunities for your hot prospects? Just associate them with a hot prospects group.

To associate opportunities with a group:

1. Click Contacts | Opportunities | New Opportunity to add a new opportunity to the database.
2. Add any relevant details to the opportunity.
3. Click the button to the right of the Associate with field. The Associate with Group/Company dialog box will appear.
4. From the list of groups and subgroups on the left, highlight a group and click the > button.
5. Click OK to return to the Opportunity dialog box.
6. Click OK to save the opportunity.

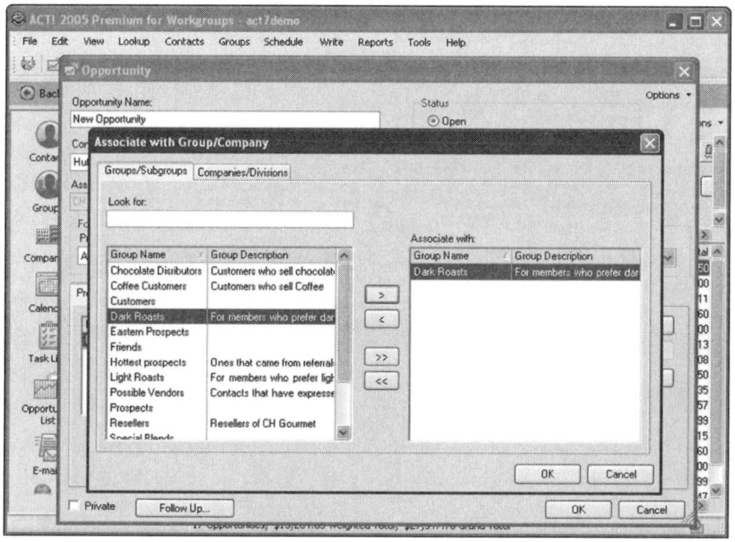

Associating an opportunity with a group

View opportunity history items

Right-click any opportunity in the Opportunity List view and select the View Summary Report option. ACT! will display a list of the relevant history items for the opportunity.

Task D Viewing Associated Items in the Groups View

In the Groups view, you'll notice that each group has a Notes, History, Activities, and Opportunities tab—just like contacts in the Contacts view. In each of these group tabs, you can view items associated with the group.

To view associated items in the Groups view:

1. In the Groups view, go to the group record whose associated items you'd like to view.
2. Click either the Notes, History, Activities, or Opportunities tabs.
3. At the top of each tab, locate the Show for drop-down. Select the Group option to display only items specifically associated with the group.
4. Click File | Quick Print Current Window to print the information in the current tab.

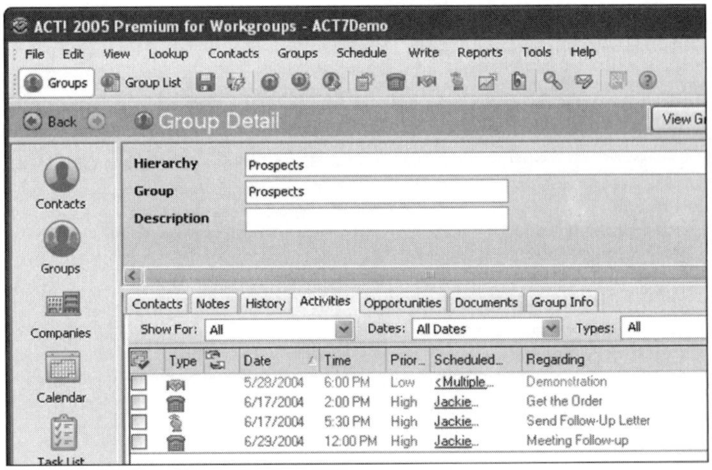

Viewing activities associated with a group

View items associated with group members

In the Groups view tabs, choose the Group Members option from the Show for drop-down to display all items associated with group members. This doesn't show items specifically associated with the group; it shows items associated with the contacts that are currently members of the group.

Chapter 8
Scheduling Activities

Navigating the Calendar Views

ACT! comes bundled with a fully-featured calendar, scalable to use as a personal calendar or as a shared office scheduling system. With ACT!, you can schedule activities with any of the contacts in your database. Because each activity is linked to a specific contact in the database, it's easy to create reports that show your activity with a group of contacts.

Task A Viewing Your Calendar

In addition to the traditional Daily, Weekly, and Monthly calendar views, ACT! 2005 offers two new calendar views: the Today view and the Work Week view. All calendar views pull data from the same database of activities, but each view can be helpful in a specific circumstance.

To view your calendar:

1. Click the Calendar option on the View bar on the left side of the ACT! interface.
2. Just below the main toolbar, you'll see the option to change calendar views. You can click the Today, Daily, Work Week, Weekly, and Monthly options to view different ranges of activity data.

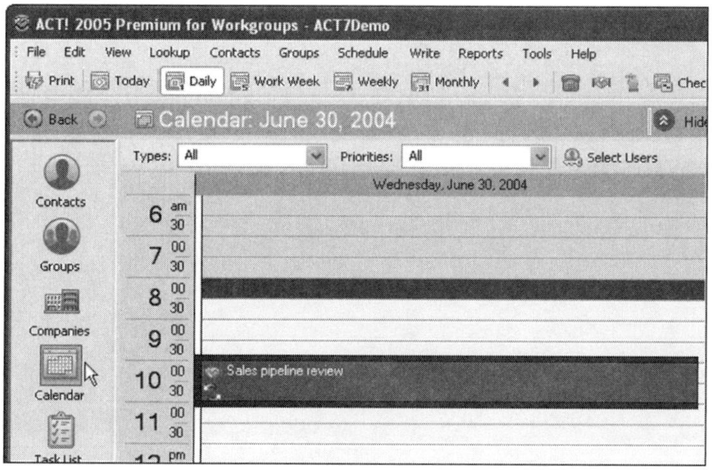

The Daily calendar

Calendar detail popups

Hover your mouse over any activity on your ACT! calendar to display basic information (like the activity subject, date, time, scheduled with contact, duration, location, and details) for that activity.

Task B Using the Mini Calendar

When was the last time you wondered on what day of the week a specific date fell? The Mini Calendar is a useful popup feature that shows dates for three months at a time. The Mini Calendar is easy to launch from anywhere in the ACT! interface.

To launch the Mini Calendar:

1. From anywhere in the ACT! interface, click View | Mini Calendar. The Mini Calendar appears.
2. Single-click a date on the Mini Calendar to view that day in the currently opened calendar view.
3. Double-click a date on the Mini Calendar to view that day's schedule in the Daily Calendar view.

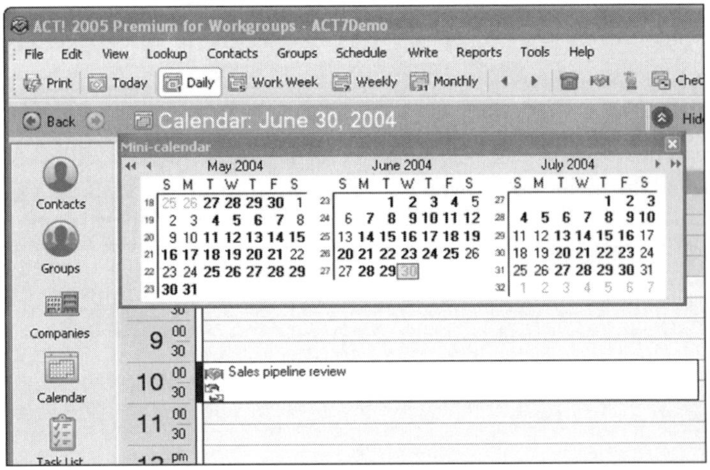

The Mini Calendar

Right-clicking in the Mini Calendar

Right-click the mouse anywhere on the Month and Year titles in the Mini Calendar to bring up a list of months. Choose one of these months from the list to quickly navigate to that month on the Mini Calendar.

Also, right-click any bold date on the Mini Calendar to get a popup list of activities for the day.

F4 for the Mini Calendar

Pressing the F4 key from anywhere in ACT! will launch the Mini Calendar. Ever wondered what day of the week the 25th falls on? Just press F4 to launch the Mini Calendar and you'll have your answer.

Task C Filtering the Calendar

The specific activities that appear on your calendar are dependent on the current calendar filter settings. The Today, Daily, Weekly, Work Week, and Monthly calendars all share the same filter, so changing filter settings in one calendar will apply the new filter to the other four calendar views.

To set the calendar filter options:

1. Click the Calendar button on the View bar to open ACT!'s calendar interface.
2. Click View | Filter Calendar View. The Filter Calendar dialog box will appear.
3. In the Users area, select up to 10 users whose activities you'd like to see on the calendar.
4. In the Type dropdown, select whether to show or hide calls, meetings, and to-dos, as well as any other activity types you've created in the database.
5. In the Priorities drop-down, select the priorities you'd like to view. If, for example, you uncheck the Low option, ACT! won't display any of the low-priority activities on your calendar views.
6. Select whether to show or hide cleared activities and private activities.
7. Click OK to apply the new filter settings.

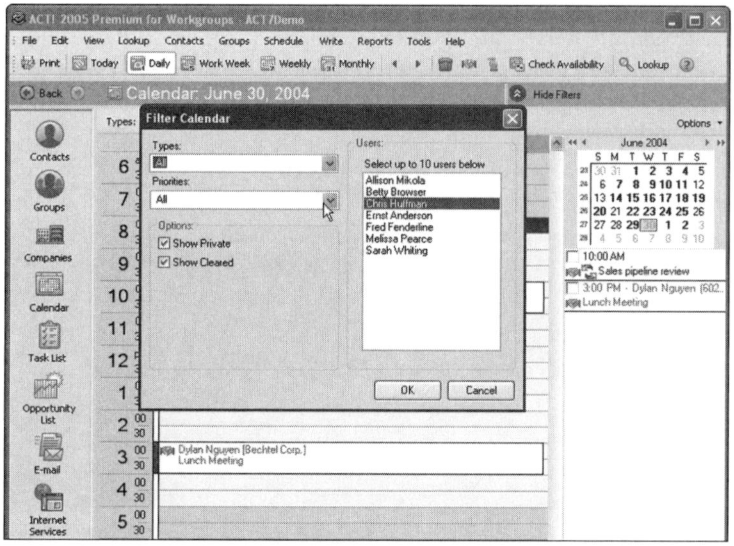

Filtering the calendar views

The activities just vanished into thin air!

If you are missing activities, make sure they haven't been filtered out. It almost goes without saying, but if you uncheck all of the options in the Types and Priorities drop-downs, ACT! will never show any activities on your calendar.

Scheduling Activities

Scheduling activities in ACT! 2005 is now a lot easier. The Schedule Activity dialog box has been redesigned to make often-used features—like the Private Activity check box field—easier to access. You also now have the option to specify the End Time and End Date for any activity.

Task A Scheduling an Activity

There are about 80 ways to schedule an activity in ACT!, and each activity scheduling method launches the Schedule Activity dialog box. Once in the Schedule Activity dialog box, you can set basic attributes for the activity.

To schedule an activity:

1. In the Contact View, lookup the contact with whom you would like to schedule an activity.
2. Click Schedule | Call, Meeting, or To-do.
3. If you'd like to schedule a custom activity type, click Schedule | Other and select the type of activity.
4. Enter a Start Date, End Date, Start Time, and End Time for your activity.
5. In the With field, you'll see that the contact you looked up in Step 1 is shown. You could change this field to schedule the activity with another contact in the database.
6. In the Regarding field, type a general description of the activity.
7. Give the activity a priority, and select a color for the activity.
8. If you'd like ACT! to ring an alarm before your activity occurs, check the Ring Alarm option.
9. If you select to show a full day banner, the activity will display as the main activity for the day in the Monthly Calendar View only.
10. Click OK. The activity will appear on your calendar.

Scheduling keyboard shortcuts

CTRL + L	Schedule Call
CTRL + M	Schedule Meeting
CTRL + T	Schedule To-do
F4	Launch the Mini-Calendar
SHIFT + F5	Launch the Daily Calendar
F3	Launch the Weekly Calendar
F5	Launch the Monthly Calendar

Task B Editing/Rescheduling an Existing Activity

You can edit an existing activity on your calendar by double-clicking it in any calendar view. Rescheduling an activity in ACT! is as simple as dragging the activity from one spot on your calendar to another.

To edit an existing activity:

1. Locate the activity in one of your calendar views.
2. Double-click the activity. The Schedule Activity dialog box will appear.
3. Change any information about this activity and click OK to save your changes.

To reschedule an activity:

1. Locate the activity you'd like to reschedule
2. Click and drag the activity to a new time slot on the calendar.

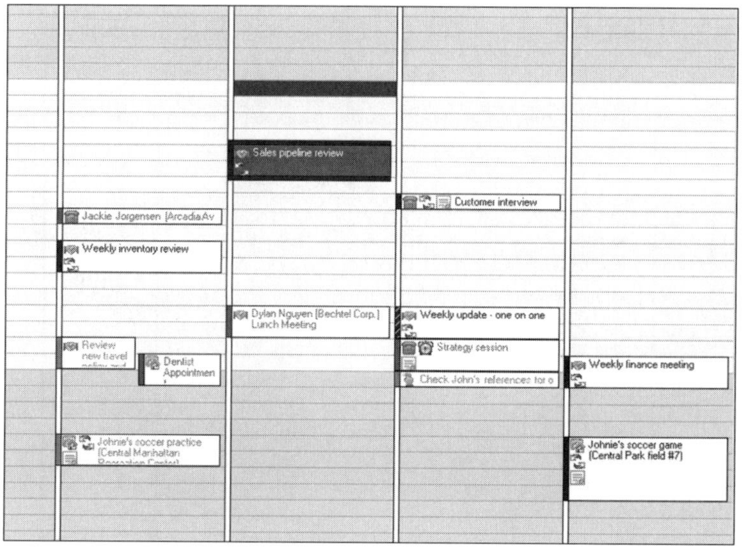

Dragging a contact from one day to another on the Work Week calendar

Schedule with your My Record

If you wish to schedule an activity with someone not in your ACT! database, you can schedule the activity with your My Record. In the With drop-down, click the My Record button to associate an activity with yourself.

Task C Adding Activity Details

If you'd like to record additional information for an activity, you can do so in the Details tab of the Schedule Activity dialog box. The Details tab will hold a note of virtually unlimited length, and you could use this area to keep meeting agendas, driving directions, or other lengthy information about the activity. In ACT! 2005, you can now add RTF formatting (bolded text, different colors, and so on) to any text in the Details tab.

Take activity details with you

- **Printed Calendars.** When you print a calendar in ACT!, you'll have the option to print all activity details on a second page.
- **Handhelds.** Most handheld links—including the ACT! Link for Pocket PC and the ACT! for Palm products—will send activity details down into your handheld device.

To add details for an activity:

1. Bring up the Schedule Activity dialog box. If you're scheduling a new activity, then click Schedule | Call, Meeting, or To-do. If you're editing an existing activity, then double-click it on the calendar.
2. Click the Details tab.
3. Type a detail of unlimited length.
4. Click the Attach button to attach a file to the activity.
5. Click OK to save your changes.

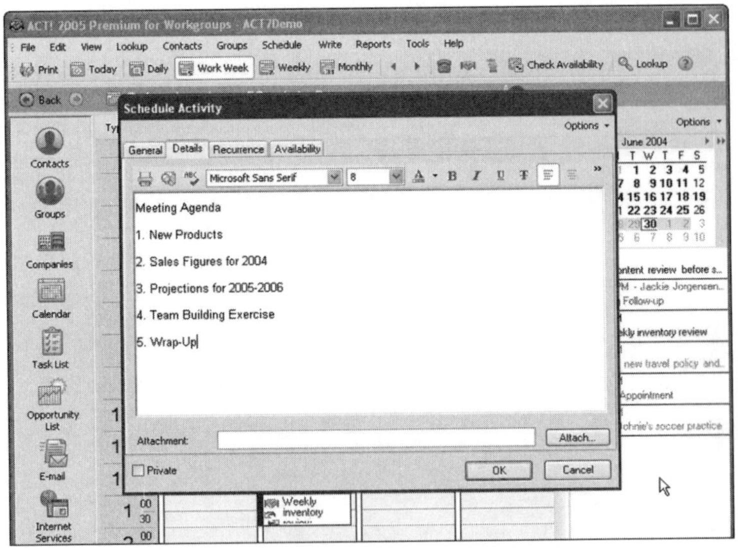

Adding details for an activity

Task D Automatically Creating an E-mail for Activity Participants

You can easily set ACT! to automatically send an e-mail to each activity participant as a reminder. When you have this option checked, ACT! will draft an e-mail to each activity participant, and the program will even attach the activity (in both ACT! and Outlook formats) to the outgoing message. Your activity participant will be able to double-click the e-mail attachment to add the activity automatically to his or her ACT! or Outlook calendar.

To automatically create an e-mail for activity participants:

1. Bring up the Schedule Activity dialog box and set the basic activity attributes. (Scheduling activities is covered in an earlier task in this chapter.)
2. In the upper-right corner of the Schedule Activity dialog box, click the Options drop-down.
3. Select the option to send an activity e-mail.
4. Click OK to schedule the activity. ACT! will automatically draft an outgoing message for all activity participants.

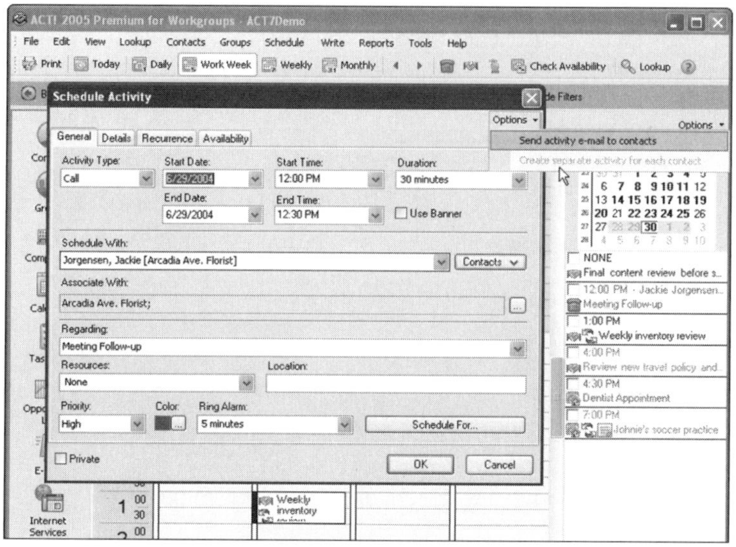

Selecting to send an activity e-mail to contacts

Configuring e-mail

Before using the Automatic E-mail feature for activity participants, you'll need to configure ACT!'s e-mail settings. Click Tools | Preferences | E-mail tab. Then, click the E-mail System Setup button to set ACT! to work with Outlook, Outlook Express, Eudora, or Internet Mail.

Task E Scheduling a Private Activity

When you need to schedule a personal activity in ACT!, you have the option of scheduling the activity as private. Private activities can't be viewed by any other ACT! user, including the administrator. Of course, if other users have access to your password and can login as you, then they might gain access to your private data.

Activity security

Private activities are much more secure in ACT! 2005. Unlike previous versions, if another user—even the administrator of the database—does not have your password, then he or she won't be able to gain access to any of your private data.

To schedule a private activity:

1. Bring up the Schedule Activity dialog box and set the basic activity attributes. (Scheduling activities is covered in an earlier task in this chapter.)
2. In the lower-left corner of the Schedule Activity dialog box, click the Private option.
3. Click OK to schedule the private activity.

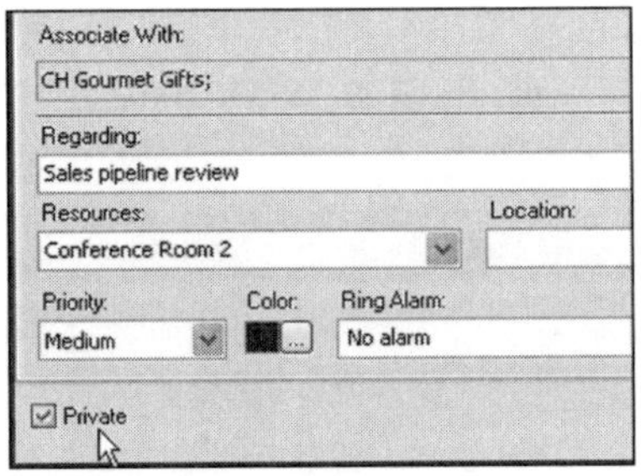

Creating a private activity

Task F Scheduling a Global Event

From time to time, you may run into events that involve most of your staff members. You can now use the new Global Events feature in ACT! 2005 to put a single timeless activity on everyone's calendar in one easy step. Trade shows, staff meetings, and special events can all be added as global events. Only users with administrator or manager access can schedule global events.

To schedule or edit a global event:

1. Click Schedule | Manage | Events. ACT! will show a list of all current global events.
2. Click the Add button to add a new global event.
3. Highlight a global event and click Edit to edit the event's properties.
4. Highlight a global event and click Delete to remove the event from the database.
5. Click Close to save your changes.

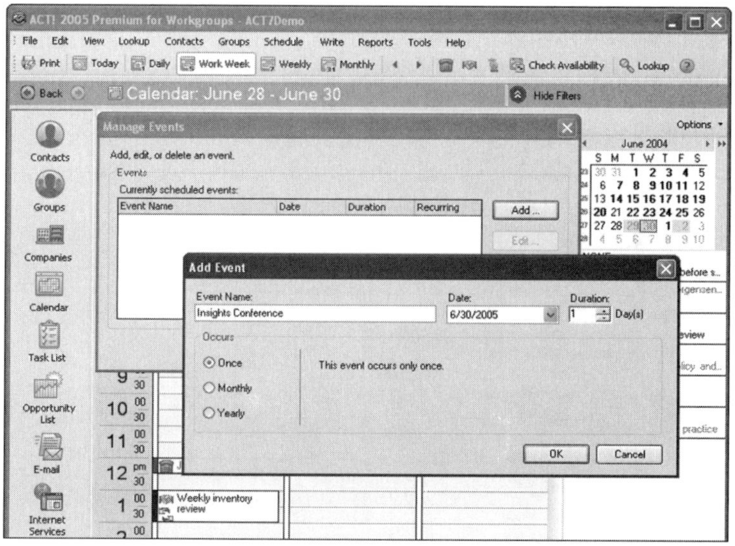

Adding a global event

Company holidays

If you add all of the company holidays as global events in ACT!, then all staff members will see that they have the day off when looking at their ACT! calendars.

Completing Activities

Once you've completed an activity, clearing it will mark the activity as having been completed on your ACT! calendar. A cleared activity will show with a strikethrough on the calendar, and it's easy to filter out cleared activities if you don't want to view them in any calendar view.

Task A Clearing an Activity

Whenever you complete an activity, it's a good idea to clear it on your ACT! calendar. When you clear an activity, ACT! places a history of the completed activity in the contact's History tab.

To clear an activity:

1. Right-click on any activity on your calendar.
2. Select the Clear Activity option. The Clear Activity dialog box will appear.
3. Update any information for the activity (if necessary).
4. If you'd like to add a quick note about the result of the activity, then click the Add Details to History option and type a note of unlimited length.
5. Click the Follow Up button to schedule another activity with the same contact.
6. Click OK to clear the activity and create a history of the activity in the contact's History tab.

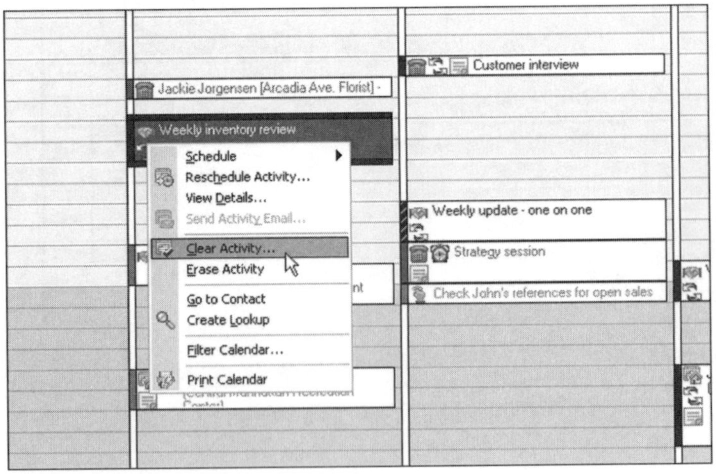

Clearing an activity in the Work Week calendar

Other ways to clear an activity

- In the Daily, Weekly, Work Week, or Monthly calendar views, click the white box next to the activities listed on the right side of the screen.
- In the Activities tab or Task List, click the white area under the check mark column.
- In any calendar view, highlight an activity and press CTRL + D.
- In any calendar view, highlight an activity and click Contact | Clear Activity.

Task B Erasing an Activity

Erasing an activity is different than clearing an activity. When you erase an activity, the call, meeting, or to-do is permanently removed from your calendar and a history of the activity is not created in the contact's History tab. If you accidentally put something on the calendar that needs to be removed without a trace, you should use this procedure to erase it.

To erase an activity:

1. Locate the activity you'd like to erase.
2. Right-click the activity in any calendar view.
3. Select the Erase Activity option.
4. Click OK to confirm the deletion. The activity will be permanently deleted from the calendar, and no activity history will be created.

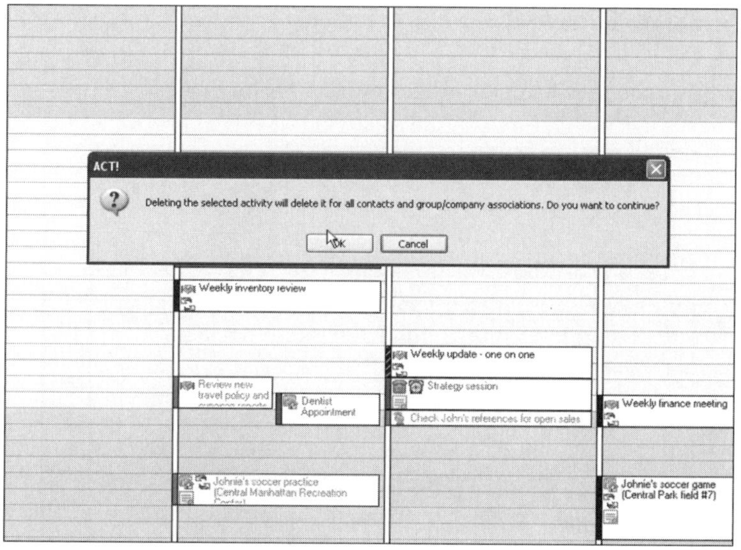

Erasing an activity

Erasing old activity data

To remove cleared activities older than a certain number of days, click Tools | Database Maintenance | Remove Old Data. Choose the option to remove cleared activities and select a number of days. Be careful when using this feature. It can't be undone, so always create a backup before removing any old data.

Task C Recording a History of an Unscheduled Activity

If someone calls, you may want to record a history of the call. But it can be time-consuming to enter the activity on the calendar and then clear it. In ACT!, you can easily record a history of an unscheduled activity. Histories of unscheduled activities will not appear as cleared activities on the calendar, but they will appear in the Notes/History tab alongside other histories of cleared activities.

To record a history of an unscheduled activity:

1. In the Contact or Contact List view, click Contacts | Record History.
2. Specify details for the history—like the history type, result, date, time, and duration.
3. In the Details text box, type a note of unlimited length to indicate the subject of the history.
4. Click OK.
5. The history item will appear in the contact's History tab.

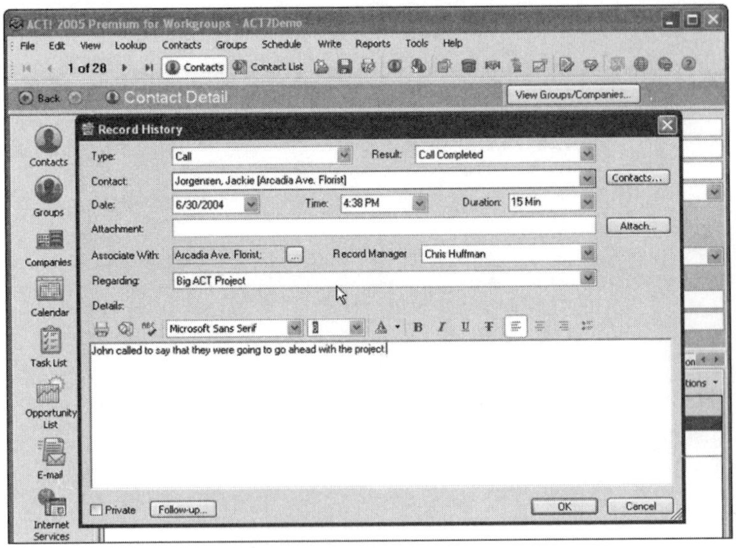

Recording a history of an unscheduled activity

CTRL + H

Pressing Ctrl + H from anywhere in the ACT! interface will record a history of an unscheduled activity.

If you press Ctrl + H in the Contact List view after tagging multiple contacts, then ACT! will record the history for each tagged contact.

Using the Task List

The Task List shows a list of activities that have been scheduled on your ACT! calendar in a useful, spreadsheet-like view. The activities that appear on the Task List are dependent on the current filter settings. Once you've customized the Task List to show just the right activities, you can print the list as a handy reference.

Task A Filtering the Task List

The activities that are shown on the Task List are dependent on the current filter settings. Filter settings can be changed in the filter area at the top of the Task List. If you don't see the filter area, click the Show Filters button in the top-right corner of the Task List.

To filter the Task List:

1. If the filter settings aren't showing, then click the Show Filters button in the upper-right corner of the Task List.
2. At the top of the Task List, locate the Dates drop-down. Use the options in the drop-down to filter the Task List to show just activities in a specific date range.
3. In the Types drop-down, select the types of activities you'd like to show.
4. In the Priorities drop-down, select the priorities you'd like to show.
5. Click the Select Users button to select the users whose activities you'd like to show.
6. Click the Options drop-down in the upper-right corner of the Task List to filter private, cleared, timeless, and Outlook activities.

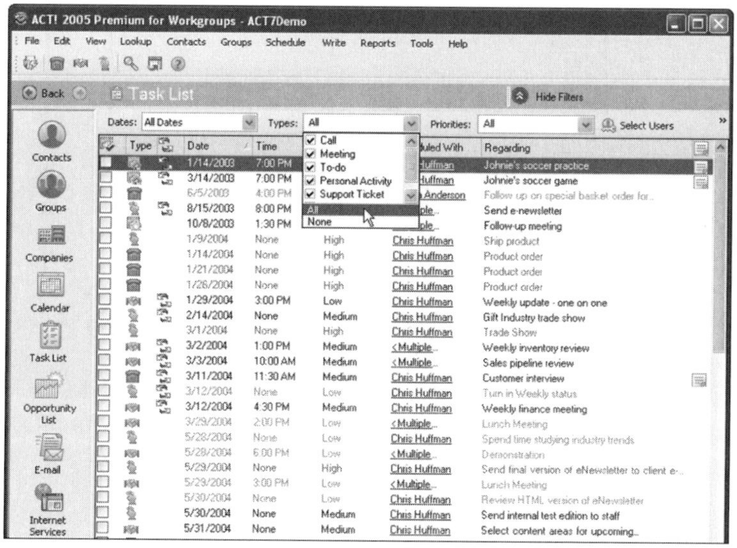

Filtering the Task List

Use the Task List for support tickets

If you're running a help desk, you could use ACT! 2005's Task List to track support tickets. Just add the support tickets as a type of activity and filter the list to show just support tickets. You'll be able to link support tickets with specific contacts, prioritize the tickets, give them a due date, and generate reports to show what your help desk has been doing.

Separate calendar filters

The filter settings in the Task List are separate from the filter settings in other ACT! calendar views. The Today, Daily, Work Week, Weekly, and Monthly calendars all share the same filter settings. The Task List, however, has its own Insert separate filter.

Task B Editing Activities in the Task List

In previous versions of ACT!, you could edit any individual activity attribute from within the Task List. In ACT! 2005, the process to change activity attributes is slightly different. Now, you'll have to double-click the activity from the Task List and edit the attributes in the Schedule Activity dialog box.

To edit an activity in the Task List:

1. Locate the activity you'd like to edit in the Task List.
2. Double-click the activity. The Schedule Activity dialog box will appear.
3. Edit any of the activity attributes and click OK to save the changes.

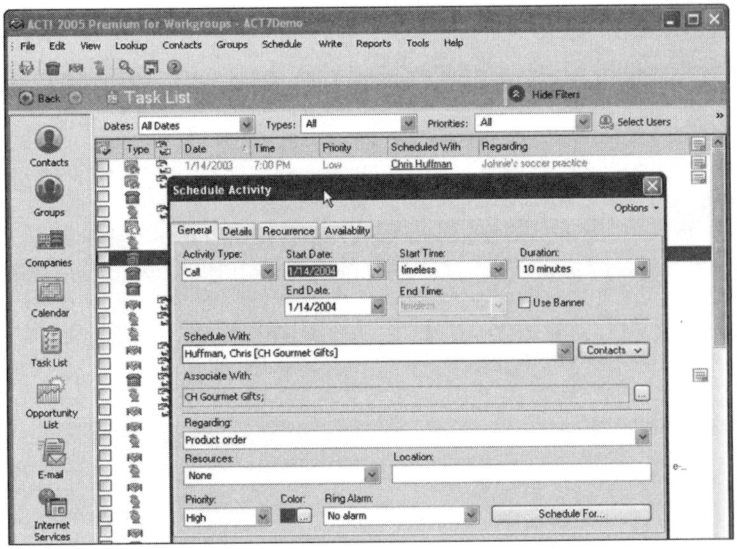

Editing an activity in the Task List

Watch where you're double-clicking!

In the Task List, you can double-click anywhere on an activity to edit the activity's attributes. If you double-click on the Start Time, ACT! displays the Schedule Activity dialog box and automatically highlights the Start Time field. If you double-click somewhere on the activity's details, then the Details tab will display. If you click on the underlined name of the contact with whom you've scheduled the activity, ACT! will take you directly to that contact's record in the Contacts view.

Task C Sorting the Task List

You can sort the Task List to show activities in a specific order. If you sort the Task List by activity type, for example, all of the calls, meetings, and to-dos will be grouped together. If you sort the Task List by date, all of the activities will appear in chronological order.

To sort the Task List:

1. Click a column header in the Task List. ACT! will sort the activities in the Task List by that column. A small arrow on the right side of the column header will indicate whether the list is sorted in ascending or descending order.
2. Click the column header again to sort the Task List in the opposite order.

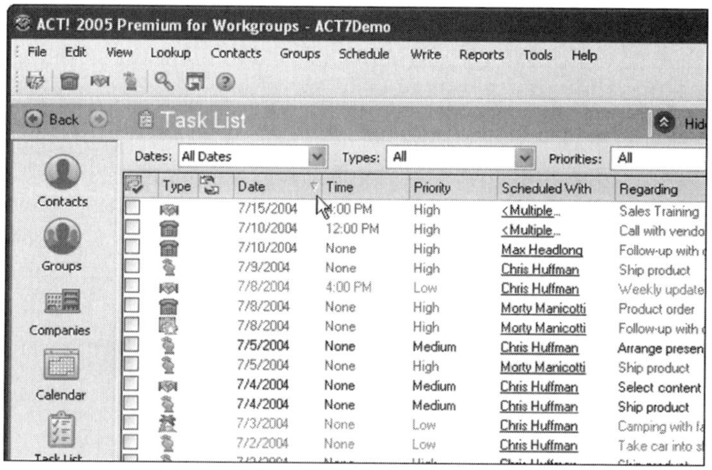

Sorting the Task List

Sort any field

In previous versions of ACT!, certain fields in the Task List were not sortable. In ACT! 2005, you can now sort the Task List by any field.

Scheduled With column

One of the columns in the Task List shows the name of the contact with whom you've scheduled an activity. If you click on the underlined contact name, then ACT! will take you directly to that contact's record in the Contact view.

Task D Changing Task List Columns

Changing Task List columns entails the same procedure as changing Contact List view columns. You can change the order and thickness of Task List columns, and you can also add and remove columns to show just the specific information you need to see in the Task List.

To change the columns showing in the Task List:

1. In the upper-right corner of the Task List, locate the Options drop-down.
2. Select the Customize Columns option. The Customize Columns dialog box will appear.
3. The list on the left will show all of the fields that aren't currently showing in the Task List but could be added.
4. The list on the right shows all of the columns that are currently displayed on the Task List.
5. To add a field to the Task List, highlight the field from the list on the left and click the > button.
6. To remove a field, highlight the field from the list on the right and click the < button.
7. To change the order of a field, highlight the field from the list on the left and click the Move Up or Move Down buttons.
8. To reset the columns to the installation default, click the Reset button.
9. Click OK to save your changes.

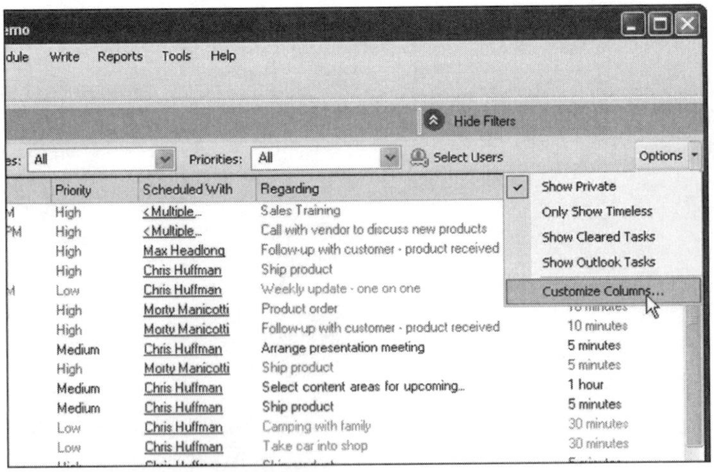

Customizing columns shown on the Task List

Managing Activity Types and Priorities

ACT! has always been able to schedule high, medium, and low priority calls, meetings, and to-dos. In ACT! 2005, you can now create your own custom activity types and priorities. If you think it would be useful to have a separate super-high priority for your activities, adding the new priority can be done in just a few clicks.

Task A Creating/Removing Activity Types

By default, ACT! 2005 databases will have six custom activity types: Calls, Meetings, To-dos, Personal Activities, Support Tickets, and Vacations. You can add an unlimited number of activity types to the database to match the specific types of activities you need to schedule.

To manage activity types:

1. Click Schedule | Manage | Activity Types. The Manage Activity Types dialog box appears.
2. To add a new activity type, click the Add button. The Add Activity type dialog box will appear.
3. Select a name for your new activity type.
4. If you want the activity type to display a custom icon, then click the Browse button.
5. If necessary, edit or add to the list of result types. The result of the activity is selected when you clear the activity.
6. Click OK to save your changes.
7. Click Close to exit the Manage Activity Types dialog box.

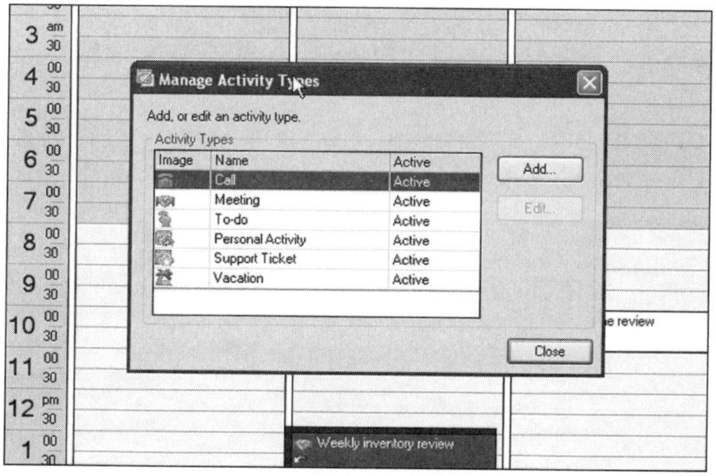

Adding custom activity types

Use custom activity types to manage billing

If you're a consultant, you might add a Billable Activity activity type to the database. Whenever you do something for a client, record it as a billable activity in the database. In the Task List, you'll be able to filter the list to show all of your billable activities for the week.

Task B Creating/Removing Custom Priorities

As we mentioned, ACT! has always been able to schedule and filter high, medium, and low priority activities. But what if you want to add a super-high priority activity? A super-high priority is not included by default. If you need to add this custom priority, you can now do so in ACT! 2005.

To manage custom activity priorities:

1. Click Schedule | Manage | Priorities. The Manage Priorities dialog box will appear.
2. Highlight any existing priority and click the Edit button to change the name of the priority. You could, for example, change the name of one of the existing inactive priorities to be a super-high priority.
3. Click the Restore Defaults button to restore ACT!'s default set of priorities.

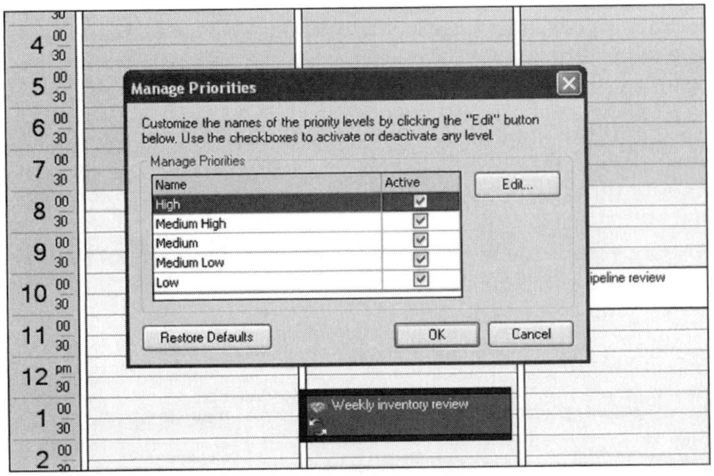

Managing custom priorities

You cannot delete custom activity types and priorities

When you need to remove custom activity types and priorities, you cannot delete them from the database. Instead, you must change their status to Inactive. Users will not be able to schedule activities with an inactive priority.

Managing Resources

If your office has shared resources, like a conference room, projector, or loaner laptop, then you'll be happy to know that you can manage and book these resources with ACT! 2005. Whenever you schedule an activity, you'll have the option of reserving a resource for the activity. And because ACT! has built-in conflict checking, you won't double-book your conference room. These features are only available in ACT! 2005 Premium Edition.

Task A Creating Resources

Before you can reserve resources in the Schedule Activity dialog box, you'll have to create the list of shared resources that your company uses.

To add/remove/edit shared resources:

1. Click Schedule | Manage | Resources. The Manage Resources dialog box will appear.
2. Click the Add button to add a new resource. Give the resource a name and choose whether or not the resource is also a location.
3. To edit a resource's name, highlight it and click the Edit button.
4. To remove a resource, highlight the resource name and click the Delete button.
5. Click OK to exit and save your changes.

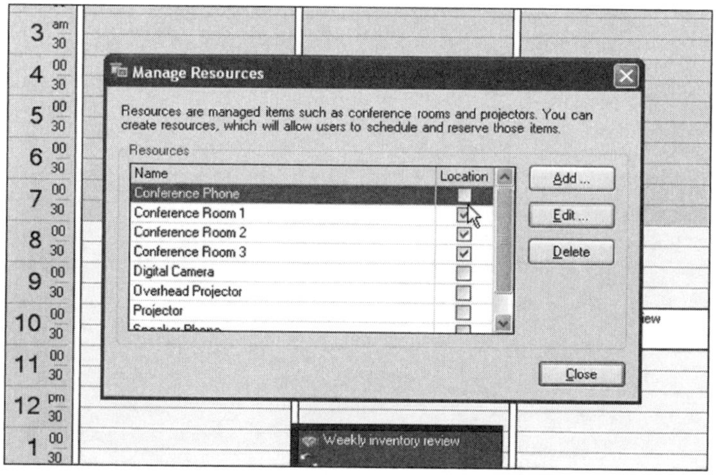

Managing resources

Task B Checking Resource Availability

If you have your conference room, projector, or other shared resource set up as a resource in ACT!, then you can check the availability of the resources within any of the calendar views.

To check resource availability:

1. In any calendar view, click the Check Availability button on the toolbar. The Check Availability dialog box will appear.
2. Click the Users/Resources button.
3. Click the users and resources whose availability you'd like to check. Click the > button to add them to the list of selected users and resources.
4. Click OK. A list of users and resources will appear in the list on the left. On the right, you'll see the availability of the user or resource.

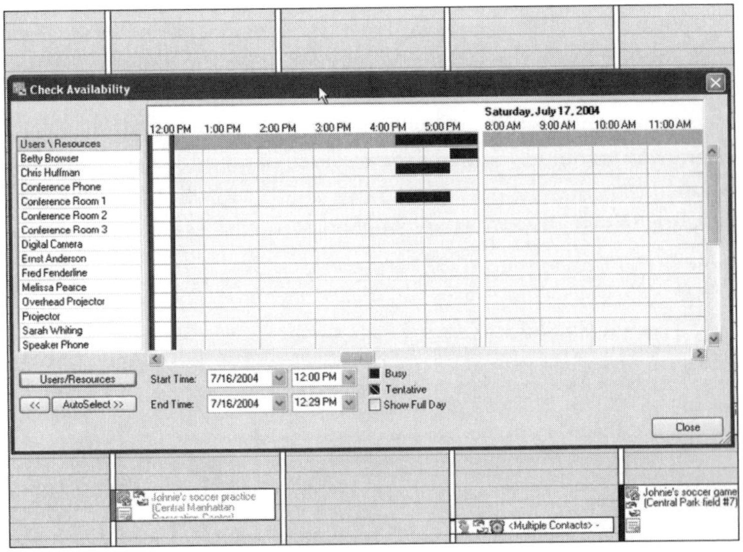

Checking availability of users and resources

Task C Scheduling a Resource

Whenever you schedule an activity on the ACT! calendar, you'll have the option of linking a resource to the activity. If, for example, your meeting will be in a specific conference room, you could link the meeting with the conference room resource. The built-in Conflict Checking feature will ensure that you don't double-book the conference room.

To schedule a resource:

1. Bring up the Schedule Activity dialog box. (There are many ways to do this, and most are covered in the first few tasks in this chapter.)
2. In the Schedule Activity dialog box, locate the Resources drop-down. Select one or more resources from this drop-down.
3. Click OK to schedule the activity. ACT! will reserve the selected resources for the entire duration of your activity.

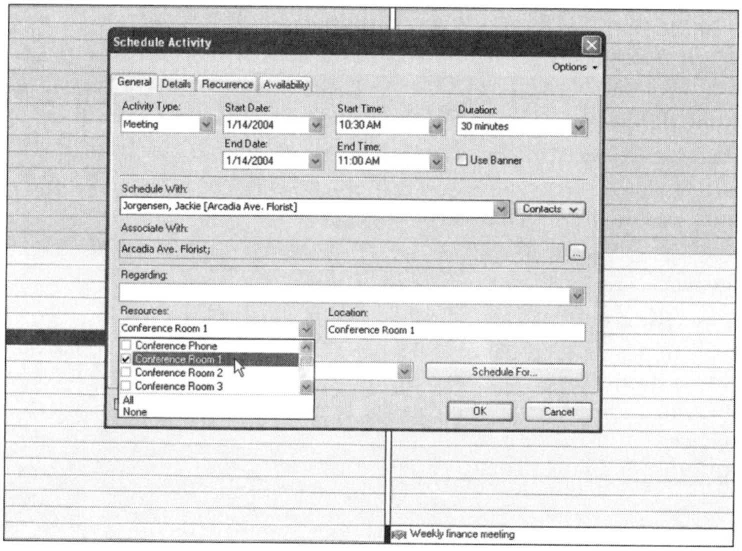

Scheduling resources for an activity

Possible types of resources

- Conference rooms
- Projectors
- Shared laptops
- Digital cameras
- Video cameras
- Video conferencing equipment
- Other office machines

Working with Multiple Activities

By using the automated scheduling features built into ACT!, you can avoid monotonous data entry when entering recurring activities or activities for multiple contacts in the database.

Task A Scheduling an Activity for Multiple Contacts

If you'd like to schedule an activity for multiple contacts in the database, you can do so easily from within ACT!. Maybe you just finished a marketing campaign, and you'd like to schedule a follow-up call with each contact targeted in the campaign? Perhaps you'd like to schedule a to-do to follow up with each of the contacts in a specific territory?

To schedule an activity for multiple contacts:

1. Click Schedule | Call, Meeting, or To-do to schedule an activity.
2. Set any needed activity attributes, like the activity Regarding, Start Time, and End Time.
3. To the right of the Schedule With drop-down, click the Contacts button.
4. Choose the Select Contacts option.
5. Select a contact from the list on the left and click the > button to add the contact to the list of selected contacts.
6. Repeat Step 5 until all contacts have been added to the list of selected contacts.
7. Click OK to return to the Schedule Activity dialog box.
8. In the upper-right corner of the Schedule Activity dialog box, click the Options button and select to schedule a separate activity for each contact. This will create a separate activity for each contact in the list of selected contacts.
9. Click OK to schedule the activity.

Schedule for the current lookup

When scheduling an activity for multiple contacts, you can easily schedule the activity for all contacts in the current lookup. In the Schedule Activity dialog box, click Contacts | Select Contacts. In the upper-left corner of the resulting dialog box, choose the Current Lookup option in the Select from drop-down. Then, click the >> button to add all contacts in the current lookup to the list of selected contacts.

Task B Scheduling a Recurring Activity

If an activity is so much fun that you feel compelled to do it regularly—like a weekly staff meeting—you can schedule it as a recurring activity in the database. Recurring activities only need to be scheduled once, but they appear on the calendar multiple times.

To schedule a recurring activity:

1. Click Schedule | Call, Meeting, or To-do to bring up the Schedule Activity dialog box.
2. Set the basic activity attributes.
3. Click the Recurrence tab.
4. Select the frequency of the recurring activity (daily, weekly, monthly, and so on) on the left.
5. Depending on the frequency you selected, various options will appear on the right side of the dialog box that will let you specify when the activity should occur.
6. In the Range area, select a start date and end date.
7. Click OK to schedule the recurring activity on the calendar.

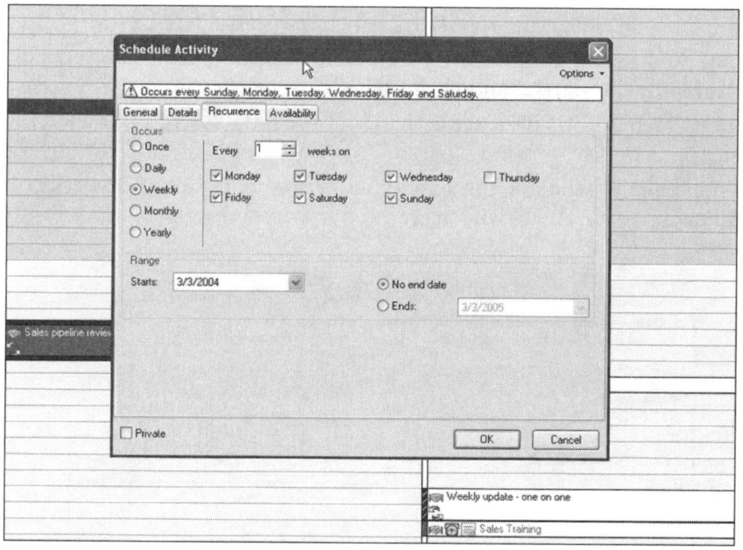

Scheduling a recurring activity

Schedule an activity for a new contact

If a contact isn't currently in your ACT! database, then go ahead and bring up the Schedule Activity dialog box. Click the Contacts button and select the New Contact option. This will allow you to create a new contact on the fly and schedule an activity with this contact.

Scheduling an Activity Series

After a marketing campaign or leading up to a specific event, you may have a series of events that need to be scheduled together. For this purpose, you can create an activity series in your ACT! database. The Activity Series feature has been greatly enhanced in ACT! 2005. Now, if you change any activity that is part of a series, ACT! will prompt you to adjust all other activities in the series.

Task A Creating an Activity Series Template

If you're running a marketing campaign, for example, you may want to follow up with a phone call five days after the campaign is started. Then, after ten days, you might schedule a to-do to send a follow-up card. Then, after 30 days, you might want to schedule another follow-up activity. All of these activities can be scheduled in one step by setting them up as an activity series.

Link activities to users

New in ACT! 2005: You can now schedule each activity in the series with a different user in the database.

To create an activity series template:

1. Click Schedule | Manage | Activity Series Templates.
2. The Activity Series Template Creation Wizard will appear. Click the option to create a new activity series and then click Next.
3. Give your activity series a name and description. Specify whether the template you're creating should be public or private. Click Next.
4. Click Add to add a new activity to the series. Specify all of the necessary settings for the activity and click OK.
5. Repeat Step 4 until all of the activities in the series have been added to the list.
6. If you'd like to schedule the activity series now, click Yes. If not, select No and click Finish. ACT! will create your activity series template.

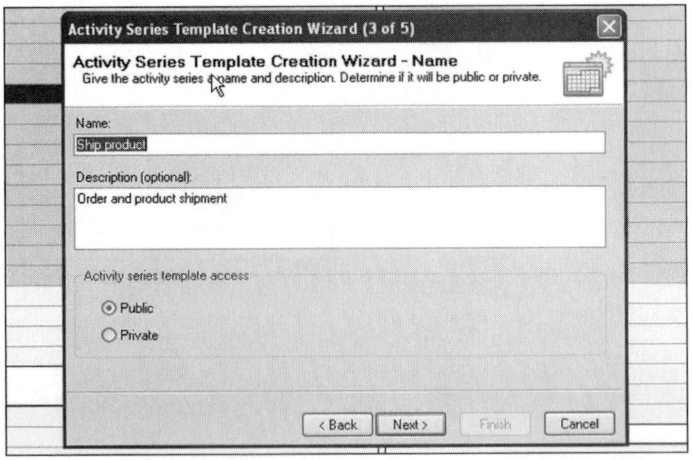

Creating an activity series template

Task B Editing an Activity Series Template

Once you've created an activity series template, you might need to fine-tune it from time to time. Editing an activity series template is as simple as creating one, and it entails a very similar process.

To edit an existing activity series template:

1. Click Schedule | Manage | Activity Series Template. The Activity Series Template Creation Wizard appears.
2. Choose to edit an existing activity series and click Next.
3. A list of existing activity series templates will display. Highlight the template you'd like to edit and click Next.
4. If necessary, modify the name and description of the template. Click Next.
5. A list of the activities in the series will appear. Use the Add, Edit, and Delete buttons to modify the list of activities. When you're finished editing the template, click Next.
6. Click Finish to save your changes.

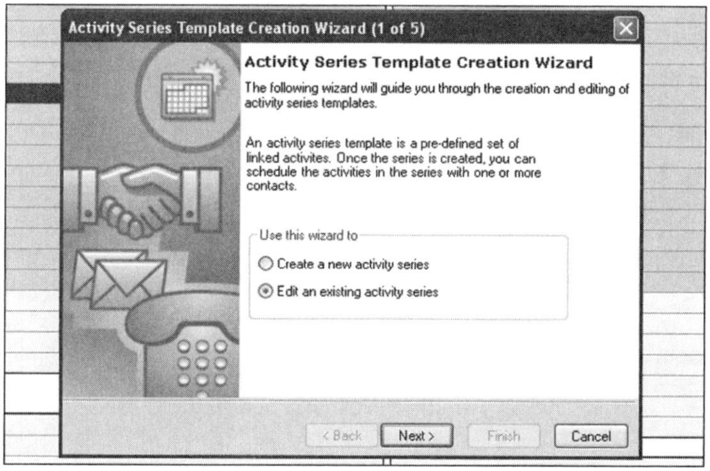

Editing an existing activity series template

Undo changes

If you need to undo changes made to an activity series template, just cancel out of the Activity Series Template Creation Wizard. ACT! will discard any changes you've made. Once you finish the Wizard and save the changes, you can't undo any changes made to the activity series.

Task C Scheduling an Activity Series

When you bring on a new customer, what do you do? Do you have a series of phone calls, follow-up letters, and other events that you do for your new customer? If so, you'll love ACT!'s Activity Series feature. By scheduling the single activity series, multiple activities for a contact in the database are placed on your calendar. You'll need to create an activity series template before attempting to schedule an activity series.

To schedule an activity series:

1. Click Schedule | Activity Series.
2. In the Activity series template drop-down, select the activity series template you'd like to schedule.
3. Select an anchor date for the activity series.
4. In the With drop-down, select the contact for whom you'd like to schedule the activity series. By default, the current contact will be selected.
5. Click OK. ACT! will schedule all of the activities in the series with your contact.

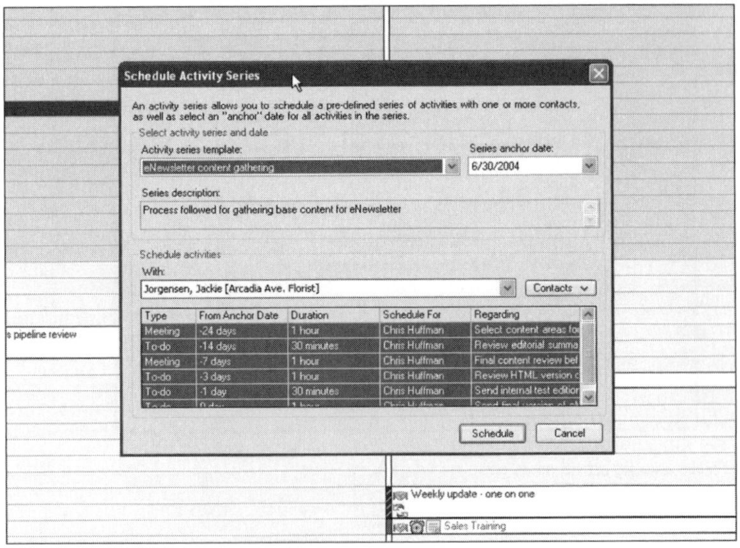

Scheduling an activity series in the Work Week calendar

Schedule an activity series with multiple contacts

If you'd like to schedule an activity series for multiple contacts, just click the Contacts button in the Schedule Activity Series dialog box and choose the Select Contacts icon. The process for scheduling an activity series with multiple contacts is very similar to the process of scheduling an activity with multiple contacts. (Scheduling activities with multiple contacts is covered in an earlier task in this chapter.)

Workgroup Calendar Features

If you use ACT! to share calendar information with your colleagues, then you'll love the new Workgroup Calendar enhancements made to ACT! 2005. You can now limit access to your calendar, send meeting invitations, and check other users' and resources' availability. Some of these features are only available in the ACT! 2005 Premium Edition.

Task A Granting Calendar Access

In previous versions of ACT!, anyone could schedule activities for another user. In ACT! 2005, you must grant calendar access to the people that you want to be able to schedule on your behalf (see sidenote for the exception to the rule). By default, none of the other Standard, Restricted, and Browse users in your database will be able to schedule activities on your calendar.

To grant another user scheduling permissions for your calendar:

1. Click Schedule | Grant Calendar Access.
2. Select a user from the list and click the Access button.
3. Select whether the user should be able to view or view and schedule activities on your calendar.
4. Click OK. Repeat Steps 2–3 with other users in the database.
5. Click OK to save your changes.

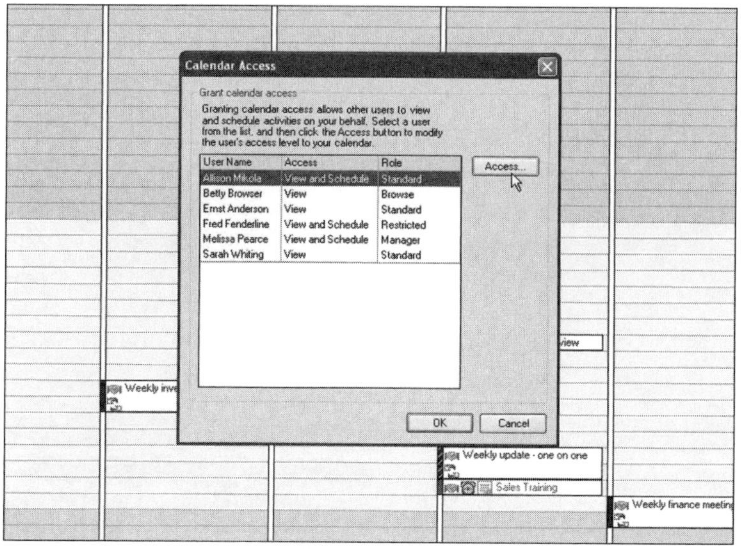

Granting calendar access

Managers and administrators

All users in the database with manager or administrator login access will be able to schedule activities on your calendar, regardless of whether or not you've granted them access to your calendar.

Task B Viewing Meeting Invitations

If you schedule an activity on behalf of another user in the database, then the activity is tentatively scheduled on that user's calendar. An invitation to attend the meeting is created for that user. At any time, users can view, accept, or reject their meeting invitations.

To view your meeting invitations:

1. In the bottom-right corner of the ACT! interface, double-click the Invitations icon.
2. The Invitations dialog box appears.
3. Highlight a meeting invitation and select to accept it, decline it, or make it tentative.
4. Click OK.

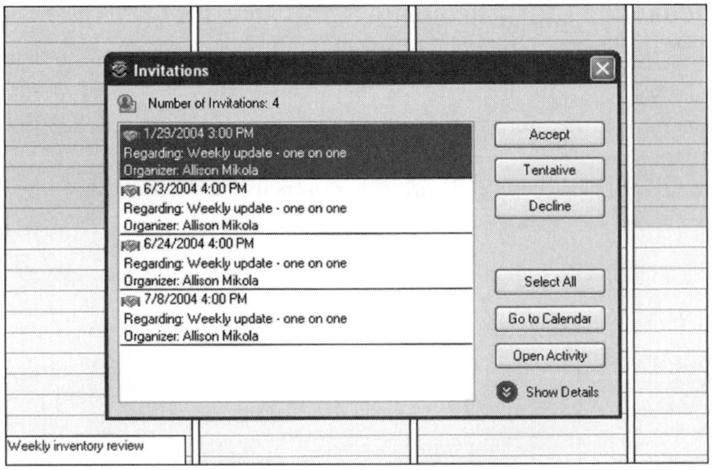

Viewing meeting invitations

Show details

In the Invitations dialog box, click the Show Details icon in the bottom-right corner of the dialog box to show more detailed information about the currently selected activity.

Automatic invitation notices

When you have new meeting invitations, a notice will appear in the bottom-right corner of the ACT! interface immediately after you open the database.

Setting Activity Preferences

Maximize the efficiency of your ACT! calendar by setting your calendar preferences. By setting ACT!'s default calendar preferences, you'll be able to configure the calendar to show information just the right way. Setting the default scheduling preferences will save you time when entering activities into the database.

Task A Setting Calendar Preferences

In the Calendar Preferences dialog box, you'll be able to set default preferences that affect the look and feel of your ACT! calendar views. You'll be able to set the week's start date, default calendar increments, what actually shows on your ACT! calendar, and other preferences.

To set your calendar preferences:

1. Click Tools | Preferences.
2. Click the Calendar & Scheduling tab.
3. Click the Calendar Preferences button.
4. If necessary, change any preferences and click OK to save your changes.

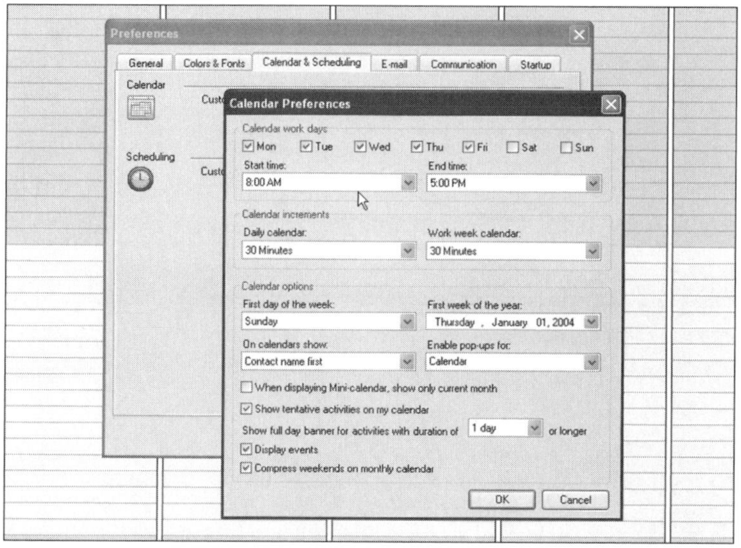

Configuring calendar preferences

Calendar preferences

- Calendar work days
- Work day start time and end time
- Calendar increments
- First day of the week
- Compress weekends on the monthly calendar
- Enable popups for other calendar views
- and more…

Worried about messing up other users' calendars?

Calendar preferences are set for each network login user. You can change the look and feel of your calendar without affecting any other users' settings.

Task B Setting Scheduling Preferences

In the Scheduling Preferences area, you can set defaults for your calls, meetings, to-dos, and other activity types. You can also set general activity settings—such as whether you'd like cleared activities to show with a strikeout or with a gray font color.

Scheduling preferences:

- Default priority, alarm lead time, and duration for each type of activity
- Auto-display drop-downs for activities
- Cleared activity appearance
- Enable/disable conflict checking
- Make new activities public/private
- Create separate activities when scheduling for multiple contacts
- Prompt to automatically schedule an activity when a new contact is created

To set your scheduling preferences:

1. Click Tools | Preferences.
2. Click the Calendar & Scheduling tab.
3. Click the Scheduling Preferences button.
4. If necessary, change any preferences and click OK to save your changes.

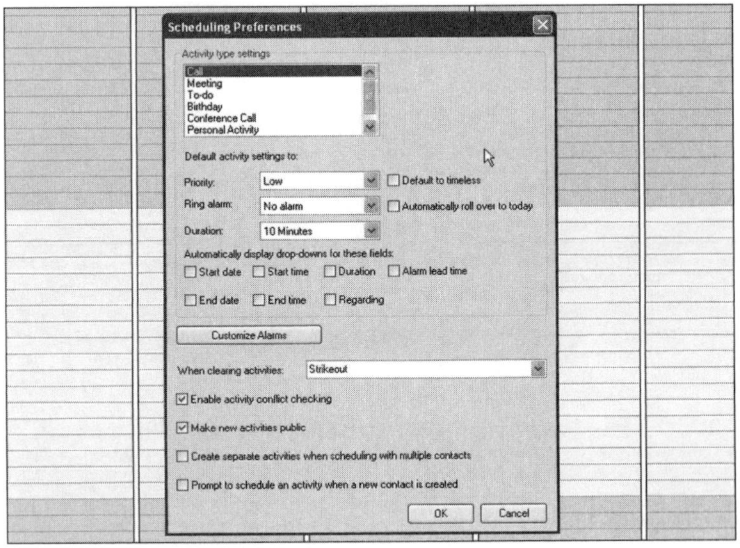

Configuring scheduling preferences

Printing the Calendar

If you don't have a Palm or Pocket PC, you might want to print a paper calendar to take with you when you're not near a computer. ACT! offers many options for printing your schedule. Calendars can be printed on standard copy paper, they can be printed on paper that will fit into your paper organizer, and they can be filtered to show just specific types of activities.

Task A Printing a Standard Calendar

With ACT!, you can print a standard daily, weekly, or monthly calendar. Calendars can be printed in portrait or landscape format, and if you have a paper-based organizer (like a Day Runner) you can print on pre-perforated paper that will fit in your organizer.

To print a standard calendar:

1. Click File | Print. The Print dialog box will appear.
2. In the Printout Type area, select to either print a Day Calendar, Week Calendar, or Month Calendar.
3. In the Paper Type area, select the type of calendar you'd like to print.
4. Click the Options button for additional calendar options.
5. Click Print to print the calendar.

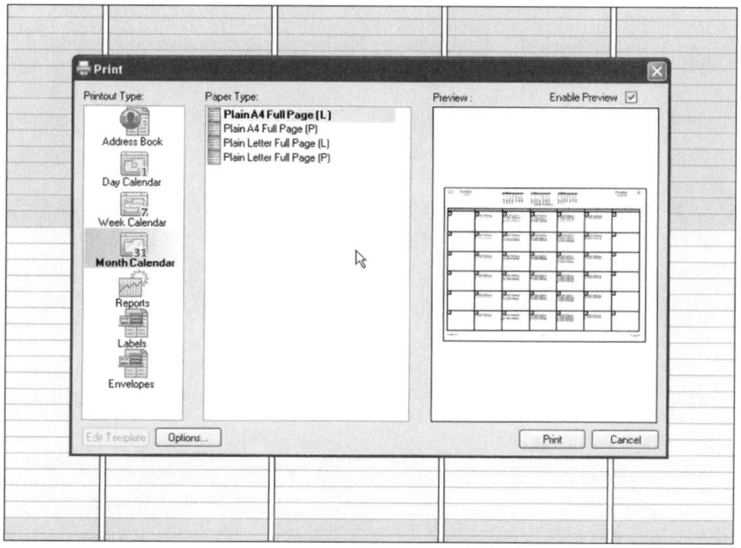

Printing a standard calendar

Calendar print options

In the Print dialog box, you'll notice an Options button in the lower-left corner. After selecting the type of calendar you'd like to print, click this Options button to set these additional settings:

- Print the company name for each activity
- Print a five-week view
- Print/omit Saturday and Sunday
- Print activity details
- Show priorities
- Filter the printed calendar

Task B Quick Print a Calendar View

New to ACT! 2005 is the ability to create a quick printout of any calendar view. If you use the Quick Print feature to print your calendar, the printout will look almost identical to the actual calendar view in ACT!.

Monthly Quick Prints

If you're printing the monthly calendar, you may need to set your printer preferences to landscape to fit all of the calendar information on one page.

To Quick Print a calendar view:

1. Go to any calendar view.
2. Click File | Quick Print.
3. The Print dialog box will appear. Select a printer and click OK.
4. ACT! will generate a quick printout of the calendar view you selected in Step 1.

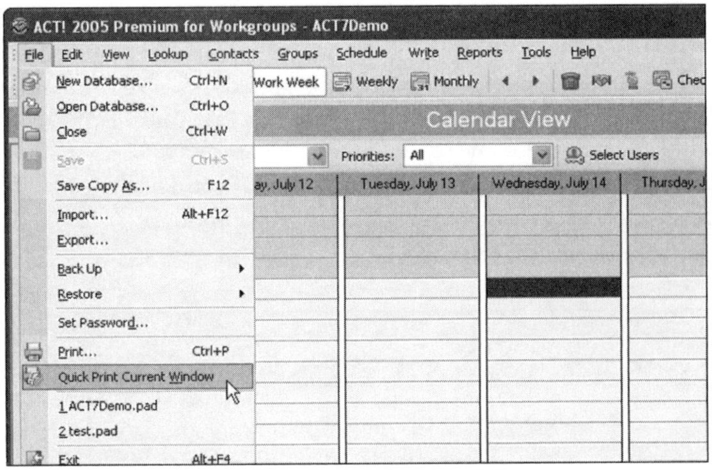

Quick Printing a calendar view

Chapter 9
Opportunity Management

Viewing Opportunities

The Opportunities feature (called Sales/Opportunities in previous versions of ACT!) has been completely overhauled in ACT! 2005. A new Opportunity view, the ability to maintain a centralized product list, the ability to add multiple products per sale, and the ability to customize user fields for new opportunities are just a few of the great new features built into this new version of ACT!.

Task A Filtering the Opportunity List

The Opportunity List is one of the best new features in ACT! 2005. The new view allows you to manage all of the opportunities in the database. The opportunities that appear in the Opportunity List are dependent on the filter you've selected.

To filter your Opportunity List:

1. Click the Opportunity List button on the View bar.
2. A list of all opportunities will appear in a spreadsheet-like format.
3. If you don't see the filter options at the top of the Opportunity List, then click the Show Filters button in the upper-right corner of the ACT! interface.
4. In the filter area, you can select to show opportunities set to close in a certain date range, with a certain status, in a certain stage of a sales process, with a specific probability or amount, or managed by a particular set of users.
5. Click the Reset button to reset the filter to show all opportunities.

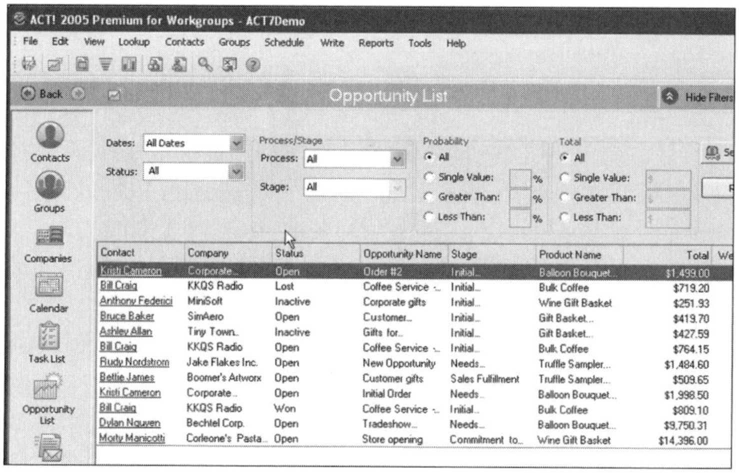

Filtering the Opportunity List view

Export to Excel

Once you've filtered the Opportunity List to show just a certain set of opportunities, you can export the list to Excel by clicking the Export to Excel button on the toolbar in the Opportunity List view.

Task B Looking Up Opportunities

You're probably used to performing lookups to find contacts in the database, but ACT! 2005 also lets you perform opportunity lookups. If you need to find all opportunities that are selling a specific product, this lookup is now easily done from the Lookup menu. If you add custom user fields to the Opportunities area, you'll be able to lookup by these fields, too!

A practical example

If you want to find all of the opportunities in the database that involve a specific product or service, you could click Lookup | Opportunities | Product. Type the name of the product and click OK. All opportunities involving that product will appear in the Opportunity List, and you can filter the list to refine the lookup further. (Filtering the Opportunity List view is covered in the preceding task in this chapter.)

To lookup opportunities by opportunity fields:

1. Click Lookup | Opportunities.
2. Select a field from the pre-defined list, or click Other to perform a lookup using any opportunity field.
3. In the Lookup Opportunities dialog box, enter your search term in the Search for area.
4. Click OK. ACT! will display all resulting contacts in the Opportunity List.

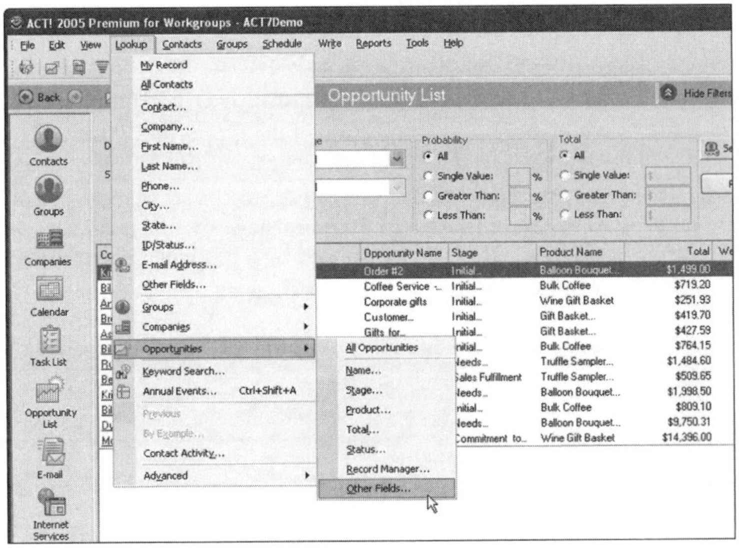

Performing an opportunity field lookup

Task C Customizing the Opportunity List Columns

The columns that display in the Opportunity List view are customizable. You can rearrange the order and thickness of the columns, and you can select to show or hide certain columns. Any changes made to your Opportunity List columns will only affect your computer, even if you are using a shared or synchronizing ACT! database.

To rearrange the columns in the Opportunity List:

1. Click the column header for any field in the Opportunity List.
2. Hold the mouse button down and drag the column header to a new spot.

To stretch or shrink columns in the Opportunity List:

1. Hover your mouse on the separator line between two column headers.
2. When your cursor turns into a double-pronged arrow, click and drag to make the column wider or shorter.

To add/remove columns in the Opportunity List:

1. Click the Opportunity List button on the View bar.
2. In the upper-right corner of the ACT! interface, click the Options drop-down and select the Customize Columns option.
3. In the Customize Columns dialog box, you can add available fields to the Opportunity List and you can change the order of the columns that are showing.

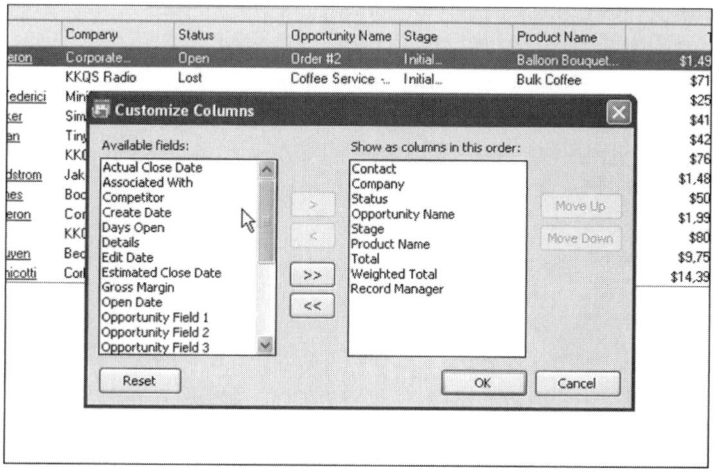

Customizing columns in the Opportunity List view

Adding and Removing Opportunities

The Sales/Opportunities feature allows you to record an upcoming sale or opportunity for a contact in your ACT! database. As you enter these opportunities, you can record specific information about the sale, such as price, quantity, main competitor, and more.

Task A Entering a New Opportunity

Adding a new opportunity to the ACT! database is the first step in managing your prospective sales with ACT!. The Opportunity dialog box has been completely redesigned in ACT! 2005, and the new layout lets you track a lot more information for each sale.

To enter a new opportunity:

1. Click Contacts | Opportunities | New Opportunity. The Opportunity dialog box will appear.
2. Name your opportunity in the Opportunity Name field.
3. In the Contact drop-down, select the contact associated with this opportunity. By default, the current contact will appear selected.
4. Choose a sales process, sales stage, probability, and estimated close date for the opportunity.
5. In the Products/Services tab, add as many products or services as you require.
6. In the User Fields tab, enter additional information about the sale. (Manager and Administrator level users can edit these tabs in Tools | Define Fields.)
7. In the Details tab, enter a note of unlimited length.
8. In the Opportunity Info tab, enter additional information about the sale, such as the Record Manager, competitor, and referral source.

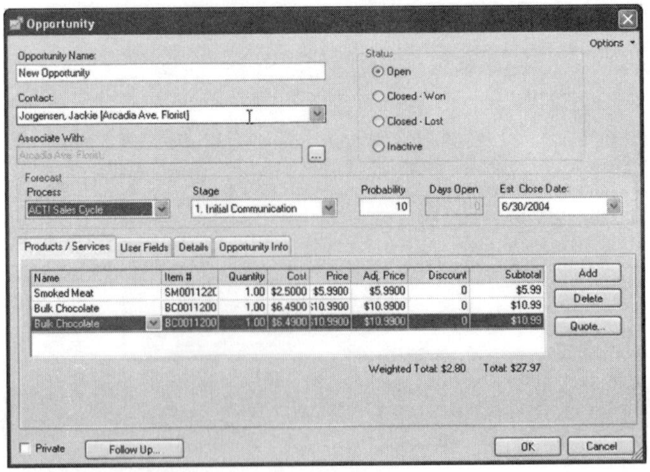

Entering a new opportunity

To schedule an activity

Do one of the following:

- Click Contacts | Opportunities | New Opportunity
- Click the New Opportunity button on the toolbar
- Click CTRL + F11

Go directly to a contact's record

Click the blue underlined contact name in the Contact column in the Opportunity List view to go directly to that contact's record in the Contacts view. Alternatively, you could right-click any opportunity in the Opportunity List and select the Go to Contact option to go directly to the contact record for the contact associated with the opportunity.

Task B Editing an Existing Opportunity

Throughout your sales process, you may need to make changes to some of the opportunities in your database. You can double-click any opportunity in the Opportunity List to change any of the field values for that opportunity.

To edit an existing opportunity:

1. In the Opportunity List view, locate the opportunity you'd like to edit.
2. Double-click the opportunity. The Opportunity dialog box for that opportunity will appear.
3. Make any changes to the fields for this opportunity and click OK.

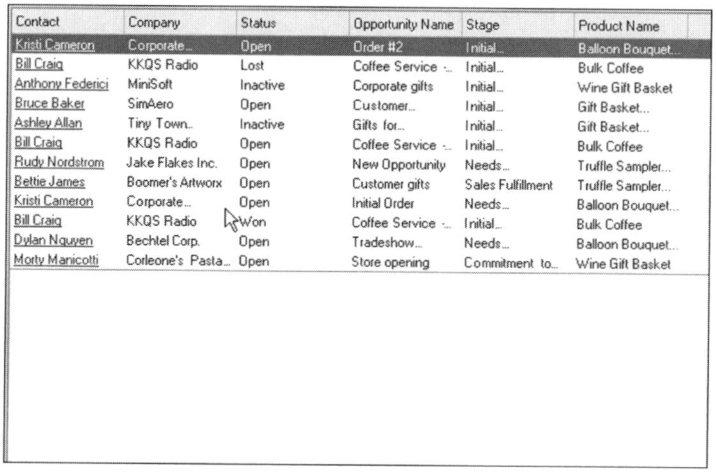

Contact	Company	Status	Opportunity Name	Stage	Product Name
Kristi Cameron	Corporate...	Open	Order #2	Initial...	Balloon Bouquet...
Bill Craig	KKQS Radio	Lost	Coffee Service -...	Initial...	Bulk Coffee
Anthony Federici	MiniSoft	Inactive	Corporate gifts	Initial...	Wine Gift Basket
Bruce Baker	SimAero	Open	Customer...	Initial...	Gift Basket...
Ashley Allan	Tiny Town...	Inactive	Gifts for...	Initial...	Gift Basket...
Bill Craig	KKQS Radio	Open	Coffee Service -...	Initial...	Bulk Coffee
Rudy Nordstrom	Jake Flakes Inc.	Open	New Opportunity	Needs...	Truffle Sampler...
Bettie James	Boomer's Artworx	Open	Customer gifts	Sales Fulfillment	Truffle Sampler...
Kristi Cameron	Corporate...	Open	Initial Order	Needs...	Balloon Bouquet...
Bill Craig	KKQS Radio	Won	Coffee Service -...	Initial...	Bulk Coffee
Dylan Nguyen	Bechtel Corp.	Open	Tradeshow...	Needs...	Balloon Bouquet...
Morty Manicotti	Corleone's Pasta...	Open	Store opening	Commitment to...	Wine Gift Basket

Double-clicking an opportunity for editing

New opportunity features

As you're entering a new opportunity, take a moment to check out the new features in the Opportunity dialog box:

- You can give each opportunity a name.
- You can define and use multiple sales processes.
- You can tie the probability percentage automatically to an opportunity's sales stage.
- You can add multiple products per sale.
- You can create a one-click quote for any opportunity.
- You can choose from more realistic opportunity status options.
- You can create custom user fields for sales.
- You can format text within the opportunity details.

History creation

Whenever you close an opportunity, ACT! will automatically create a history of the opportunity's status change in the contact's History tab. In ACT! 2005, a history is also created when you change the estimated close date.

Task C Closing an Opportunity

Once an opportunity has been either won or lost, you can close the opportunity in ACT!. It's a good idea to close your opportunities when they're no longer active because you can then easily filter out all of the won, lost, or inactive opportunities in the Opportunity List.

To close an opportunity:

1. In the Opportunity List view, locate the opportunity you'd like to close.
2. Right-click the opportunity.
3. Select Close Opportunity. ACT! will bring up the Opportunity dialog box for your opportunity.
4. In the Status area, select whether you won or lost the sale. New to ACT! 2005 is a third option that lets you put the opportunity into an inactive status.
5. Enter the actual close date for the opportunity.
6. Update any other fields in the Opportunity dialog box, as needed.
7. Click OK.

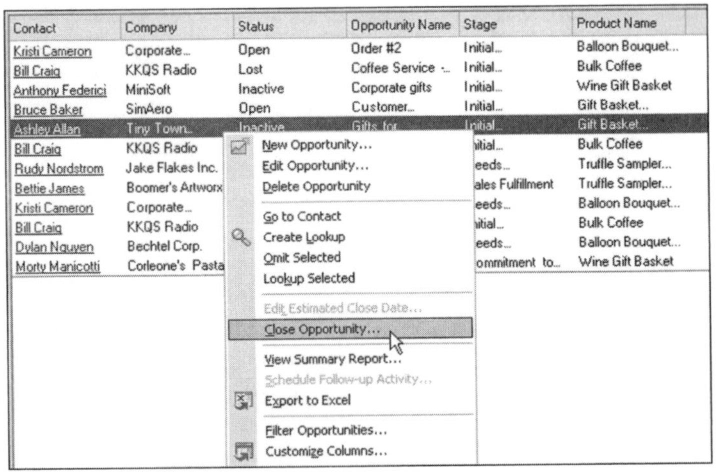

Closing a won or lost opportunity

Task D Deleting an Opportunity

When you need to remove an opportunity from the database, deleting it will get rid of it without any trace in your contact's History tab. You should close most sales when they become won, lost, or inactive. For more information on closing an opportunity, see the previous task in this chapter.

To delete an opportunity:

1. In the Opportunity List, locate the opportunity you'd like to delete.
2. Highlight the opportunity.
3. Click Contacts | Opportunities | Delete Opportunity. The opportunity will be permanently removed from the database.

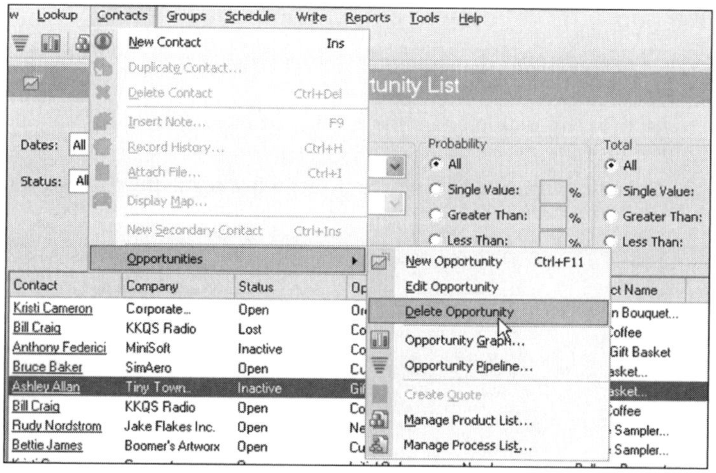

Deleting an opportunity.

Viewing associated histories

Right-click any opportunity in the Contact List view and select the View Summary Report option to bring up a list of all contact history items that have been created as a result of this sale.

Generating Quotes

If you're selling a product or service, many customers will require a written quote before they'll write a check. With a single click, you can now generate a quote for any opportunity in the database. You must have Microsoft Word and Microsoft Excel installed on your computer to use the Quoting features.

Task A Writing a Quote for an Opportunity

Quotes generated for opportunities in the database will open in Microsoft Word with an embedded Excel spreadsheet. When you print a quote for a contact, you'll have the option to create a history of the quote in the History tab.

To write a quote for an opportunity:

1. Add a new opportunity. (See the beginning of this chapter for details on how to add a new opportunity to the database.)
2. In the Opportunity dialog box (where you edit the attributes of the sale) click in the Products/Services tab.
3. Click the Quote button. ACT! will generate a quote for the opportunity.

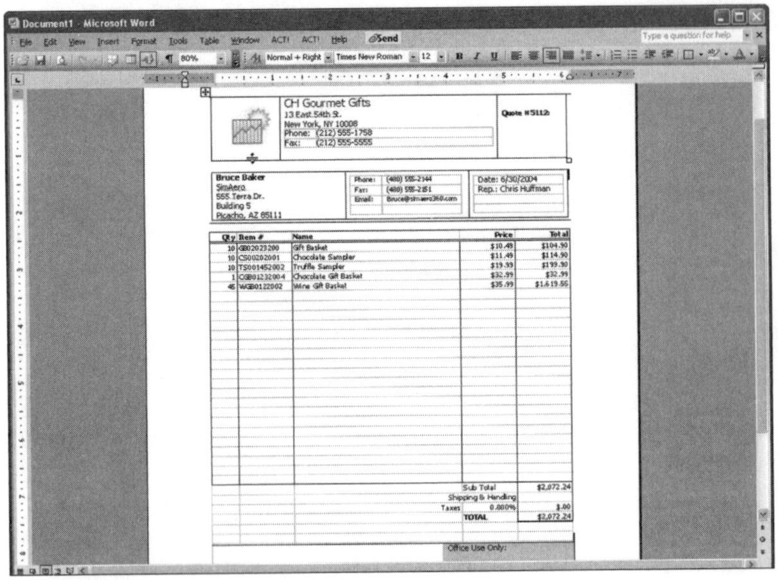

Generating a quote for an opportunity

Quoting takes time

It may seem like ACT! takes a long time to generate a quote, especially on a slow computer. When you click the Quote button, ACT! must:

- open Excel
- add product data to the Excel spreadsheet
- open Word and incorporate contact field data into the quote
- embed the Excel workbook into the Word document
- close Excel

It may seem like ACT!'s performance is sluggish, but it's actually a lot faster than it would be if you had to perform all of these steps manually.

Task B Editing the Quote Template

When you generate a quote for an opportunity, ACT! bases the quote on an editable template in your database supplemental files folder. Editing the template lets you customize the quote to match your company's look and feel. Because the quotes generated by ACT! have an embedded Excel spreadsheet, you may have to edit both the Word template that generates the quote and the Excel template that is embedded into the quote.

To edit the Word quote template:

1. In ACT!, click Write | Edit Template.
2. In your default template folder, select the Quote.adt file and click Open.
3. The quote will open in Microsoft Word for editing.

To edit the embedded Excel quote template:

1. In Microsoft Excel, click File | Open. Browse to open your default template folder. By default, this is My Documents\ACT for Win 7\Databases\[database name]-database-files.
2. Open the Quote.xls file for editing in Excel.

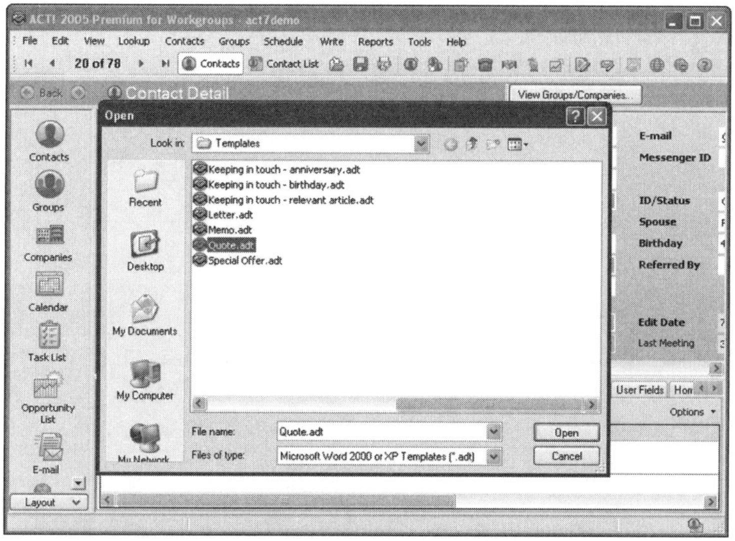

Editing the Quote.adt file

Database supplemental files template folder

In Windows Explorer, browse to the folder that houses your ACT! database. (By default, this is My Documents\ACT\ACT for Win 7\Database.) Within that folder, there will be a folder called [databasename]-database-files. Within this folder, you'll find a folder for attachments, backup files, layouts, queries, reports, and templates. These folders make up your database supplemental files system, and you can configure ACT! to set them to synchronize to remote users.

Exporting Opportunities to Excel

One of the most powerful opportunity-reporting features is the new link between the Opportunity List and Microsoft Excel. With a single click, you can export the currently filtered opportunities into an Excel spreadsheet that has pre-created pivot tables to help you drill down the data.

Task A Exporting the Opportunity List to Excel

Before exporting the Opportunity List to Excel, it's probably a good idea to perform a lookup of the specific contacts you'd like to see. Alternatively, you could filter the Opportunity List to show just a specific set of opportunities.

Toolbar button

You can also click the Export to Excel button on the toolbar to export the Opportunity List to Microsoft Excel.

Some users can't export

Browse, Restricted, and Standard users cannot export to Excel. This feature is only available to Managers and Administrator users.

To export the Opportunity List to Excel:

1. In the Opportunity List view, set the filter to show just the opportunities you'd like to export to Excel. (See the beginning of this chapter for information on filtering the Opportunity List.)
2. Customize the columns in the Opportunity list to display the fields you'd like to export to Excel. (To do this, click the Options button in the upper-right corner of the Opportunity List view and choose the Customize Columns option.)
3. Click Tools | Export to Excel.
4. The Opportunities List will appear in a Microsoft Excel spreadsheet.

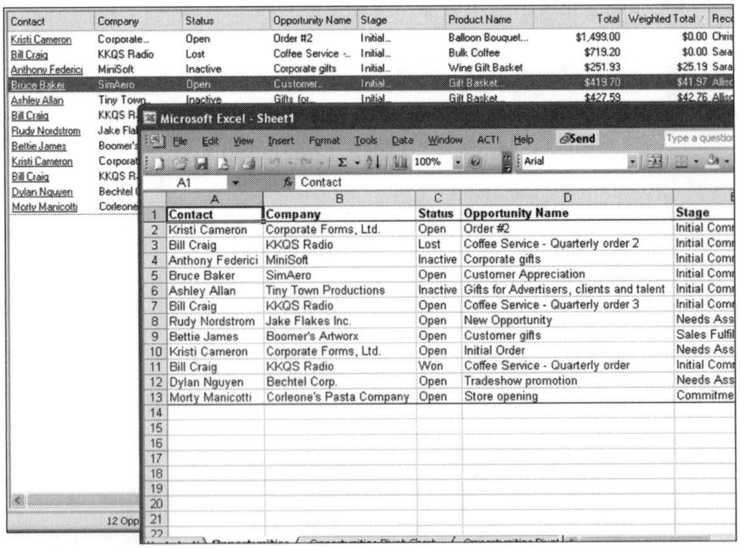

Exporting the Opportunity List view to Excel

Task B Viewing Excel Pivot Tables for Opportunity Data

After exporting your Opportunity List to Microsoft Excel, you'll notice that ACT! automatically sets up a pivot table and pivot chart. Pivot tables give you a great way to sort and total the opportunity data that has been exported to Excel.

To view pivot tables and charts for your opportunity data:

1. Ensure that the filter in your Opportunity List view is set to include all of the opportunities that you would like to analyze in an opportunity pivot.
2. Click Tools | Export to Excel.
3. When the Excel spreadsheet opens, click the Opportunities Pivot Chart worksheet to view a visual representation of the spreadsheet data.
4. Click the Opportunities Pivot worksheet to report on sum totals of the opportunity data in the spreadsheet.

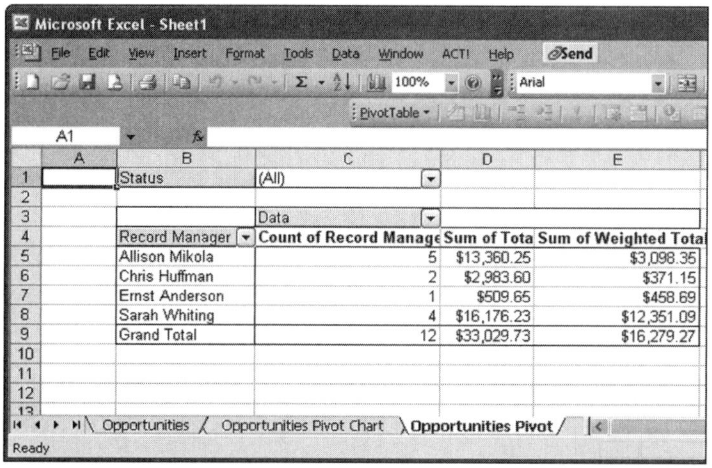

Manipulating opportunity data in an Excel pivot table

Managing the Sales Process

ACT! 2005 now lets you create multiple sales processes, each with its own unique set of sales stages. If you're selling multiple products that each follow a slightly different sales process, this will definitely help your sales reporting.

Task A Creating a Sales Process

When you create a new sales process, you'll have to define a set of sales stages for the process.

To create a sales process:

1. Click Contacts | Opportunities | Manage Process List.
2. In the area on the left, click the Create Opportunity Process option.
3. Give your new opportunity process a name and description. Click Next.
4. Click Add to add a new opportunity stage for the process. Add a stage name, description, and default probability.
5. Repeat Step 4 until all of your stages have been added.
6. Click Finish.

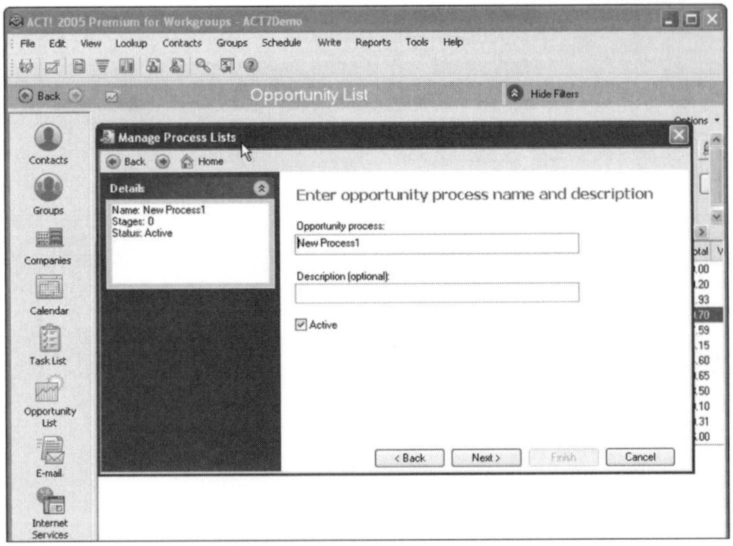

Creating a new sales process

Deleting a sales process

You cannot delete a sales process if any of your open sales are using it. If you edit a sales process, you'll have the option of making the process inactive.

Task B Modifying an Existing Sales Process

From time to time, you may need to modify an existing opportunity process. You can add stages, remove stages, change probability numbers linked to stages, and make the entire sales process inactive.

To modify an existing opportunity process:

1. Click Contacts | Opportunities | Process List.
2. Highlight the opportunity you'd like to edit and click the Edit Opportunity Process option in the blue area on the left.
3. If necessary, edit the opportunity process name and description. Click Next.
4. Click Add to add a new opportunity stage for the process.
5. To remove a stage, highlight it and click the Delete button.
6. Click Finish.

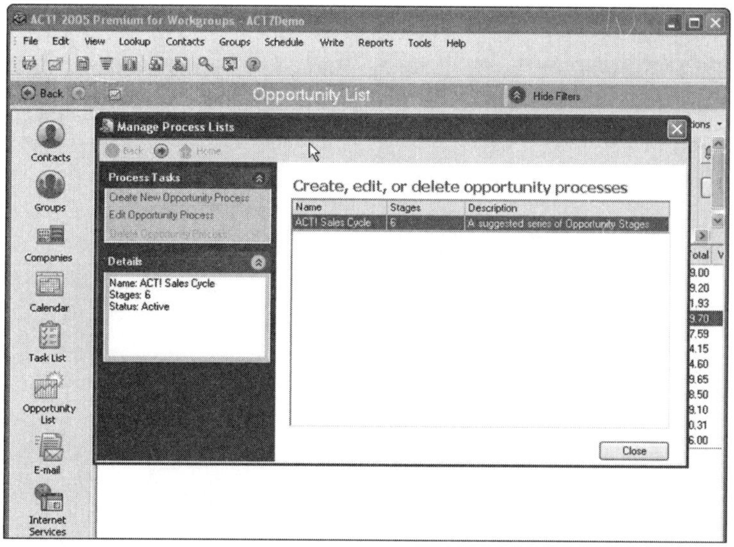

Modifying an existing sales process

Deleting opportunity stages

If you have any open opportunities at a particular opportunity stage, you won't be able to delete the stage.

Lookups reset any filter

If you perform a lookup by sales stage or any of the other opportunity fields, ACT! will automatically reset your filters in the Opportunity List view.

Task C Looking Up Contacts by Opportunity Stage

If you want to find all of the contacts in your database that are at a certain opportunity stage, you can either perform a lookup on the opportunity stage field or you can filter the Opportunity list to show just contacts at the sales stage.

To perform a lookup by sales stage:

1. Click Lookup | Opportunities | Stage.
2. In the Search for area, type the name of the sales stage you'd like to find.
3. Click OK. All of the opportunities at the stage will appear in the Opportunity List.

To filter the Opportunity List view by sales stage:

1. In the Opportunity List, locate the Process/Stage area in the filter settings.
2. From the Process drop-down, select an opportunity process.
3. In the Stage drop-down, you'll be able to select the opportunities that you'd like to filter in or out of the Opportunity List view.

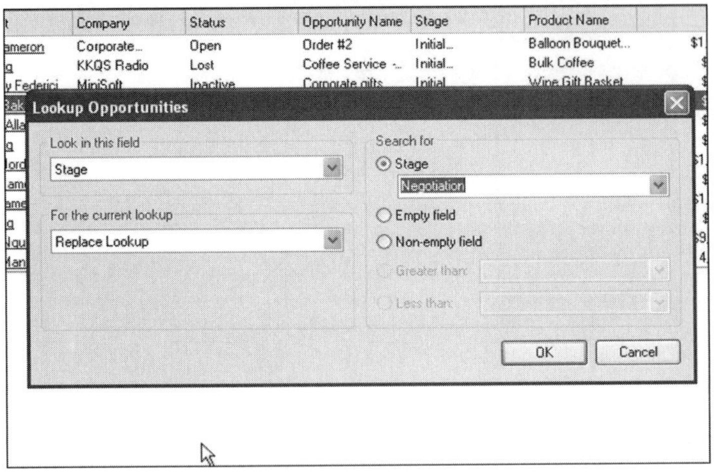

Performing a lookup of opportunities by sales stage

Maintaining a Product List

In ACT! 2005, you can maintain a centralized list of all products and services that your company sells. Along with the list of product names, you can store item numbers, internal costs, and customer costs.

Task A Adding Items to the Product List

As you add new products and services to your list of offerings, add these items to your centralized product list in ACT! as well. Doing so makes it easy to create opportunities that involve the products in your master list.

To add new items to the centralized product list:

1. Click Contacts | Opportunities | Manage Product List. The Manage Product List dialog box will appear, and you'll see a list of all products already in the list.
2. Click the Add button to add a new product.
3. Give the product a name, item number, internal cost, and selling price.
4. Repeat this process until all of your products and services have been added to the centralized list.

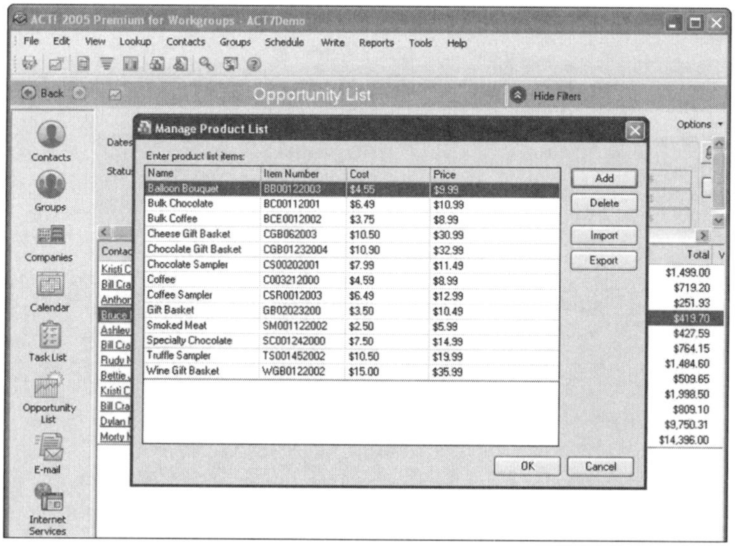

Managing the centralized product list

Importing your product list

If you have a list of products and services in Microsoft Excel, you can save this product list as a .TXT or .CSV text file. These file formats can be imported into the master list of products. To import new products, click Contacts | Opportunities | Manage Product List.

Different selling prices

If you have different selling prices for each customer, enter a standard high-end price in the Price field. Then, as you're adding each item to an opportunity, you'll have the opportunity to reduce the selling price by a percentage or fixed number.

Task B Modifying the Product List

At any time, you can modify the list of products and services. Modifying the master product list follows the same general process as adding new items to the list.

To modify the product list:

1. Click Contacts | Opportunities | Manage Product List.
2. Locate the product you'd like to modify. Click in any of the product fields (Name, Item Number, Cost, Price) to modify that field.
3. Repeat this process until all of your products and services have been updated.

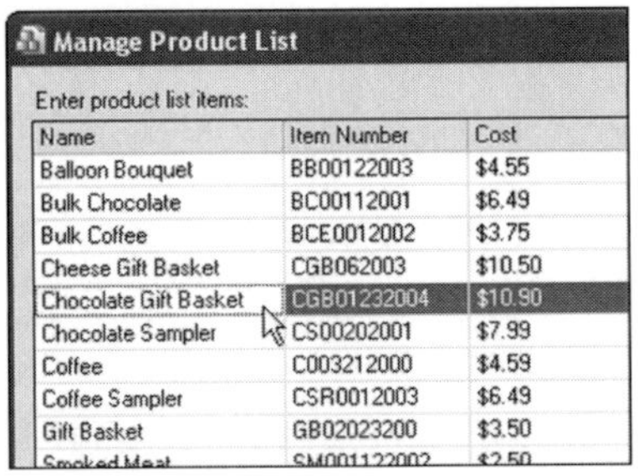

Editing items on the product list

Managing price increases

If you have periodic price increases for your products or services, you'll want to modify the selling price for each product in the master list.

Delete products

If you discontinue a product or service, you can remove it from the master list by highlighting it and clicking the Delete button. Only Manager and Administrator users can maintain the product list, and deleting a product from the list doesn't affect any existing opportunities.

Task C Importing a Product List

If you already have a list of products and services, importing the list will save a lot of data entry time. The easiest way to import a product list is to open it in a program like Microsoft Excel and save as a .CSV or .TXT text file.

To import a product list:

1. Click Contacts | Opportunities | Manage Product List. The Manage Product List dialog box will appear.
2. Click the Import button. The Import Products dialog box will appear.
3. Click the Browse button and double-click the .CSV or .TXT file you'd like to import.
4. Click the Import button.

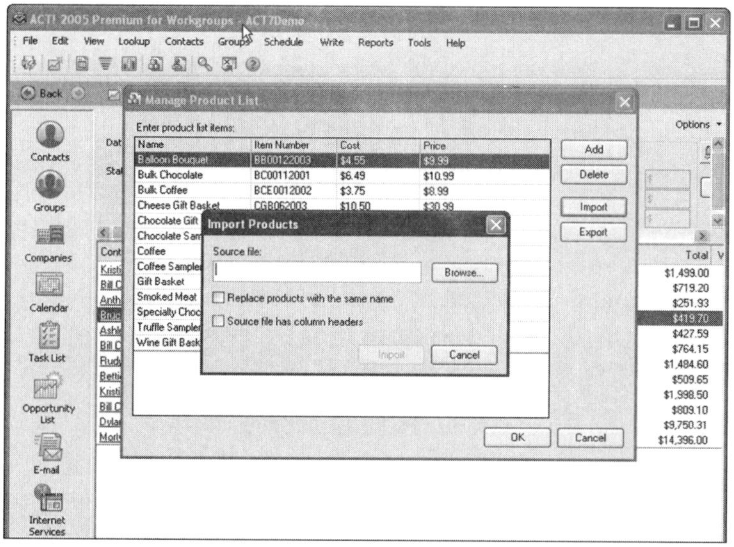

Importing products from a text file

Duplicate matching

When importing a list or products or services, click the Replace products with the same name option in the Import Products dialog box to turn on ACT!'s Duplicate Matching feature.

.CSV or .TXT

You can only import .CSV or .TXT text files into ACT!. The easiest way to get a properly formatted text file is to create your list in Microsoft Excel. In the Excel spreadsheet, create a column for product name, item number, cost, and price. Populate all information and save as a comma-separated values (.CSV) file or a tab-delimited text (.TXT) file.

Custom Opportunity Fields

If you have specific information that needs to be tracked for each sale, you can customize any of the eight opportunity user fields to house this data. Since you can easily lookup activities based on the contents of any user field, this feature will help you categorize your opportunities.

Task A Changing the Opportunity User Fields

You'll need administrator-level access to the database to modify any fields, including the opportunity user fields. You only have eight user fields in the database, so customize them carefully.

To change the name of an opportunity user field:

1. Log into the database as an administrator.
2. Click Tools | Define Fields.
3. In the drop-down at the top of the Define Fields dialog box, select the Opportunities option.
4. In the field list, select one of the opportunity user fields.
5. In the blue area on the left side of the screen, click the Edit Field option.
6. In the Field name area, change the name of the field (if necessary).
7. In the data field type drop-down, select a field type. In the Customize field behavior area, select additional options for the field. Click Next.
8. Specify a default field value, field format, and field length. Click Next.
9. Add a trigger for the field, if necessary. A *trigger* is a program or action (like an activity series) that is launched after you modify the information in the field.
10. Click Finish and exit the Define Fields dialog box.

Locking the database

Defining fields will lock the database, so you'll need to edit the opportunity user fields during a time when all users can log out of the database.

Where are the custom opportunity fields?

The customizable opportunity user fields are located in the User Fields tab of the Opportunity dialog box. To bring up the Opportunity dialog box, click Contacts | Opportunities | New Opportunity.

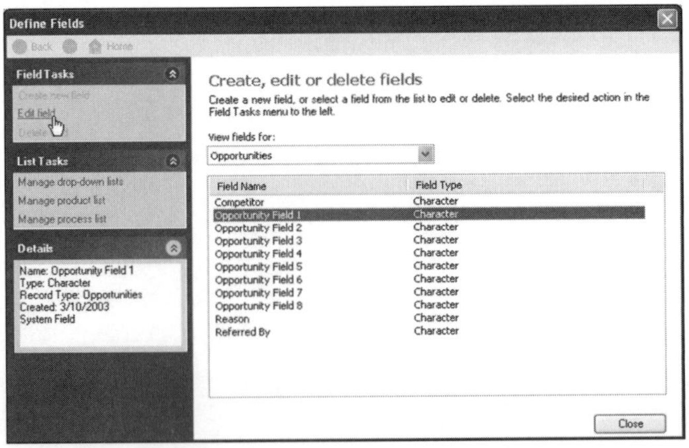

Editing the customizable opportunity fields

Running Opportunity Reports

The real power of the Opportunities feature lies in ACT!'s sales reporting functionality. With ACT!'s Sales Reporting features, you can print lists of opportunity data, and you can even produce opportunity graphs and pipeline funnels. ACT! ships with about a half dozen sales reports. You can use these out-of-the-box reports, edit them to include your custom fields, or create entirely new reports.

Task A Running Opportunity Reports

The seven basic opportunity reports that ship with ACT! will probably meet most of your basic reporting needs. Before creating a customized opportunity report, check to see if one of the out-of-the-box reports will work.

To run an opportunity report:

1. If you need to limit the contacts whose opportunity data is included in the report, then perform a lookup of these contacts you'd like to include in the report.
2. Click Reports | Opportunity Reports. From the resulting list, select the opportunity report you'd like to run. The Define Filters dialog box will appear.
3. Select an output method, a contact range, and any necessary filters. (See Chapter 17, "Reports," for more information on filtering reports.)
4. Click OK.

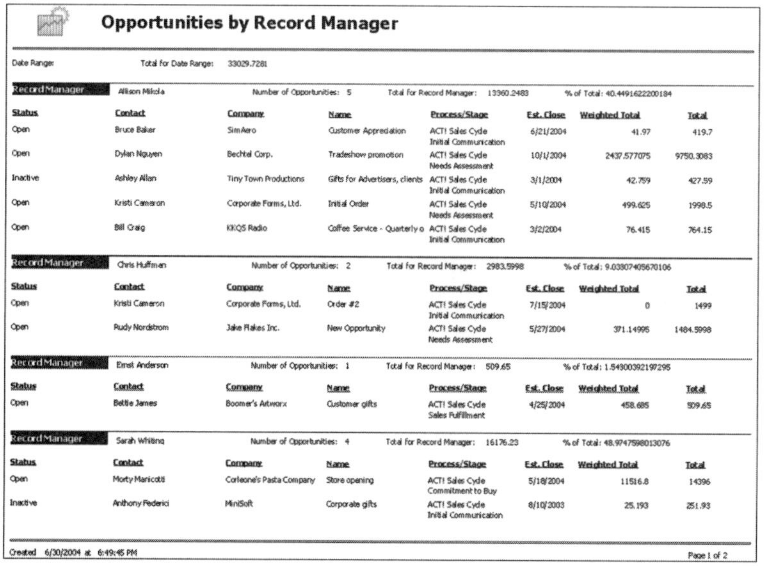

Opportunities by Record Manager

Date Range: Total for Date Range: 33029.7281

Record Manager Allison Mikola Number of Opportunities: 5 Total for Record Manager: 13360.2483 % of Total: 40.4491622200184

Status	Contact	Company	Name	Process/Stage	Est. Close	Weighted Total	Total
Open	Bruce Baker	SimAero	Customer Appreciation	ACT! Sales Cycle Initial Communication	6/21/2004	41.97	419.7
Open	Dylan Nguyen	Bechtel Corp.	Tradeshow promotion	ACT! Sales Cycle Needs Assessment	10/1/2004	2437.577075	9750.3083
Inactive	Ashley Allan	Tiny Town Productions	Gifts for Advertisers, clients	ACT! Sales Cycle Initial Communication	3/1/2004	42.759	427.59
Open	Kristi Cameron	Corporate Forms, Ltd.	Initial Order	ACT! Sales Cycle Needs Assessment	5/10/2004	499.625	1998.5
Open	Bill Craig	KKQS Radio	Coffee Service - Quarterly o	ACT! Sales Cycle Initial Communication	3/2/2004	76.415	764.15

Record Manager Chris Huffman Number of Opportunities: 2 Total for Record Manager: 2983.5998 % of Total: 9.03307405670106

Status	Contact	Company	Name	Process/Stage	Est. Close	Weighted Total	Total
Open	Kristi Cameron	Corporate Forms, Ltd.	Order #2	ACT! Sales Cycle Initial Communication	7/15/2004	0	1499
Open	Rudy Nordstrom	Jake Flakes Inc.	New Opportunity	ACT! Sales Cycle Needs Assessment	5/27/2004	371.14995	1484.5998

Record Manager Ernst Anderson Number of Opportunities: 1 Total for Record Manager: 509.65 % of Total: 1.54300392197295

Status	Contact	Company	Name	Process/Stage	Est. Close	Weighted Total	Total
Open	Bettie James	Boomer's Artworx	Customer gifts	ACT! Sales Cycle Sales Fulfillment	4/25/2004	458.685	509.65

Record Manager Sarah Whiting Number of Opportunities: 4 Total for Record Manager: 16176.23 % of Total: 48.9747598013076

Status	Contact	Company	Name	Process/Stage	Est. Close	Weighted Total	Total
Open	Morty Maricotti	Corleone's Pasta Company	Store opening	ACT! Sales Cycle Commitment to Buy	5/18/2004	11516.8	14396
Inactive	Anthony Federici	MiniSoft	Corporate gifts	ACT! Sales Cycle Initial Communication	8/10/2003	25.193	251.93

Created 6/30/2004 at 6:49:45 PM Page 1 of 2

The Opportunities by Record Manager report

Complex opportunity reports

You can use Crystal Reports to create complex reports using ACT!'s Opportunity data. There are a few good programs on the market that will help interface ACT! with Crystal Reports. Go to http://www.actaddons.com for a list of reporting add-on products.

Task B Filtering Opportunity Reports

You can filter any of the opportunity reports to show just the specific information you need to see on the report. You might want to print a report that only includes data managed by a specific user. Or you might want to change the sorting of the report. Perhaps you want to limit the report to include only opportunities set to close in a specific date range? All of this can be done using the report filter settings.

To filter an opportunity report:

1. Click Reports | Opportunity Reports, and select the report you'd like to run. The Define Filters dialog box will appear.
2. Select whether or not to show open opportunities, closed/won opportunities, or lost opportunities.
3. In the Date Range drop-down, select a date range to filter the report to include just information set to close in a specific time period.
4. In the right column, select the users whose data should be included in the report.
5. Click OK to run the report.

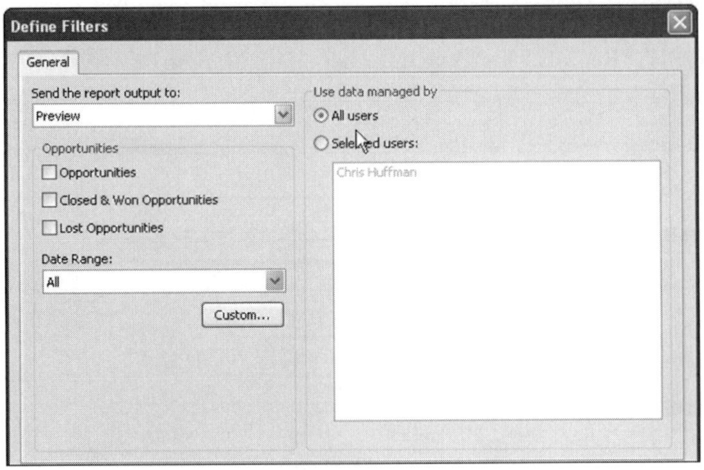

Defining the filter for a report

Lookup first

Before running a sales report, you might want to perform a lookup of contacts. Then, in the Run Report dialog box, you can select the Current Lookup option in the General tab to run the report just for sales that have been associated with contacts in the current lookup.

Task C Running an Opportunity Graph

ACT! can generate an *opportunity graph*, a visual representation of the opportunities in your database. You can customize an opportunity graph to show a specific set of information, and ACT! makes it easy to copy and paste the graph into a document or PowerPoint presentation.

To run an opportunity graph:

1. Click Report | Opportunity Reports | Opportunity Graph.
2. The Graph Options dialog box appears. In the Create graph for area, select a range of contacts whose opportunity data should be included in the graph.
3. In the Graph area, select the type of opportunities to include in the graph.
4. In the Display data for area, select the users whose opportunities should be included.
5. In the Dates to graph area, select a date range.
6. In the Value to graph area, select whether to graph by sales volume or by total number of units.
7. Type header and footer text in the Header/Footer area.
8. Click Graph to display the opportunity graph.
9. Use the buttons on the right side of the opportunity graph to save, copy, or print the image.

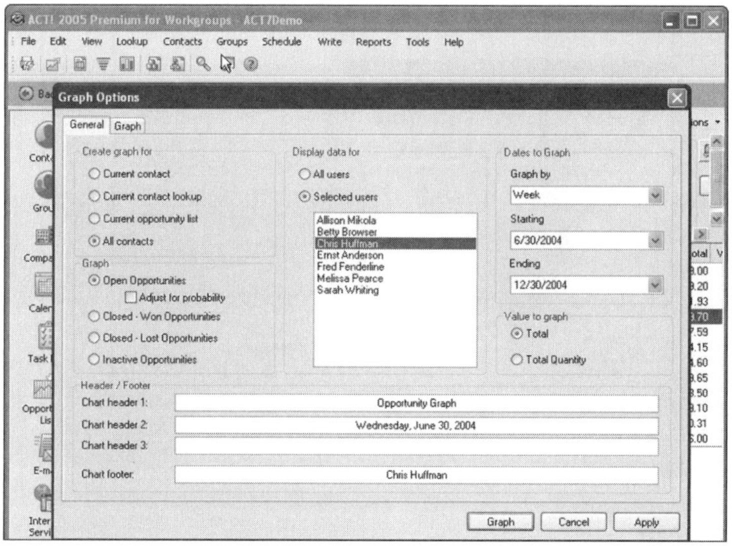

Specifying options for the opportunity graph

Making changes to a graph

After you've clicked the Graph button to create an opportunity graph, you can edit the options for the graph by clicking the Options button. Doing so will take you back to the Graph Options dialog box, where you'll be able to make any changes to the graph setup.

Task D Running an Opportunity Pipeline

The Opportunity Pipeline graphic shows a visual representation of the number of opportunities you currently have in each stage in the sales process. In the Opportunity Pipeline Options dialog box, you can color-code the stages and select which contacts' and users' opportunities should be included in the pipeline.

To run an Opportunity Pipeline graph:

1. Click Reports | Opportunity Report | Opportunity Pipeline. The Opportunity Pipeline Options dialog box will appear.
2. In the Create graph for area, select the range of contacts to use in the report.
3. In the Display data for sales managed by area, select whose opportunities you'd like to include in the pipeline.
4. In the Assign colors area, select the colors you'd like to use for each stage in the sales process.
5. Click Graph. The Opportunity Pipeline will appear.
6. Use the buttons on the right to save, copy, and print the pipeline report.

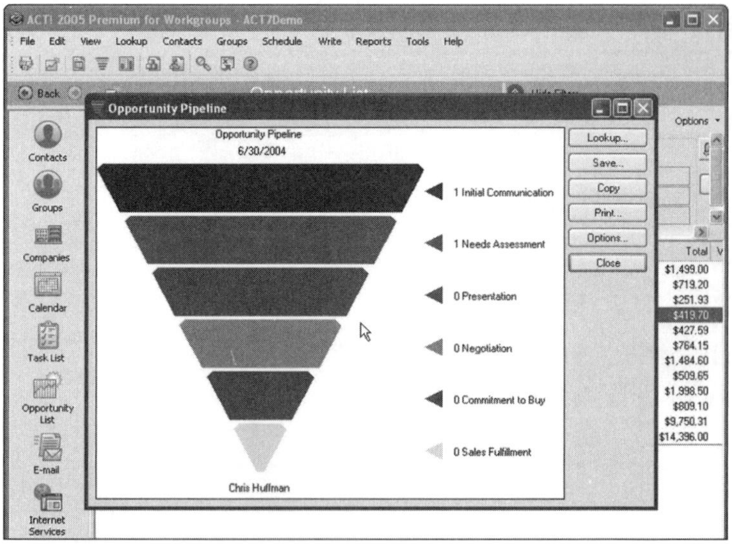

The Opportunity Pipeline graph

Sales pipeline report

After running a graphical opportunity pipeline, you might want to run an opportunity pipeline report to show details about each opportunity grouped by sales stage. Click Reports | Opportunity Reports | Pipeline Report.

A perfect pipeline every time

Before you get too excited about your perfectly-shaped pipeline, you should know that the pipeline will look like a perfect funnel regardless of the number of activities at each stage in your sales process. The funnel graphic is not dynamic.

Chapter 10
Letters, Envelopes, and Labels

Setting Letter Preferences

Before writing letters to your ACT! contacts, you'll need to set a few word processor preferences. You'll need to specify a default word processor and select a default folder for saving documents written to ACT! contacts.

Task A Setting the Default Word Processor

The Communication tab of the Preferences dialog box is where you'll set preferences for ACT!'s word processing and faxing features. In the General tab, you can set the default locations for ACT!'s ancillary files, such as documents.

To set the default word processor:

1. Click Tools | Preferences. The Preferences dialog box appears.
2. Click the Communication tab.
3. In the Word processor drop-down, select either Microsoft Word or The ACT! Word Processor.
4. Click OK.

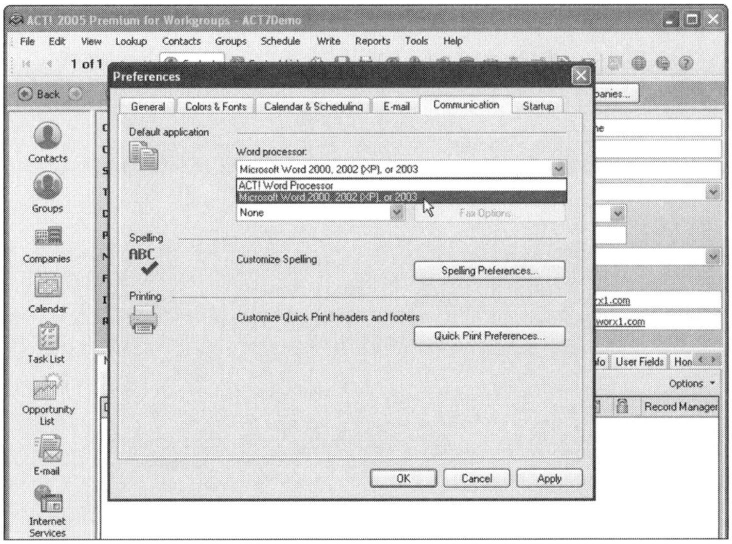

Setting the default word processor

Supported Microsoft Word Versions

- Word 2000
- Word 2002 (XP)
- Word 2003

Writing a Template-Based Letter

From ACT!'s Write menu, you can write template-based letters to any contact in your ACT! database. Template letters will appear in the default word processor—either the ACT! Word Processor or Microsoft Word. When letters created from within ACT! are printed in the Word Processor, a history of the letter having been sent can be automatically created in the History tab for your contact. Best of all, field information from your ACT! database can be sent over into your letters, so you'll never have to re-type someone's address in a letter again.

Task A Writing Letters, Memos, and Fax Cover Pages

ACT! gives you the option of writing letters, memos, and fax cover pages from the Write menu.

To write a letter, memo, or fax cover page:

1. Go to the contact for whom you'd like to create a letter, memo, or fax cover page.
2. Click Write | Letter to write a letter.
3. Click Write | Memo to write a memo.
4. Click Write | Fax Cover Page to write a fax cover page.
5. The letter, memo, or fax cover page will appear in your default word processor.

Writing a letter to a contact

What's happening in the background?

When you click Write | Letter, ACT! launches a letter that's based off a template in the template folder of your database supplemental files folder. (By default, the database supplemental files system is located within My Documents\ACT\ACT for Win 7\Databases\.) You may want to edit the letter, memo, or fax cover page template that ACT! uses by default. Use the list below to figure out the name of the file that ACT! uses to create these documents:

Letter

- letter.tpl (AWP)
- letter.adt (Word)

Memorandum

- memo.tpl (AWP)
- memo.adt (Word)

Fax Cover Page

- faxcover.tpl (AWP)
- faxcover.adt (Word)

(AWP = ACT! Word Processor)

(Word = Microsoft Word 2000, 2002, or 2003)

Task B Writing Other Template-Based Letters

If you have created customized letter templates, then it's easy to write documents based on these letter templates to your ACT! contacts. Creating custom templates is covered in this chapter. To create a new custom template, click Write | New Letter/E-mail Template.

To write other template-based letters:

1. Go to the contact for whom you'd like to create a document.
2. Click Write | Other Document (from template).
3. Locate the template you'd like to use as the basis for the document.
4. Highlight the document template and click the Open button. ACT! will create a document for your current contact based on the template you selected.

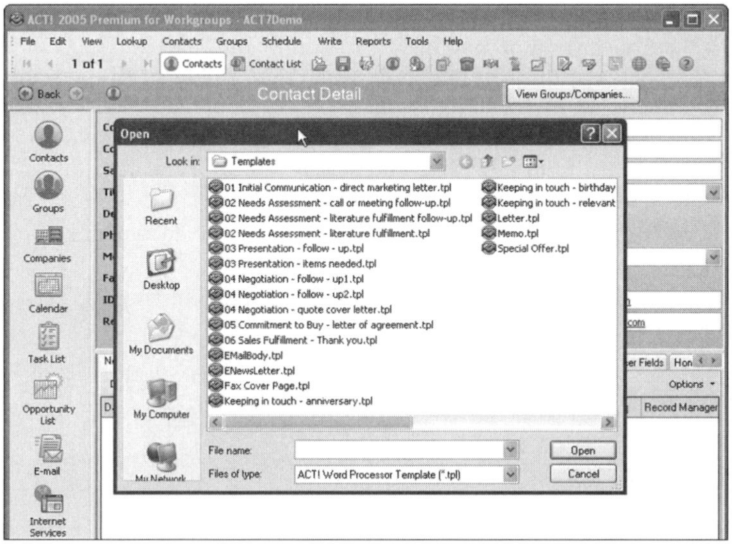

Selecting a letter template

Synchronize templates

ACT! 2005 now supports synchronization of supplemental ACT! documents such as document templates and attached documents. When setting up a remote sync database, you'll have the option to synchronize these files with the remote user.

Turning off the envelope printing prompt

To turn off the envelope printing prompt that appears each time you print a document created from within ACT!, click Edit | Preferences. In the General tab, uncheck the option labeled When printing letters, prompt to print an envelope.

Task C Creating a History of a Letter Sent

Whenever you print a document that has been created for an ACT! contact, Microsoft Word (or the ACT! Word Processor) will automatically prompt you to create a history of the letter. If you choose to create a history of the letter having been sent, ACT! can automatically associate the history with the contact to whom you wrote the document.

To create a history of a letter:

1. Write a template-based letter to an ACT! contact. For example, you could click Write | Letter to write a basic letter.
2. In the default word processor, click File | Print to print the document.
3. Verify your printer settings and click OK to print the document. The Create History dialog box appears.
4. In the Regarding field, type the main subject of the document you're printing.
5. Click the Attach document to history option if you'd like ACT! to create a hyperlink between the history item in your contact's Notes/History tab and the document. (If you choose this option, you'll be able to double-click the history item in ACT! to bring up a copy of the letter.)
6. Click the Create button. If you chose to attach the document to history, you will be prompted to save the document.
7. ACT! will prompt you to save the document. Save the document somewhere on your local computer or network.
8. A history of the letter having been sent will be created in your ACT! contact's History tab.

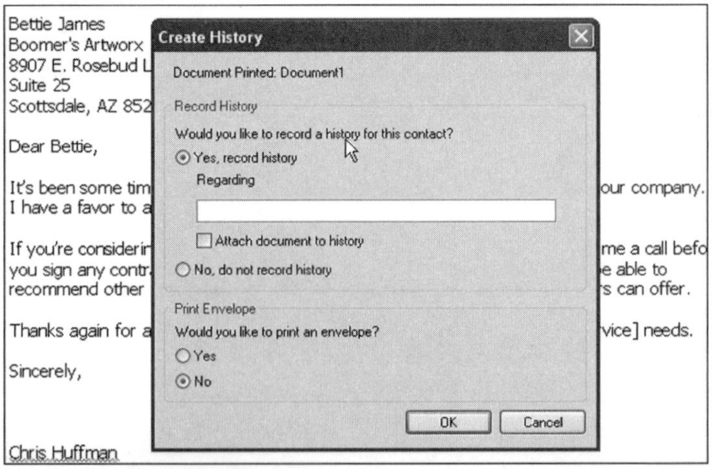

Creating a history of a letter sent

Printing Envelopes

Once you've created a letter for one of your ACT! contacts, you might want to print an envelope for this contact. You can easily print envelopes of any size in ACT! 2005.

Task A Printing Standard Envelopes

Most business envelopes are standard COM #10 size. You can print a COM 10 envelope using this simple procedure.

To print a standard COM #10 envelope for a contact:

1. Go to the contact for whom you'd like to print an envelope.
2. Click File | Print. The Print dialog box appears.
3. In the Printout type area on the left, select the Envelopes option.
4. In the white block, highlight the Envelope #10 option.
5. Click Print. The Define Filters dialog box appears.
6. In the Create report for area, select whether you'd like to print envelopes for the current contact, the current lookup, or all contacts in the database.
7. In the Send the report output to area, select whether you'd like to send the envelopes directly to the printer or whether you'd like to preview the envelopes before printing them.
8. Click OK. The envelopes will either print or appear in the preview, depending on the option you selected in Step 7.

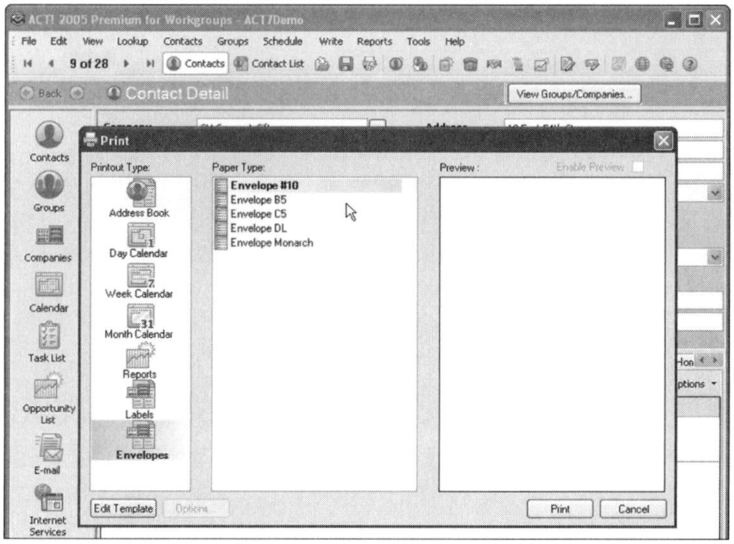

Printing an envelope

Return addresses

The default COM 10 envelope template includes field placeholders that show your return address in the upper-left corner of printed envelopes. If you're printing on pre-printed envelopes, you may need to remove the return address from the envelope template. Click File | Print, and then select the Envelopes option, highlight an envelope template, and click the Edit Template button. In the Template Editor, delete the return address and save.

Task B Creating Envelope Templates

ACT! ships with many envelope template options, but you may need to print on non-standard envelopes. ACT! includes the built-in ability to create new envelope templates of any size. This feature is especially useful for printing on holiday cards.

To create an envelope template:

1. Click Reports | New Template.
2. ACT! launches the Report Editor and the New Report dialog box will appear.
3. In the Report Types column, choose the Contact Reports option.
4. In the Templates column, choose the Contact Envelopes option. Click OK.
5. Select the height and width of your envelope. Click OK.
6. When the Report Designer appears, use the Field button on the Toolbox to add field placeholders to the envelope.
7. Click File | Save As to save a copy of the envelope.

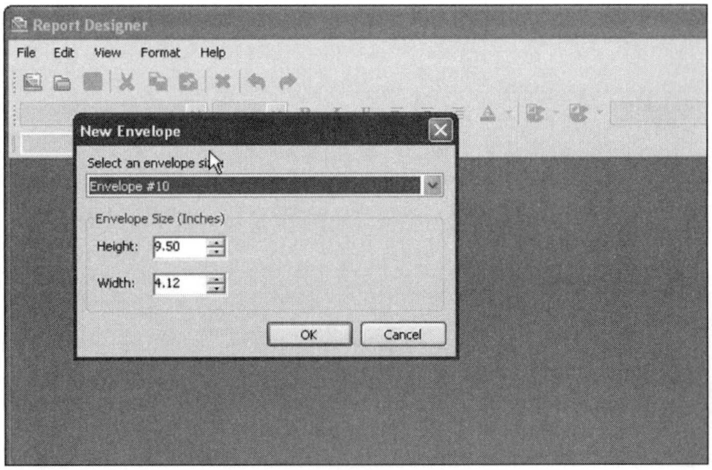

Creating a new report template

Task C Editing Envelope Templates

By default, all ACT! envelope templates include a return address. If you're printing on pre-printed company envelopes, then you'll need the ability to edit ACT!'s standard envelope templates to not include the return address.

To edit an envelope template:

1. Click File | Print. In the Printout type area, choose the Envelopes option.
2. Highlight the envelope template you'd like to edit and click the Edit Template button.
3. The Template Editor appears. Click View | Toolbox to show the list of icons that will allow you to add fields, icons, and pictures to the template.
4. Click View | Properties Window to show the Properties window. The Properties window will display all editable attributes for the currently selected object on the template.
5. Make any necessary changes to the template and click File | Save or File | Save As to save.

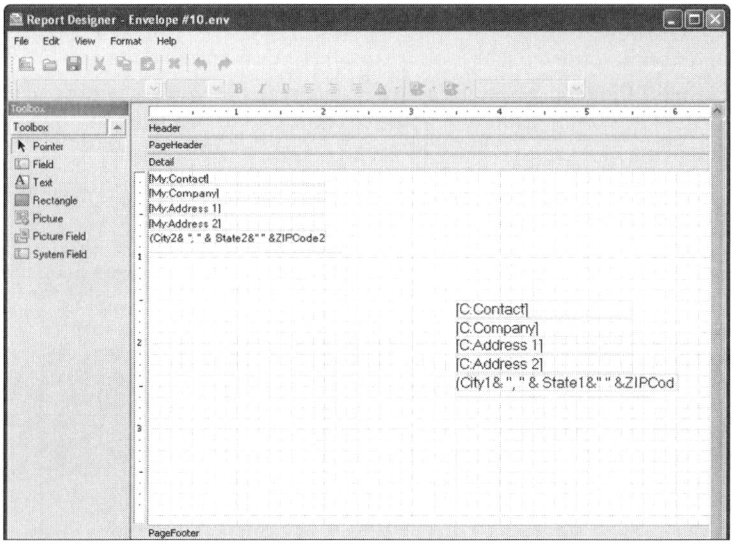

Editing an envelope template

Adding a concatenated "City, State Zip" field

To add the City, State, and Zip fields to an envelope template, place each field somewhere on the report template. Click View | Properties Window, and the Properties window will appear on the right. Highlight the City, State, and Zip fields and change the Visible option to No for each field. Also in the Properties window, edit the property name so there are no spaces. (Do not use the Delete key when editing the property name. Use only the backspace key.) Then, place a system field on the template where you want to print the City, State, and Zip fields. Highlight this system field. In the Properties window, enter the following expression: **(City1&","&State1&" "&ZIPCode1)**

Envelope template files

Envelope templates are saved as .env files in the Reports folder of the database supplemental files system. (By default, the Database supplemental files are kept in My Documents\ACT\ACT for Win 7\Databases\.) If you have envelope templates that were created in a previous version of ACT!, then click Tools | Convert ACT! 3-6 Items to convert them to ACT! 2005 format.

Printing Labels

Printing many envelopes is easy if you have a printer that can easily accommodate large numbers of envelopes. If your printer doesn't feed multiple envelopes, you may find it easier to print mailing labels. ACT! can print on most standard Avery shipping labels. If you have a custom-sized label, you can create your own label template.

Task A Printing Standard Avery Labels

ACT! ships with many standard Avery label templates, and you can use these templates to print mailing labels for your contacts.

Singing the 5160 blues

If you've printed on Avery 5160 (3 across and 10 down) labels with previous versions of ACT!, you've probably been frustrated that ACT! would only print four lines of text on the label. This wasn't very useful if you use the second address line! In ACT! 2005, you can fit five lines of text on the label.

To print labels on standard Avery label sheets:

1. Go to the contact for whom you'd like to print a label.
2. Click File | Print. The Print dialog box will appear.
3. In the Printout Type area on the left, select the Labels option.
4. In the white block, highlight the Avery label size you'd like to use.
5. Click Print. The Define Filters dialog box appears.
6. In the Create report for area, select whether you'd like to print labels for the current contact, the current lookup, or all contacts in the database.
7. In the Send the report output to area, select whether you'd like to send the labels directly to the printer or whether you'd like to preview them before printing.
8. Click OK. The labels will either print or appear in the preview, depending on the option you selected in Step 7.

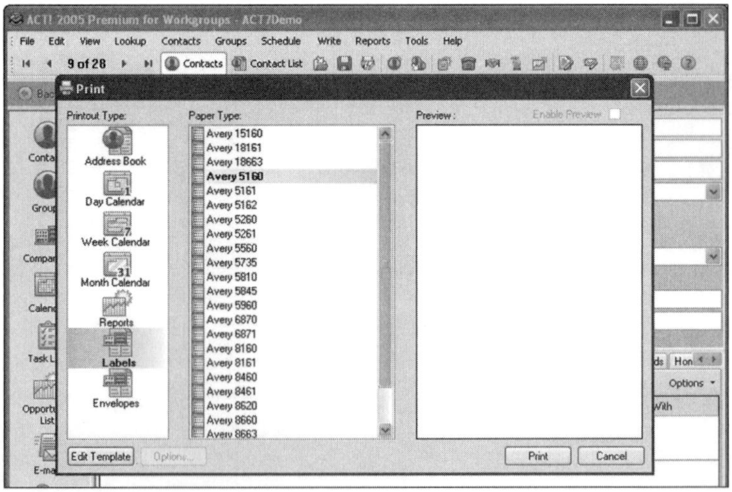

Printing labels for contacts

Task B Creating Non-Standard Label Templates

If you need to print a label size not listed in the default list in ACT!, you can create your own custom label template. This ability to create non-standard label templates is especially useful if you have pre-printed company shipping labels.

To create non-standard label templates:

1. Click Reports | New Report Template. ACT! launches the Report Editor, and the New Report dialog box appears.
2. In the Report Types column, choose the Contact Reports option.
3. In the Templates column, choose the Contact Labels option. Click OK.
4. From the drop-down at the top of the Create Label dialog box, select an Avery label size. Alternatively, you could manually specify the margins, label size, spacing, and number of labels.
5. Click OK to launch the Label Template Editor.
6. Use the Fields option on the Toolbox to add field placeholders to your label.
7. When you're finished designing the label, click File | Save As to save the template.

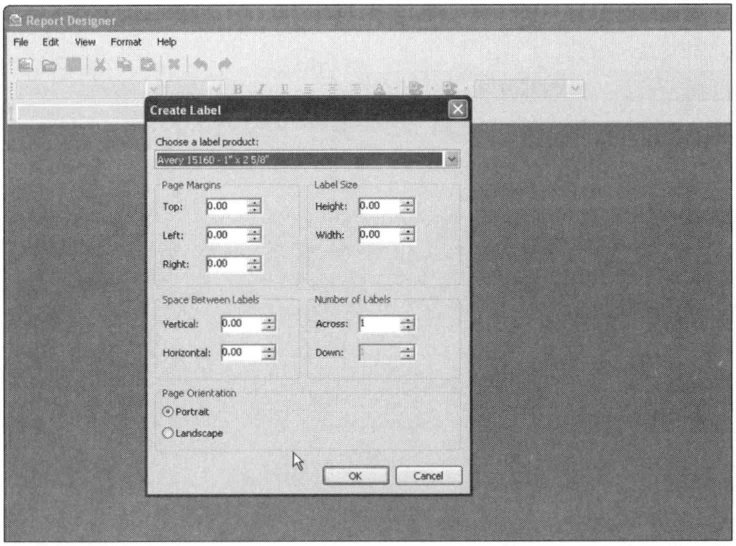

Creating a custom label template.

Label template files

Label templates are saved as .LBL files in the Reports folder of your database supplemental files system.

Name tags

If you're hosting an event, you can use ACT!'s Label feature to print name tags for your guests.

Chapter 11
Performing a Mail Merge

Creating Letter Templates

Editing an ACT! document template is as easy as editing a regular document in your word processor. When editing a document template, though, you have the ability to embed field placeholders into the text of the template. When the template is then written for a contact in your database, ACT! will replace the field placeholders with data from the ACT! database.

Task A Creating a Letter Template from Scratch

Letters written from within ACT! are based on templates. ACT! ships with a few simple letter templates—such as the letter, memorandum, and fax cover page—but you don't really realize the real power of ACT!'s letter-writing features until you create your own letter templates.

To create a letter template from scratch:

1. Click Write | New Letter/E-Mail Template. A blank template will appear in Microsoft Word or the ACT! Word Processor.
2. Make any necessary changes to the template.
3. When the template is complete, click File | Save As from within the Word Processor to save the template for later use.

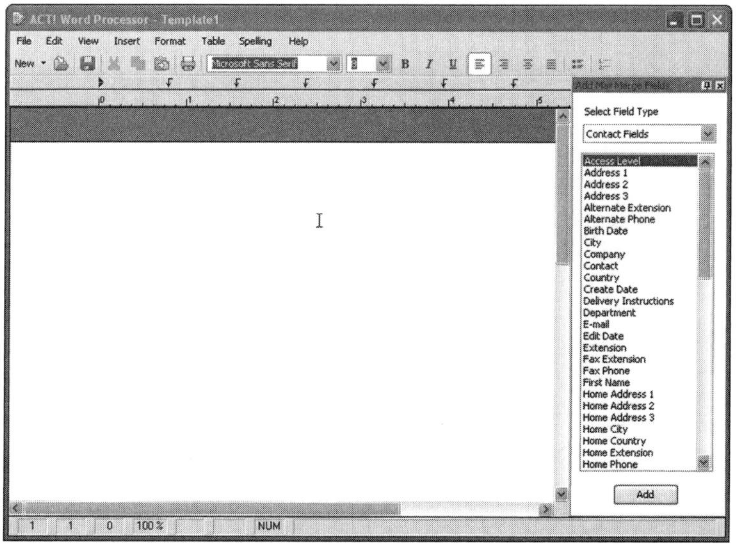

Editing a template in the ACT! Word Processor

Word processing preferences

Before editing any templates, click Edit | Preferences. In the General tab, make sure the correct word processor—either Microsoft Word or the ACT! Word Processor—is set as the default word processor. If, for example, the ACT! Word Processor is set as your default word processor, you won't be able to create new ACT! document templates in Microsoft Word.

File types

ACT! document templates created in Microsoft Word have an .ADT extension.

Task B Editing an Existing Letter Template

From time to time, you may need to make modifications to your letter templates. You may also need to create new letter templates that look similar to existing letter templates. Editing an existing template can be a lot faster than creating a new one from scratch. If you've already created, for example, a template formatted to use your letterhead margins and letter style, you'll find that it's easier to edit the existing template and save it with a new name than it is to recreate the template from scratch.

To edit an existing letter template:

1. Click Write | Other Document (from template).
2. A list of available templates on your system will appear. Browse and select the template you'd like to edit. The template will appear in your default word processor. Make any necessary changes.
3. Click File | Save to save the changes to your template.
4. Click File | Save As to save the template with a new name.
5. Close the word processor.

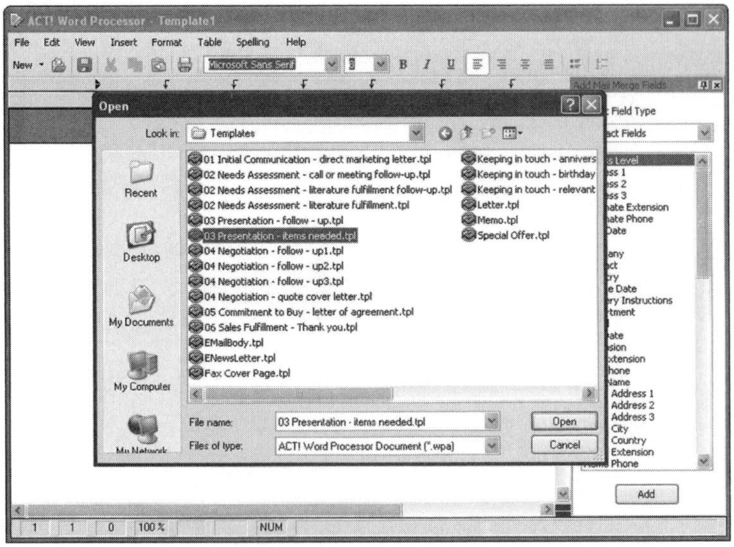

Opening an existing letter template

Switching word processors?

There's no easy way to convert document templates from ACT! Word Processor format to Microsoft Word format. If you're switching from the built-in word processor to Microsoft Word, you'll find that using Cut and Paste is the fastest way to recreate the templates in Word.

Working with Letter Templates

When editing an ACT! document template, you have the full editing capabilities of your word processor. The ACT! Word Processor provides fairly limited document editing capabilities, but you'll be able to design just about any document if you use Microsoft Word as your default word processor.

Task A Inserting Field Placeholders

When editing a document template in the ACT! Word Processor or Microsoft Word, you'll notice that a Mail Merge Fields dialog box hovers over your word processor. You can use this dialog box to insert field placeholders in the template. Inserting a My Record field placeholder will pull data from the My Record of the currently logged-in user in ACT!. (To find your My Record, click Lookup | My Record in ACT!.)

To insert field placeholders into a letter template:

1. Edit an ACT! document template. (To do this, click Write | Edit Template and select the template you'd like to edit.)
2. In your default word processor, place the cursor where you'd like to insert a field placeholder.
3. In the Mail Merge Fields dialog box, select the field you'd like to insert.
4. Click the Insert button. The field placeholder for the field you selected will be placed in your template.

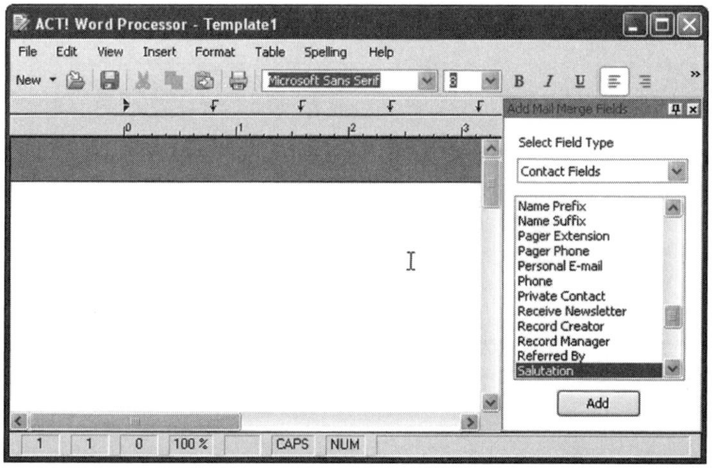

Inserting placeholders from the list of available fields

Gone...but not forever

If you close the Mail Merge Fields dialog box while editing a document template, you can always bring it back up by clicking Insert | ACT! Mail Merge Fields.

Task B Inserting My Record Field Placeholders

Inserting a My Record field gives you more flexibility when deploying the template to other users in your company or workgroup.

For example, you might want to include a closing in a letter template. Instead of adding your name to the closing, add a field placeholder for your My Record. Then, you'll be able to give the template to your co-workers. When a co-worker writes a document based on this template, your co-worker's name (pulled from his or her My Record) will appear in the closing.

To insert a My Record field placeholder into a letter template:

1. Edit an ACT! document template.
2. In your default word processor, place the cursor where you'd like to insert the My Record field placeholder.
3. In the Mail Merge Fields dialog box, choose the My Record field option.
4. Select the field you'd like to insert.
5. Click the Insert button. A field placeholder for the field you selected will be placed in your template.

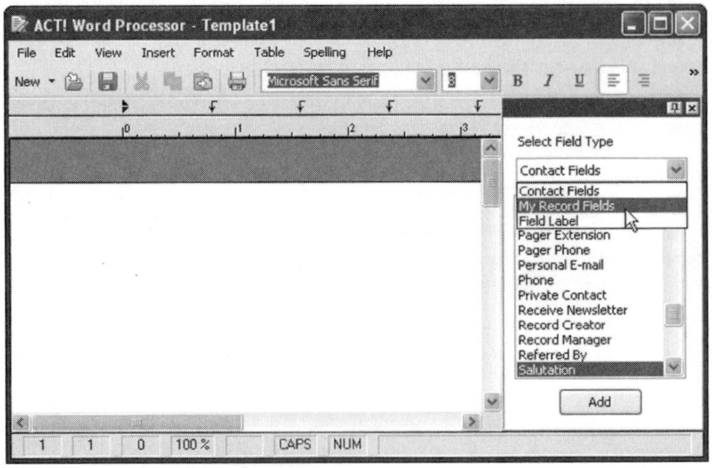

Inserting My Record field placeholders

Task C Testing Letter Templates

Once you've created a document template, it's a good idea to run it for a single ACT! contact to test that the formatting is correct and the field placeholders work properly.

To test a letter template:

1. Create and save the letter template.
2. In ACT!, click Write | Other Documents.
3. Browse and select the document template you'd like to test.
4. Click Open. The letter will be created in your default word processor for your current contact.

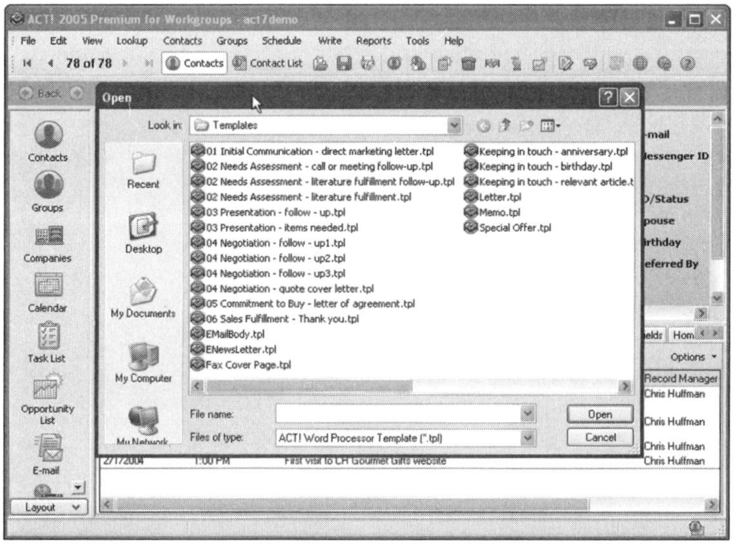

Writing a custom letter template

Default folder

When you click Write | Other Documents in ACT!, ACT! will display a list of templates in your default document template folder.

You can change the location of the default document template folder by clicking Edit | Preferences. In the General tab, select Document Templates from the File type drop-down. Then, click the Browse button to select a new default folder.

Using the ACT! Word Processor

If you don't have Microsoft Word installed on your computer, or if Microsoft Word's performance is sluggish on your computer, you may opt to use the built-in ACT! Word Processor when writing letters to ACT! contacts. The ACT! Word Processor is pretty basic, and its learning curve is relatively small if you've used other word processing programs.

Task A Configuring Page Setup Options

In the Page Setup area of the ACT! Word Processor, you'll be able to set the size of paper for the current document or template. You'll also be able to set the paper orientation and margins.

To configure the page setup options in the ACT! Word Processor:

1. Open a document or template in the ACT! Word Processor. To do so, click Write | New Document or Write | Letter/E-Mail Template.
2. Click File | Page Setup.
3. When the Page Setup dialog box appears, select the paper size, orientation, and margins for the document or template.
4. Click OK to save the changes.

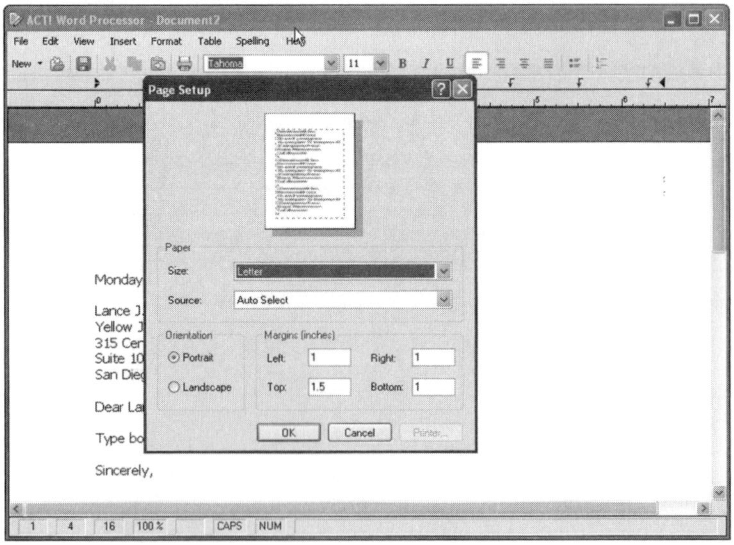

Configuring page setup options

Choose a word processor now

If you're just starting out with ACT!, decide now whether you'll use the ACT! Word Processor or Microsoft Word as your default word processor.

Switching default word processors later is not simple. You'll have to recreate all of your templates from scratch.

Task B Formatting Text

In the ACT! Word Processor, you can specify the font, size, color, and style for any text in a document. You'll find that the formatting options in the ACT! Word Processor are comparable to those in WordPad, the word processor included with Windows.

To format text in the ACT! Word Processor:

1. Highlight text in the ACT! Word Processor.
2. Click Format | Font.
3. In the Font dialog box, select text formatting options such as the font, font size, font color, and so on.

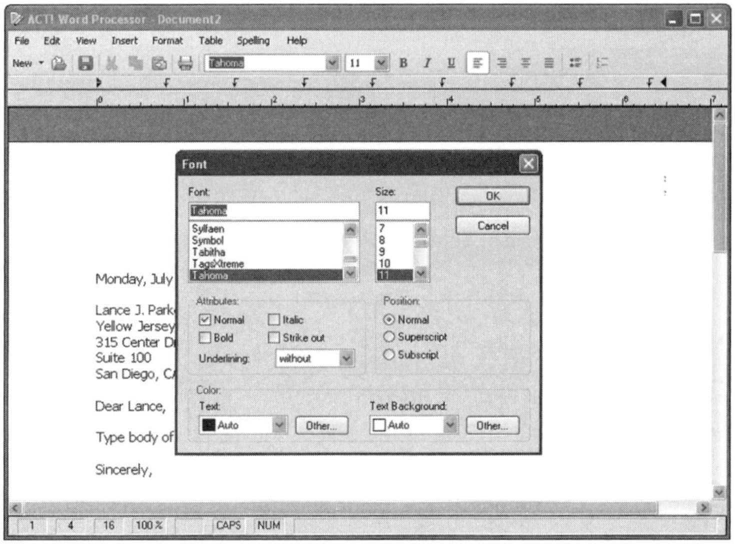

Setting font properties

Use the toolbar

Many text formatting options are also available on the toolbar. Commonly used features, like Bold, Underline, text justification, and font selection are all on the standard toolbar in the ACT! Word Processor.

Formatting shortcut keys

Many standard Windows formatting shortcut keys—such as Ctrl+B for bold, Ctrl+I for italics, and Ctrl+U for underline—will work in the ACT! word processor.

What's a paragraph?

The ACT! Word Processor defines a paragraph as anything between two hard returns. A paragraph could be a grouping of sentences, or it could be just a line of text.

Task C Formatting a Paragraph

Setting paragraph options for text in the ACT! Word Processor will allow you to configure the indentation, spacing, and alignment of the current paragraph.

To set paragraph formatting options in the ACT! Word Processor:

1. In the ACT! Word Processor, click the cursor somewhere in the paragraph you'd like to format.
2. Click Format | Paragraph.
3. When the Paragraph dialog box appears, select indentation options in the Indents area.
4. Select whether you'd like to single or double-space the paragraph in the Line Spacing area.
5. In the Alignment area, select whether you'd like to left-, center-, right-, or full-justify the text.
6. In the Distances area, select the spacing before and after the paragraph.
7. Click OK to save the changes.

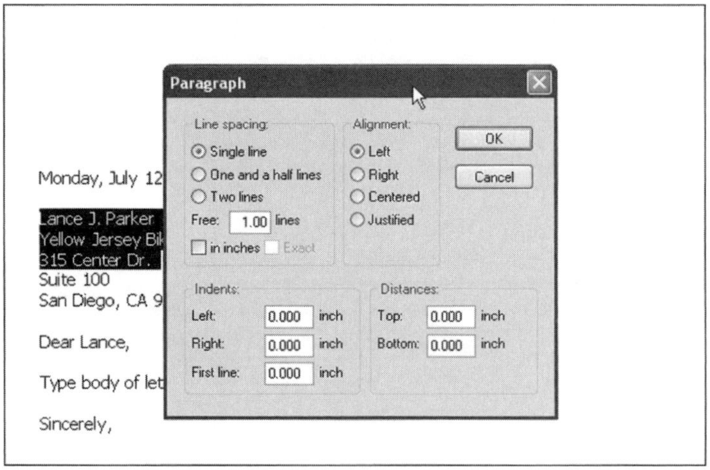

Setting paragraph options

Task D Inserting Tables

Previous versions of the ACT! Word Processor did not support tables; this was a bit problematic for anyone looking to design complex letter or e-mail templates. The ACT! 2005 Word Processor now supports tables, just like Microsoft Word.

To insert a table in the Word Processor:

1. In the ACT! Word Processor, click Table | Insert | Table.
2. Select the number of columns and rows for your table. Click OK. ACT! will insert the table into your document.
3. To change the formatting (line color, text distance, background color, and so on) of the table, place your cursor inside the table and click Table | Table Format.

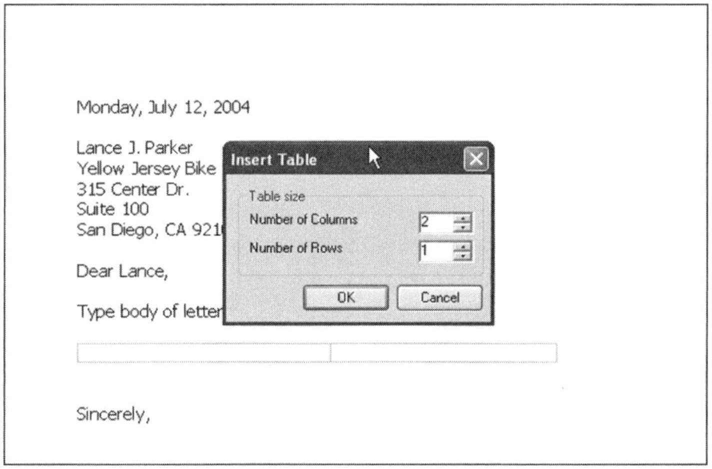

Inserting a table into a document

Why use tables?

If you're designing an ACT! Word Processor template for use as e-mail templates, inserting a table into your template can make it easier to design great-looking e-mails.

Task E Spell Checking a Document

When you have misspelled words in your document—even if the misspellings are unintentional—the credibility and effectiveness of your message diminishes exponentially with each misspelled word. ACT! has a built-in spell checker that will help you avoid an embarrassing mistake.

A better spell check

In previous versions of ACT! the spelling dictionary that shipped with the product would often mis-flag correctly-spelled words as misspelled. You'll find that the new spelling dictionary in ACT! 2005 is a lot more accurate.

To spell check an ACT! Word Processor document:

1. Create a document, document template, or e-mail template in the ACT! Word Processor.
2. Click Spelling | Check Document. The ACT! Spell Check dialog box appears.
3. ACT! will cycle through all possibly misspelled words in the document.
4. For each possibly misspelled word, select whether to replace the word with a word from the list of suggested words, skip the word, or add the word to the dictionary.

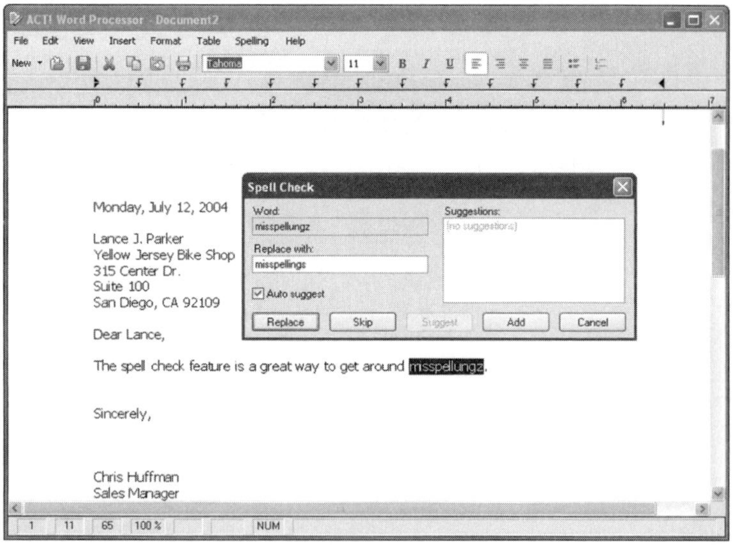

Spell checking a document

Sending a Mail Merge

Before actually performing a mail merge, you'll want to make sure your data is good and complete. You'll also want to make sure that you've identified the recipients for the merge.

Task A Preparing for a Mail Merge

Rarely will you send a mass letter to everyone in your database. Most of the time, you'll send the letter to a specific subset of the database. ACT! gives you the ability to send a mail merge to the current lookup or to a specific group or subgroup in the database.

To identify the recipients for a mail merge:

1. Perform a lookup of the contacts you'd like to include in the merge.
2. In the Contact List view, select the Tag Mode.
3. Tag any contacts that should be omitted from the mail merge.
4. Click the Omit Tagged button.

or

1. Create a group for your mail merge.
2. Add all of the intended merge recipients to this group. (To do this, click Groups | Group Membership | Add Selected to Group.)

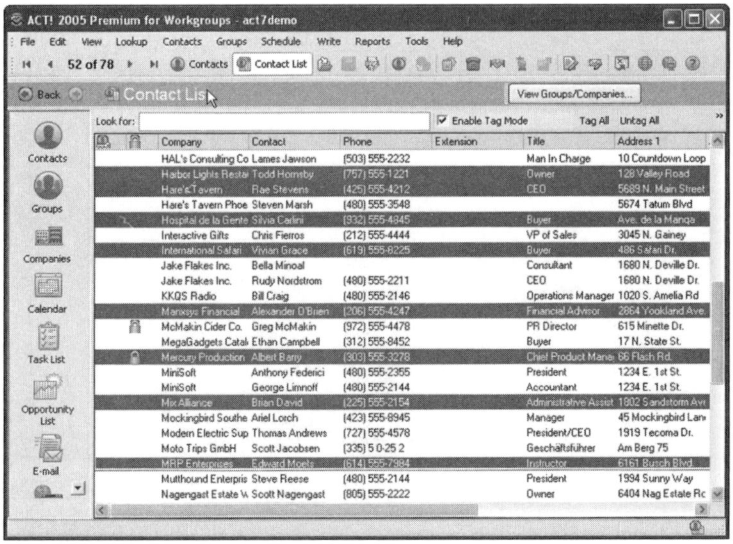

Tagging contacts in the Contact List view

Newsflash! Not everyone wants your junk mail

You may have customers that don't wish to receive your mailings. It might be a good idea to establish a method for identifying these contacts in your database. Here are two strategies:

- **Using groups.** You could keep all contacts who wish to receive mailings in a group. When a contact expresses a desire to be removed from your mailing list, simply remove the contact from the group.
- **Using fields.** Add a field to your database to indicate whether or not each contact would like to receive mass correspondence. You could use the new YES/NO field type to accomplish this.

Task B Ensuring Complete Data for a Mail Merge

If you've added field placeholders to the template you're about to use as the basis for your mail merge, you'll want to ensure that you have good data in these fields.

Use caution when merging

If you're including data from your ACT! database in a mail merge, make sure you don't have bad, inappropriate, or sensitive data in the fields you use for a mail merge.

For example, if a negative comment about a client of yours is mistakenly entered into a field that you use in a mail merge, you could end up sending that insensitive comment directly to your client.

To narrow your lookup or group to include only contacts that contain data in a specific field:

1. Perform a lookup of the contacts that will be included in your mail merge.
2. If you plan to send the mail merge to a group, then perform a lookup of the contacts in the group. To do this, click the View Groups/Companies button in the upper-right corner of the ACT! interface and select the group or subgroup.
3. Click Lookup | Other Fields.
4. Select a field you plan to use in the mail merge.
5. Click the Empty field option.
6. Click OK.Your current lookup will now include just the contacts who do not have any information in the field you selected in Step 4.

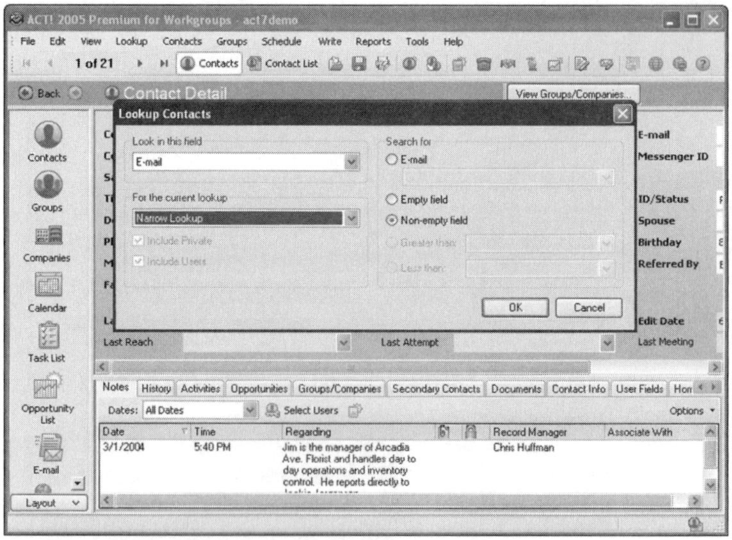

Narrowing a lookup to just include contacts with an e-mail address

Sending a Mail Merge

When you need to send a letter to more than one contact in your ACT! database, you can use the Mail Merge feature in ACT! to send a template-based letter in one short procedure.

Task A Performing a Mail Merge

By following the simple steps in the ACT! Mail Merge Wizard, you can write a single template-based letter to multiple contacts in an ACT! database. If you've used the Mail Merge features in other programs, you'll probably find that ACT!'s Mail Merge is much more user-friendly.

To perform a mail merge:

1. Perform a lookup of contacts or create a group of contacts for your mail merge. (Refer to Chapter 5 for more information on lookups and Chapter 7 for information on groups.)
2. Click Write | Mail Merge. The Mail Merge Wizard will appear.
3. Click Next through the first screen of the Mail Merge Wizard.
4. Select the Word Processor option and click Next.
5. Click Browse and select the template you'd like to use as the basis for the mail merge. Click Next. (Refer to Chapter 10 for information on creating letter templates.)
6. Select the range of contacts who should receive the mail merge. Click Next.
7. Click Finish. The merged letters will appear in the default word processor.

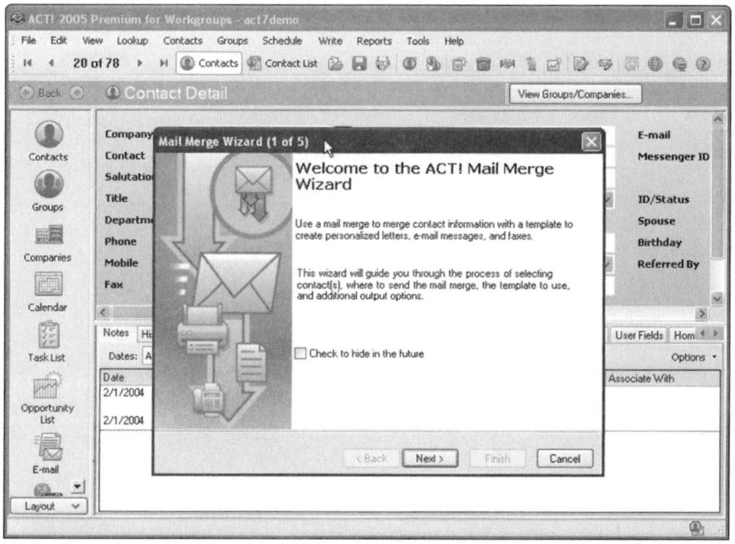

Performing a mail merge

Task B Printing Letters and Creating a Letter Sent History

After performing a mail merge in ACT!, you can have ACT! automatically create a history item in the Notes/History tab for each letter recipient. Just print the merged letter, and ACT! will prompt you to create a history for all contacts included in the mail merge.

To record a history for mail merge recipients:

1. Perform a mail merge and send the output to the word processor.
2. Print the resulting word processor document.
3. When the Create History dialog box appears, enter the main subject of the mail merge in the Regarding area.
4. Click Create. A history of the letter sent will be added to each recipient's History tab.

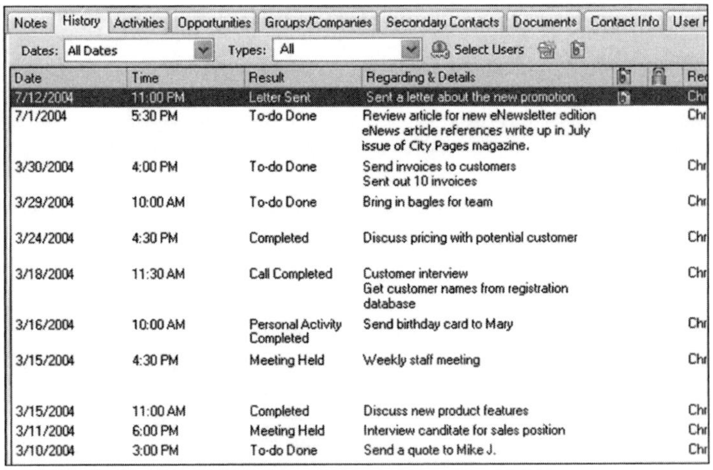

A Letter Sent history item

The merge history isn't attached

Creating a history of a mass letter will put a line in the Notes/History tab for each letter recipient to remind you of the letter sent. Unlike histories created for single letters, you won't be able to double-click the mass letter history to open a copy of the sent letter.

Chapter 12
Document and File Management

Documents Tab

The Documents tab has replaced the Library tab in ACT! 6.0. The new tab performs the same basic function of associating documents with your ACT! contacts, but it is a lot more stable than the ACT! 6.0 Library tab. You can now attach an unlimited number of documents to any contact.

Task A Adding a Document

Before you can begin to manage documents in the Documents tab, you'll need to add documents to the tab. Each contact in the database has his or her own Documents tab.

To add a document to the Documents tab:

1. In the Contact view, lookup a contact.
2. Click the Documents tab.
3. Click the Add Document button at the top of the Documents tab.
4. Select the document you'd like to add. The document will be listed in the Documents tab.

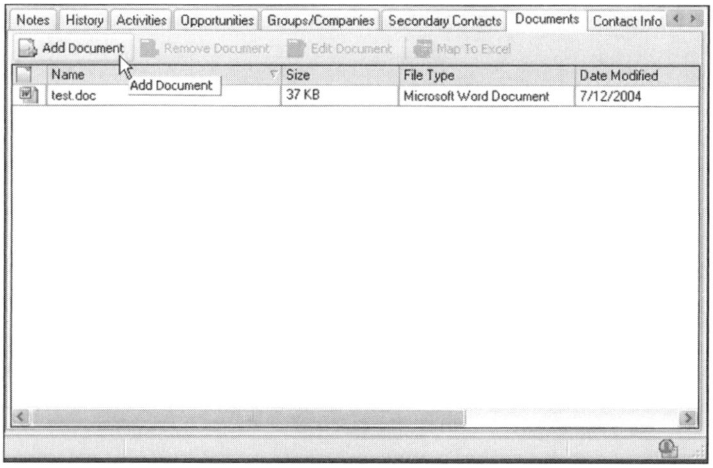

Adding a document to the Documents tab

Documents are attached

When you add a document to the Documents tab, the document is copied into your database supplemental files. If you have set up synchronization to also synchronize files in the supplemental files system, then the files in the Documents tab will synchronize to and from remote users. See Chapter 21, "Synchronization," for more information on synchronization.

Task B Removing a Document

If you no longer want a document to be associated with a contact in your database, then simply remove the document from the list in the Documents tab. Removing the document from the Documents tab will also delete the document from the Attachments folder in your database supplemental files folder, so make sure you have a backup if the document is important.

Removing a file?

Removing the document from the Documents tab will delete the document from the Attachments folder in your database supplemental files folder. Unless you have another backup copy of the document, removing the document could permanently delete it from your computer.

To remove a document from the Documents tab:

1. Click the Documents tab in the Contact view.
2. Highlight the document you'd like to remove from the list.
3. Click the Remove Document icon in the toolbar at the top of the Documents tab.
4. ACT! will ask you to confirm the removal. Click Yes. The document will be removed from the Documents tab and ACT! will delete the document in the database supplemental files system.

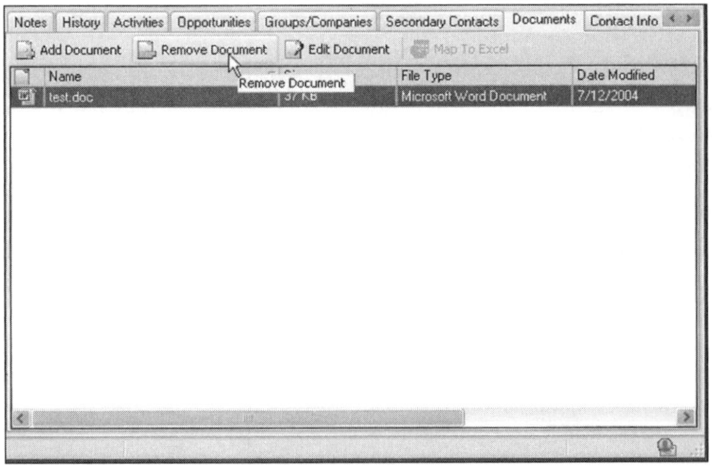

Removing a document from the Documents tab

Task C Viewing an Attached Document

You can quickly open any document that has been attached to an ACT! contact in the Documents tab. Documents will open in the program associated with their extension on your computer (.DOC files will open in Microsoft Word, .XLS spreadsheets will open in Microsoft Excel, and so on).

To view an attached document:

1. In the Documents tab, locate the document you'd like to view.
2. Highlight the document.
3. Click the View Document button at the top of the Documents tab. ACT! will launch the document for editing.

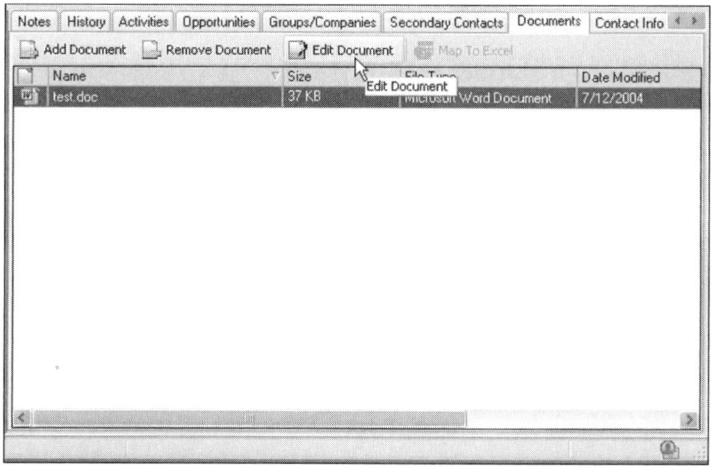

Editing a document in the Documents tab

Mapping to Excel

You can link the contents of ACT! fields to cells in an Excel spreadsheet by clicking the Map to Excel button at the top of the Documents tab.

Attaching Files

You can attach any file on your hard drive or network to a contact in your ACT! database. Attached files can be viewed in the History tab alongside histories of events that have occurred with your contact. If you need to share these files with your colleagues, you may opt to attach files in the Documents tab.

Task A Attaching a File to a Contact

Attaching a file doesn't actually physically attach the file to your ACT! database; it merely provides a hyperlink to a spot on your local computer or network where your file has been saved. If you move a file that has been attached to an ACT! contact record, ACT! won't be able to find its new location. If you're using a multi-user database, you won't be able to see files that your co-workers have attached to their individual hard drives.

To attach a file to a contact record:

1. Click Contacts | Attach File.
2. Browse to the folder that houses the file you'd like to attach and double-click the file. The document will appear as an attachment in the History tab.

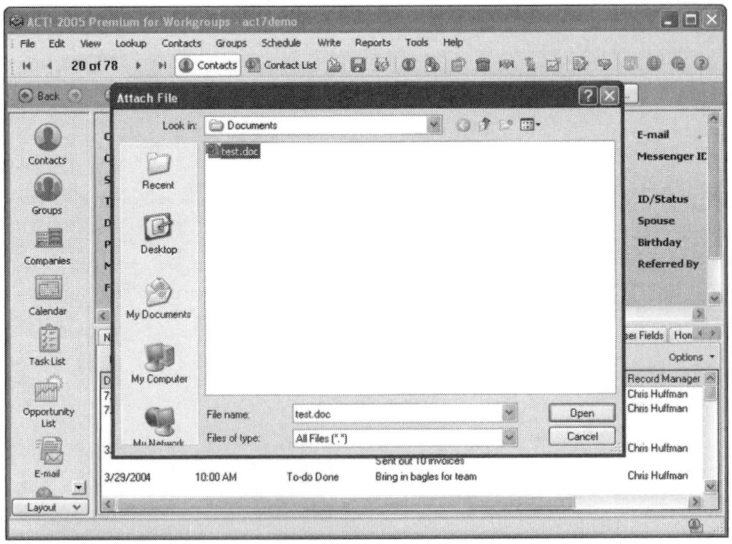

Attaching a file to a contact in the History tab

Sharing documents in a multi-user environment

If you're sharing an ACT! database with other users, and if you want other users to be able to double-click and launch files you've attached to contacts, then your attached files must be stored on a shared network drive.

If, for example, you were to attach a file on your local desktop, other users would receive an error if they attempted to launch the file from the Notes/History tab on their computers.

Task B Launching an Attached File

You can quickly launch any attached file from within the History tab. ACT! will launch the file in the default program for the file type on your computer.

To launch an attached file:

1. In the History tab, locate the attached file.
2. To the right of the Regarding & Details column, you'll see an attachment column. Click the attachment icon for the file you'd like to launch.

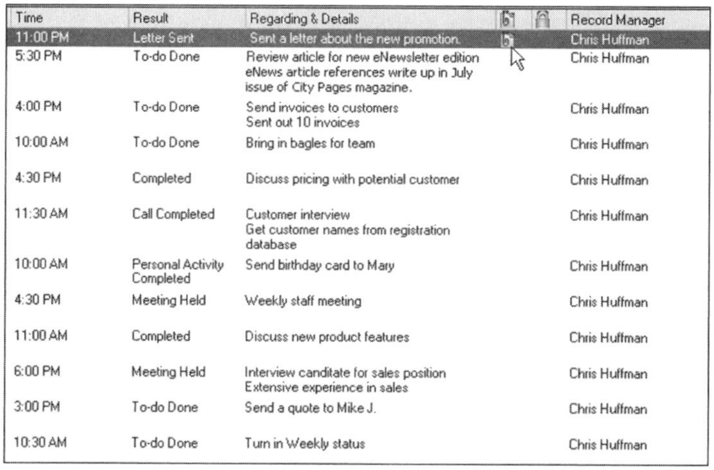

Time	Result	Regarding & Details			Record Manager
11:00 PM	Letter Sent	Sent a letter about the new promotion.			Chris Huffman
5:30 PM	To-do Done	Review article for new eNewsletter edition eNews article references write up in July issue of City Pages magazine.			Chris Huffman
4:00 PM	To-do Done	Send invoices to customers Sent out 10 invoices			Chris Huffman
10:00 AM	To-do Done	Bring in bagles for team			Chris Huffman
4:30 PM	Completed	Discuss pricing with potential customer			Chris Huffman
11:30 AM	Call Completed	Customer interview Get customer names from registration database			Chris Huffman
10:00 AM	Personal Activity Completed	Send birthday card to Mary			Chris Huffman
4:30 PM	Meeting Held	Weekly staff meeting			Chris Huffman
11:00 AM	Completed	Discuss new product features			Chris Huffman
6:00 PM	Meeting Held	Interview canditate for sales position Extensive experience in sales			Chris Huffman
3:00 PM	To-do Done	Send a quote to Mike J.			Chris Huffman
10:30 AM	To-do Done	Turn in Weekly status			Chris Huffman

Launching an attached file in the History tab

Documents tab

If you'd like your attached documents to synchronize with remote users, then consider attaching them to a contact in the Documents tab. This automatically adds the documents to the database supplemental files folder.

Chapter 13
Viewing and Composing E-mail

Setting E-mail Preferences

ACT! can be configured to work as a stand-alone e-mail client. It can also be set to work with many popular e-mail programs, like Microsoft Outlook and Outlook Express. Once you've configured ACT!'s e-mail functionality, you can check and send your e-mail directly from within ACT!. You can also write template-based e-mails and send mass e-mails to your contacts.

Task A Setting ACT! to Work as a Stand-alone E-mail Client

Before you send any e-mails from within ACT!, you'll need to set a few basic e-mail preferences. These preferences will tell ACT! how to send e-mails, what signature to use, and how to record a history of e-mails that have been sent to your contacts.

To configure ACT! to check your POP3 E-mail account:

1. Click Tools | Preferences.
2. Click the E-mail tab.
3. Click the E-mail System Setup button. The E-mail Setup Wizard will appear.
4. Click Next to get past the confirmation screen.
5. Click the Internet Mail button and click Next.
6. Click the Add button to add a new e-mail account. The Internet Mail dialog box will appear.
7. In the User Information tab, fill in the account name, real name, organization, e-mail address, and reply address.
8. In the Outgoing Mail Server tab, specify your SMTP server name.
9. In the Incoming Mail Server tab, fill in the POP3 server name, username, and password.
10. Click OK to return to the E-mail Setup Wizard. Click Next. Click Finish to complete the Wizard.

Lotus Notes users

ACT! 6.0 integrated with Lotus Notes, but this functionality was taken out of the 2005 product.

Task B Setting ACT! to Work with Microsoft Outlook

You can set ACT! to piggyback on top of Outlook for e-mail. When you do this, the ACT! e-mail interface will always show your current inbox and folder from Outlook. E-mails sent from within ACT! will be transferred to Outlook, where they'll appear in the Sent Items folder.

Supported versions

ACT! 2005 only works with Outlook 2000, 2002 (XP), and 2003. Outlook 97 users will need to upgrade to take advantage of ACT!'s Outlook integration.

To set ACT! to work with Microsoft Outlook:

1. Click Tools | Preferences.
2. Click the E-mail tab.
3. Click the E-mail System Setup button. The E-mail Setup Wizard appears.
4. Click Next to get past the confirmation screen.
5. Click the Microsoft Outlook button and click Next.
6. If all of the Microsoft Outlook settings are acceptable, click Next.
7. Click Finish. When ACT! launches e-mail, it will use Outlook as its backend e-mail client.

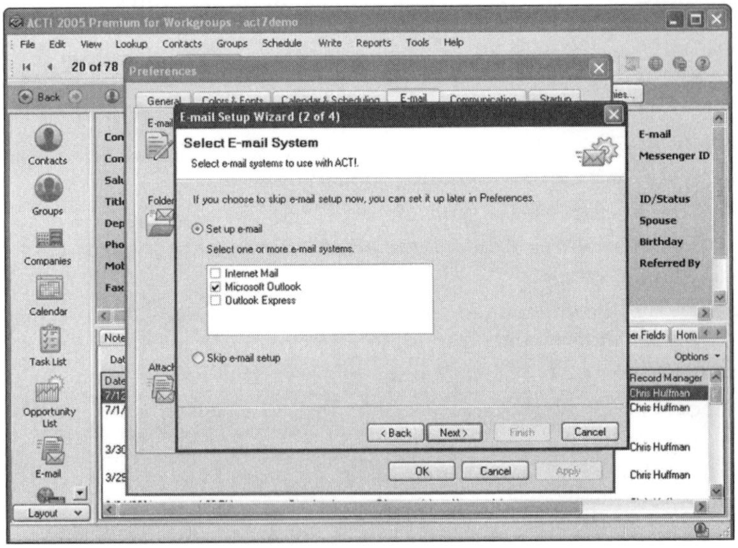

Selecting Microsoft Outlook as the default e-mail system

Task C Setting E-mail Signatures

When you send an e-mail from the ACT! e-mail client, you might want a standard string of text, commonly referred to as an *e-mail signature*, inserted at the end of each message. In the e-mail preferences, you can manage your signatures.

To configure an e-mail signature:

1. Click Edit | Preferences.
2. Click the E-mail tab.
3. Click the Composing Options button.
4. Click the Signatures button.
5. Click Add to add a new signature. Give the signature a name and edit the text of the signature in the bottom text area.
6. Click OK three times to return to the main ACT! interface.

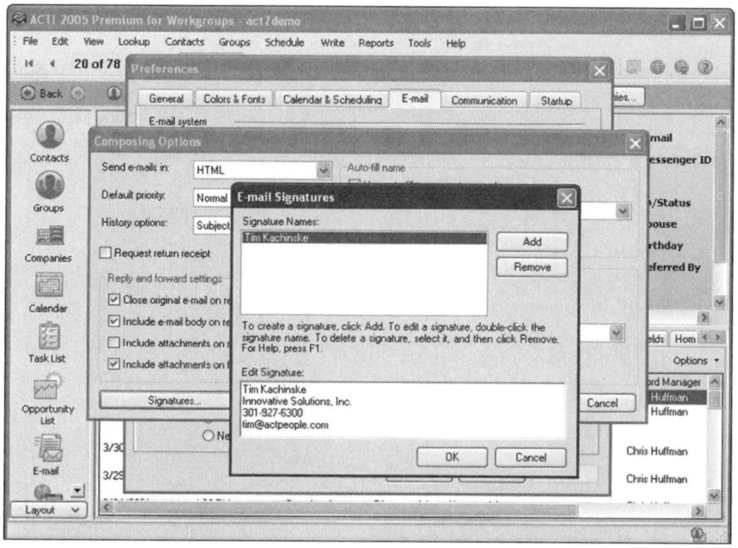

Creating an e-mail signature

Outlook signatures

If you have ACT! set to work with Outlook as its backend e-mail client, then you'll still need to specify a separate e-mail address in ACT!. ACT! will not pick up your Outlook signature when sending messages to ACT! contacts in the ACT! e-mail interface.

Task D Setting E-mail Composing Options

Many of the preferences that affect the behavior of the ACT! e-mail client are hidden in the Composing Options area of the e-mail preferences. In the Composing Options area, you can specify how to auto-fill names in the To field of e-mail addresses, how to create history items for outgoing e-mail messages, and more.

To set the e-mail composing options:

1. Click Edit | Preferences.
2. Click the E-mail tab.
3. Click the Composing Options button.
4. On the left side of the Composing Options dialog box, specify the default format for outgoing messages, the default priority, the default history creation options, and the reply/forward options. On the right, specify auto-fill and name resolution options.
5. Click OK.

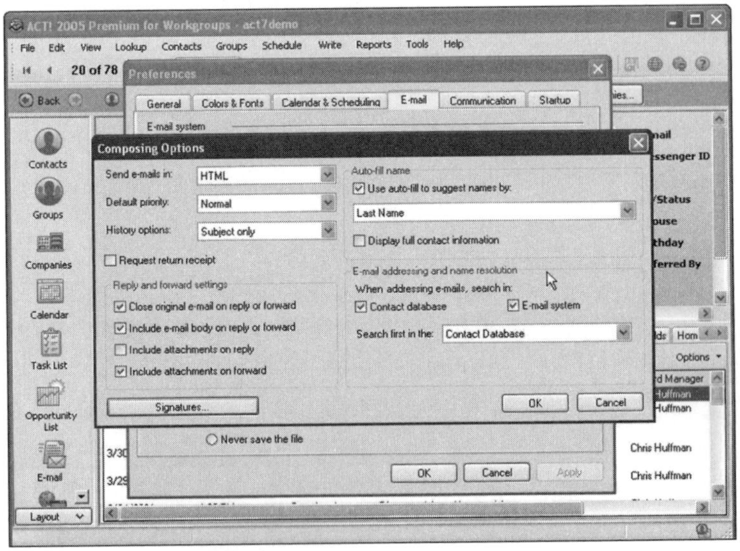

Setting e-mail composing options

Default e-mail history creation options

- **None**. No history will be created for outgoing e-mails to your ACT! contacts.
- **Subject Only**. A history will be created that shows the subject line of your outgoing messages.
- **Subject + Message**. A history will be created that shows the subject and the entire message body. Only the text will appear. (Graphics and text formatting will not appear in the history.)
- **Attach to Contact(s)**. ACT! will save a copy of your outgoing message as a file in the Attachments folder in the database supplemental files folder for the currently-opened database.

Viewing E-mail in ACT!

If you've used Microsoft Outlook or Outlook Express, you'll feel right at home in the ACT! e-mail interface. Many of the ACT! e-mail buttons and features are in the same place in Outlook and Outlook Express. You can launch the ACT! e-mail interface by clicking the E-mail button on the left navigation bar.

Task A Checking Your Messages

You can view your e-mail messages right within the ACT! interface. If you've set ACT! to work with Outlook or another supported e-mail program, then ACT!'s e-mail interface will show the same messages and folders you see in the supported e-mail program.

To check your messages in ACT!:

1. Click the E-mail button on the left navigation bar. ACT!'s e-mail interface will appear.
2. Click the Send/Receive button. ACT! will poll your e-mail account, and any new messages will appear in the Inbox.

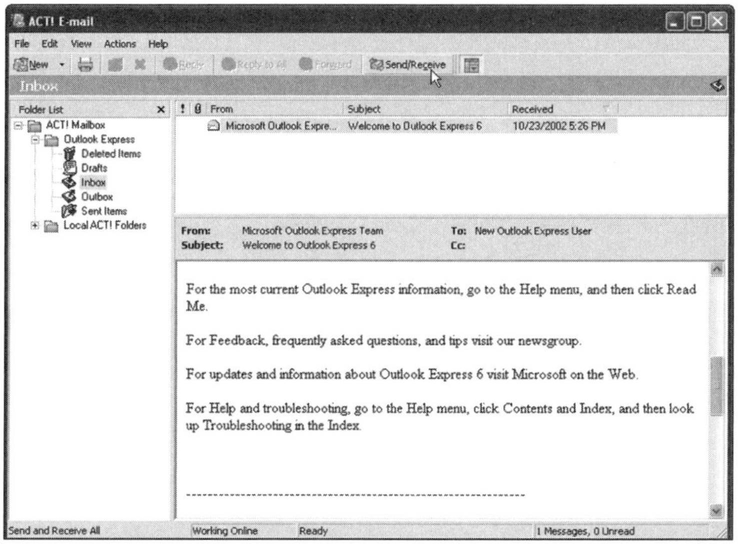

Viewing e-mail in the ACT! e-mail interface

Preview pane

In the ACT! e-mail interface, click View | Preview Pane to show and hide the Preview pane. When the Preview pane is selected, you'll see a preview of the currently highlighted e-mail message in the lower pane of the e-mail interface.

Task B Creating New E-mail Folders

You can organize your e-mail messages with ACT!'s Folders feature. ACT! gives you the ability to add as many folders as you need, and you can use these folders to organize your messages for easy retrieval.

Maintaining two e-mail accounts?

If you're using ACT! with Outlook (or another supported e-mail program), then checking your ACT! e-mail will also check your Outlook (or other) e-mail.

Moving messages to a folder

To move a message from your Inbox to a folder, drag the message from the Inbox onto the folder from the list of folders on the left side of the ACT! e-mail interface.

To create a new e-mail folder:

1. Go to the ACT! e-mail interface by clicking the E-mail button on the left navigation bar.
2. Highlight a folder from the list of folders on the left. The new folder will become a subfolder of this folder.
3. Click File | New | Folder.
4. Type the name of the folder and click OK.

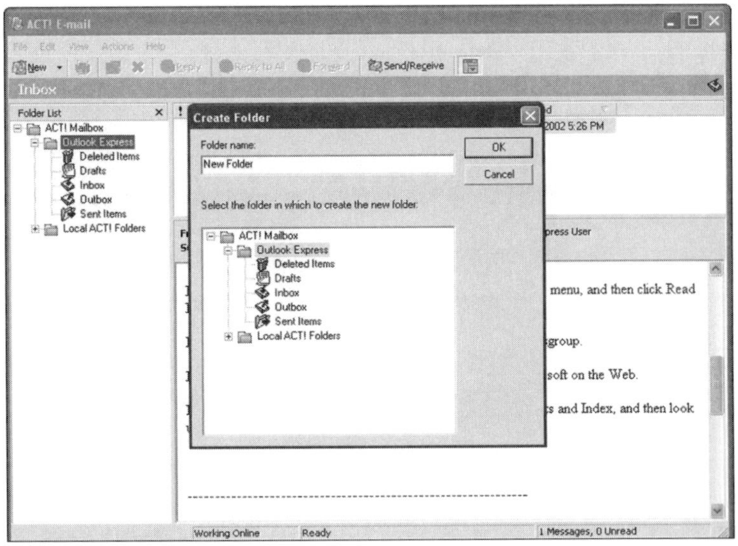

Creating a new e-mail folder

Composing an E-mail in ACT!

ACT!'s built-in e-mail functionality allows you to send e-mail to your ACT! contacts right from within the ACT! interface. There are two major advantages to using the ACT! e-mail functionality: 1) A history of each outgoing e-mail created from within ACT! is created in the History tab for the e-mail recipient, and 2) ACT! gives you the ability to write single or mass template-based HTML e-mails.

Task A Composing a Message to an ACT! Contact

You can create a message to any ACT! contact from within the ACT! e-mail interface. When you create a message to a contact, ACT! can automatically create a history of the outgoing message in the contact's History tab.

To compose a message to an ACT! contact:

1. Go to the ACT! e-mail interface by clicking the E-mail button on the left navigation bar.
2. Click the New button to create a new message.
3. When the new message appears, click the To button to select the message recipients.
4. Highlight a contact from the list on the left and click the To button to add the contact to your recipient list. Repeat this step until all of your recipients have been selected.
5. Click OK.
6. In the Create History drop-down, select the type of history you'd like to create for this e-mail. (See the "Setting E-mail Composing Options" task in this chapter for an explanation of the history creation options.)
7. Give your e-mail message a subject and body and click the Send button.

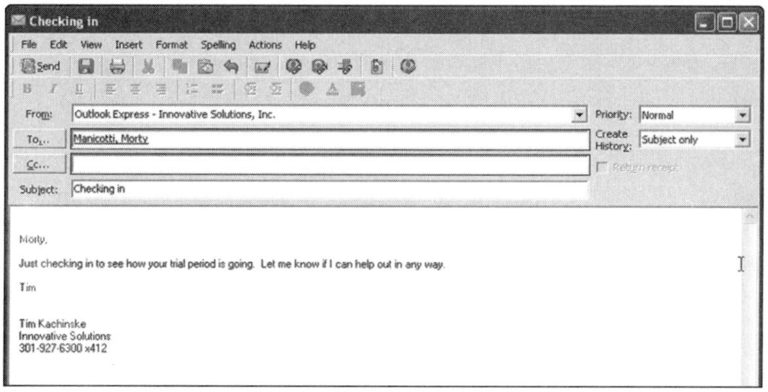

Composing a message to an ACT! contact

Instantly create a blank e-mail

In the Contacts view, click the blue underlined text in the E-mail Address field to instantly create a new blank e-mail for the contact.

E-mail recipient options

Click the New button in the ACT! e-mail interface to create a new message. After clicking the To button, choose the Current Lookup, Groups, or Companies option to send an e-mail to multiple contacts at once.

Task B Composing a Message to a Non-ACT! Contact

You may need to write e-mail messages to contacts that you don't want to add to the ACT! database. ACT! allows you to send e-mails to non-ACT! contacts from within the ACT! e-mail interface. This functionality is especially important if you are using the ACT! e-mail interface as your primary e-mail client.

Automatic name resolution

When you enter an e-mail address into the To field in an e-mail, ACT! will automatically check to see if the contact exists in either your address books or the database. You can set the name resolution settings by clicking Tools | Preferences. In the E-mail tab, click the Composing Options button.

To compose a message to a non-ACT! contact:

1. Go to the ACT! e-mail interface by clicking the E-mail button on the left navigation bar.
2. Click the New button to create a new message.
3. In the To field, type the contact's e-mail address.
4. Type a subject and message body.
5. Click Send.

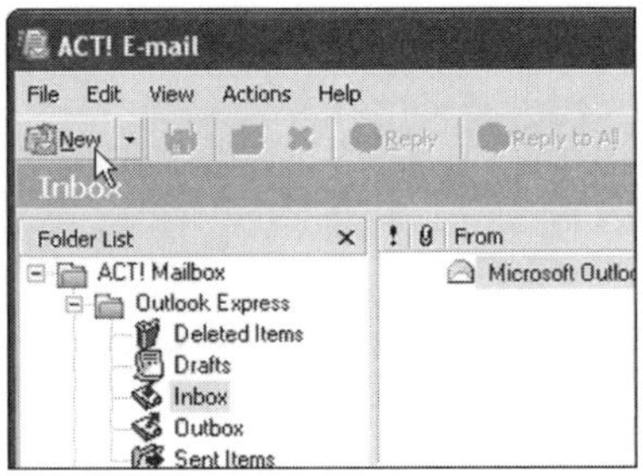

Creating a new message

Recording a History for Outgoing E-mails

When sending an e-mail to ACT! contacts, you can set ACT! to record a history of the outgoing e-mail in the History tab. History entries look just like regular notes—except that they're housed in the History tab instead of the Notes tab.

Task A Setting the Default E-mail History Options

Whenever you send an e-mail from within the ACT! e-mail interface, a history of the e-mail can be created in your contact's History tab. As you compose new messages, you'll notice a Create History drop-down in the upper-right part of the e-mail message. If you always want the history option to default to Attach to Contact(s), you can choose the default setting in the e-mail preferences.

To set the default e-mail history options:

1. Click Tools | Preferences.
2. Click the E-mail tab.
3. Click the Composing Options button.
4. In the History options drop-down, select the type of e-mail history you'd like to create by default. See the tip on this page for an explanation of the e-mail history options.
5. Click OK twice to return to the ACT! interface.

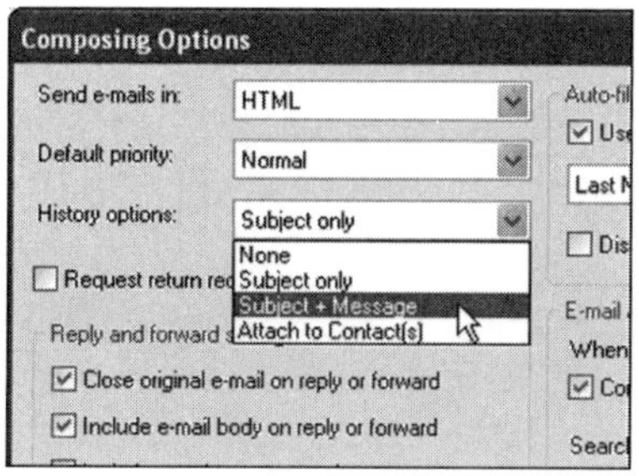

Specifying the history creation options

E-mail history creation options

- **None.** No history will be created for outgoing e-mails to your ACT! contacts.
- **Subject Only.** A history will be created that shows the subject line of your outgoing messages.
- **Subject + Message.** A history will be created that shows the subject and the entire message body. Only the text will appear. (Graphics and text formatting will not appear in the history.)
- **Attach to Contact(s).** ACT! will save a copy of your outgoing message as a file in the default e-mail folder. ACT! will attach this file to your history item, and you'll be able to double-click the attachment icon for the history to bring up a copy of the e-mail message.

Task B Recording a History for Outgoing E-mails

Each time you create an e-mail in the ACT! interface, you'll have the option to record a history of the outgoing e-mail message. Each new e-mail message in ACT! has a Create History drop-down, and as you write e-mail messages, you'll have the option to select the type of history that should be created for the e-mail.

Composing in Outlook?

In Outlook, you can automatically record a history of outgoing e-mails by sending the messages to contacts in your ACT! Address Book in Outlook.

Attach to Contact(s)

If you choose the Attach to Contact(s) history option, ACT! will save a copy of your outgoing e-mail message in the default e-mail folder. When you double-click the history attachment, ACT! will bring up this saved copy of the message. Even if you delete the message from your Sent Items folder, the history will remain in ACT!.

To record a history for outgoing e-mails:

1. Click the E-mail button on the left navigation bar to open the ACT! e-mail interface.
2. Click the New button to create a new message.
3. In the Create History drop-down, select the type of history that you'd like to create for the contact. (See the tip from the preceeding task for an explanation of the history creation options.)
4. Type a subject and body for the message.
5. Click OK. ACT! will send the message, and a history will be created.
6. Go to the contact's History tab. You'll notice that an E-mail Sent history item has been created to document the fact that you sent the e-mail message.
7. If you chose the Attach to Contact(s) option, double-click the attachment icon to view a saved copy of the e-mail.

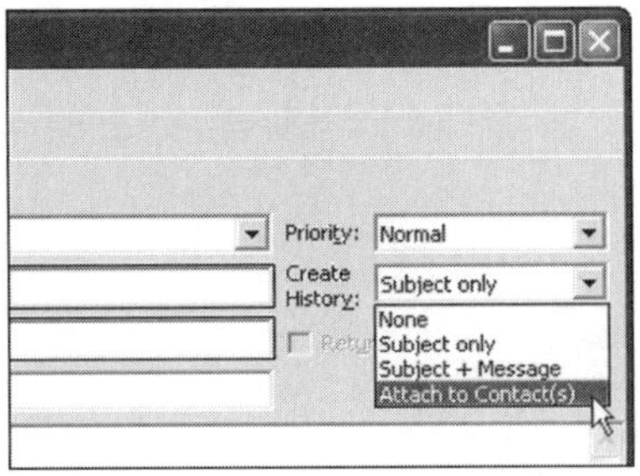

Recording a history for an outgoing e-mail

Chapter 14
Sending Mass E-mails

Working with E-mail Templates

In ACT! 6.0, ACT! used a separate graphical mail template for e-mail merges. ACT! 2005 has wiped out the need for this separate e-mail template, and form e-mails in the new version are created using regular word processor templates.

Task A Creating an E-mail Template

Before sending a mass e-mail, you'll need to create an e-mail template in your default word processor. You should design the e-mail template to look like your outgoing e-mail; where you want to incorporate personalized information from ACT! fields, you'll be able to insert field placeholders.

To create an e-mail template:

1. Click Write | New Letter/E-mail Template. The default word processor will appear.
2. Design the e-mail template. Include tables, graphics, and text as needed.
3. Use the Mail Merge Fields dialog box to add field placeholders to the text. When you actually write the e-mail to a contact, ACT! will replace the field placeholders with the actual contents of fields in the database.
4. Click File | Save As to save the template. If you're using Microsoft Word, ACT! will save the e-mail templates as .ADT files. If you're using the ACT! Word Processor, the program will save them as .TPL files.

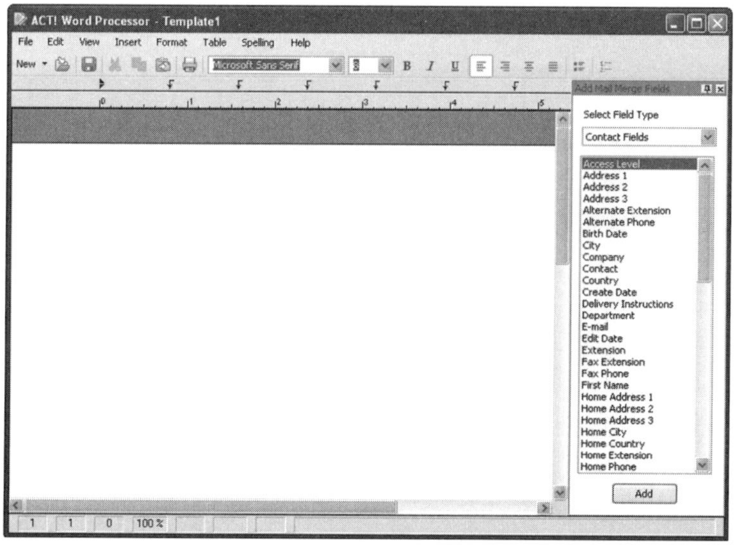

Creating a new e-mail template

The default word processor

You will need to create e-mail templates in your default word processor. You can set ACT! to work with either the ACT! Word Processor or Microsoft Word by clicking Tools | Preferences and selecting the Communication tab.

Task B Editing and Existing E-mail Templates

Rather than create an e-mail template from scratch, you might want to use one of the existing templates on your system as the basis for a new e-mail template. ACT! ships with about a dozen pre-designed e-mail and letter templates. If these templates aren't what you're looking for, then check out High Impact E-mail, a program that integrates with ACT! and includes thousands of pre-designed e-mail templates. Point your Web browser to http://www.templatezone.com for more information.

To edit an existing e-mail template:

1. Click Write | Edit Template. A list of available templates will appear.
2. Select a template and click Open. The template will appear in the default word processor.
3. Make any necessary changes to the template.
4. Click File | Save As to save the template.

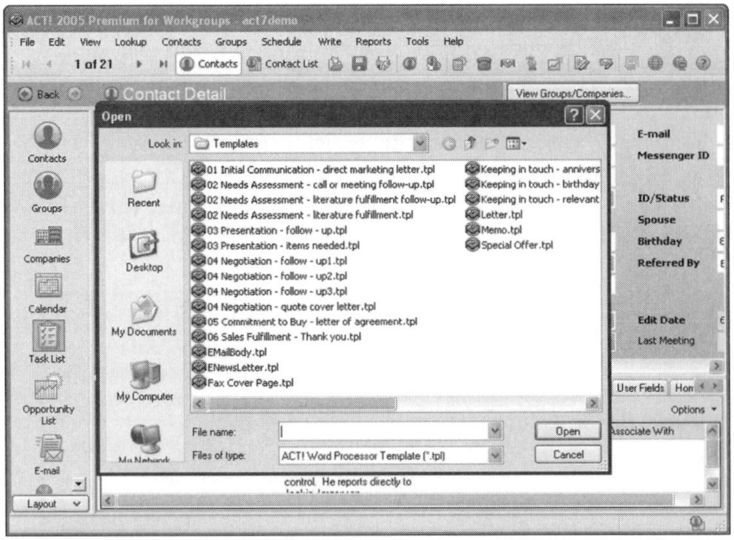

Opening an existing e-mail template

.ADT or .TPL

After clicking Write | Edit Template, ACT! will show templates available for your default word processor. If you have ACT! set to Microsoft Word, then only .ADT files will be displayed. If you're using the ACT! Word Processor, then only .TPL templates will show. To change your default word processor, click Tools | Preferences | Communication Tab.

Emailbody.adt/tpl

When you click Write | E-mail in ACT!, the program actually creates a new e-mail based on a template. You can edit this default e-mail template by changing the e-mailbody.adt file (or e-mailbody.tpl if you're using the ACT! Word Processor).

Formatting E-mail Templates

Both the ACT! Word Processor and Microsoft Word provide an interface that you can use to design an HTML-formatted e-mail template. Using either program, you can change font sizes, add pictures, create hyperlinks, create tables, and more. The instructions in this section assume that you are using the ACT! Word Processor as your default word processor. If you are using Microsoft Word, see the tips in the margins for equivalent directions.

Task A Formatting Basic Text

As you're editing an ACT! e-mail template, you might want to emphasize some of the text in the template. In the ACT! Word Processor, you can change the font, size, alignment, and color for any text.

To format basic text in the ACT! Word Processor:

1. Click Write | Edit Template and open the e-mail template you'd like to edit.
2. Highlight text in the e-mail template.
3. Click Format | Paragraph to set line spacing, alignment, indents, or paragraph distances for the text.
4. Click Format | Font to specify the font type, size, attributes, and color.
5. To create a bulleted or numbered list, click Format | Bullets & Numbering | Attributes.

Microsoft Word users

Click Format | Font to edit font attributes. Click Format | Paragraph to edit paragraph attributes. For bulleted lists, click Format | Bullets & Numbering.

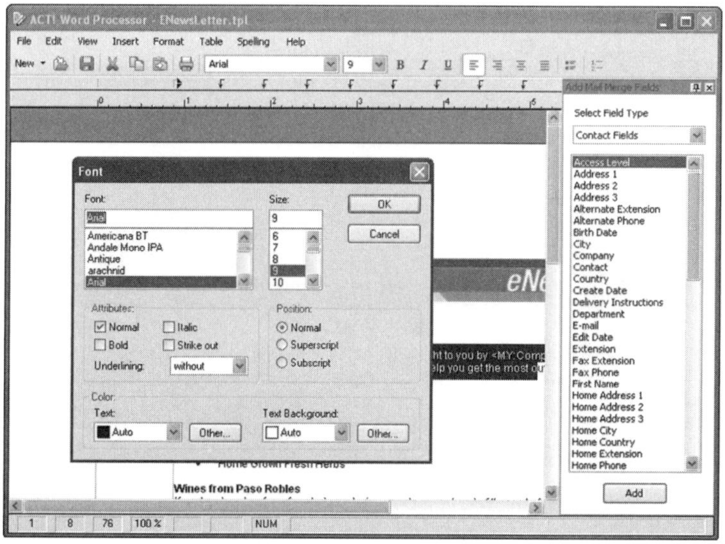

Formatting text in an ACT! e-mail template

Task B Inserting E-mail Merge Field Placeholders

As you design an e-mail template, you can add field placeholders to the text. When you perform an e-mail merge to contacts in your ACT! database, the field placeholders will be replaced with data from each individual contact's record.

To insert a field placeholder:

1. Click Write | Edit Template and open the e-mail template you'd like to edit.
2. Position the cursor in the spot where you'd like to add a field placeholder.
3. If the Mail Merge Fields list does not appear on the right side of the ACT! Word Processor, click View | Mail Merge Fields.
4. From the Mail Merge Fields list, select a field and then click the Add button.

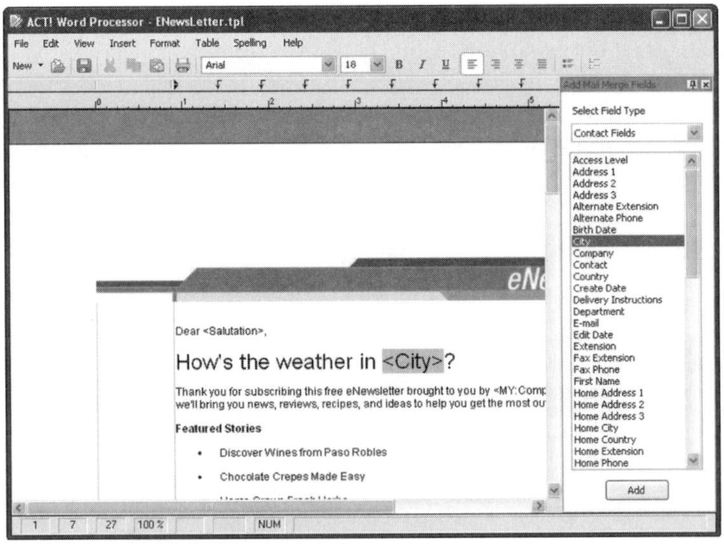

Inserting a field placeholder for the City field

Microsoft Word users

In Word, the Mail Merge Fields dialog box appears as a separate dialog box. If you can't see it, click Insert | ACT! Mail Merge Fields.

Inserting My Record fields

Select the My Record field option in the Mail Merge Fields area to insert field placeholders that will pull data from your My Record in ACT!. This feature is especially useful for the closings in letters. Instead of inserting a person's name in the closing, insert the My Record's contact field. Then, the closing will display the name of the person writing the letter, and everyone in your office will be able to use the same template to write a letter.

Task C Inserting an Image

You can insert graphic files into any ACT! template. These graphics are then embedded into your outgoing messages. Keep in mind that if the recipient of your e-mails cannot accept HTML e-mail, the plain text version of your e-mail may look odd.

To insert an image into an e-mail template:

1. Click Write | Edit Template and open the e-mail template you'd like to edit.
2. Click Insert | Image.
3. If you would like the image to be inserted in the text of the document, select the Character Position option.
4. If you would like the image to be left-aligned, right-aligned, or centered, select the Fixed Position option.
5. Locate and double-click the graphic file you'd like to insert. Note that you might need to select the type of graphic (.JPG, .BMP, .GIF, and so on) from the Files of type drop-down before it will appear in the Open dialog box.

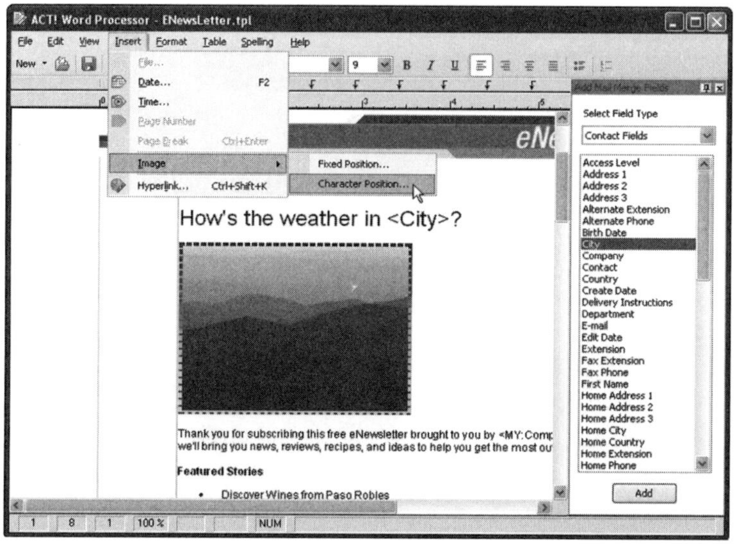

Inserting an image into an e-mail template

Microsoft Word users

Click Insert | Image | From File to insert a .JPG or .GIF image into an e-mail template.

Image size matters

Before embedding any images into your e-mail templates, you should make sure the graphics are optimized. It's a good idea to use Adobe Photoshop's Save for Web feature to reduce the size of the images. If you send a message with large graphic files, chances are good that your server will reject the e-mail merge.

Task D Adding a Table

Previous versions of the ACT! Word Processor did not support tables, and this was a major problem for anyone looking to create advanced e-mail templates. The table functionality in ACT! 2005 gives you the ability to create columns of text within an e-mail template. This feature is especially useful for creating e-mail newsletters.

Microsoft Word users

Click Table | Insert | Table to add a table to your document.

To add a table to an e-mail template:

1. Click Write | Edit Template and open the e-mail template you'd like to edit.
2. Place the cursor in the spot where you'd like to add a table.
3. Click Table | Insert | Table.
4. Select the number of columns and rows.
5. Click OK.
6. The table will appear in the template. Place the cursor inside the table and click Table | Table Properties to edit the table's attributes.

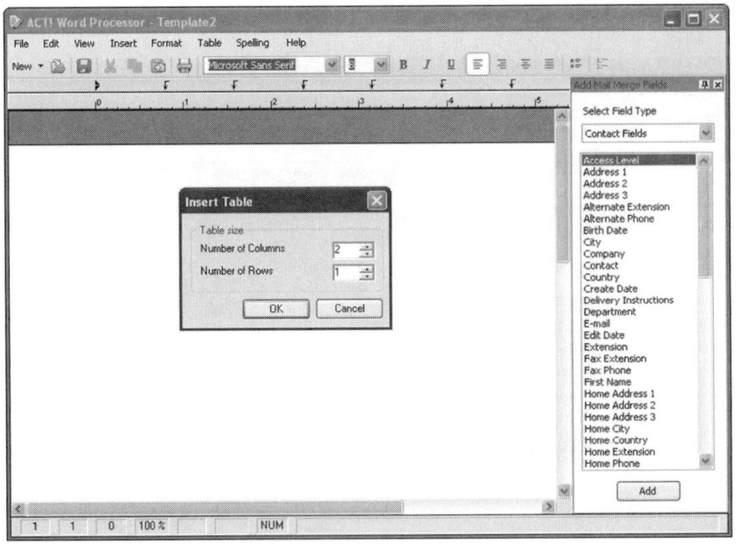

Inserting a table into an e-mail template

Task E Adding Hyperlinks to a Template

Hyperlinks embedded into an HTML e-mail give you an easy way to direct the e-mail recipients to your Web site for more information. You can make any text in an e-mail template hyperlinked. When the recipient clicks on any hyperlinked text, he or she will be automatically taken to the Web site you specify.

To add a hyperlink to a template:

1. Click Write | Edit Template and open the e-mail template you'd like to edit.
2. Highlight the text you'd like to hyperlink.
3. Click Insert | Hyperlink.
4. In the Linked To field, type or paste a Web address.
5. Click OK.

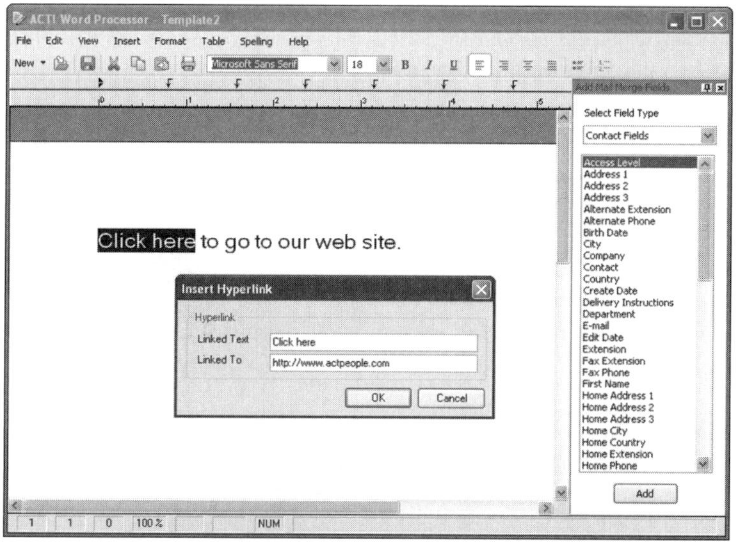

Creating hyperlinked text in an e-mail template

Microsoft Word users

Click Insert | Hyperlink to add a hyperlink to the text of your e-mail template.

Sending a Mass E-mail

Most mass e-mail is never read by the intended recipients. Even if your message is important, many people will delete your e-mails if it's apparent that the e-mail went out to hundreds of other people. With ACT!'s mass e-mails, each message is sent individually and includes personalized contact information pulled from the ACT! database. When your ACT! contact receives a mass e-mail sent from within ACT!, he or she won't know it went out to hundreds of other people.

Task A Performing a Mail Merge

Before actually sending an e-mail merge from your computer, you'll need to make sure that your outgoing mail server can handle the number of e-mails you plan on sending. Most non-business ISPs only allow 20 or so e-mails to be sent at a time.

To perform a mass e-mail merge:

1. Click Write | Mail Merge.
2. When the welcome screen of the Mail Merge Wizard appears, click Next.
3. Select the E-mail option and click Next.
4. Click the Browse button and select the template you'd like to use for this e-mail merge.
5. Select the range of contacts to include in the e-mail merge. Your options are: Current Lookup, Current Contact, All Contacts, Selected Group, or Selected Company. Click Next.
6. Type a subject for the e-mail, select a history creation option, and attach any necessary files to the mass e-mail. Click Next.
7. Specify how you'd like to deal with missing e-mail addresses. Click Next.
8. Click Finish.

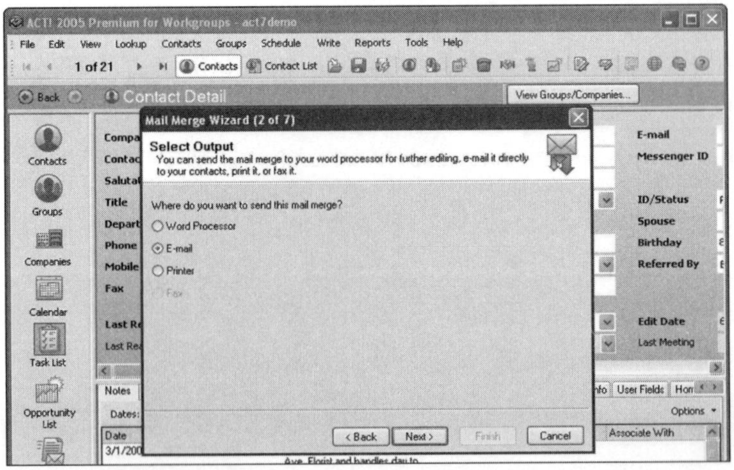

Performing a mass e-mail merge

Mass e-mail subject

One of the mass e-mail options in the Mail Merge Wizard lets you specify the subject of the outgoing e-mail. This subject is not a personal note to yourself; rather, it's the subject of the outgoing message that will display in your recipients' inboxes. The moral of this story: Don't write anything in the Subject area that you wouldn't want the recipients to see.

Chapter 15
Outlook Integration

Setting Outlook's ACT! Settings

You can create an ACT! Address Book in Outlook and then send e-mails to the ACT! Address Book contacts from within Outlook. After sending a message to an ACT! Address Book contact, ACT! will record a history of the e-mail in the contact's Notes/History tab—even if ACT! isn't open.

Task A Creating an ACT! Address Book in Outlook

To set up a link between ACT! and Outlook, you'll need to create an ACT! Address Book in Outlook. This will allow you to send e-mails directly to your ACT! contacts from within Outlook—without even opening ACT!.

To create an ACT! Address Book in Outlook 2002/2003:

1. Click Tools | E-mail Accounts. The E-mail Accounts dialog box will appear.
2. Select to add a new directory or Address Book and click Next.
3. Select the Additional Address Books option and click Next.
4. Select ACT! 2005 Address Book and click Next. Your ACT! Address Book options will appear.
5. Click the Browse buttons to select ACT! databases to add to your ACT! Address Book in Outlook. You can add up to three databases for inclusion in the Address Book.
6. When you're finished, click OK to create your Address Book. You will need to restart both Outlook and ACT! before using your new Address Book.

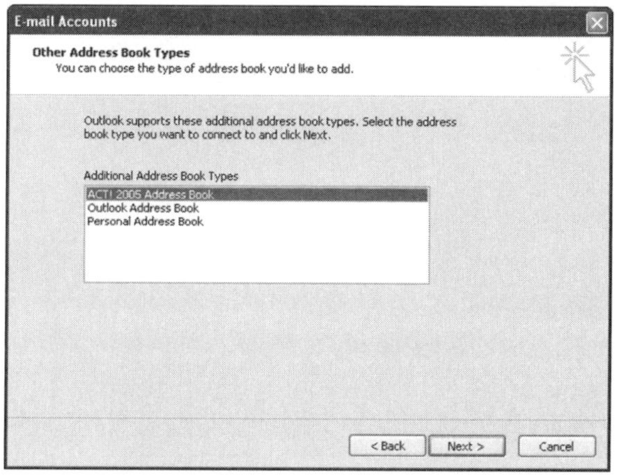

Creating an ACT! Address Book

An important first step

Most of the lessons in this section require that you have an ACT! Address Book created in Outlook. If you don't create an ACT! Address Book in Outlook, you won't be able to send e-mails to your ACT! contacts from within Outlook.

Outlook 2000 users

The process of adding an ACT! Address Book is slightly different in Outlook 2000: Click Tools | Services, and then click the Add button. Select the ACT! Address Book option and click OK. Browse to select up to three ACT! databases, and then click OK to save the changes.

Task B Setting Default Attachment Options

When you send messages in Outlook to your ACT! Address Book contacts, Outlook will create a history of the e-mail in ACT!. Before you begin using this feature, you might want to set the default history creation options. History creation options are:

- **Do not save e-mail to history**. No history will be created for outgoing e-mails to your ACT! contacts.
- **Date, time, and subject**. A history will be created that shows the subject line of your outgoing messages.
- **Date, time, subject, and message text**. A history will be created that shows the subject and the entire message body. Only the text will appear. (Graphics and text formatting will not appear in the history.)
- **Entire e-mail as an attachment** ACT! will save a copy of your outgoing message as a .msg file in your default attached e-mail folder. You'll be able to double-click the icon for the history that's created for each outgoing e-mail, and ACT! will display the saved copy of the e-mail that was sent.

Attachment toolbar

The attachment preferences you select in Tools | Options will apply to all messages sent to your ACT! Address Book contacts. You can choose to change this attachment option for each individual message sent by clicking View | Toolbars | ACT! History in a new Outlook message.

To set the default attachment options:

1. In Outlook, click Tools | Options.
2. You should have an ACT! tab in your Options dialog box like the one shown in the figure on this page. If you don't have an ACT! tab, you should set up an ACT! Address Book.
3. Select the attachment options you'd like to set for e-mails that are sent to ACT! contacts from within Outlook.

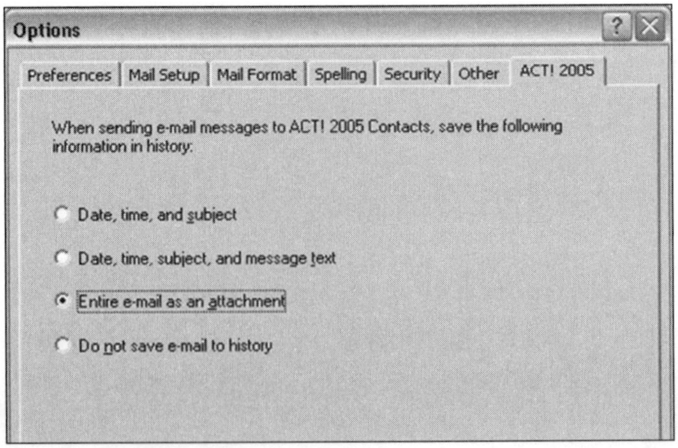

Setting the default attachment options in Outlook

Sending E-mails to ACT! Contacts

When sending messages from within Outlook, you can now attach a history of the message to an ACT! contact. To do this, you'll need to send the message to an ACT! contact from the ACT! Address Book.

Task A Sending an E-mail to an ACT! Contact

Before attempting this task, you must set up an ACT! Address Book in Outlook. If you want Outlook to save a history of your e-mail in the Notes/History tab for your contact, then you must send the e-mail to a contact in your ACT! Address Book in Outlook.

To send an e-mail to an ACT! contact:

1. In Outlook, click the New button to create a new e-mail message.
2. Click the To button to select a recipient from the Address Book.
3. The Select Names dialog box will appear. In the top part of this dialog box, under the header Show Names from the, make sure ACT! Address Book is selected.
4. Select an ACT! contact from the list on the left side of the dialog box. Click the To, Cc, or Bcc buttons to add the ACT! contact to the recipients list.
5. Click OK to begin composing the message.

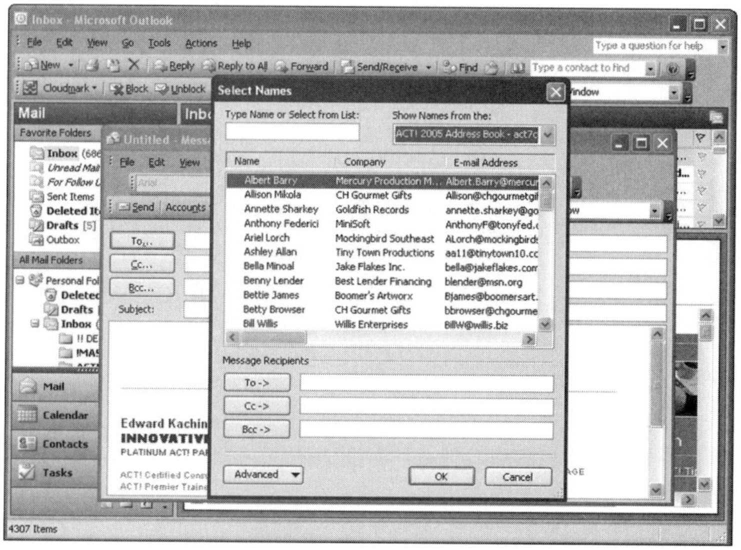

Selecting a recipient from the ACT! Address Book

Missing contacts

If you're missing ACT! contacts in the ACT! Address Book, check (in ACT!) to see if the contact has an e-mail address. The ACT! Address Book will only show ACT! contacts with an e-mail address in the ACT! e-mail address field.

Task B Checking E-mail Properties for an ACT! Contact

If you're sending an e-mail to an ACT! Address Book contact from within Outlook and you don't have ACT! open, you may want to check the e-mail properties for the ACT! Address Book contact before sending the message. Doing so gives you an opportunity to verify the e-mail address of the contact before your e-mail is sent.

To check e-mail properties for an ACT! contact:

1. Follow the steps in Task A to create an e-mail message for one of your ACT! Address Book contacts.
2. Double-click the underlined e-mail address in the address bar. The properties for the contact will appear.
3. You can review the contact's name, company name, and e-mail address and the database that Outlook is using to pull the contact's information.

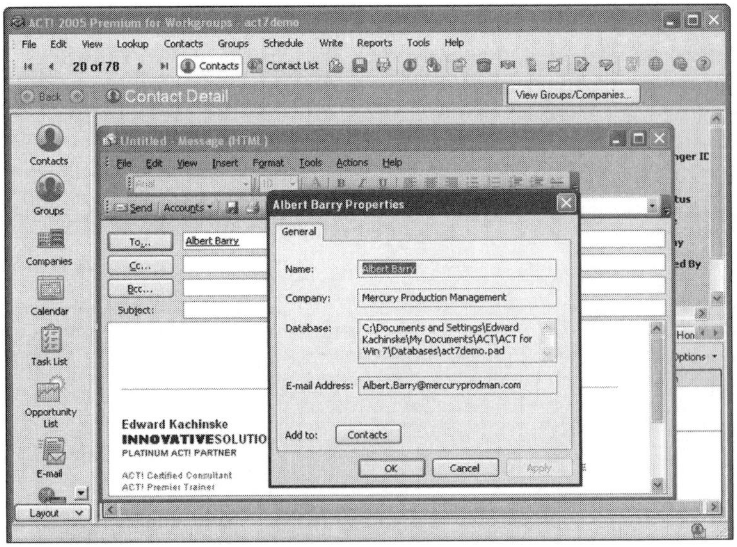

Viewing the properties of an ACT! Address Book recipient

Add to your Personal Address Book

After viewing the properties of an ACT! Address Book contact, click the Personal Address Book button to add the ACT! contact to your Outlook Personal Address Book.

Task C Specifying Message History Options

In a previous lesson, you learned how to set the default history creation options for outgoing messages to your ACT! Address Book contacts. In this lesson, you'll learn how to change the history options for an individual e-mail you're sending.

To specify message history options:

1. In Outlook, create a new message and address it to one of your ACT! Address Book contacts.
2. Click View | Toolbars | ACT! 2005 History.
3. The ACT! History toolbar will appear for your new outgoing e-mail. (It will also appear the next time you create a new message in Outlook.)
4. From the drop-down in the ACT! History toolbar, select the e-mail attachment option you'd like to set for this individual outgoing e-mail.
5. Send the message.

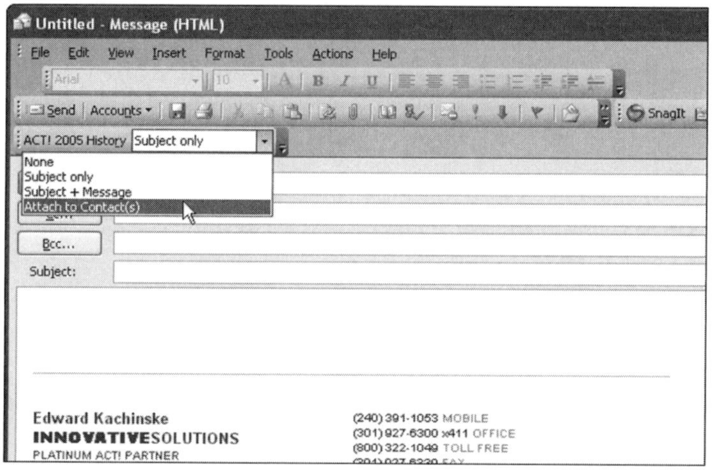

Specifying message history options in Outlook

Not always functional

After you add the ACT! History toolbar to outgoing messages in ACT!, it will appear for e-mails sent to ACT! Address Book and non-ACT! contacts. If you're sending an e-mail to a non-ACT! contact in Outlook, just ignore the ACT! History toolbar. It's only functional for e-mail sent to ACT! Address Book contacts.

> **Configure the ACT! Address Book**
>
> You must have set up an ACT! Address Book to perform these steps. Adding an ACT! Address Book is covered in an earlier task in this chapter.

Attaching Existing Outlook Messages to ACT! Contacts

In previous lessons, you've seen how to attach outgoing Outlook messages to ACT! contacts. In this section, you'll learn how to attach existing messages (in your inbox, sent items folder, or other folders) to ACT! contacts.

Task A Attaching a Single E-mail to an ACT! Contact

If you have an important message in your Outlook inbox, you might want to attach the message to a contact in ACT!. ACT! makes it easy to attach any existing message to a contact in any of the three databases in your configured ACT! Address Book.

To attach a single e-mail to an ACT! contact:

1. In Outlook, double-click an e-mail in your inbox (or other folder).
2. When the e-mail opens, click the Attach to ACT! Contacts icon on the toolbar.
3. You'll be prompted to select a database. Select the database that contains the contact you'd like to use.
4. The Select Contact(s) dialog box appears. Select an ACT! contact from the list on the left and click Add.
5. Click OK. ACT! will attach the e-mail message to your contact.

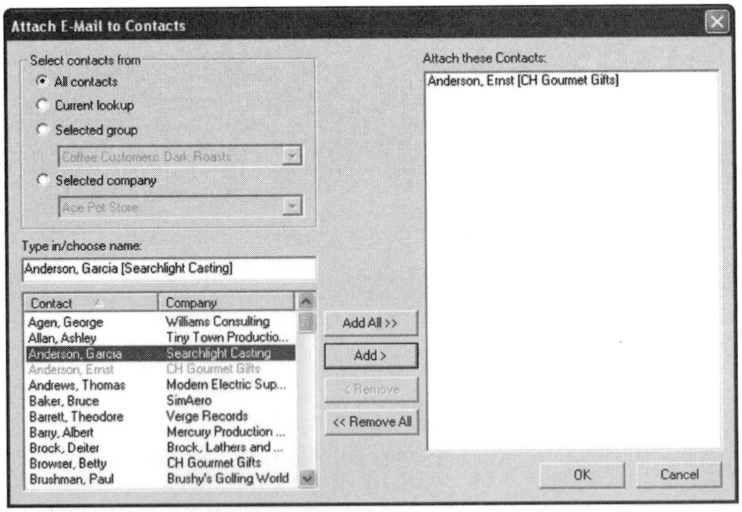

Attaching a single message to an ACT! contact

Task B Attaching Multiple E-mails to an ACT! Contact

You may want to attach more than one e-mail to an ACT! contact. When this is the case, you can attach multiple e-mails in an Outlook folder to a contact in your ACT! database in one simple procedure.

To attach multiple e-mails to an ACT! contact:

1. Hold down the Ctrl key and click multiple e-mails in an Outlook folder. This highlights all messages you click.
2. Click the Attach to ACT! Contacts icon on the toolbar.
3. You'll be prompted to select a database. Select the database that contains the contact you'd like to use.
4. The Select Contact(s) dialog box appears. Select an ACT! contact from the list on the left and click Add.
5. Click OK. ACT! will attach each message you highlighted to your contact.

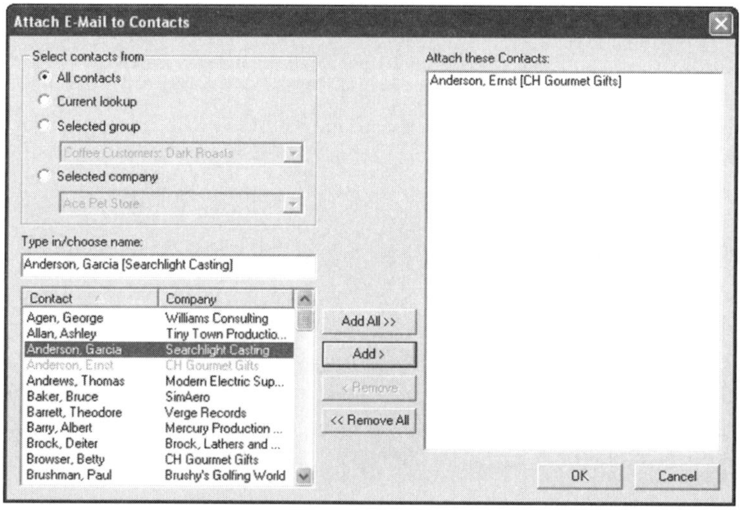

Attaching multiple messages to an ACT! contact

Using multiple databases?

After clicking the Attach to ACT! Contacts button on the toolbar, you'll have the opportunity to select from up to three databases. The e-mail(s) will be attached to the database you select.

If you don't see all of your ACT! databases listed after clicking the Attach to ACT! Contacts icon on the toolbar, then you'll need to set up the additional databases in your ACT! Address Book.

Sharing ACT! and Outlook Activities

If you use an ACT! calendar and your colleagues use an Outlook calendar, there's no problem—it's easy to share your Outlook and ACT! calendars. Updating your ACT! and Outlook calendars is a manual process, and you'll need to remember to perform an update from time to time. Activities scheduled in ACT! or Outlook won't automatically transfer between programs without your manual intervention.

Task A Updating ACT! and Outlook Activities

Each time you update your ACT! and Outlook calendars, activities from the current ACT! database will be transferred into Outlook. Activities scheduled with the currently logged-in user in Outlook will be transferred to the ACT! calendar. ACT! activities viewed in Outlook are read-only, and Outlook activities shown on the ACT! calendar will not be editable from within ACT!.

To update your ACT! and Outlook activities:

1. In ACT!, click Tools | Outlook Activities | Update. The Update Calendars dialog box will appear.
2. In the Update area, select whether to perform a one-way or two-way synchronization.
3. In the For these dates area, select a date range. ACT! will only update activities in this date range.
4. Click Update.

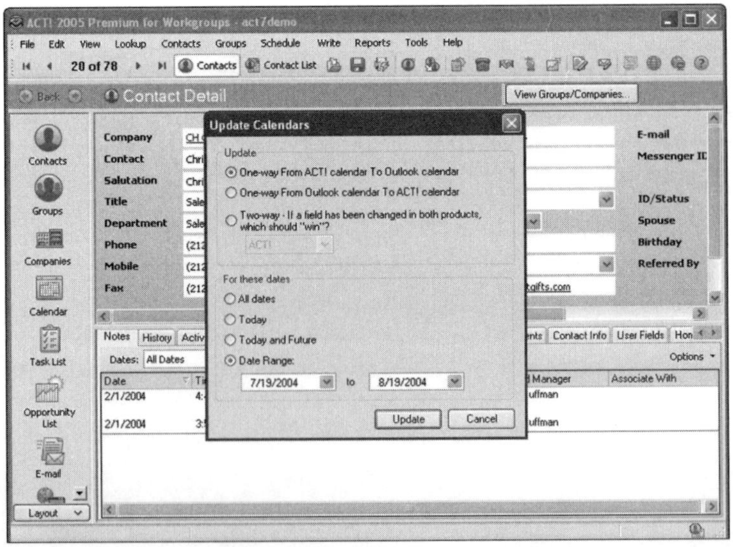

Updating the ACT! and Outlook calendars

Editable activities

In previous versions of ACT!, activities that were shared between the ACT! and Outlook calendars were read-only in the non-native calendar. So, for example, if you sent an activity from ACT! to Outlook, you wouldn't be able to modify the activity in Outlook. Now, in ACT! 2005, shared activities are editable in both ACT! and Outlook.

Task B Removing Shared ACT!/Outlook Activities

At any point, you can easily remove all Outlook activities from your ACT! database. You can also remove any ACT! activities from your Outlook calendar.

To remove shared ACT!/Outlook activities:

1. Click Tools | Outlook Activities | Remove All Activities.
2. Select whether you'd like to remove ACT! activities from Outlook and/or Outlook activities from ACT!.
3. Click OK to remove the activities.

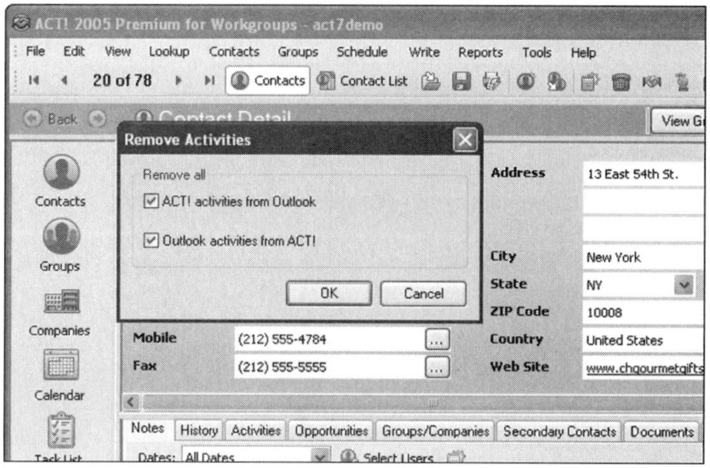

Removing Outlook activities from the ACT! calendar

Updating Outlook activities

If you remove shared activities, they remain in the original program. At any time, you can click Tools | Outlook Activities | Update to share them again.

Chapter 16
Internet Integration

Internet Services

In previous versions of ACT!, the Internet Services view appeared as a Web browser built into the ACT! interface. Now, ACT! interfaces directly with Internet Explorer to give you easier Web-browsing capabilities. If you find a site of interest, you can easily attach it to an ACT! contact record.

Task A Attaching a Web Page to a Contact

When you click the Internet Services button on the View bar, ACT! will launch a session of Internet Explorer. Because you launched the Web browser from within ACT!, you'll have the option to attach the current page to a contact in your database. All attached Web pages will appear in the contact's History tab.

To attach a Web page to a contact:

1. Click the Internet Services button on the View bar to launch ACT!'s Web browser, and browse to the Web page you'd like to attach.
2. Click the Attach button on the Internet Explorer toolbar.
3. Select a contact from the list on the left, then click the > button to add the selected contact to the attachment list.
4. Click OK. The current Web page will be automatically attached to the contact(s) you selected.

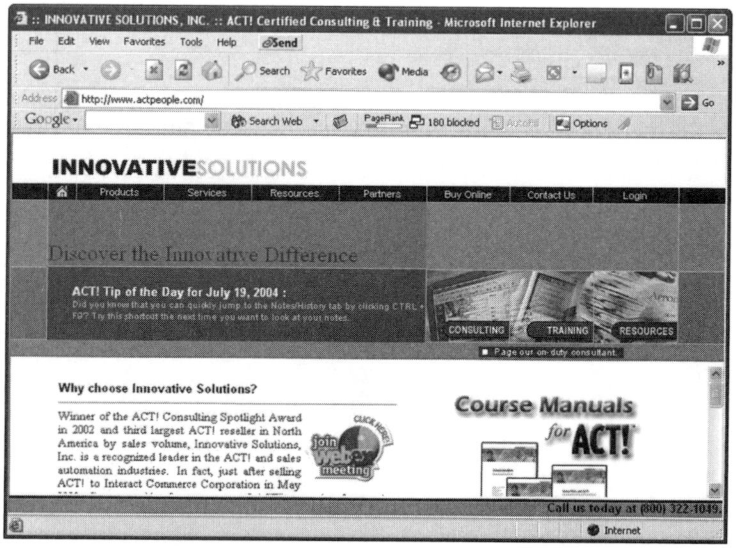

Viewing a Web page in Internet Explorer

Where are the attached Web pages saved?

By default, ACT! saves your attached Web pages in the Netlinks folder within your default ACT! database folder. To see where your Netlinks folder is, click Tools | Preferences and select Internet Links from the File Type drop-down in the General tab. If you change computers, be sure to back up this directory, or all of your saved Internet sites will disappear.

Task B Viewing an Attached Web Page

When you attach a Web page to an ACT! contact, the Web page and associated graphics are saved in your database's Attachments folder. The attached Web page will appear as an item in your History tab.

To view an attached Web page:

1. Go to the contact for whom you've attached a Web page.
2. Click the History tab.
3. Locate the Web page attachment item in the History tab.
4. Double-click the Attachment icon to bring up a copy of the saved Web page. The attachment column is to the right of the Regarding & Details column.

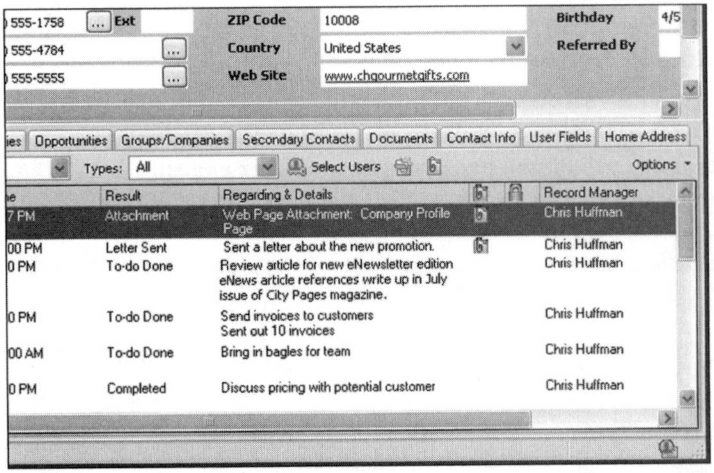

Viewing attached Web pages in the History tab

Task C Launching Web Sites in URL Fields

Whenever you click in a URL (Web site) field in ACT!, the program will launch your contact's Web site in the default Web browser. You can also click the Internet Services button on the View bar to launch the browser, where you'll be able to type any Web Insert address manually.

To launch a Web site from a URL field:

1. Locate a contact's Web Site field.
2. Click the blue underlined text inside the field. ACT! will open the Web site in the default Web browser.

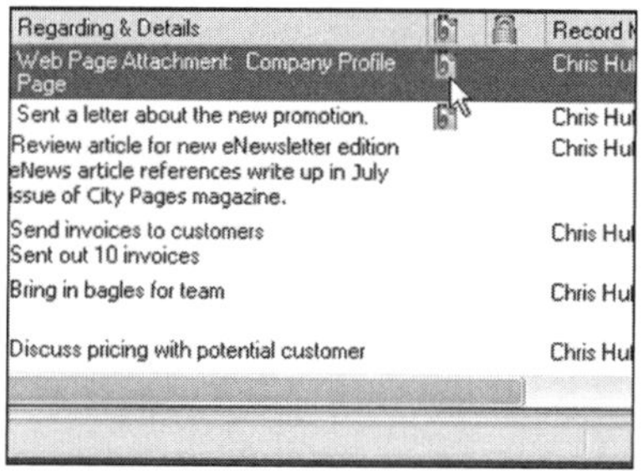

The Web page attachment icon

Need to edit the Web Site field?

When you click inside the Web Site field, ACT! launches the contact's Web site in the Internet Services view. But what if you want to edit the contents of the Web Site field?

To edit a Web Site field, right-click somewhere inside the Web Site field and select the Edit Web Site option. Alternatively, you can hover the mouse over the field for four seconds until an edit cursor appears. Then, left-click in the field to edit the e-mail address. These editing tricks work with the E-mail Address field, too.

Maps and Driving Directions

After a legal dispute with Yahoo!, driving directions and mapping functionality was removed from ACT! 6.0. In ACT! 2005, ACT! has reestablished this time-saving feature. ACT! now integrates with MapQuest for maps and driving directions.

Task A Generating a Map for a Contact

Using the built-in link to MapQuest Maps, you can easily generate a map for your contact. When you launch a map using the link on the View | Internet Links menu, ACT! generates a map using your current contact's address.

Internet connection required

Driving directions are processed online using MapQuest's online driving directions feature, so you'll need an Internet connection to use this feature.

To generate a map for a contact:

1. Go to the contact for whom you'd like to generate a map.
2. Click View | Internet Services | Internet Links | MapQuest Maps. ACT! will launch Internet Explorer, and the MapQuest map for your current contact will appear.

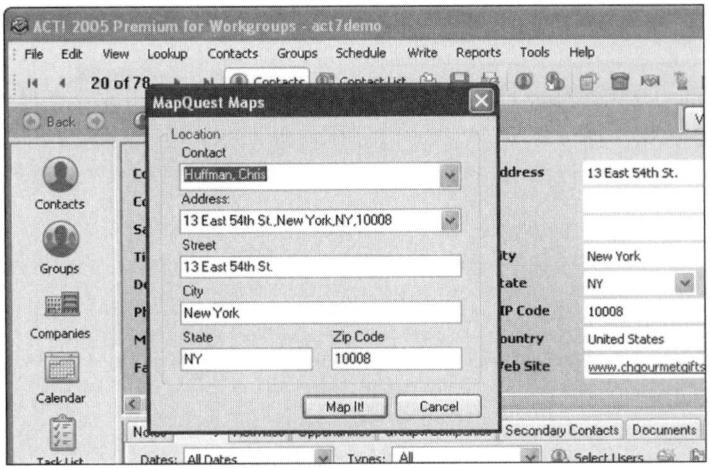

Generating a MapQuest map for a contact

Task B Generating Driving Directions

When you generate driving directions from within ACT!, you won't have to retype any addresses. ACT! will automatically fill in your address and the address of your current contact.

To generate driving directions:

1. Go to a contact's record in ACT!.
2. Click View | Internet Services | Internet Links | MapQuest Driving Directions.
3. ACT! will verify your address and your contact's address. If the addresses are correct, click OK. The MapQuest Driving Directions will appear in Internet Explorer.

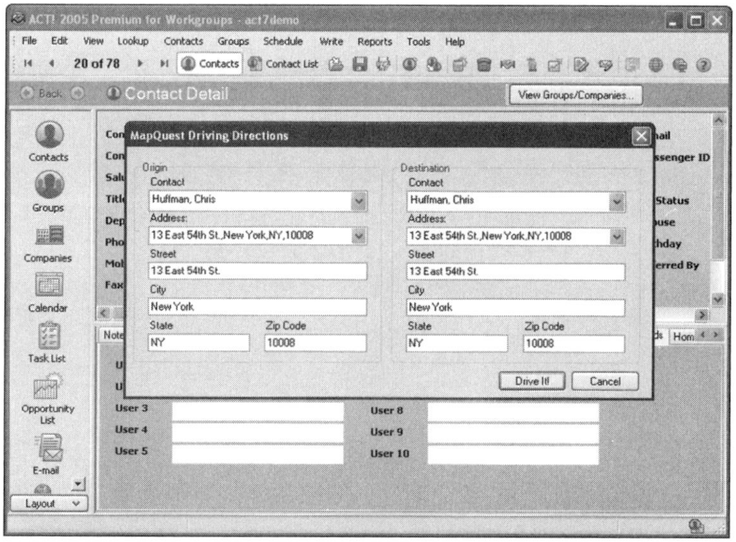

Generating MapQuest driving directions

Always double-check the directions

It's a good idea to double-check any directions generated from the built-in links to MapQuest. The driving directions are fairly accurate, but road construction, new roads, and other conditions might prevent you from taking a particular route.

Chapter 17
Reports

Running Reports

So you've amassed a huge collection of information about your customers. So what? What good is it if you can't produce customized or specific reports on this data? ACT!'s Report Writer gives you the ability to create just about any sort of basic report that lists information on your contacts. You can pull information from ACT!'s fields, your custom fields, notes, histories, opportunities, activities, and more.

Task A Running a Standard Report

ACT! ships with about two dozen pre-designed reports that will probably meet most of your reporting needs. If you're new to ACT! reports, you should probably run a contact report to see the sort of information that can be included in an ACT! report. The contact report includes basic field, activity, and notes/history information for a contact. It's a good report to run if you want to print basic information for your contact and take it offsite.

To run a standard report:

1. Click the Reports menu.
2. Select a standard report to run. (If you need examples, try running a Contact, Notes/History, or Activities/Time Spent report.)
3. In the General tab, select a report output method from the drop-down menu.
4. In the Create report for area, select a range of contacts to include in the report. Your options are: Current Contact, Current Lookup, or All Contacts.
5. In the Use data managed by area, select the users whose data should be included in the report.
6. Click OK. The report will appear or print, depending on the output method you selected.

Need better reporting?

If your needs are more complex than ACT! can accommodate, try Stonefield Query (http://www.stonefieldquery.com) or Crystal Clear Reports (http://www.crystalclearreports.com). Or for even more reporting add-ons, go to http://www.actaddons.com.

Task B Running a Custom Report

In addition to running the standard reports included with a basic ACT! installation, you can also run reports that you've customized on the system. You can only run these customized reports if you or someone in your workgroup has already created them. Creating custom reports is covered in a later task in this chapter.

To run a custom report:

1. If you wish to run the custom report just for contacts in the current lookup, perform that lookup.
2. Click Reports | Other Contact Reports. The Define Filters dialog box appears.
3. In the Send the report output to drop-down, select how you'd like the report to appear.
4. In the Create report for area, select a range of contacts. When you run the report, only contacts in this range will be included.
5. Click OK. The report will print, save to a file, or appear in the preview area, depending on the output method you selected.

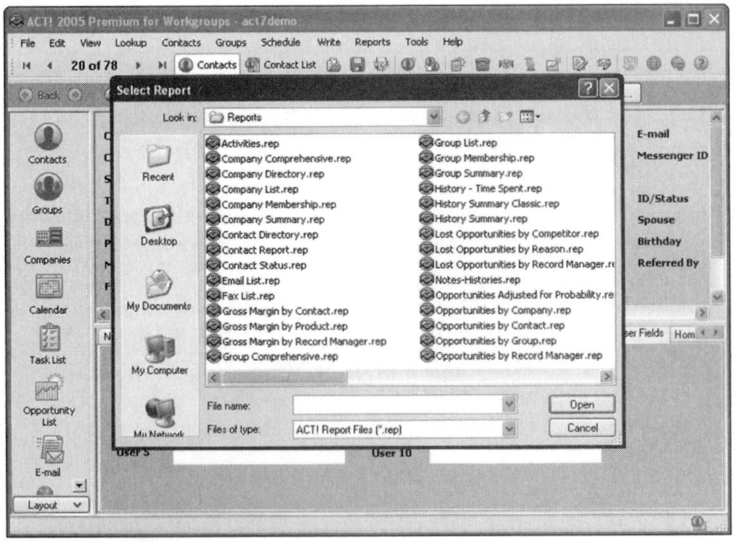

Running a custom report

Output to PDF

If you plan to send the report to others in your workgroup, set the output method to PDF. Your colleagues will need to have the Acrobat Reader installed on their computers to view the report.

Export to Excel

In the Contact List view, arrange the columns and contacts to show just the most relevant information. Then, click Tools | Export to Excel. All of the information showing in the Contact List view will be transferred to an Excel spreadsheet. You can edit this spreadsheet, but changes will not be sent back into ACT!.

Filtering a Report

To include or exclude specific information in your reports, you'll want to take advantage of the Filter tab in the Run Report dialog box. This is especially important when you're printing reports that contain activities, notes, histories, attachments, or opportunities.

Task A Filtering an Activity Report

Filtering an activity report will give you the ability to produce a report that contains just specific types of activities. You can filter to show activities in a given date range. Or you could show just activities that have been scheduled with specific users in the database. You can also include/exclude specific activity types and priorities.

To filter an activity report:

1. Click Report | Activities. The Define Filters dialog box will appear.
2. In the General tab, select an output method from the drop-down.
3. Also in the General tab, select a range of contacts whose data should be included in the report.
4. Click the Activity tab to show the activity filter options.
5. In the Activities area, select whether or not to display calls, meetings, to-dos, or cleared or custom activities.
6. In the Date range drop-down, select a range of activities to include in the report.
7. In the Use data managed by area, select the users whose activities should be included in the report.
8. Click OK to run the report.

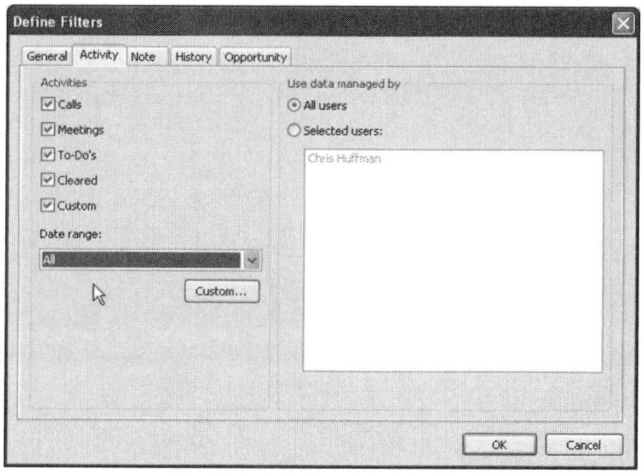

Filtering an activity report

Output to Rich Text Format

If you want to be able to edit the report once it has been created, set the output method to Rich Text Format (RTF). This will save the report in a format that you can open in Microsoft Word to edit.

A practical example: call reports

Let's say you select the All Contacts option in Step 3. In Step 5, you select to show only calls and completed activities. In Step 6, you select the Last Week option. Finally, in Step 7, you select to show just activities for a specific user. In this case, ACT! will create a call report that shows all open and completed calls made last week by your employee.

History Summary Classic report

If you need to analyze the number of history items created for each contact, try running the History Summary Classic report. Broken down by individual contact, this report will show the number of attempted calls, completed calls, meetings held, and letters sent.

Task B Filtering a History Report

Filtering a note or history report gives you the ability to select whether to show or hide notes, histories, attachments, and e-mails. You can also select a date range for the notes and histories you'd like to include in the report, and you can select the users whose data you'd like to include.

To filter a history report:

1. Click Report | History Time Spent. The Define Filters dialog box will appear.
2. In the General tab, select an output method from the drop-down.
3. Also in the General tab, select a range of contacts whose data should be included in the report.
4. Click the History tab to show the history filter options.
5. In the Histories area, select whether or not to show history items, sent e-mail items, or attached file items in the report.
6. In the Date range drop-down, select a range of histories to include in the report.
7. In the Use data managed by area, select the users whose activities should be included in the report.
8. Click OK to run the report.

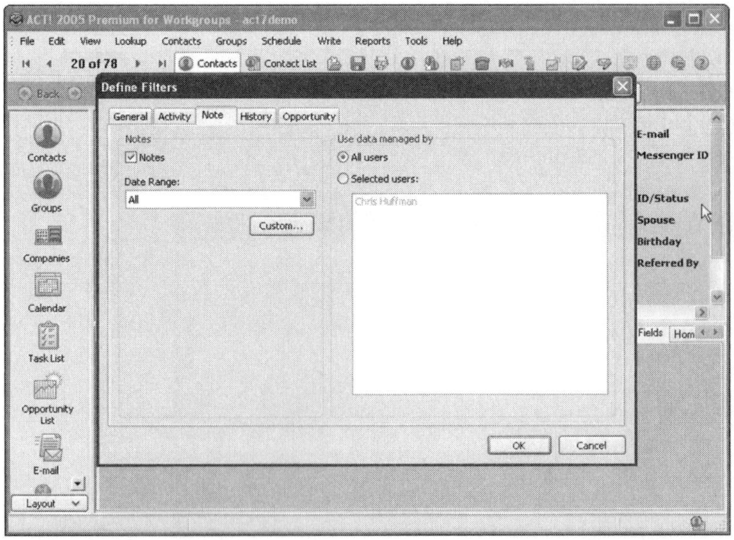

Filtering a note or history report

Task C Filtering an Opportunity Report

You can filter any of the sales reports to show just the specific information you need. You might want to print a report that only includes data for a specific user. Or you might want to change the sorting of the report. Perhaps you want to limit the report to include only information in a specific date range? All of this can be done using the report filter settings.

To filter an opportunity report:

1. Click Reports | Opportunity Reports.
2. Select the opportunity report you'd like to run.
3. The Define Filters dialog box appears. In the Opportunities area, select the types of opportunities you'd like to include in the report.
4. In the Date Range area, select a relative date range (today, last week, last month, and so on) for the data you'd like to include in the report. Select the Custom button to select a specific date range.
5. In the Use data managed by area, select the users whose opportunities should display on the report.
6. Click OK to run the report.

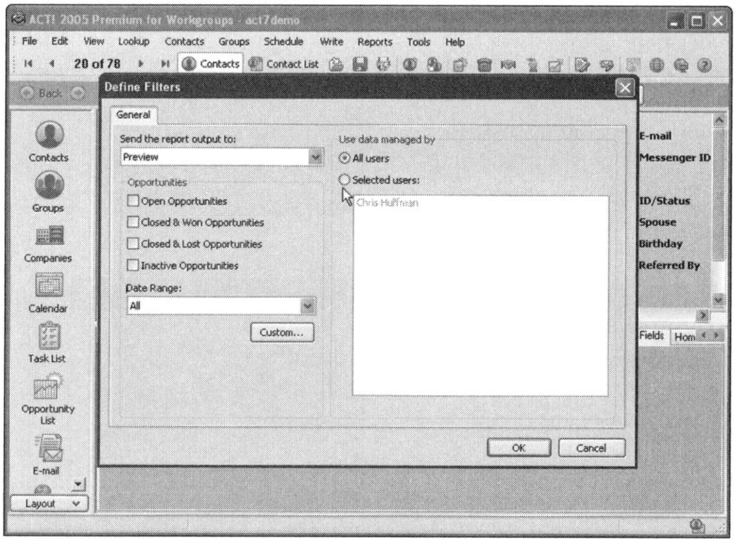

Filtering an opportunity report

Lookup first

Before running a sales report, you might want to perform a lookup of contacts. Then, in the Define Filters dialog box, you can select the Current Lookup option in the General tab to run the report just for sales that have been associated with contacts in the current lookup.

Creating a Report Template

ACT! ships with a number of custom report templates. The existing reports will suffice for most users' reporting needs. However, once you've devoted thousands of staff hours to entering data into an ACT! database, you may want more reporting flexibility than the standard ACT! reports provide.

Task A Creating a Report Template from Scratch

If none of the out-of-the-box report templates resemble the report you're trying to create, then you should create a new report template from scratch. This feature probably has the biggest learning curve of any in this book, but for what it's worth, the Report Writer in ACT! is probably the simplest report writer you'll come across.

Other reporting add-ons

Check out http://www.actaddons.com for a complete listing of all reporting add-ons that work with ACT!.

To create a report template:

1. Click Reports | New Template. The New Report dialog box in the Report Designer will appear.
2. On the left side of the New Report dialog box, select the general type of report you'd like to create.
3. On the right, a list of available basic templates will appear. Highlight the template that most closely resembles the template you'd like to create. If you do not want to use a pre-designed template format, select the first option, Empty Contact Report.
4. Click OK. The report will appear in the Report Designer. You're now ready to add objects, fields, and sections to the report. Adding content to a report is covered later on in this chapter.

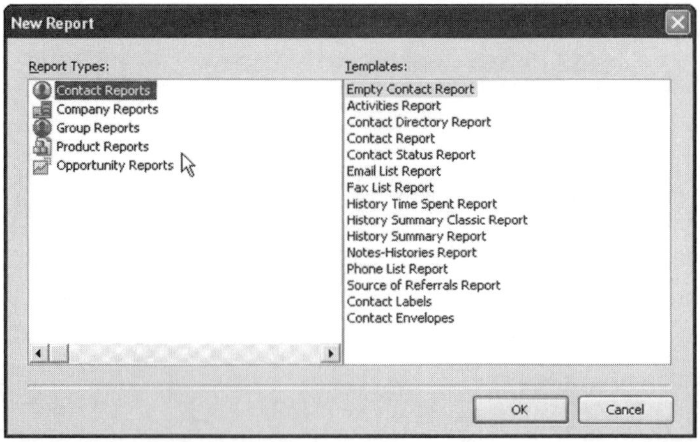

Creating a new report template

Task B Editing an Existing Report Template

If one of the out-of-the-box ACT! reports resembles the report you're trying to create, it's a good idea to edit the existing report template and save it with a new name.

To edit an existing report template:

1. Click Reports | Edit Template.
2. Browse and double-click the report template you'd like to edit.
3. The report template will appear in the Layout Designer. Make any necessary changes to the template.
4. Click File | Save As to save the report with a new name.

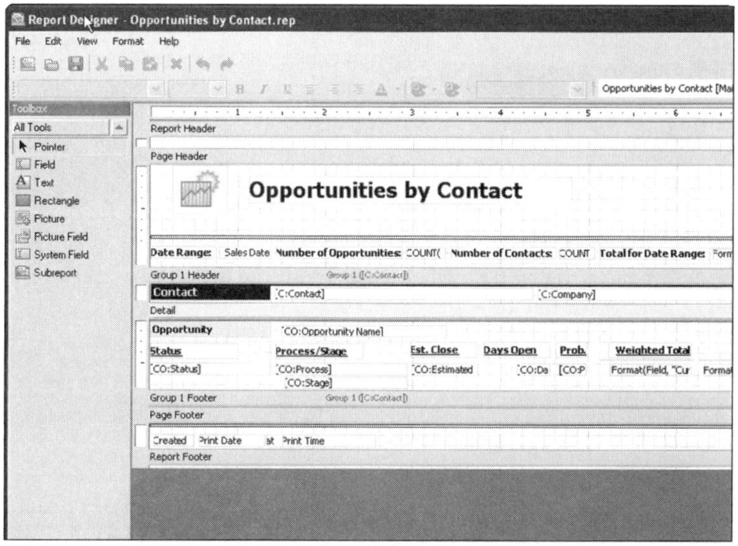

Editing an opportunity report

Converting existing reports

If you need to edit a report template that was created in a previous version of ACT!, you'll need to convert the reports to 2005 format before following the steps in this task. To convert an ACT! 3–6 report template to 2005 format, click Tools | Convert ACT! 3-6 Items.

Adding Objects to a Report

As you design a customized report, you'll find that adding objects may give you more flexibility to organize your report and make it look good. Using the buttons on the Tool Palette, you can add text objects, shapes, and backgrounds to any section. You can also add graphics to make an otherwise boring report sizzle.

Task A Adding Fields

Adding fields to any section of your report will pull data from a part of the ACT! database. You can add contact, note, history, opportunity, activity, group, secondary contact, product, and company fields to the database. You can even add summary fields that will produce sums and other basic mathematical calculations.

Adding multiple fields

You can add multiple fields to your report at once. Hold down the Ctrl key and select multiple fields from the list in the Select Field dialog box. When you click the Add button, all highlighted fields will be added to the report template.

Choose the right field

As you add fields to a report, make sure you're adding the right kinds of fields to each section. You'll add contact fields to a contact section, notes fields to a notes subreport, activity fields to an activity subreport, and so on.

To add fields to a report:

1. If the Toolbox is not showing on the left side of the Report Designer, click View | Toolbox.
2. In the Toolbox, click the Field option.
3. In the area on the Report Designer where you'd like to add a field, click and drag space for the field placeholder.
4. The Select Field dialog box will appear. From the drop-down, select the type of field you'd like to add.
5. Highlight the field name and click the Add button.

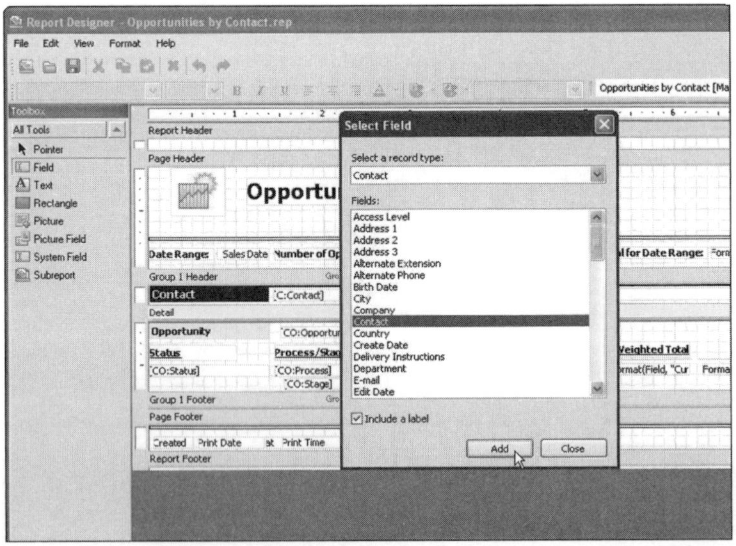

Inserting a field placeholder into a report template

Task B Adding Text Objects

As you design a customized report, you'll find that adding objects may give you more flexibility to organize your report and make it look good. Using the buttons on the Toolbox, you can add text objects, shapes, and backgrounds to any section.

To add text objects to a report:

1. If the Toolbox is not showing on the left side of the Report Designer, then click View | Toolbox.
2. In the Toolbox, click the Text option.
3. Click and drag the space on the report that you would like to devote to the text box. The empty text box will appear on the report.
4. Double-click the text box to edit its text.

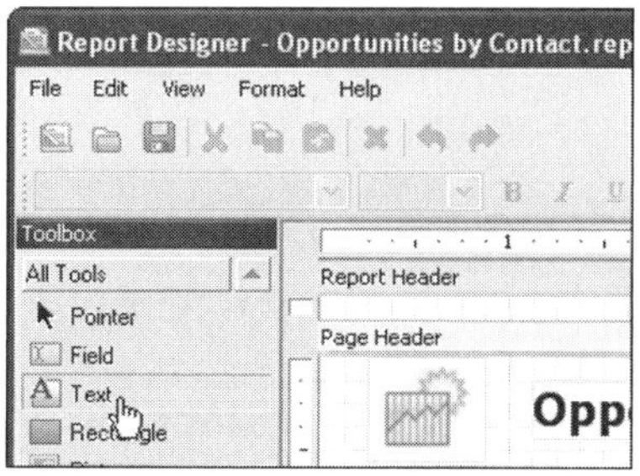

Using the Text tool to add text to a report

Changing font attributes

Highlight any text box and use the text attribute options on the toolbar to make the text bolded, aligned, or colored. Alternatively, you could highlight the text box and click View | Properties Window to show all font options.

Task C Adding Lines and Shapes

You can also add graphics to make an otherwise boring report pop. In the Report Designer, you can use basic the rectangle drawing object to better organize and present the information in a report.

To add drawing objects to a report:

1. If the Toolbox is not showing on the left side of the Report Designer, click View | Toolbox.
2. In the Toolbox, click the Rectangle option.
3. Draw a rectangle on the report template.
4. Double-click the rectangle to edit its background color and line style.
5. Click View | Properties Window to view additional options for the rectangle formatting.

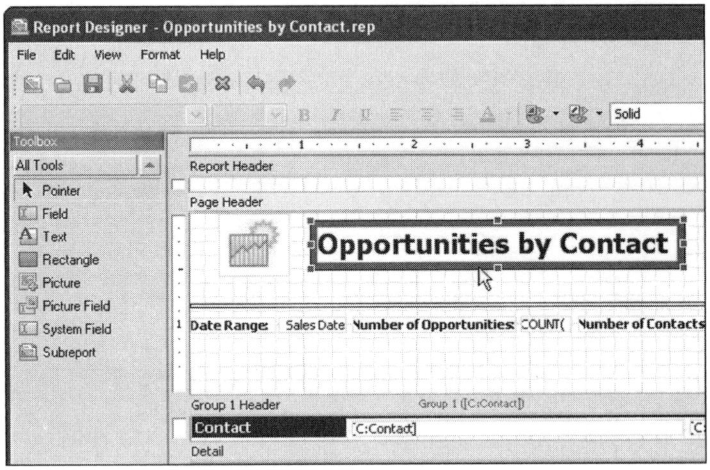

Drawing a box around the report title

Drawing a line

You might notice that the line-drawing feature is no longer available in ACT! 2005. You can still draw lines by drawing a rectangle and then, in the Properties window, selecting to make the line only one pixel high.

Task D Using the Properties Window

You can use the Properties window to change the attributes for any selected object in the Report Writer. If you need to change the text color, line color, background, height, or width of a field or object, you should perform the edit in the Properties window. The feature does not display by default, so you'll need to follow these instructions to show the window.

To display the Properties window:

1. Click Tools | Properties Window.
2. The Properties window will appear on the right side of the Report Designer.
3. Click an object on the report template.
4. The properties for that object will appear in the Properties window.

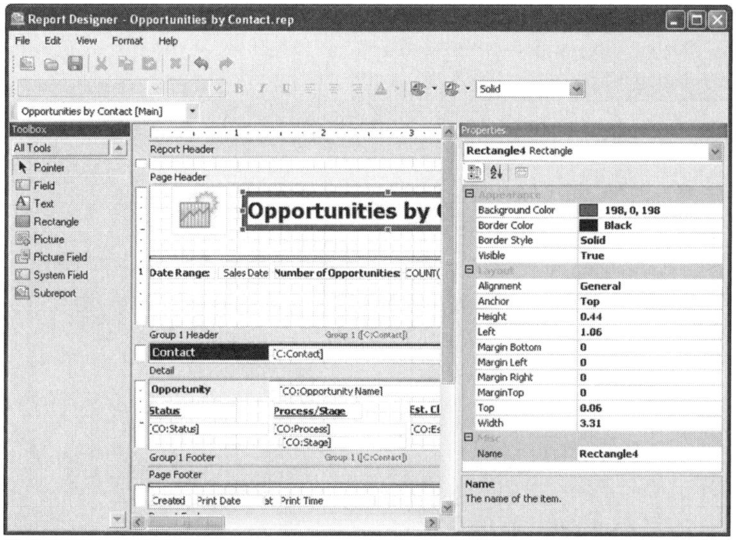

Using the Properties window to change object attributes

Screen resolution

While working in the Report Designer, it might be a good idea to bump up your screen resolution to at least 1024 × 768. When the Toolbox and the Properties window are both displayed, the actual workspace in the Report Designer is minimal in any resolution lower than 1024 × 768.

Testing Reports

Before saving a report, you'll want to test the report to ensure that it produces the right kind of information listing. You can test-run a report right from within the Report Designer.

Task A Testing a Report in the Report Designer

If you've made changes to an existing report, or if you'd like to see if a new report produces the kind of document you're after, you should run the report before saving it.

To test a report in the Report Designer:

1. Bring up the report you'd like to edit in the Report Designer.
2. Click File | Run.
3. The Define Filters dialog box will appear. Select all of the filter options for this report, if any, and click OK to run the report.

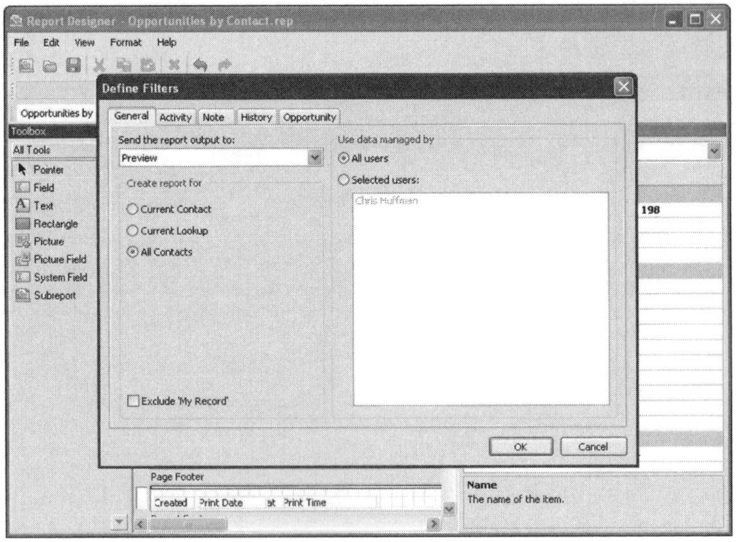

Running a report in the Report Designer

Chapter 18
Interface Customization

Menu and Toolbar Customization

ACT! allows complete customization of menus and toolbars. You can add new items—such as executable programs, templates, or internal ACT! commands—to the menus and toolbars. You can also remove items from the menus and toolbars. If you make any mistakes, don't worry—resetting the menus and toolbars back to the factory default is a snap!

Task A Creating a Custom Command

If you want to add a program, template, or other non-ACT! command to the menus or toolbars, you'll first need to create a custom command for the item.

To create a custom command:

1. Click Tools | Customize | Menus & Toolbars. The Customize Menus and Toolbars dialog box will appear.
2. Click the Custom Commands tab.
3. Click the New button.
4. In the Command name field, specify the name for your custom command.
5. In the Tooltip text field, type the text that you'd like to see appear when hovering the mouse over a toolbar button for this command.
6. Click the Browse button to select the program, document, or template that will be executed when the custom command is run.
7. Click the Add Command button to add the command to the list of custom commands.
8. Click Close to exit.

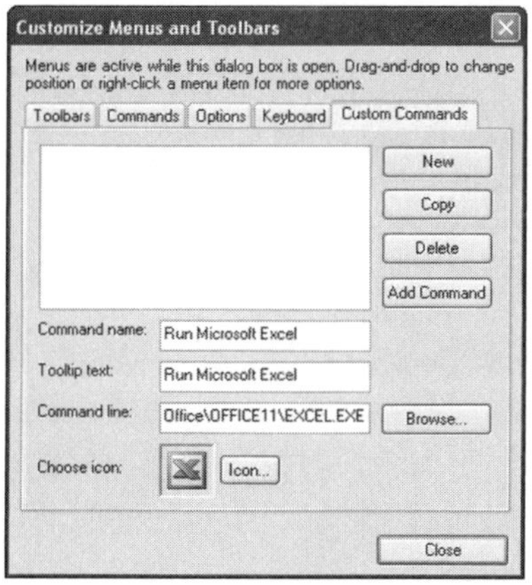

Creating a custom command

Macros

In previous versions of ACT!, you could create a macro and add it as a custom command to the toolbar. Macros were removed from ACT!'s feature set in Version 2005. You could use a program like Macro Magic to get the same sort of functionality.

Custom command icons

In the Custom Commands tab, click the Icon button to specify a icon for the command. In your favorite search engine, do a search for .ICO icon files to find libraries of icons that you can use for this purpose.

Showing different toolbars

In the Customize Menus and Toolbars dialog box, click the Toolbars button and check any toolbar that you'd like to view in the current ACT! view.

Task B Adding a Command to the Menus and Toolbars

Once you've created a custom command, you can add it to any of the ACT! menus or toolbars. You can also rearrange any of the existing menu and toolbar commands.

To add commands to the menus:

1. Click Tools | Customize | Menus & Toolbars. The Customize Menus and Toolbars dialog box will appear.
2. Click the Commands tab.
3. Select a category from the list on the left. (If you're trying to add a custom command, select the Custom Command option.) On the right, a list of commands associated with the category you selected will appear.
4. Click a command and drag it to a location on the menus or toolbars.
5. Click Close to save your changes.

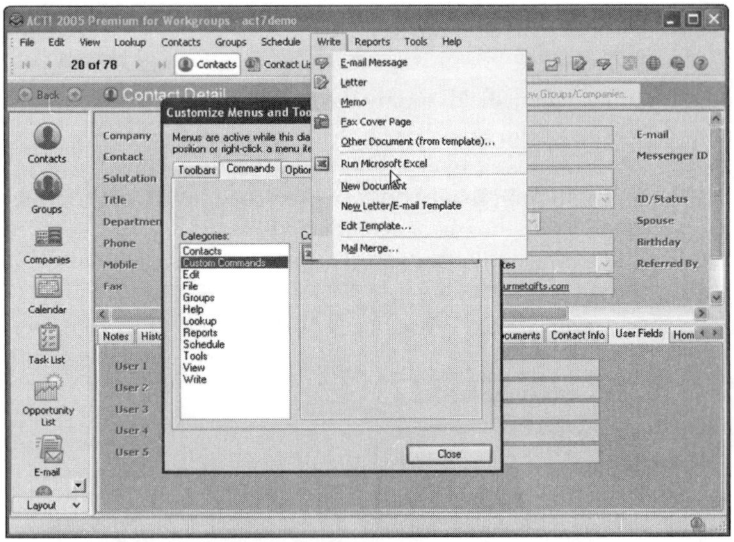

Dragging a custom command onto the Write menu

Task C Creating a Custom Keyboard Shortcut

ACT! ships with a number of keyboard shortcuts for commonly-used functions. You can redefine any existing keyboard shortcut, or you can create your own new shortcuts to run functions or custom commands within ACT!.

To create a custom keyboard shortcut:

1. Click Tools | Customize | Menus & Toolbars. The Customize Menus and Toolbars dialog box will appear.
2. Click the Keyboard tab.
3. From the list on the left, highlight a category. A list of commands in the category will appear on the right. If the command already has a keyboard shortcut assigned, it will appear to the right of the command name.
4. Highlight a command and click the Assign Shortcut button.
5. Press a shortcut key combination.
6. Click OK.
7. Repeat this process until all of your new keyboard shortcuts have been assigned.
8. Click Close to save your changes.

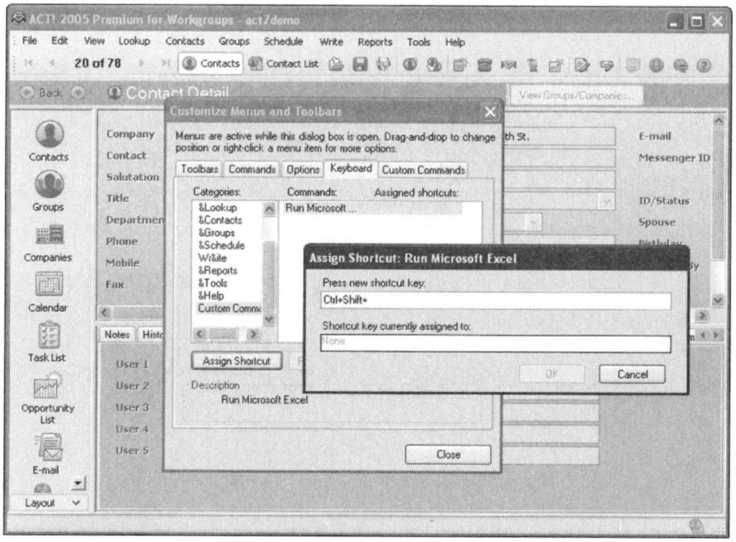

Assigning a shortcut to a custom command

Reset to undo mistakes

If you make mistakes in the keyboard shortcut area, just click the Reset button in the Keyboard tab of the Customize Menus and Toolbars dialog box. This will reset your keyboard shortcuts to the default settings.

Task D Resetting Menus and Toolbars

Customizing the menus and toolbars can be lots of fun, but if you go overboard and make unnecessary changes, you might want to reset the menus and toolbars back to the default settings. You can do this with a single click, but be aware that this process will reset all of the changes you've made. You won't be able to pick and choose which settings should be reset.

Add-on products

If you've installed ACT! add-on products that have modified the menus or toolbars, you may need to reinstall them after resetting the menus and toolbars. For a comprehensive list of add-on products, point your Web browser to http://www.actaddons.com or http://www.actsolutions.com.

To reset the menus and toolbars:

1. Click Tools | Customize | Reset Menus & Toolbars.
2. A confirmation screen will appear. If you want to reset the menus and toolbars, click OK.
3. All menu and toolbar customization (except custom commands) will be reset to the default settings.

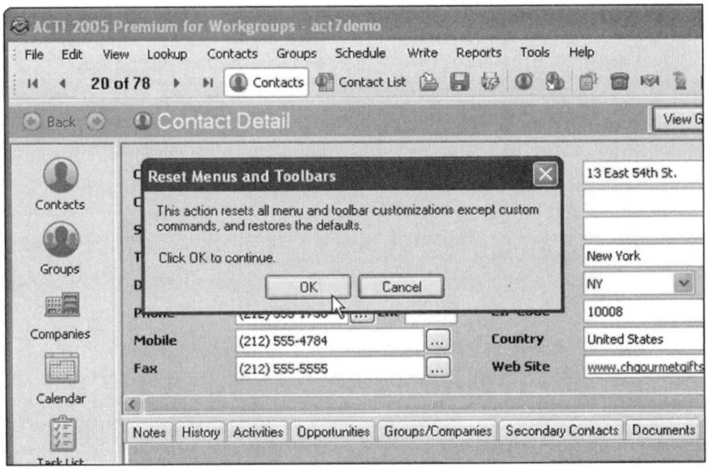

Resetting menus and toolbars

Navigation Bar Customization

On the left side of the ACT! interface, the navigation bar lets you easily switch between ACT!'s views. In previous versions of ACT!, this navigation bar didn't have as many customization options. So many new views—such as the Companies view and Company List view—have been added to ACT! 2005 that they've included a mechanism for changing the size, placement, and order of the icons on the navigation bar.

Task A Changing Navigation Bar Options

Right-clicking anywhere on the navigation bar will bring up a list of options for how the navigation bar displays its icons. You can choose to show small or large icons, to show different sets of icons, or to customize the specific icons that appear on the navigation bar.

To change the navigation bar options:

1. Right-click anywhere in the left navigation bar.
2. Select to show either small or large icons.
3. Select to show the standard, expanded, or classic menu. The standard menu is the default for ACT! 2005. The expanded menu shows most icons. The classic menu looks more like the navigation bar menus in previous versions of ACT!.

Selecting to show the classic menu

Reset the navigation bar

If you make changes to the navigation bar that you'd like to undo, right-click anywhere in the navigation bar and select the Customize option. Then, click the Reset button.

Task B Customizing Navigation Bar Icons

If the standard, classic, or expanded navigation bar menus don't fit your specific need, you can customize the navigation bar to show just the icons you need in the order you specify.

To customize the navigation bar icons:

1. Right-click anywhere in the navigation bar and select to show either the standard, expanded, or classic menu. (This lets you select which menu scheme to customize.)
2. Right-click anywhere in the navigation bar again and select the Customize button.
3. A dialog box appears, showing the list of available commands. Drag any command to a spot on the navigation bar.
4. To change the order of icons on the navigation bar, click an icon and drag it to a new spot.
5. To remove an icon from the navigation bar, click and drag the icon into the list of available icons in the Customize dialog box.
6. Click Close to save your changes.

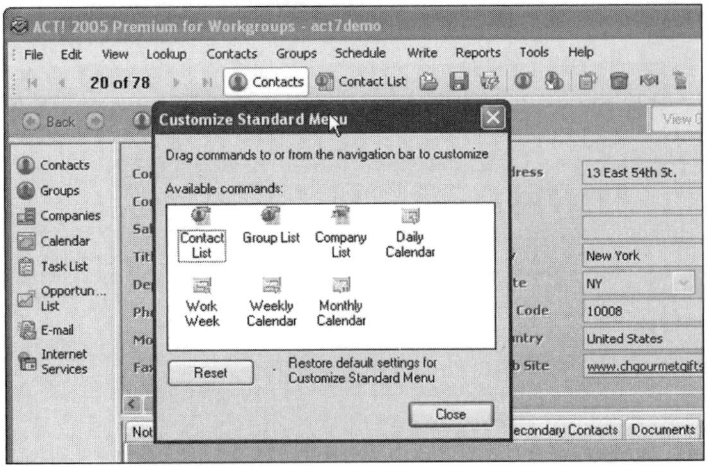

Customizing the navigation bar icons

Standard navigation bar

The standard navigation bar shows only the essential views. You'll see a Companies view, but you won't see a Company List view. You'll see a Contacts view, but you won't see a Contact List view. You'll see a Calendar view, but you won't see any of the specific calendar views.

When you go into the Company view, you'll see the option to launch the Company List view in the top toolbar. When you go into the Calendar view, you'll see the option to launch the Daily, Work Week, Weekly, and Monthly Calendar views in the top toolbar.

Chapter 19
Database Maintenance and Administrator Tools

Back Up and Restore

This lesson is by far the most important one included in this book. You should always back up your database regularly, and how often you decide to back up should depend on how much data you can afford to lose. If you can afford to lose a week's worth of data, you should back up weekly. If you can afford to lose only a day's worth of data, you should back up daily. If you can afford to lose a year's worth of data, then by all means, only back up your database once a year.

Task A Backing Up Your Database and Supplemental Files

The built-in backup process included with ACT! 2005 will make a compressed .zip backup of your database and all of the database supplemental files. Unlike previous versions of ACT!, you can't restore ACT! 2005 backup .zip files with WinZip. You'll have to restore them using the ACT! Restore feature.

To back up your database and supplemental files:

1. Click File | Backup | Database.
2. Click the Browse button to specify a filename and location or the compressed backup file.
3. If you want to password-protect the backup file, check the Password protect file option.
4. Click OK. ACT! will create the backup file.
5. Move the backup file to an offsite secure location if possible.

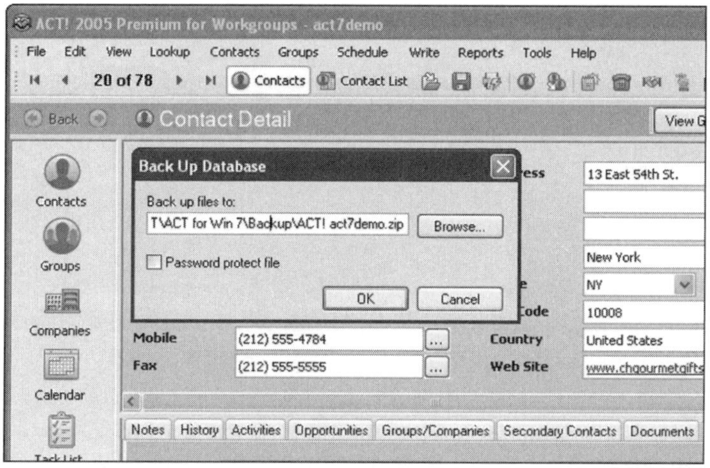

Backing up a database

Keep an offsite backup

If all of your backup files are stored on a single computer, what will you do if the computer's hard drive crashes? Copy your backups onto a CD and keep them in a media fireproof safe. Alternatively, you could use one of the many online backup services to keep offsite copies of your database and backup files.

Back up personal files

Click File | Backup | Personal File to make a backup of the ACT! personal supplemental files. These files include documents, internet links, and custom dictionaries. Other files—such as layouts, templates, reports, queries, and document tab attachments—are kept in the database supplemental files system and are included in the database backup.

Task B Restoring a Backup

If you have a backup of an ACT! 2005 database, you can restore it onto any computer with ACT! 2005 installed. When you restore a backup file, the database files and the supplemental files (reports, layouts, queries, and so on) are all restored.

To restore a backup:

1. Click File | Restore | Database.
2. Select the type of database restoration you'd like to complete. If in doubt, choose the Restore as option. (See the tip for a description of the options.)
3. Click OK.
4. Click Browse and select the backup file you'd like to restore.
5. Click OK.
6. If prompted, specify the name, location, username, and password for the database you'd like to restore.
7. Click OK. ACT! will restore the backup file.

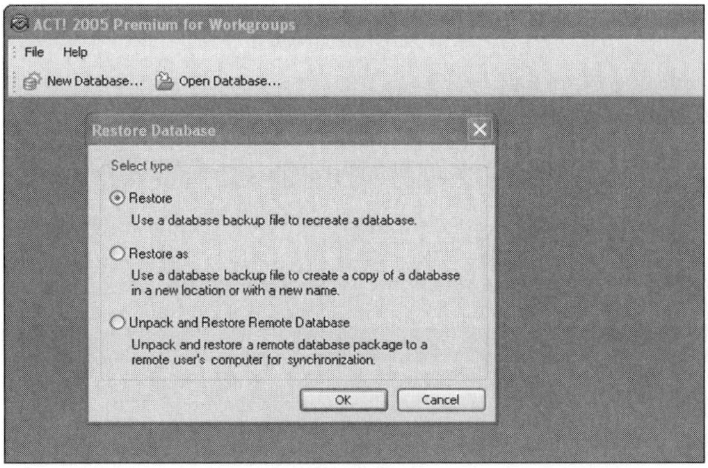

Restoring a database

Restore options

- **Restore.** Use this option if you are restoring a backup of a database that exists on the current computer.
- **Restore as.** Use this option if you're restoring a backup of a database onto a new computer or with a new name on the same computer.
- **Unpack and Restore Remote Database.** Use this option to restore a remote synchronizing database.

Fixing Database Corruption

If you're experiencing problems with an ACT! database, you might want to run the Check and Repair feature on it. This new feature in ACT! 2005 will analyze the most commonly corrupted areas of your database for problems. It can also rebuild the index files for the database, which will make your database perform better.

Task A Checking and Repairing the Database

The Check and Repair feature performs two functions. It will check the database for errors, and it will reorganize the index files to give you optimal database performance. Before starting this task, make sure you have a recent backup of your database.

To check and repair a database:

1. Click Tools | Database Maintenance | Check and Repair.
2. Select whether or not to perform an integrity check or a reindex.
3. Click OK. ACT! will check and repair the database.

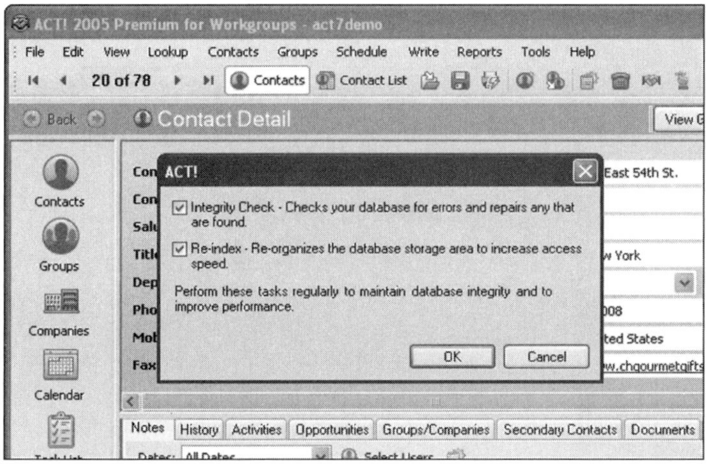

Checking a database for errors

Severe corruption

If you suspect that your database is severely damaged, you might need to contact an ACT! Certified Consultant. For a list of local ACT! CCs, go to http://www.act.com/acc.

Removing Old Data

Removing old data from an ACT! database will permanently delete the data. If you do not want to delete any data from your ACT! database, then cleaning up old data should not be part of your routine maintenance schedule. However, if you do not want to see old data in your database—or if your database has become too large—you may find the Remove Old Data option quite useful.

Task A Removing Old Data

Removing old data from the database will remove from the database specific types of data that are older than a specified number of days. Make a backup of your database before trying this.

Types of data

The following types of old data can be removed using this feature: notes, histories, cleared activities, closed opportunities, open/inactive opportunities, and document tab entries.

To remove old data:

1. Click Tools | Database Maintenance | Remove Old Data.
2. Select the types of data you'd like to remove.
3. For each checked item, specify a number of days. ACT! will remove all data older than this number of days. For example, if you wanted to get rid of everything more than a month old, you would specify 31 days.
4. Click OK.

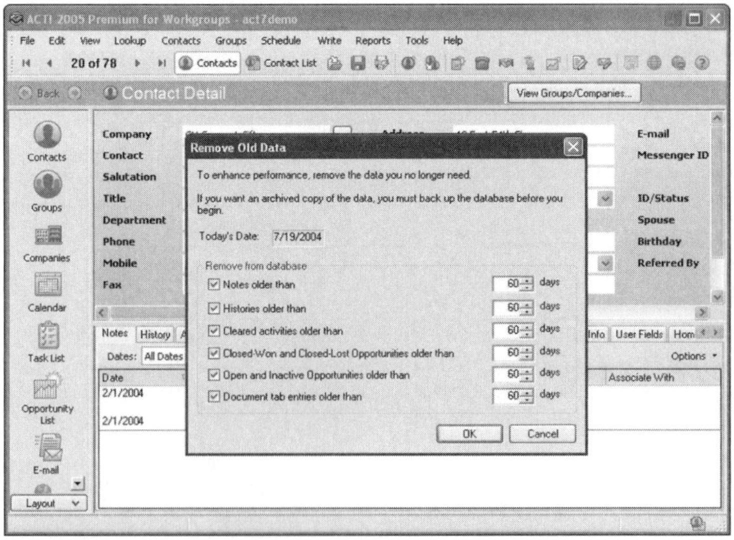

Removing old data from a database

Using the ACT! Diagnostic Tool

Hidden among ACT!'s program files, the ACT! 2005 Diagnostic Tool (ACTDIAG) is one of ACT!'s best-kept secrets. ACTDIAG has shipped with every copy of ACT! since Version 3.0. The new ACT! Diagnostic Tool for ACT! 2005 has a number of tools to help manage the SQL instance of ACT!.

Task A Viewing Server Information

One of the great things about the ACT! 2005 Diagnostic Tool is its server diagnostic tools. With ACTDIAG 2005, you can view information about the SQL server, network settings, and error logs.

To view server information with ACTDIAG:

1. Launch ACTDIAG. To do so, double-click the actdiag.exe file in the ACT! 2005 installation folder. On most computers, this is c:\program files\act\act for win 7\.
2. On the left menu, click the Server button. The server options will appear.
3. In the Server Information area, you can view basic server information, such as the server name, SQL build, and SQL edition.
4. In the Error Logs area, you can view error logs created by the ACT! instance of SQL.

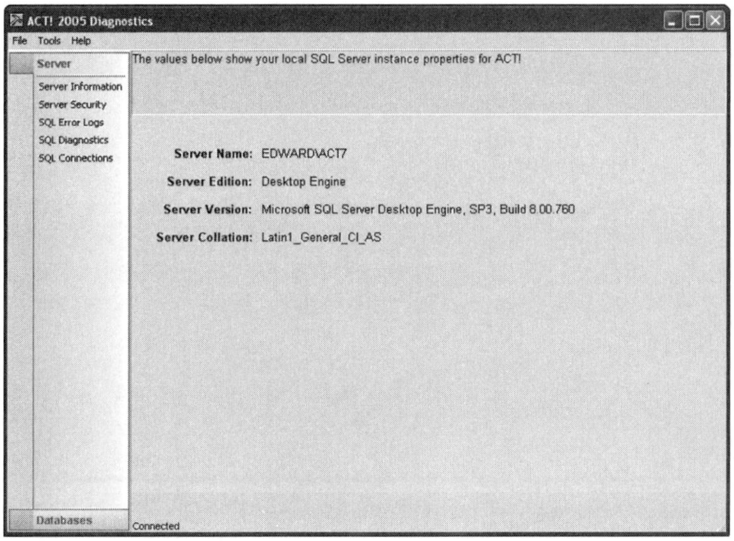

Viewing basic server information in the ACT! Diagnostic Tool

Task B Viewing Database Audit Logs

New in the ACT! 2005 Diagnostic Tool is the ability to view audit logs for the database. These audit logs will let you know when administrative tasks—such as synchronization, backup, restore, and database maintenance—have been performed on your database.

What is audited?

Database checkup, backup, restore, reindex, lock, unlock, pending purge, delete orphan data, event log purge, purge attachments, sync definition, sync database, sync logs purge, database configuration settings modified, and combine contacts.

To view the database audit logs:

1. Launch ACTDIAG. To do so, double-click the actdiag.exe file in the ACT! 2005 installation folder. On most computers, this is c:\program files\act\act for win 7\.
2. On the left menu, click the Databases button. The database options will appear.
3. Click the Audit Logs option.
4. From the Database drop-down, select the database whose audit logs you'd like to view.
5. From the Event Types drop-down, select the type of maintenance feature you'd like to audit. (See the tip for a list of features that are audited.) ACT! will show each time the maintenance was performed, who performed it, and when it was performed.

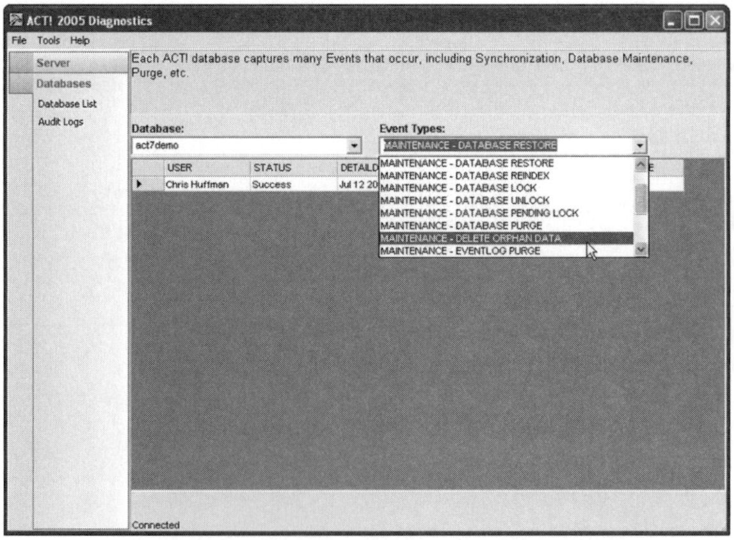

Viewing database audit logs

Task C Deleting a Database

Because ACT! databases now use a Microsoft SQL backend, deleting them is a bit more complicated than merely deleting the database files. You can use the ACT! Diagnostic Tool to delete any ACT! database and properly unregister it with the SQL Server. This feature is similar to the Tools | Database Maintenance | Delete database feature built into ACT!, but the ACTDIAG Delete feature allows you to delete a database that is not currently open.

To delete a database:

1. Launch ACTDIAG. To do so, double-click the actdiag.exe file in the ACT! 2005 installation folder. On most computers, this is c:\program files\act\act for win 7\.
2. On the left menu, click the Databases button. The database options will appear.
3. Click the Database List option.
4. Right-click the database you'd like to delete and click the Delete option. ACT! will properly delete the database. The database supplemental files will not be deleted.

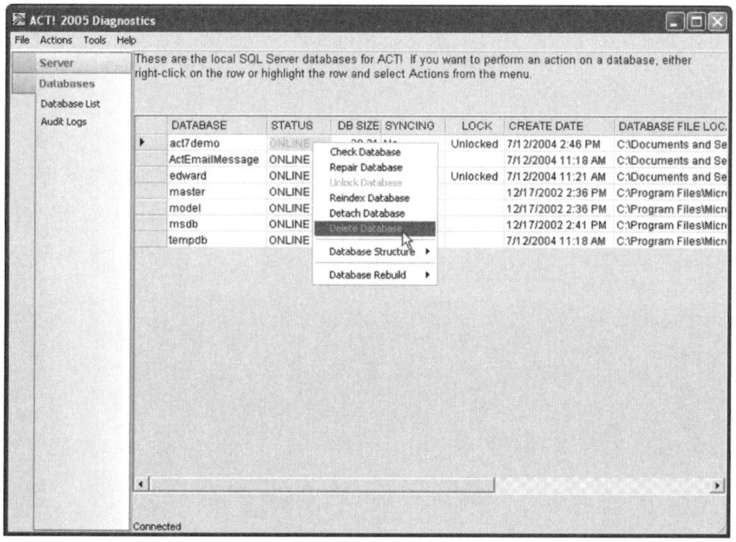

Deleting a database

Be careful!

Unless you really know what you're doing, you shouldn't try to delete an ACT! database. Even if you are an experienced database administrator, it's a good idea to make a backup of everything before you delete a database.

Chapter 20
Database Creation and Design

Database Creation

Your computer can house a virtually unlimited number of ACT! databases. Creating a new database is easy and entails the steps outlined in this lesson. As a general rule of thumb, you should create the database on your server. If you're only going to access the database from your computer, then you should create the database on your local workstation.

Task A Creating a Local Database

When you create an ACT! 2005 database, a number of files are created. The actual SQL database consists of an ADB and ADF file. ACT! also creates a .PAD file, which is a pointer to the ACT! database. Each ACT! database also has a series of database supplemental files.

To create a local database:

1. Open ACT! on the local computer (or the server) and click File | New Database.
2. The New Database dialog box will appear. Specify a name for the new database.
3. Click the Browse button to specify the folder where you'd like ACT! to house the database and supplemental files.
4. Specify a username and password for the database.
5. Click OK. ACT! will create the new database.

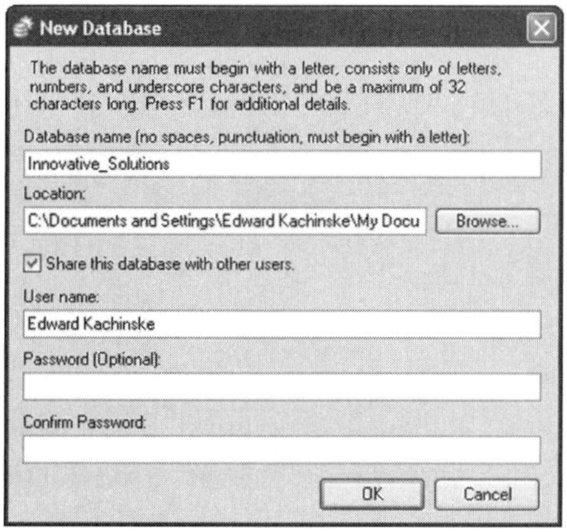

Creating a new database

Database supplemental files

When you create a new database, a series of supplemental file folders are created. These supplemental files include reports, templates, queries, layouts, and more.

Database names

The database name in ACT! 2005 is subject to SQL naming rules, so it cannot contain any spaces. Instead of using spaces in the database name, you might elect to use an underscore character.

Task B Sharing a Database

When you create a database on your local computer or network, you can elect to share the database with other users on your network. In previous versions of ACT!, you could simply open the .DBF file of the database from any network computer. However, in ACT! 2005, you must select to share the database from within the ACT! application.

To share a database with other network users:

1. Open the database you'd like to share.
2. Click Tools | Database Maintenance | Share Database.
3. Click OK to confirm that you'd like to share the database and supplemental files with other network users.
4. Locate the .PAD file for your database. It should be in the same folder as the main database files. Copy this file to a spot on your network that is accessible by other users. The .PAD (pointer to ACT! database) acts as a shortcut to direct ACT! to the SQL server housing the ACT! database.
5. From another workstation, open ACT! and click File | Open Database. Browse to the folder that houses the .PAD file and double-click it.

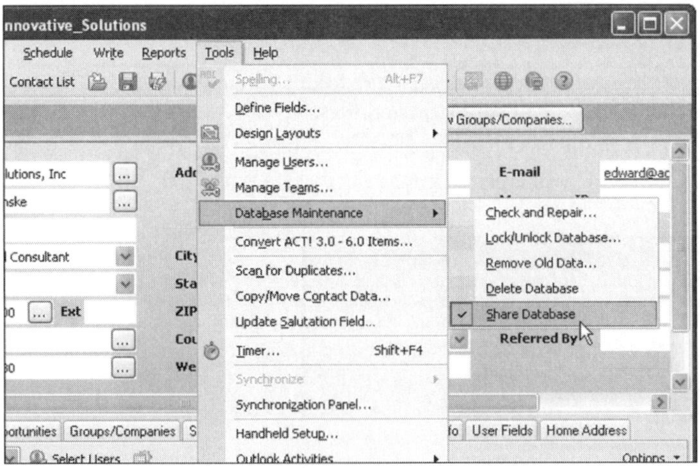

Sharing the database with other users on the network

Supplemental files security

The supplemental files folders will become shared folders when you follow the process outlined in this lesson. By default, everyone on the network will be given full control of these folders. All of the ACT! users will need full control access to these folders, but your system administrator may wish to restrict access to this set of folders just to those using the ACT! database.

Database folder

The folder that houses the actual ACT! database (the .ADF and .ADB files) does not need to be shared with other users. Only the .PAD file needs to be in a shared folder.

Task C Moving a Database

In previous versions of ACT!, you could move a database simply by copying the database files from one folder to another. In ACT! 2005, you should use the Backup and Restore feature. If you simply copy the database files, the database may not register properly with the SQL server.

To move a database:

1. Make a backup of the database. To do so, open the database and click File | Backup. The backup process will create a .ZIP backup file of the database and supplemental files. If you have a lot of data in your database, this file could be quite large—perhaps even too large to fit on a CD.
2. Copy the backup file to another computer.
3. Go to the computer where you will restore the database. Open ACT! and click File | Restore. Select the Restore As option and follow the instructions to restore the database to a different folder on the new computer.
4. Delete the original database. To do so, open it and click Tools | Database Maintenance | Delete Database.

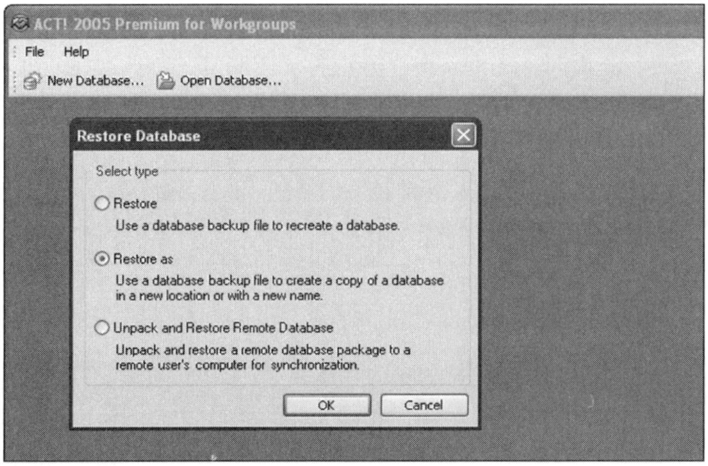

Restoring a database using the Restore as feature

Moving databases on the same computer

If you need to move the database to a different location on the same computer, simply copy the database and delete the original database. To make a copy of the database, click File | Save Copy As. Click Tools | Database Maintenance | Delete Database to delete the currently open database.

User Management

Each person accessing your database should be set up with his or her own username in ACT!. It's important to ensure that all of your users are logging in with a unique login username because each time an action is performed in the database—such as adding a note or recording a history of an event—the action is associated with a user account. Unlike in previous versions of ACT!, the number of named users allowed is restricted by your licensing serial number.

Task A Adding Users

You must have administrator access to your database to add, edit, or delete users. When adding a user to your database, you will be prompted to assign a My Record to the user. The My Record is the contact in ACT! that contains information about the user. Each user must have a My Record, and you should make sure that your users' My Records contain complete field information.

To add a user to the database:

1. Click Tools | Manage Users.
2. Click the Create New User option on the left.
3. The Create New User Wizard will appear. If the user already exists as a contact in your database, click the Create User from Contact option. If not, choose the Create New User option. Click Next.
4. If you chose to create the new user from a contact, you'll need to select the contact and click Next.
5. If you chose to create the new user from scratch, then enter the user's contact name, username, password, and security role. Click Next.
6. Specify whether or not the user can login to the database, sync with handheld devices, and access the framework. Click Next.
7. If needed, add the user to teams. Click Finish to add the user.

ACT! 2005 versus ACT! 2005 Premium for Workgroups

ACT! 2005 (the product sold in retail computer stores) has an MSDE (Microsoft SQL Desktop Edition) backend and is limited to ten named users. If you have more than ten users, you'll need to upgrade to ACT! 2005 Premium for Workgroups.

Locking the database

When you perform most administrative tasks in the database—such as defining users—ACT! will lock all users out of the database. You may need to schedule these tasks during off hours to avoid interrupting your users.

Task B Deleting Users

Whenever you delete an ACT! user, you will be required to either delete all of the information associated with the user or reassign it to another user. If you have former employees whose information you'd like to retain, you might consider deleting their login usernames and reassigning all of their information to a user called Former Employee. You might also opt to leave all of the former employees in your database and simply make their logins inactive. Either way, you'll need administrator access to the database to delete a user.

To delete a user:

1. Click Tools | Manage Users.
2. Highlight a user from the list.
3. Click the Delete User option on the left side of the Manage Users dialog box.
4. You'll be prompted to either delete the records managed by this user or reassign them to another user. (Be careful about doing this, and make sure you have a backup before proceeding!)

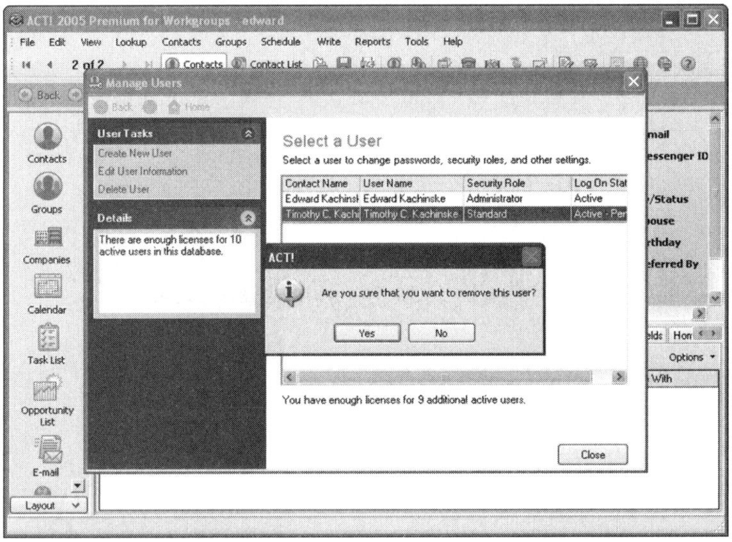

Deleting a user from the database

Warning!

If you delete a user in the database, ACT! will either

- delete all information (contacts, notes, histories, activities, and so on) associated with the user, or
- reassign all information associated with the user to another user in your database.

Be sure to back up before deleting any users. There's no easy Undo button for undoing the damage caused by a mistakenly deleted user.

No login prompt?

If you only have one active user in a database, ACT! will not prompt you for a username or password when opening the database. If you have two or more users, you will need to supply a valid username and password. You will also need to supply a username and password if your single login user has a password.

Forgot the password?

Cracking database passwords in previous versions of ACT! was fairly easy. Cracking an ACT! 2005 database password is nearly impossible. Best Software, the makers of ACT!, have trusted access to the SQL database and can open any ACT! database. For a fee, they'll remove the passwords from your database.

Task C Editing an Existing User

From time to time, you may need to edit an existing user's attributes—you may need to make one of your users an administrator, or you might want to disable someone's login rights. Editing an existing user's attributes is as simple as adding or deleting a user.

To edit an existing user:

1. Click Tools | Manage Users.
2. Highlight a user from the list and click the Edit User option on the left side of the Manage Users dialog box.
3. Edit the username, password, and security level. Click Next.
4. Select whether the user is active or not. Click Next.
5. Add the users to any teams. Click Finish to save your changes.

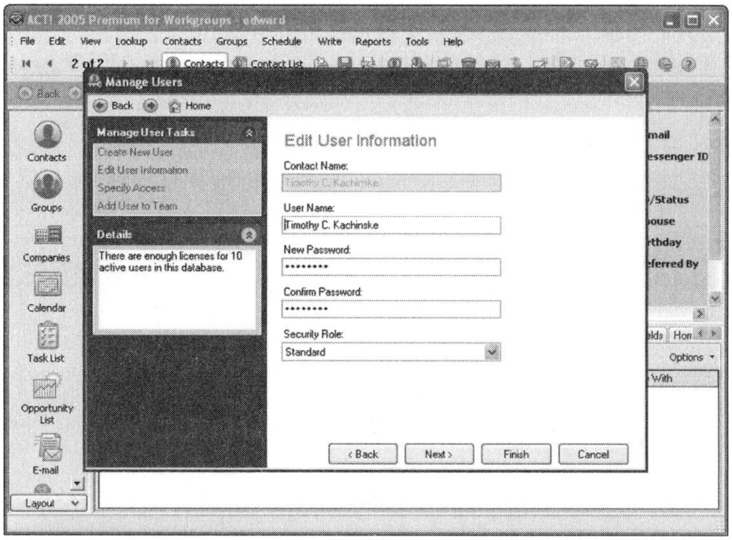

Editing user information

Field Customization

You have specific information you'll want to track in ACT!, and you can enter this information into customized fields. In this lesson, you'll practice adding fields to the database. You should back up your database before adding fields. If ACT! crashes while modifying the database schema, you could suffer an irreparable loss of data.

Task A Adding Fields to the Database

You can add a variety of character, numeric, date, phone, time, address, memo, picture, yes/no (checkmark), and currency fields to your database. You'll want to make sure your field structure closely matches your data to increase the quality of the data your users enter into ACT!.

To add a field to the database:

1. Click Tools | Define Fields.
2. Click the Create New Field option on the left side of the Define Fields dialog box.
3. Specify a field name, type, and behavior. Click Next.
4. If you are adding a character field, you will need to specify a default value, field format, and length. If you are adding a different field type, the options that appear will depend on the field type. Click Next.
5. Set the field triggers. Triggers are actions (programs, activity series, and templates) that are executed when you place the mouse in a field, when changing the field value, or when your cursor leaves a field.
6. Click Finish. The new field will be added to the database.

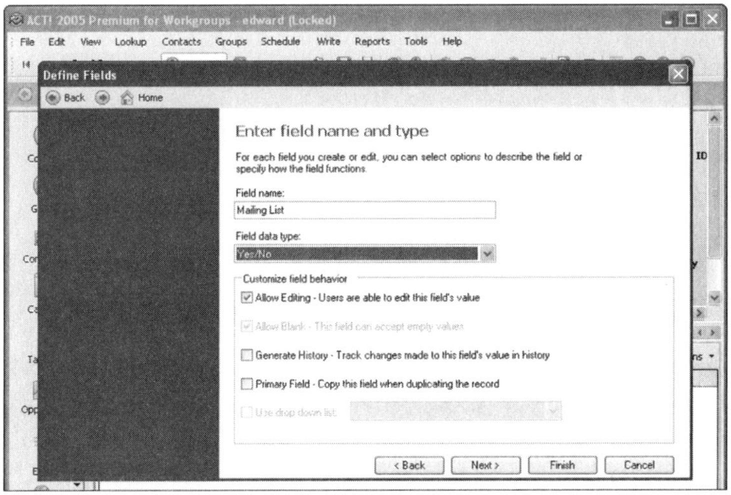

Adding a new field to the database

Locking the database

Adding fields to the database requires that you lock the database. If any users are logged into the database when you attempt to add a field, ACT! will prompt you to lock the database.

New field types in 2005

- Yes/No Fields (Checkmark)
- Memo Fields (Unlimited length character fields)
- Address Fields
- Picture Fields
- E-Mail
- Decimal

Task B Editing Field Attributes

Once you've added a field to the database, you can edit its attributes in the Define Fields dialog box. Be careful when editing field attributes—you could irreversibly modify your contact data. For example, if you reduce the number of characters a field will allow, some of your data could be cropped to the new length limit.

To edit a field's attributes:

1. Click Tools | Define Fields.
2. Highlight a field from the list.
3. Click the Edit List option on left side of the Define Fields dialog box.
4. Go through the rest of the Define Fields Wizard to edit the field's attributes.
5. Click Finish when you're done.

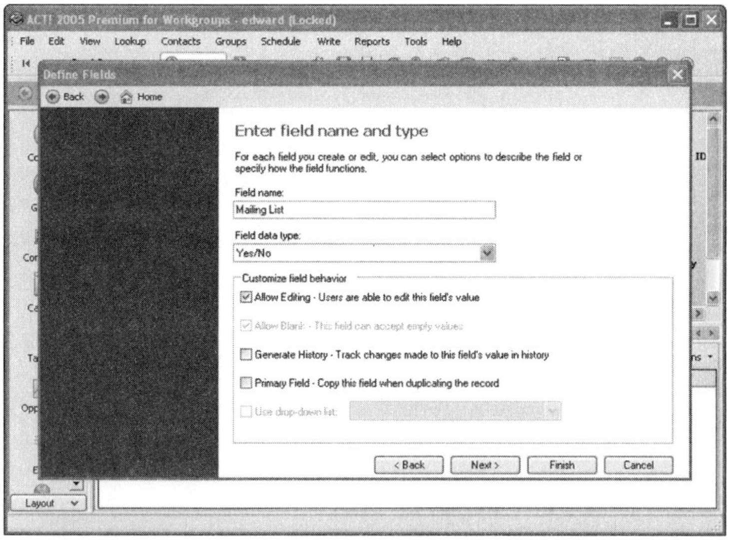

Editing an existing field

Activity series triggers

You can now set any field to launch an activity series when you change the value in the field. Just select the Activity Series option from the drop-down in the Set Triggers area of the Define Fields Wizard.

Forbidden modifications

Some field changes can't be made in ACT! 2005. Character fields, for example, cannot be converted to phone fields. Also, many of the system fields in the database, like the company field, cannot be deleted.

Task C Managing Drop-Downs

ACT! 2005 maintains a centralized list of drop-downs in the Define Fields area. If you need to add a drop-down to a field, you'll need to create the drop-down before adding or editing the field. Any drop-down can be linked to multiple fields.

To create a drop-down and add it to a field:

1. Click Tools | Define Fields.
2. On the left side of the Define Fields dialog box, click the Manage drop-down lists option. A list of all field drop-down lists in the database will appear.
3. On the left side of the Define Fields dialog box, click the Create drop-down list option.
4. Give the drop-down list a name, type, and description.
5. If you want non-administrator users to be able to edit drop-down items, then check the Allow users to edit items in this list option.
6. If you want the drop-down list items to be self -building, then check the Automatically add new items option. Click Next.
7. Click the Add button and add items to the drop-down list.
8. Click Finish.
9. Add a new field to the database or edit an existing field. In the first step of the Define Fields Wizard, you'll have the option to use a drop-down list for the field.

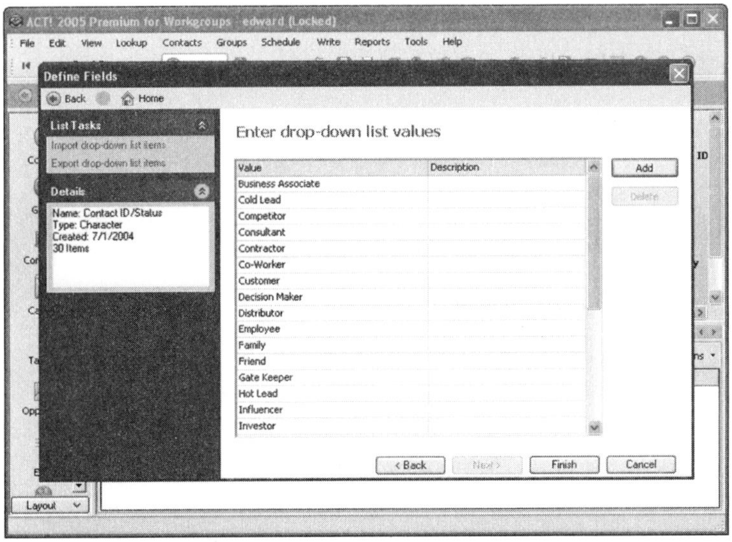

Adding values for a drop-down list

Multi-select drop-downs

If you want users to be able to select multiple values from the drop-down lists, then click the Allow Multi-select option when defining the field. You'll configure this setting when defining the field, not when you're defining the drop-down list.

Administrators only

Only users with administrator-level logins in ACT! can define fields.

Drop-down descriptions

The description of each drop-down item will appear for your reference in the drop-down if you select the Show Descriptions option. You might add descriptions to the items in your drop-down if each item in the drop-down was a product number or code and you needed a longer explanation of the product or code than would fit in your field.

Task D Deleting Fields from a Database

Deleting fields from a database is a permanent action. You can't undo a field deletion, so be sure to have a backup of your data before proceeding. Deleting a field will delete the field for all users, and the field will be deleted on any remote users' databases when they synchronize.

To delete fields from a database:

1. Click Tools | Define Fields.
2. Select a field from the list that appears.
3. Click the Delete field option on the left side of the Define Fields dialog box.
4. Click Yes to confirm the deletion.

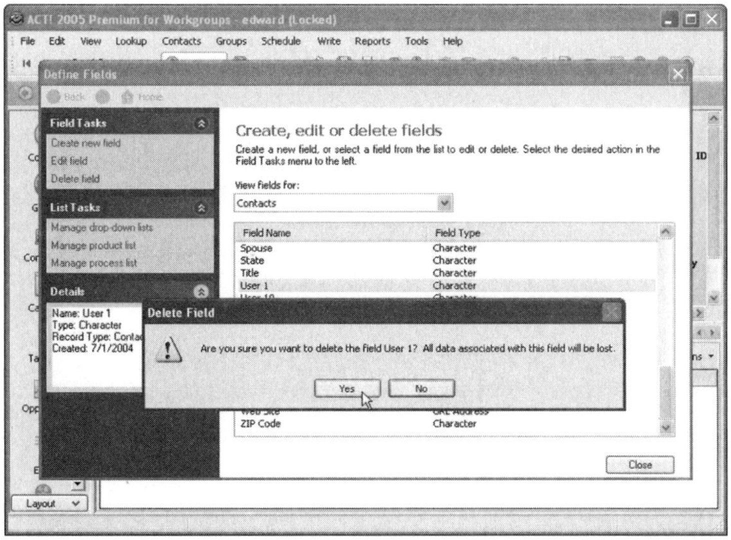

Deleting a field

System fields

None of the core ACT! contact fields can be deleted. These fields—such as Company, Contact, Address, and so on—are protected. If you no longer wish to use any of the core contact fields, you could remove them from your layout.

Layout Customization

The layout in ACT! is the file that determines the placement, the order, and other attributes of the fields you see in the Contact and Groups views. Whenever you add a contact, group, or company field to your database, you'll need to add it to the layout. There are three types of layouts: contact layouts, group layouts, and company layouts. The layouts are stored in the layout folder within the database supplemental files system.

Task A Opening the Layout Designer

ACT! ships with a number of pre-designed layouts. You can use these layouts, you can edit the layouts to meet your specific needs, or you can create your own layouts from scratch. If you're looking to edit a layout, you'll need to begin by opening the Layout Designer.

To open the Layout Designer:

1. Click Tools | Design Layouts.
2. Select to design contact, group, or company layouts.
3. The Layout Designer will appear. You can now add new fields to the layout, remove existing fields from view, or change the general look and feel of the layout.

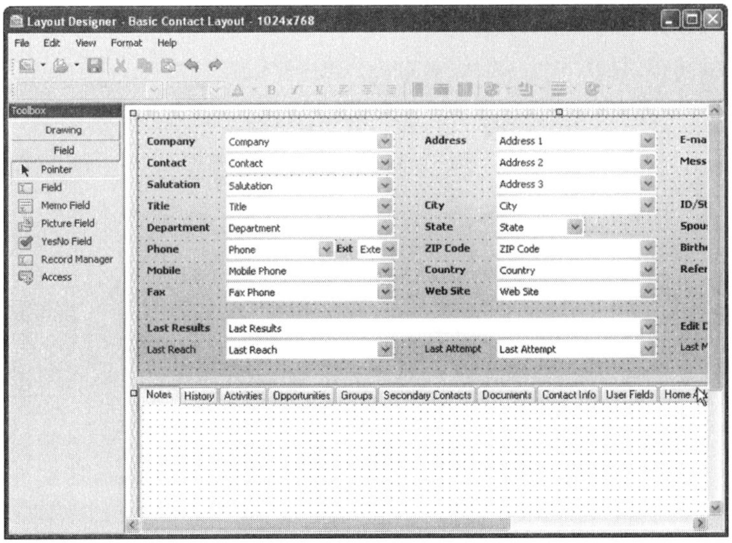

Designing a layout

Administrators and managers only

Only administrators and managers can create or edit layouts.

Layout file extensions

- Contact layouts: .CLY files
- Group layouts: .GLY files
- Company layouts: .ALY files

Task B Adding Fields to a Layout

After you've added fields to your database, you can add them to your contact, group, or company layout. To add a new field, you'll need to be in the Layout Designer, and you'll need to have the Toolbox showing. If the Toolbox does not display on the left side of the Layout Designer, click View | Toolbox.

To add fields to a layout:

1. In the Layout Designer, select the Field option on the Toolbox. (The Toolbox should display on the left side of the Layout Designer. Click View | Toolbox to show it.)
2. In the Field section of the Toolbox, select the type of field you'd like to add to the layout.
3. Using the mouse, draw a rectangle in the area on the layout where you'd like the field to display.
4. The Select Field dialog box will appear. This dialog box shows all of the fields that are currently in the database but have not yet been added to the layout. (You can't add a single field to multiple spots on the layout.)
5. Highlight a field from the list and click the Add button.
6. Repeat the process until all of your fields have been added. Click Close to return to the Layout Designer.

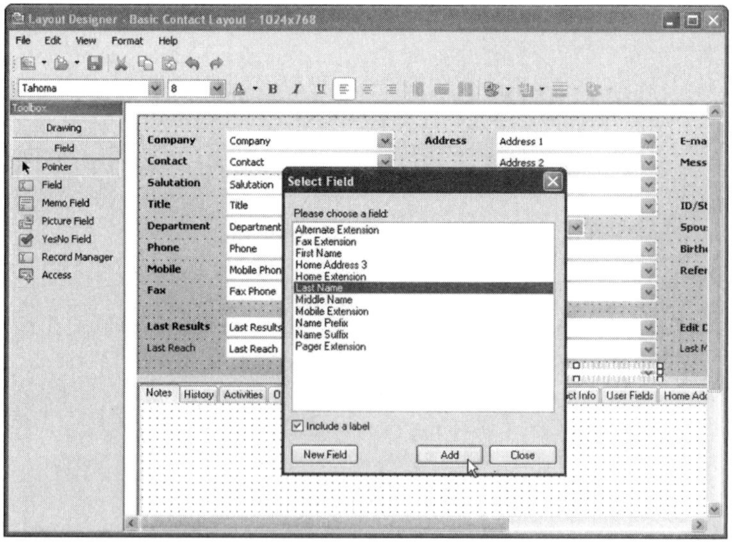

Adding a field to a layout

Add new fields

New in ACT! 2005, you can now add a field within the Layout Editor. If, halfway through designing a layout, you realize that you need to add an extra field or two, follow the process to add the field to the layout. Instead of selecting an existing field, click the New Field button to launch the Define Fields dialog box.

Multiple fields

You can add multiple fields to your layout at once. Hold down the Ctrl key and select multiple fields from the list in the Fields dialog box. When you click the Add button, all highlighted fields will be added to the layout.

Task C Managing Tabs

In the Layout Designer, you can control the order and behavior of the tabs in the lower pane of these views. Now in ACT! 2005, you can hide system tabs—such as the Opportunities tab—and you can add as many fields as will fit on your monitor.

To manage tabs in the Layout Designer:

1. Click Edit | Tabs.
2. To add a tab to the layout, click the Add Tab button.
3. To hide a tab, highlight the tab and click the < button to add it to the list of hidden tabs.
4. To change the order of a tab, highlight the tab and click the Move Up or Move Down buttons.
5. Click OK to save your changes.

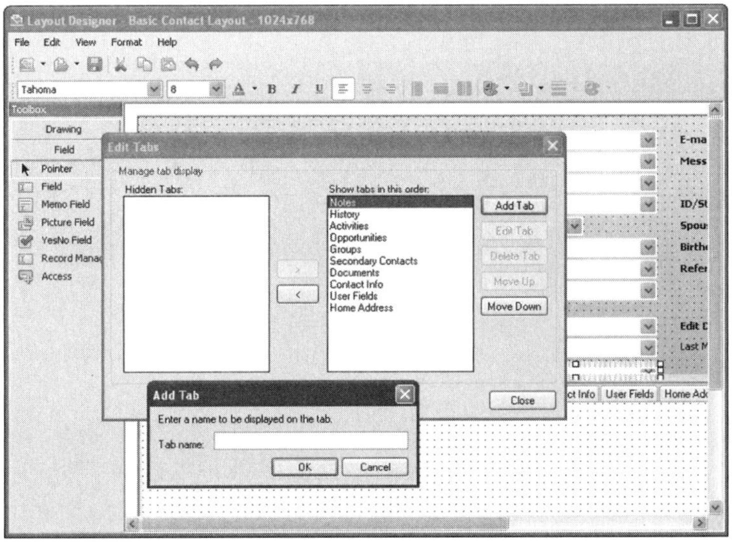

Adding a new field tab

Change the font on the tabs

You can now change the font properties for the text that displays on the tabs. Click View | Properties Window to display the Properties window. From the drop-down at the top of the Properties window, select the Tabs (Tab Control) option. In the area below the drop-down, change the font properties.

Background color

You can use the Properties window to control the background color. Just open the Properties window and click somewhere on the background to bring up the background properties.

Task D Adding Objects to a Layout

As you design a customized layout, you'll find that adding objects may give you more flexibility to organize your layout and make it look good. Using the buttons on the Toolbox, you can add text objects, shapes, images, and more to any layout. Click View | Toolbox to display the Toolbox if it is not already showing on the left side of the Layout Designer.

Properties window

The Properties window, a new feature in ACT! 2005, will show all of the attributes for any object on the layout—including shapes, fields, text boxes, and images. Click View | Properties Window to display the Properties window.

To add a shape to the layout:

1. In the Drawing section of the Toolbox, click either the Rectangle or Ellipse button.
2. Draw the object anywhere on the layout.

To add a text box to the layout:

1. In the Drawing section of the Toolbox, click the Text button.
2. Draw a text area somewhere on the layout and begin typing.

To add an image to the layout:

1. In the Drawing section of the Toolbox, click the Image button.
2. Draw a rectangle on the layout to indicate where you'd like to add the image.
3. Browse to select a graphic file to insert.

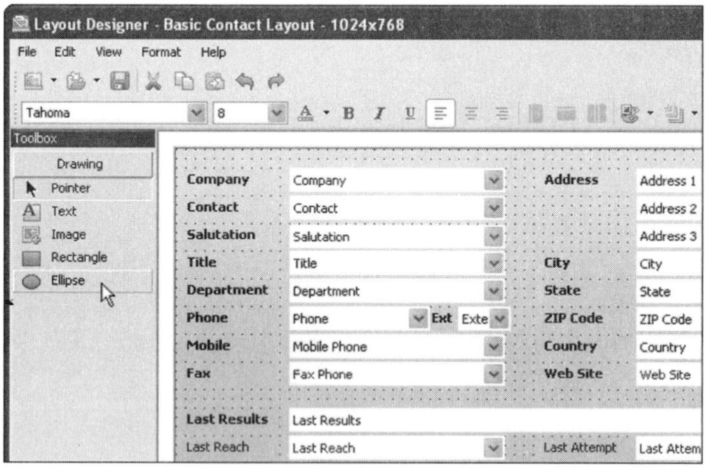

Using the Ellipse tool to draw a shape on the layout

Task E Setting Field Entry Order

In the Contacts, Groups, or Companies views, you can press the Tab key to move from one field to another. If you add fields to the database, or if you're reorganizing the existing fields, you may need to reset the field entry order. The field entry settings are kept in the layout.

To set the field entry order:

1. In the Layout Designer, click View | Tab Stops | Show Tab Stops. A small red box will appear to the right of each field.
2. Click View | Tab Stops | Clear. The small red boxes will disappear.
3. Click once on each field. As you click each field, the small red box will appear for that field. Inside this small red box will be the field entry order number for the field.
4. When you're finished, click View | Tab Stops | Show Tab Stops to return to the Layout Designer.

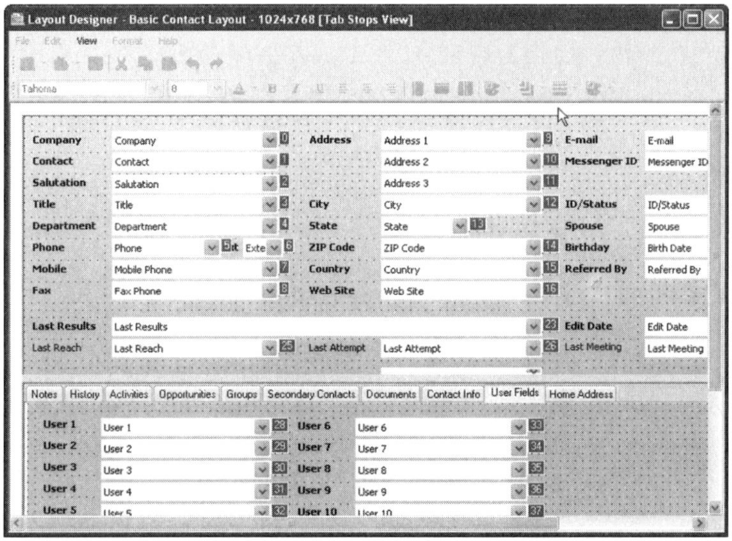

Setting field entry order

Enter Stops

The Tab Stops determine the order that ACT! will cycle through fields as you click the Tab key. The Enter Stops do the same, but they determine the field that ACT! will jump to when pressing the Enter key. Click View | Enter Stops | Show Enter Stops to view your enter stops. It's probably a good idea to put an Enter Stop on the most important fields.

Setting Preferences

Many of the user-specific settings in ACT! are consolidated in the Preferences dialog box. All of the preferences described in this section are specific to an individual workstation, and each user can have his or her own different preferences.

Task A Setting General Preferences

The General tab of the Preferences dialog box is where you'll set preferences for ACT!'s quoting, file location, name, and duplicate checking preferences. In previous versions of ACT!, you could set the location of many ancillary files that are now included in the database supplemental files system. Many of these folders—such as the templates, queries, and reports folders—are now controlled by the database supplemental files system.

To set ACT!'s general preferences:

1. Click Tools | Preferences.
2. Click the Quote Preferences button to set ACT!'s quote numbering preferences.
3. Click the File type drop-down to select a file type and click the Browse button to select ACT!'s default database folder for that file type.
4. Click the Name Preferences button to select the name prefix and suffix options.
5. Click the Salutation Preferences button to specify the format of the default value that is filled into the salutation field when entering a contact on your computer.
6. Click the Duplicate Checking button to enable or disable duplicate checking. In this area, you can also specify up to three fields that ACT! will use to identify duplicates.

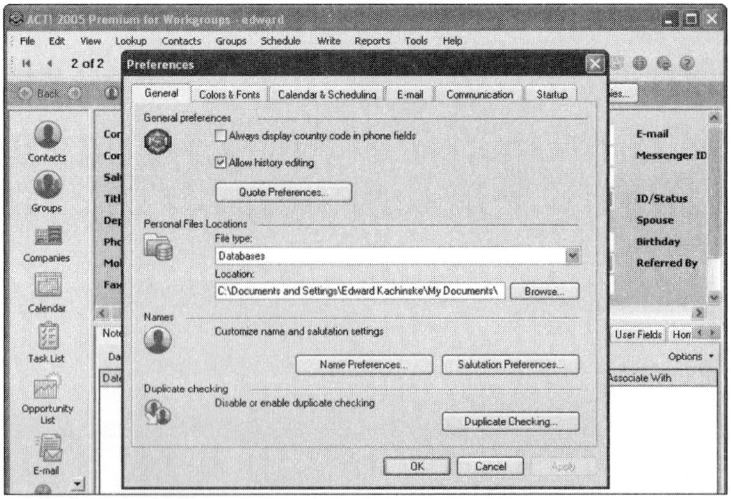

Setting general preferences

Disable duplicate checking

Before performing an import, it might be a good idea to check the duplicate checking preferences on your machine. If duplicate checking is enabled, then ACT! will check each incoming contact; if the contact already exists in the database, then ACT! will merge the incoming contact with the existing contact.

Task B Setting Color and Font Preferences

You can customize the look and feel of many parts of ACT!'s user interface by changing the color and font preferences. You should review this section if you have trouble seeing the small print in the list views, or if you are looking to change the screen fonts or background colors in any parts of the ACT! interface.

To set color and font preferences:

1. Click Tools | Preferences. The Preferences dialog box will appear.
2. Click the Colors & Fonts tab.
3. In the white block on the left side of the Colors & Fonts tab, select the part of the ACT! interface you'd like to customize.
4. On the right side of the Colors & Fonts tab, you'll be able to change the default font, color, and background color for the tab or view you selected in Step 3.
5. If you'd like to show grid lines in any of the list views or tabs, select the tab or view and click the Show grid lines option.

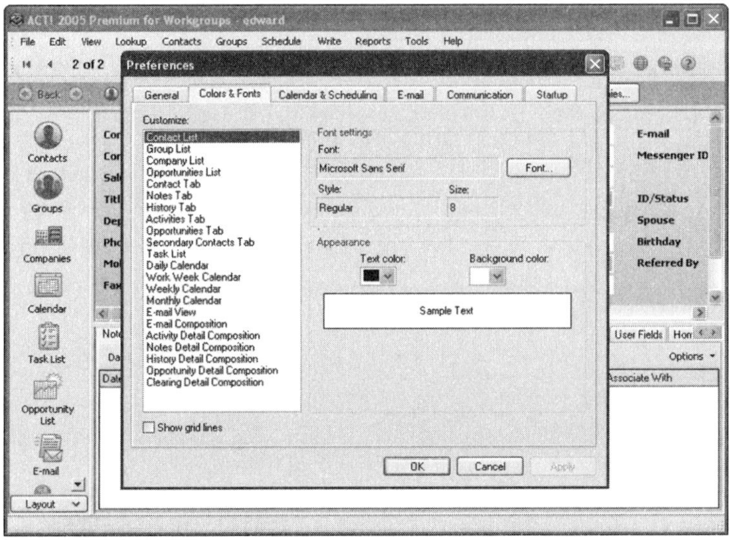

Setting color and font preferences

Machine-specific preferences

All color and font preferences are specific to your machine. If you change the font attributes for any part of the ACT! interface, those changes will not appear on anyone else's machine in a multi-user environment.

Calendar preferences

- Default calendar work days
- Default calendar increments
- First day of the week and week of the year
- Calendar display options
- Calendar popup options

Scheduling preferences

- Default priority, alarm lead time, and duration for each activity type
- Auto drop-down options for activities
- Alarm sound
- Cleared activity settings
- Activity creation settings

Task C Setting Calendar and Scheduling Preferences

In the calendar preferences, you'll be able to set default preferences that affect the look and feel of your ACT! calendar views. You can set the week's start date, default calendar increments, what actually shows on your ACT! calendar, and other preferences. You can set defaults for each activity type, and you can set some general activity settings—like whether you'd like cleared activities to show with a strikeout or with a gray font color.

To set calendar and scheduling preferences:

1. Click Tools | Preferences. The Preferences dialog box will appear.
2. Click the Calendar & Scheduling tab.
3. Click the Calendar Preferences button to configure the default settings for your calendar.
4. Click the Scheduling Preferences button to configure the default settings for activities scheduled on your calendar.

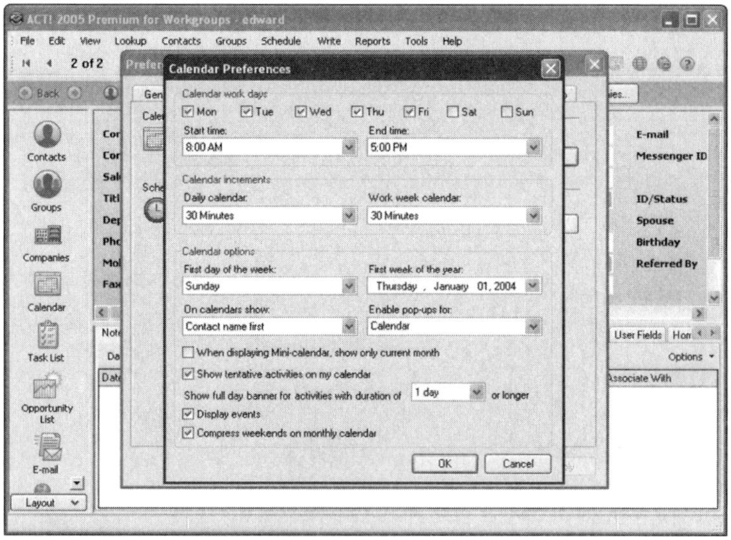

Setting calendar preferences

Task D Setting Communication Preferences

ACT!'s Word Processor, faxing, spelling, and Quick Print preferences have been consolidated into one tab in ACT! 2005. For most users, the most important settings in the Communication tab will be the Word Processor settings. ACT! supports Microsoft Word and the built-in ACT! Word Processor.

To set communication preferences:

1. Click Tools | Preferences. The Preferences dialog box will appear.
2. Click the Communication tab.
3. In the Word Processor drop-down, select to use either the ACT! Word Processor or Microsoft Word as the default word processor.
4. In the Fax software drop-down, select your default fax program. (See the margin tip.)
5. Click the Spelling Preferences button to specify ACT!'s spell check behavior.
6. Click the Quick Print Preferences button to specify font, header, and footer settings for the company, group, opportunity, contact, notes, history, and activity Quick Print features.

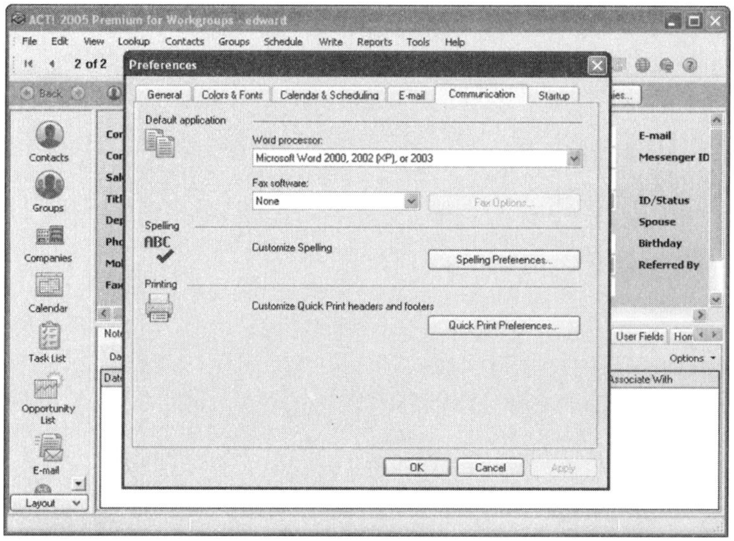

Setting communication preferences

Enable faxing

To enable ACT!'s WinFax integration, you will need to buy an add-on product from ASDS Computer. Visit http://www.asdscomputer.com for pricing and ordering information. Without this add-on product, the faxing options in the Communication tab will be disabled.

Supported Word versions

- Word 2000
- Word 2002 (XP)
- Word 2003

Task E Setting Startup Preferences

It's a good idea to set the default startup settings for each of your ACT! users. The most important preference in the Startup tab is the default database option. Out of the box, ACT! always opens the last correctly opened database. If you save a copy of your database and open it, ACT! will always attempt to open that copy until you click File | Open and open the original database. Specifying the default startup database will ensure that you're always opening the correct database.

To set the default startup options:

1. Click Tools | Preferences. The Preferences dialog box will appear.
2. Click the Startup tab.
3. In the Record Creation Settings area, select the default contact access security level for contacts, groups, and opportunities.
4. In the Startup database area, click the Named database option and browse to select a default startup database.
5. If you'd like to have ACT! automatically check for online program updates, check the Automatically check for updates every option.

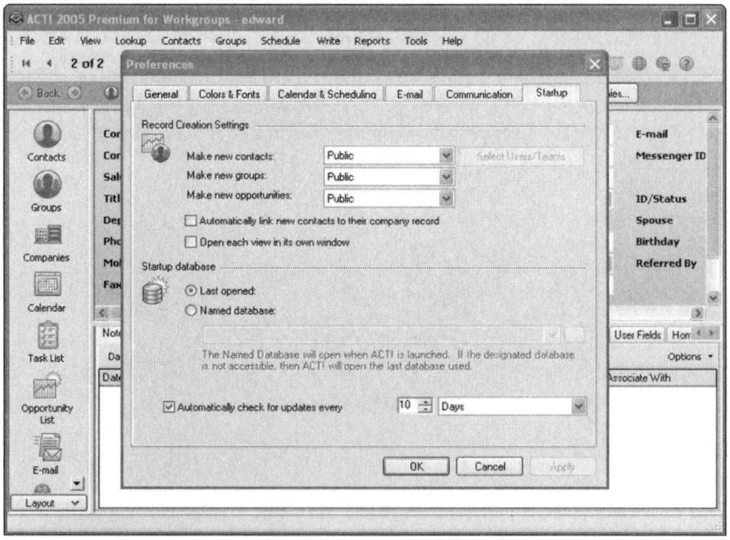

Setting default startup preferences

Default contact access

In the Startup tab, you can select the default startup contact access for new contacts entered by a user. Locate the Make new contacts drop-down in the Startup tab. Select Limited Access, and click the Select Users/Teams button. In the resulting dialog box, you'll be able to specify the users or teams that will have access to new contacts entered by a user. This setting does not change the contact access level for contacts already entered into your database.

Importing and Exporting

From time to time, you may need to import a list of data into your ACT! database. ACT! can import from tab-delimited and comma-delimited text files, dBASE compatible files, Palm Desktop data, Outlook, and other ACT! 3, 4, 5, 6, and 2005 databases. You may also need to export contacts in your ACT! database. ACT! can export basic contact information to a comma- or tab-delimited text file.

Task A Controlling Duplicate Merging During Imports

It may be a good idea to turn off duplicate checking before you import any contacts into your ACT! database. Whenever you import contacts into an ACT! database, ACT! automatically checks to see if each contact exists in the ACT! database. ACT! uses three fields to determine whether the contact is a duplicate: Company, Contact, and Phone. When ACT! finds a duplicate, it merges the existing ACT! record with the record you're importing.

To set the duplicate checking options:

1. Click Tools | Preferences.
2. In the General tab, click the Duplicate Checking button.
3. If you would like ACT! to check for duplicates when importing contacts, check the Enable duplicate checking in the database option.
4. If you have duplicate checking enabled, select up to three fields for ACT! to use when checking for duplicate contacts.

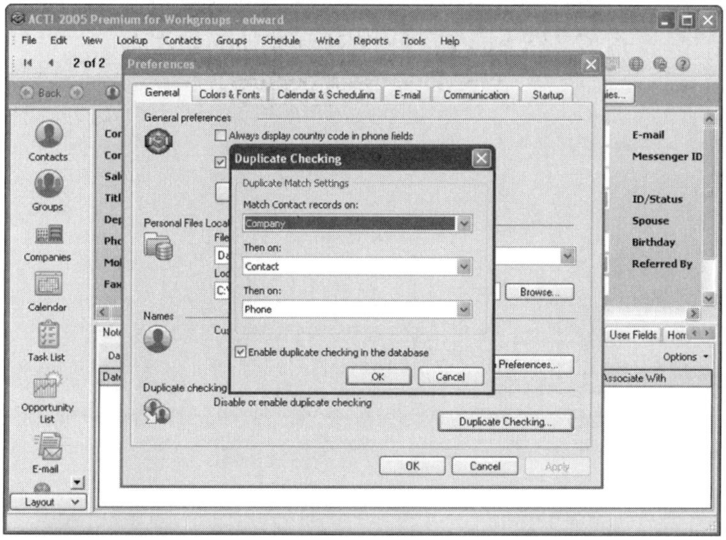

Setting the default duplicate matching fields

MigrateAdmin

If you need to perform advanced imports with ACT! 2005, check out MigrateAdmin, a cool utility from ASDS Computer, at http://www.asdscomputer.com.

Task B Importing a Text File

Just about every database program has the built-in ability to import and export delimited text files. There are two types of text files ACT! can import: tab-delimited files (.TXT files) and comma-delimited files (.CSV files).

To import a text file into your database:

1. Click File | Import.
2. When the welcome screen appears, click Next.
3. In the top drop-down, select the Text Delimited option.
4. Click the Browse button and double-click the text file you'd like to import. If you're importing a .CSV file, you'll need to select Comma Separated Values from the Files of type drop-down in the Open dialog box. Click Next.
5. Select to import either contact records, group records, or company records. If in doubt, choose the contact records option. Click Next.
6. Select whether you're importing a comma- or tab-delimited text file and choose to either import or ignore the first record in the text file. Click Next.
7. Select the Do not use a predefined map option and click Next.
8. Configure your field maps and click Finish.

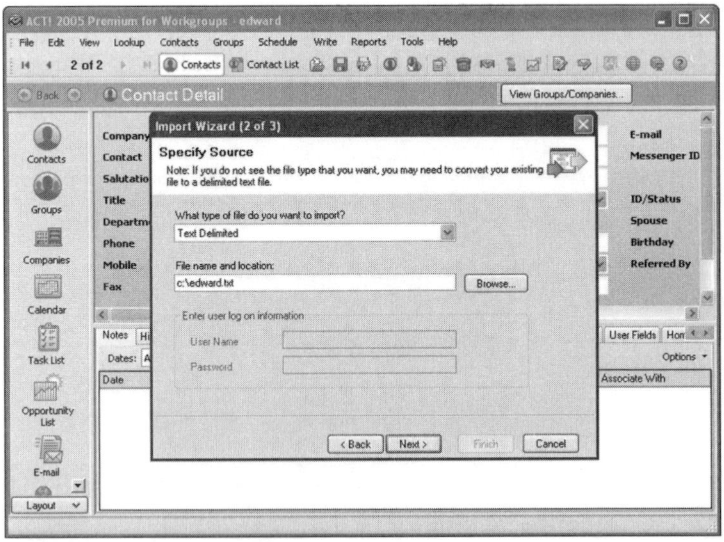

Importing a text file

Check data integrity

Before importing a text file, open the text file in Microsoft Excel and double-check the integrity of the data. You may also find it useful to add an extra column in Excel and auto-populate it with a unique word that you'll import into a data source field in ACT!. This way, you'll be able to easily look up all of the data in ACT! that you imported from this file.

Goldmine conversion service

Best Software offers a Goldmine conversion service. This service will convert all of your existing contacts, notes, activities, and more. Go to http://www.act.com and click the Database Services option for more detailed information.

Task C Exporting Contact Data

If you need to transfer your data into another database, send it to a mailing house, or look at it in another program like Excel, you'll need to know how to export contacts in your ACT! database to a text-delimited file.

To export contact data to a text file:

1. Click File | Export.
2. When the welcome screen appears, click Next.
3. In the top drop-down, select to export to a text-delimited file.
4. Click Browse and specify a filename and location for the text file. Click Next.
5. Select to export contact records, and specify the range of contacts that should be exported. Click Next.
6. Select to export a comma- or tab-delimited file, and choose the bottom option if you'd like to export field names.
7. Specify the fields to export.
8. Click Finish.

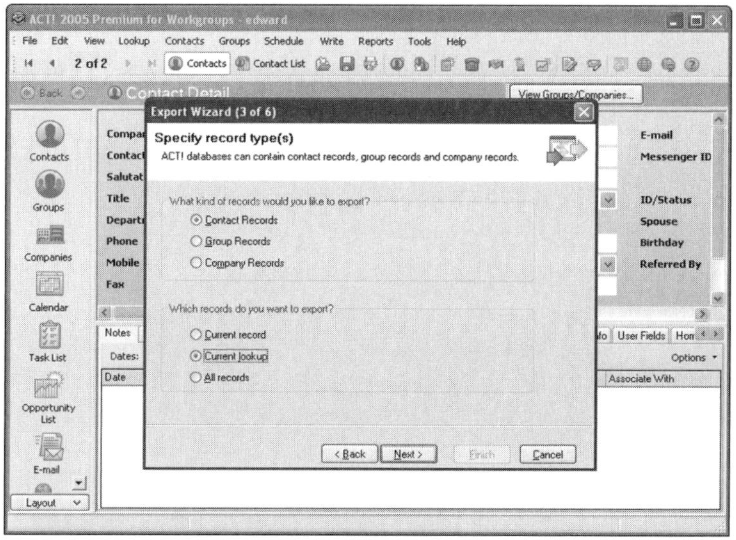

Exporting data to a text file

Exporting selected records

Perform a lookup of the contacts you'd like to export. Then, start the export. In the Export Wizard, one of your options will be to Only export the Current Lookup.

Export to Excel

In the Contact List view, configure the list to show just the fields you'd like to export. Then, perform a lookup of contacts. Click Tools | Export to Excel, and the information displayed in the Contact List view will automatically appear in Excel.

Chapter 21
Synchronization

Information for ACT! 3-6 Users

If you've synchronized ACT! in previous versions, you've probably been frustrated with the process. Older versions of ACT! synchronization required that ACT! send synchronization packets back and forth between all of the remote databases, and the setup process was cumbersome. In ACT! 2005, the synchronization process has been completely redesigned.

Main Differences Between ACT! 6.0 Sync and 2005 Sync

Synchronization in ACT! 2005 has been completely overhauled. User-to-user synchronization has been entirely replaced with a direct IP synchronization, and the concept of a "Send All" sync is gone. Because the databases connect directly with each other, you'll never have to wonder if a remote sync packet was ever applied to your master database.

How does ACT! 2005 sync differ from 6.0?

- A direct IP/HTTP connection is made with the server in ACT! 2005.
- The concept of a collection group was taken out and was replaced by a synchronization set model.
- Field level synchronization has been implemented instead of the traditional record level sync.
- When you delete a contact in a remote database, the contact is now automatically deleted in the master.
- The synchronization process can run on the server as a service.
- Multiple master databases can be synchronized on one server.
- Security is enforced throughout the entire synchronization process.
- Synchronization actually works now!

Setting Up Synchronization

Before setting up remote database synchronization, you'll need to combine all existing ACT! data into one master database. You should then open the master database on the server and perform the steps outlined in this section.

Task A Enabling Synchronization

Before any of the synchronization options will be available in your main database, you must first enable synchronization in the Synchronization Panel. This process is only done on the master database. Remote databases, by virtue of the fact that they were restored as remotes, will be automatically configured to synchronize.

Multi-tiered synchronization

ACT!'s synchronization model only allows you to have one main database per synchronization environment. All remote users synchronize into this central database.

To enable synchronization on a master database:

1. Open your main database. All data for remote users should exist in this database.
2. Click Tools | Synchronization Panel.
3. Click the Enable Synchronization option.
4. All of the other synchronization options for this database will now be available.

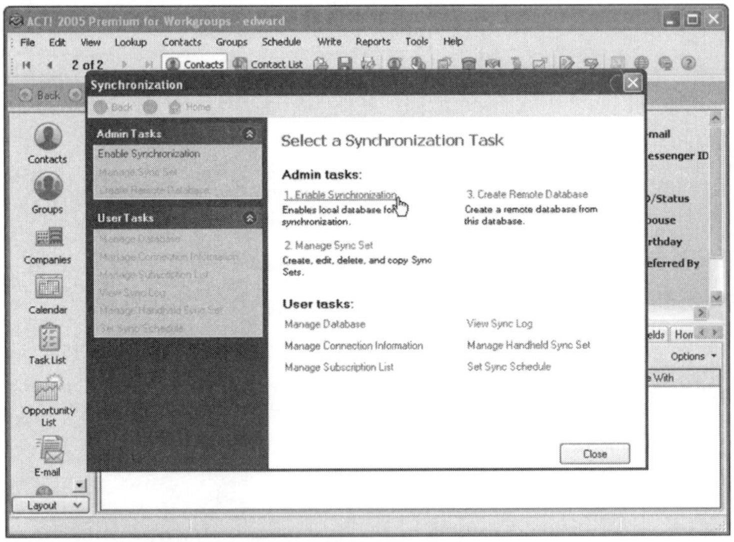

Enabling a master database for synchronization

Task B Creating a Sync Set

Before you create any remote synchronizing ACT! databases, you'll need to first create a sync set. The sync set defines the range of contacts that a remote database should receive in the synchronization. The sync set also defines the users that will be logged into the remote database. You should define a separate sync set for each remote user; the sync sets can be configured to either send all records to the remote user or just the contacts that match an advanced query.

To create a sync set:

1. Click Tools | Synchronization Panel.
2. Click the Manage Sync Set option.
3. Click the Create New Sync Set option on the left side of the Synchronization dialog box.
4. Give the sync set a name and description. Click Next.
5. Select the user(s) that should have login rights to the remote database and click the > button to add them to the list on the right. Click Next.
6. If you would like the remote database to receive all contacts in the database, then choose the Synchronize all available contacts option. If you want to define a range of contacts for the remote database to receive, then select the Define Sync Set criteria option.
7. If you chose to create a sync set criteria, click the Create Criteria button. The advanced query interface will appear. If you create an advanced query in this window, ACT! will only synchronize contacts that match the query.
8. Click Finish.

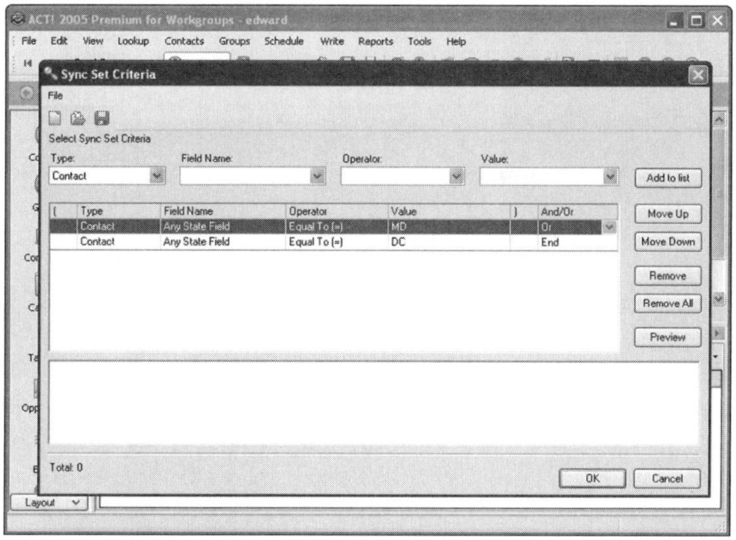

Defining the sync set criteria

Sync sets are dynamic

Let's say that you have ten salespeople on staff. You've created a salesperson field in the database. For each remote user, you create a sync set that will only send the contacts with a specific value in the salesperson field to each remote user.

If you add a new contact to the database, and if you choose the user's name from this salesperson field, ACT! will automatically synchronize that contact down to the remote user because the contact matches the sync set criteria. If you change the value in the salesperson field for an existing contact, ACT! will automatically remove the contact from the original salesperson's database and reassign it to the new salesperson.

Prerequisites

Before managing a subscription list, you must

- enable synchronization
- define a sync set for the user whose subscription list you'd like to modify

Changing the subscription list

Both the administrator and the remote user can modify the subscription list. Even if the contact is not part of the sync set, a remote user has the option to add the contact to the subscription list if the user has access to the contact.

Task C Managing the Subscription List

The administrator can set up a sync set criteria (see Task B) to configure which contacts should display in a remote database. In addition to this sync set criteria, you can add additional contacts to the list that appears on a remote database by adding them to the subscription list.

To manage the subscription list:

1. Click Tools | Synchronize.
2. Click the Manage Subscription List option.
3. Select a sync set and click Next.
4. For the sync set, ACT! will display all of the contacts that could be displayed on the remote database. A check mark will appear in the Sync Set column for each contact that is currently displayed in the remote database.
5. On the left side of the Synchronization dialog box, click the Add Contacts to Sync Set option to manually add contacts to the subscription list. Any contacts manually added to the subscription list will display in the remote database.

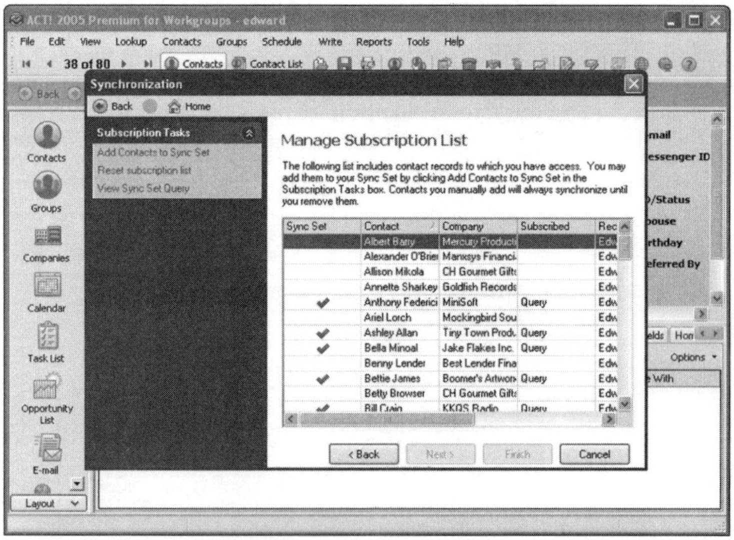

Adding contacts to the subscription list

Task D Creating a Remote Database

Once synchronization has been enabled on your master database and a sync set has been configured for each remote database, you can create the remote databases. This task must be performed on the server, and it may take a while on large databases. ACT! will create the remote databases as .RDB backup files that can be restored onto any computer running ACT!.

To create a remote database:

1. Click Tools | Synchronize.
2. Click the Create Remote Database option.
3. Enter a name for the remote database. Note that this name must be unique within the server and synchronization environment.
4. Click the Browse button to select a location where ACT! will create the remote database backup file. Click Next.
5. Select a sync set to use for this remote database. Click Next.
6. Select whether or not to allow database supplemental files (layouts, reports, templates, and so on) to synchronize.
7. Select whether or not to allow attachments (items added to the Documents tab in the Contacts view) to synchronize.
8. Set the database expiration period. Click Next.
9. Select whether the remote database will synchronize via network or HTTP synchronization. Only change the other server settings if instructed to do so by your network administrator. Click Next.
10. If you would like to password-protect the remote database backup (.RDB) file, select the option to password-protect.
11. Click Finish. ACT! will create the remote database backup file in the location you specified.

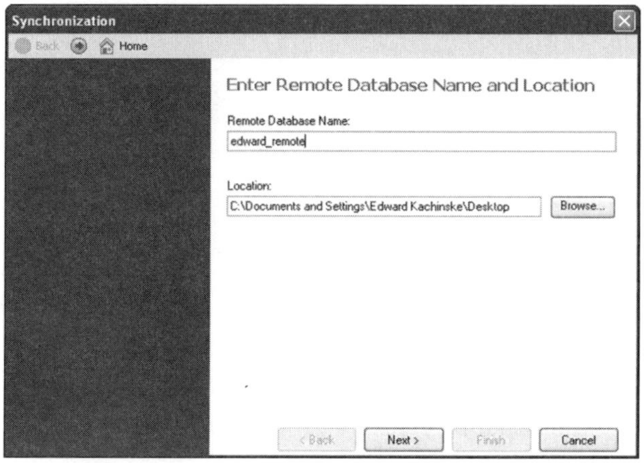

Creating a remote database

Database expiration warning!

Databases in ACT! 2005 will expire if not synchronized with the master database regularly. When setting up a database, you have the option to set expiration for a remote database. Choose this option carefully. If you choose to expire a database after 30 days, and if one of your users goes for 31 days without synchronizing, the database will never synchronize with the mater database again. In this situation, you would have to export the data back into the master database and rebuild the remote.

Supplemental files

If you choose to not synchronize database supplemental files, you will not be able to change your mind later on without rebuilding the remote database.

Task E Restoring a Remote Database

Once you have defined a sync set and created a remote database, you'll need to restore this remote database backup file onto your remote user's computer. This will require that you physically copy the .RDB file from the server onto the remote computer.

To restore a remote database:

1. Copy the .RDB file onto the remote computer.
2. Open ACT!.
3. Click File | Restore | Database.
4. Choose the Unpack and Restore Remote Database option. Click OK.
5. Click the top Browse button and locate the .RDB file.
6. If you would like to restore the database in a different folder than the one displayed, click the bottom Browse button to specify a new location. Click OK. ACT! will restore the database and its supplemental files.
7. Click File | Open to open the database.

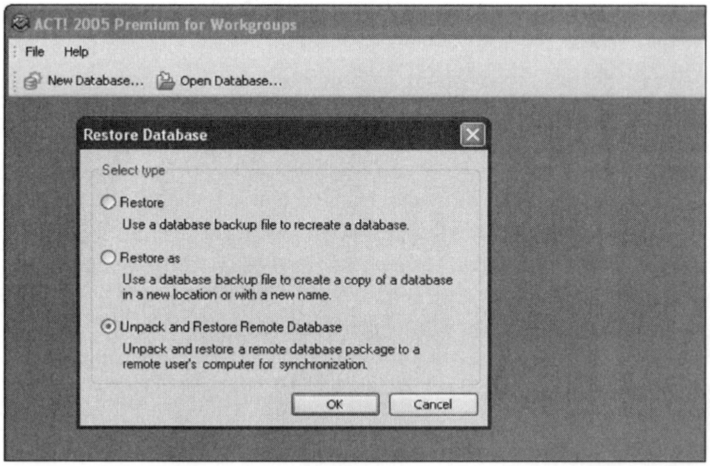

Restoring a remote database on a remote computer

Moving the .RDB

For large databases, the remote database backup (.RDB) file may be quite large—possibly too large to fit on a CD. This may present a logistical challenge when configuring your remote users, so be sure to plan ahead.

Performing a Sync

In ACT! 2005, synchronization is always initiated from the remote users. On the network server, you'll run the network or Internet (HTTP) sync service that will listen for incoming sync requests. Whenever a remote user synchronizes, the remote database will make a direct connection with the server and updated information will be sent in both directions.

Task A Installing the Sync Service

You can install either the network or Internet sync services on the ACT! server. These small programs, when running, will listen for incoming sync requests from your remote users. If your server is outside the firewall, you should use the Internet sync service. If your server is inside the firewall, and your remote users are on the local network or VPN, you should install the network sync service.

To install the sync service:

1. Insert the ACT! installation CD #1.
2. Select the ACT! Synchronization Services option.
3. Select to install either the network sync service or the ACT! Internet service.
4. The InstallShield Wizard for the sync service will appear. Follow the on-screen instructions to install, and accept all of the default settings.
5. Click Start | Programs | ACT! Network Sync Service | ACT! Network Sync. (Or Internet sync, if you're outside the firewall.)
6. The ACT! Network Sync Service options will appear. Click Add to a database. In the Database Machine field, type the name of your main ACT! server.
7. In the Database Name field, type the name of your master ACT! database.
8. Click OK.
9. Click the Start Sync Service button. ACT! will monitor for incoming sync requests.

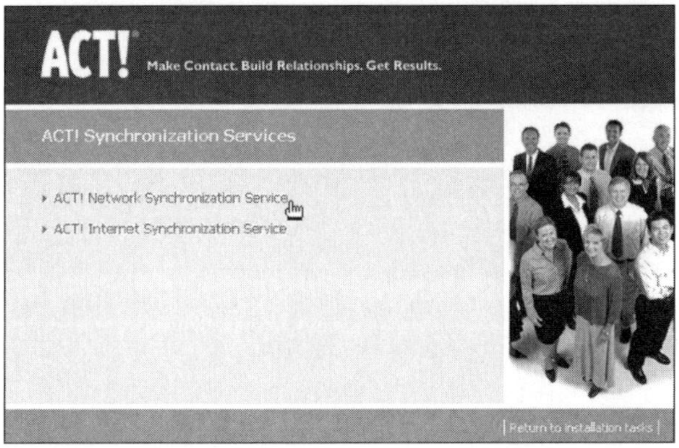

Installing the synchronization service

View currently running services

You can view all of the services running on your computer by clicking Start | Control Panel. Double-click the Administrative Tools option. Then, double-click Services.

Synchronizing multiple databases

In the sync service options area, you can add multiple databases. If you are maintaining multiple databases on a server, all databases can listen for incoming sync requests at the same time.

Task B Performing a Synchronization

If the sync service is running on your server, you should be able to perform a manual synchronization from any workstation on the network or with access to your Internet sync server. The synchronization is always initiated from the remote database.

To perform a synchronization:

1. On the remote computer, click Tools | Synchronize | Synchronize Now. ACT! will initiate the synchronization between your database and the server database.
2. While the Sync in Progress dialog box is displayed, you can continue working on your database.
3. Click the Auto minimize in taskbar option if you'd like ACT! to automatically minimize the Sync in Progress dialog box.
4. When the synchronization is complete, the Sync in Progress dialog box will simply go away.

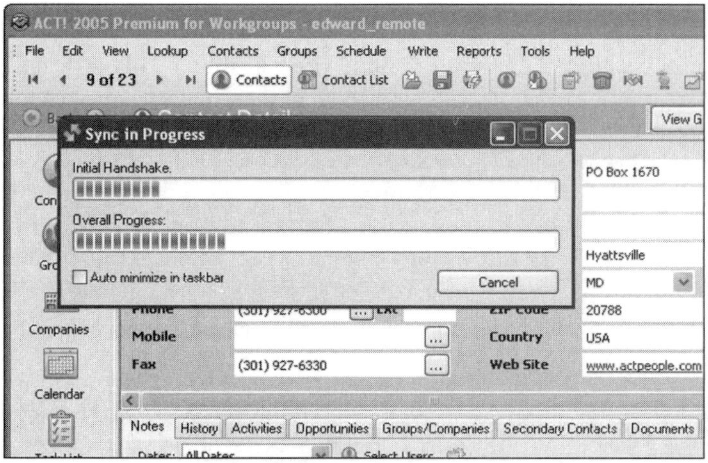

Performing a synchronization on a remote database

Set a sync schedule

If you want to have ACT! automatically synchronize on a schedule, click Tools | Synchronization Panel and click the Set Sync Schedule option.

Task C Setting an Automatic Sync Schedule

It's easy to set an automatic sync schedule to keep in regular contact with the master database. You can set ACT! to synchronize hourly, daily, weekly, or monthly at a specific time. Note that the synchronization will only be performed if ACT! is open on the remote computer and the sync service is running on the server.

To set an automatic sync schedule:

1. Click Tools | Preferences.
2. Click the Set Sync Schedule option.
3. Select to set either an hourly, a daily, a weekly, or a monthly sync. On the right side of the Synchronization dialog box, select the specific options for the frequency of the automatic sync.
4. In the Start Date and Start Time drop-downs, select the first occurrence of the sync.
5. Click Finish.

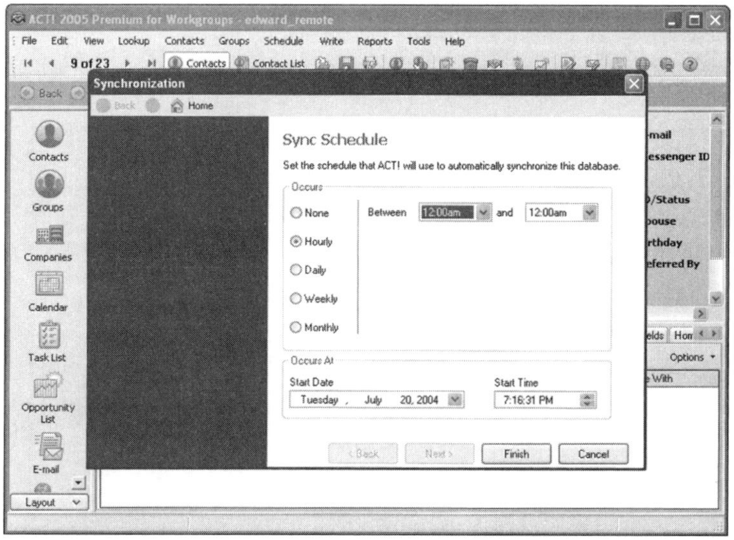

Setting an automatic sync schedule

Administering Synchronization

From time to time, you may need to re-create a remote database or troubleshoot synchronization problems. The tasks outlined in this section will help you perform the most often-used sync administrative tasks.

Task A Re-creating a Remote Database

If a database passes its expiration date, gets corrupted, or is lost for whatever reason, you may need to re-create the remote database. ACT! 2005 includes a feature that will re-create any remote database using the information currently in the master database. When ACT! re-creates the remote database, it will produce an .RDB database backup file. You'll then need to unpack and restore the backup file to the remote computer.

Creating a database

The steps outlined in this task assume that you have already set up a remote database. If you are setting up a remote database for the first time, you'll need to use the Create Remote Database option in the Synchronization Panel to create an .RDB remote database package.

To re-create a remote database:

1. On the server database, click Tools | Synchronization Panel.
2. Click the Manage Database option.
3. Highlight a remote database and click the Re-create Database option.
4. Select a location for the remote backup database file.
5. Click OK.

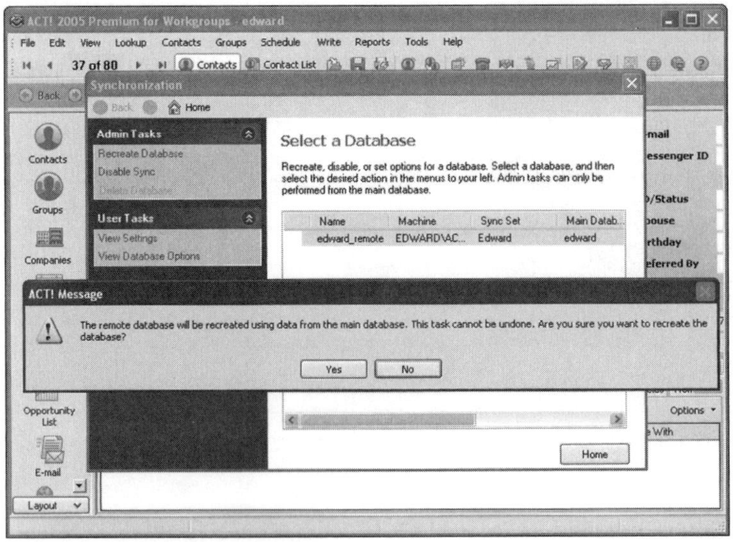

Recreating a remote database on the server console

Task B Viewing the Synchronization Log

If you need to keep tabs on who is synchronizing with your master database and what information is being transferred during the synchronizations, you can consult the synchronization log on the ACT! server.

To view the synchronization log:

1. Click Tools | Synchronization Panel.
2. Click the View Sync Log option. The synchronization log will appear. The log contains detailed information about each synchronization session.

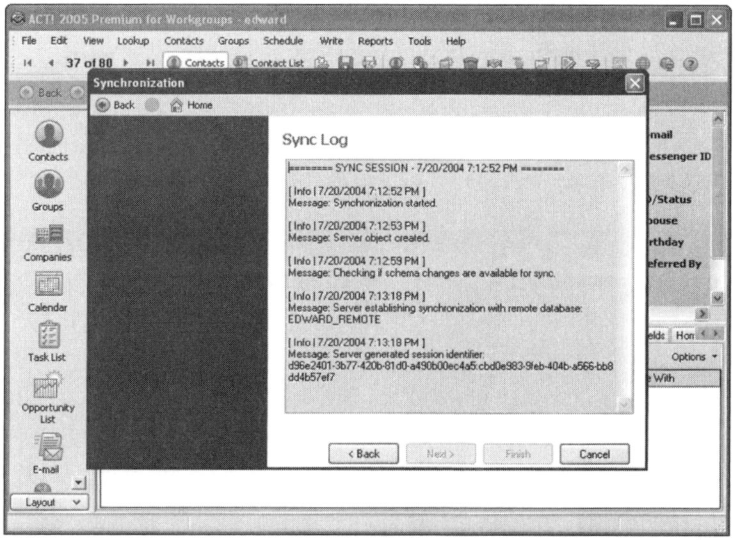

Viewing the synchronization log

Copy to Word

In the Synchronization Panel, the window for viewing the sync log is relatively small. Right-click in the sync log viewing area and choose the Select All option. Then, right click and select the Copy option. Paste the text into a Word document, and you'll have a larger viewing area with search capabilities.

ACT! 6.0 users

Previous versions of ACT! kept synchronization log information in the Notes/History tab of the My Record of the synchronizing user; this information didn't synchronize to remote users. The new consolidated sync log feature is a refreshing change for longtime ACT! users.

Task C Looking Up Synchronized Records

The sync logs will show you how many contacts, notes, activities, and so on were transferred during any of the sync sessions. But you might need more detail. It's sometimes useful to know specifically what data was synchronized up from a remote user in a certain time frame.

Looking up a sync set

Click Lookup | Advanced | Sync Set to perform a lookup of all contacts that are included in a remote user's sync set.

To lookup synchronized records:

1. Open your master database on the server.
2. Click Lookup | Advanced | Last Synchronized. The Last Synchronized dialog box appears.
3. Select the Last Session option or select a date range. (ACT! will find all contacts modified by remote users and synchronized up to the master database during this time frame.)
4. Select to search for note, opportunity, history, activity, or contact updates.
5. In the Database drop-down, select a remote database.
6. Click Find Now.

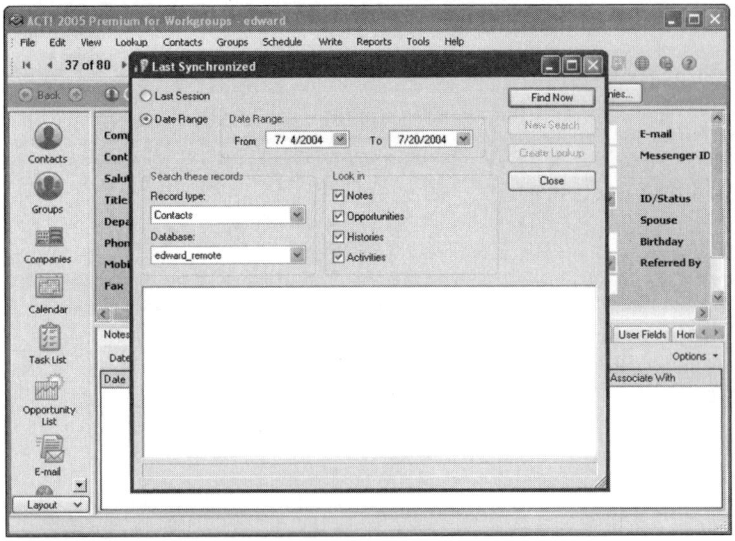

Looking up contacts synchronized up to the master database in a date range

Chapter 22
Support and Troubleshooting

Support for ACT!

ACT! has over five million users worldwide, and with such a strong user base comes a strong support network. If you run into problems with your database, chances are good that there's a help option available that meets your price requirements.

Task A Finding ACT! Certified Consultants (ACT! CCs)

There are more than 700 ACT! Certified Consultants in the world. About half of them are located in the United States, but if you live elsewhere in the world, chances are good that there will be at least a few in your area.

To find your local ACT! Certified Consultant:

1. Point your Web browser to http://www.act.com/acc.
2. Follow the on-screen instructions to locate an ACT! CC in your country, state, or city.
3. If you do not have Internet access, locate the listing of ACT! CCs inside the ACT! box.

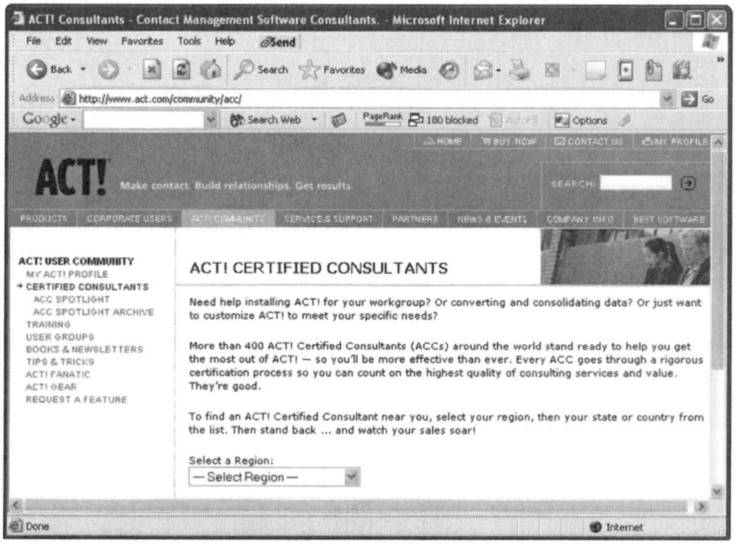

The ACT! Certified Consultant search page

Choosing the right ACT! CC

Before settling on a specific ACT! CC, take a moment to call everyone in your area. Most ACT! CCs specialize in a particular aspect of ACT!, so you'll want to be sure to find one that's right for you. Expect to pay $150–$200/hour for a seasoned consultant.

Task B Finding ACT! Premier Trainers

Within the ACT! Certified Consultant's community, many ACT! CCs also hold the ACT! Premier Trainer designation. ACT! Premier Trainers specialize in delivering custom ACT! training services on your site or in a dedicated facility. At press time, the ACT! Premier Trainer program was limited to the United States and Canada.

To find an ACT! Premier Trainer in your area:

1. Point your Web browser to http://www.act.com/apt.
2. Follow the on-screen instructions to locate an ACT! Premier Trainer in your area.
3. If you do not have Internet access, locate the listing of ACT! CCs inside the ACT! box.

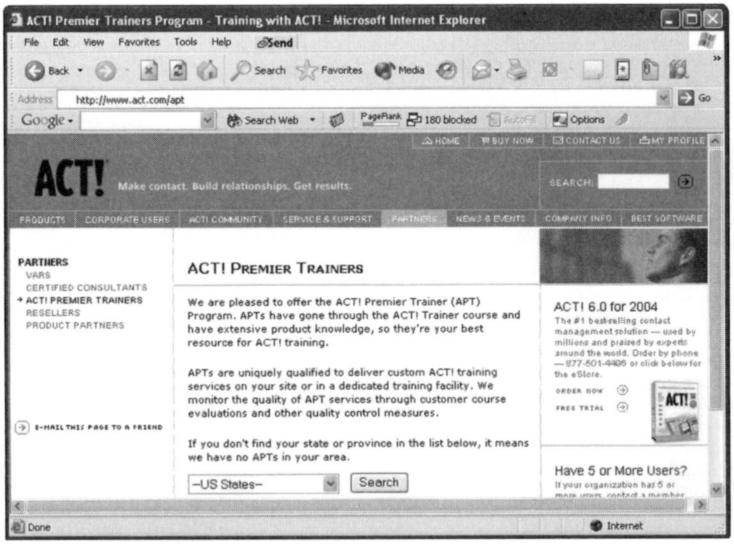

The ACT! Premier Trainer search page

Regional training centers

Many regional training centers, like CompUSA and New Horizons, offer ACT! training classes. Be careful about setting your expectations for these generic ACT! training classes, though. You can often accomplish more by hiring an ACT! Premier Trainer for a couple of hours than you can sitting through a full day generic training class.

Task C Finding ACT! Advantage Technical Support

ACT! offers many options for call-in technical support. The most cost-effective way to get support from ACT! is usually to join an ACT! Advantage program. ACT! Advantage members can call technical support an unlimited number of times within a year timeframe, and they get extra freebees—like discounts on database repair services and password removal services.

To find ACT! technical support options:

1. Call the ACT! Support Sales Department at (800) 992-4564.
2. To find support information on the Web, point your Web browser to http://www.act.com. Click the Service & Support option and select Support Plans.

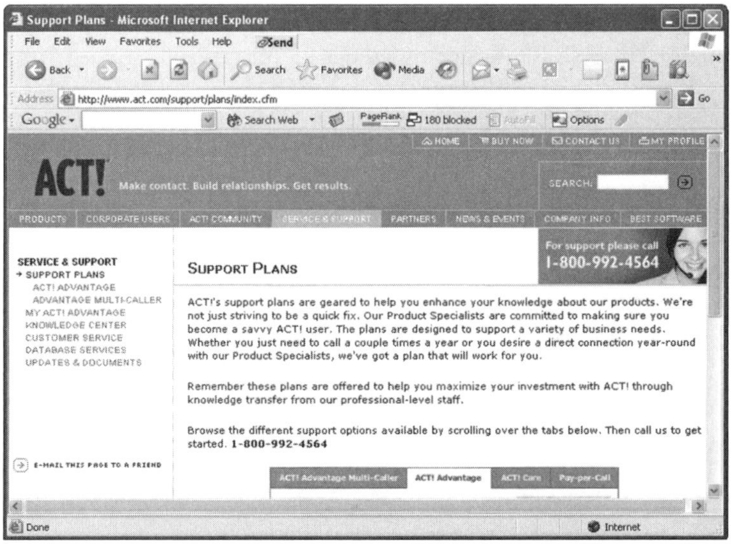

The ACT! technical support page

Technical support costs

At the time of printing, ACT! offered the following plans for technical support contracts:

- **ACT! Advantage**. Unlimited calls for a single user. $299/year.
- **ACT! Advantage Multi-Caller**. Unlimited calls for five users. $599/year.
- **ACT! Care**. Up to 5 calls per year. $199/year.
- **Pay-Per-Call**. $50.00 for the first 10 minutes. $5.00 for each additional minute.

Troubleshooting

The ACT! Knowledge Base contains a collection of tens of thousands of documents, workarounds, bug fixes, and other useful items. If you've encountered a problem, crash, or feature need, chances are good that your issue is documented in the searchable ACT! Knowledge Base.

Task A Searching the Knowledge Base

The ACT! Knowledge Base is an online searchable database of documents related to ACT!. Before calling technical support, it's a good idea to search the Knowledge Base for your issue. Most of the time, you can fix problems with the database using information in the Knowledge Base.

To search the ACT! Knowledge Base:

1. Point your Web browser to http://www.act.com/search.
2. The searchable Knowledge Base appears. Enter a keyword, error message, or phrase to search for documents related to your issue.
3. If you get too many results, try narrowing the search to just a specific product (like ACT! 2005 for Windows or ACT! for Web) and try the search again.

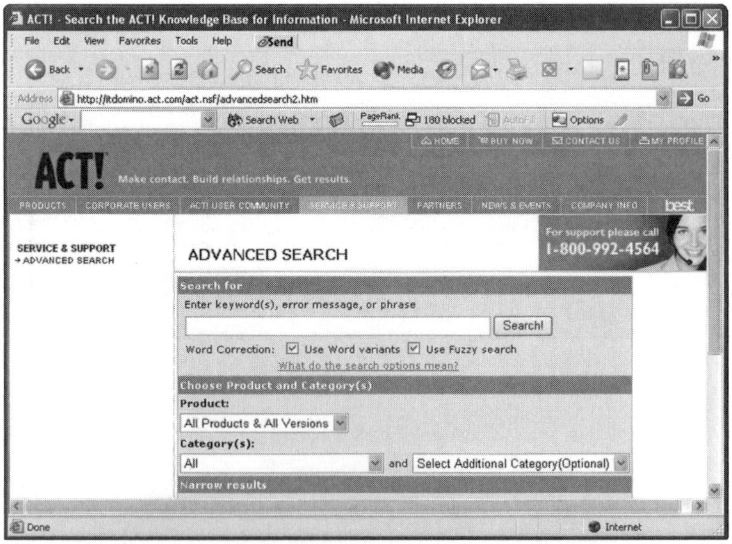

The ACT! Knowledge Base

ACT! user groups

Most metropolitan areas have locally-sponsored ACT! user groups. To find a user group in your area, go to http://www.act.com/usergroups.

Appendix
ACT! Add-Ons

One of the greatest things about ACT! is the fact that there are literally hundreds of add-on products that give the program added functionality. Because ACT! is used by four million users (and those are just the ones that paid for the product!) there's a huge market to fill the holes where ACT! lacks functionality.

There are two major collections of ACT! add-on products on the Web: the ACT! Add-On Store and ACT! Solutions.

The ACT! Add-On Store

http://www.actaddons.com
(800) 806-5288

The ACT! Add-On Store contains the largest collection of ACT! Add-on products. The store is run by Sharon Randall of SJR Productions, a longtime ACT! fanatic and all-around great person. In 2004, Sharon won the Lifetime Achievement Award from Best Software for her contributions to the add-on community over the past 15 years. Sharon's ACT! Add-On Store has a full service call center that provides customer service, and their friendly staff can answer most questions about ACT! add-on products.

ACT! Solutions

http://www.actsolutions.com

The official Best Software add-on Web site sells only the major add-on products for ACT!. The selection isn't as good as you'll find at the ACT! Add-On Store, but the site is still worth a visit.

Noteworthy Add-Ons

Of the many hundreds of ACT! add-ons available at the ACT! Add-On Store and ACT! Solutions Store, a few are exceptional and worthy of a special mention in this book. In the sections below, we will outline a few of the best ACT! add-on vendors. Within each add-on vendor section, we'll discuss the best add-ons from the vendor.

ASDS Computer

http://www.asdscomputer.com
info@asdscomputer.com
(888) 202-3573

ASDS Computer is by far the market leader for strong, robust ACT! add-on products. One reason for this is that the company snagged two of the most talented ACT! programmers, Duane Anderson and Jason Risch.

For previous versions of ACT!, ASDS created AutoAdmin, a program that automatically performed basic administrative tasks on a scheduled basis.

ASDS MedleyAdmin ($99)

MedleyAdmin is absolutely hands-down our favorite ACT! 2005 add-on product. Of the hundreds of available ACT! add-ons, it's one of only a few that we actually use in our office.

The program is a collection of really cool and useful tools that enhance the ACT! 2005 experience. In the industry, we've unofficially labeled this add-on "ACT! 2006" because it includes almost all of the features that *should* have been included in ACT! 2005 but weren't. A few of the best features included in MedleyAdmin are:

- **Tabs within Tabs**. The program includes a control that lets you create a tab within a tab or within the upper pane of the contact layout.
- **Personal Dashboard**. This feature gives you a centralized view within ACT! that displays critical daily information.
- **AutoFill City/State Fields**. Enter the zip code, and MedleyAdmin automatically fills in your city and state field based on the information entered into the zip code field.
- **Group/Company Improvements**. For those who have used ACT! in the past, the new Groups view interface is really annoying. That's because ACT! took away the tree-like structure that used to display subgroups under their parent groups. MedleyAdmin includes a tool that will replace ACT!'s new interface with a much more usable alternative. Also included in the product is a group/company calendar view.
- **Group Lookup Improvements**. If you ever need to do lookups of contacts in multiple groups, or if you need to find groupless contacts, MedleyAdmin adds this functionality.
- **Mass Update Contact Access**. This feature alone is well worth the price of the product. With MedleyAdmin, you can automatically update the contact access security levels for multiple contacts at once.

ASDS MigrateAdmin ($299)

MigrateAdmin converts data from other sources into ACT! 2005. At the time of this printing, MigrateAdmin had conversion support for GoldMine and Access. If you're importing either of these data types, then MigrateAdmin is a must-have.

MigrateAdmin is an intuitive wizard-based application that lets you convert data into ACT! 2005 format. Within the program's migration wizard, you can make adjustments for field types and field lengths, and you can even create new ACT! fields on the fly. The wizard also lets you split or concatenate fields as needed.

Best of all, MigrateAdmin converts all basic contact data as well as custom fields, histories, notes, activities, and sales data.

ASDS DocAdmin ($149)

If you're looking to create a paperless office, DocAdmin will be your best friend. The program allows you to scan documents into the Documents tab of ACT! 2005 with a single mouse click. It automatically names the file and attaches it to the ACT! contact record in PDF format. Only one DocAdmin license is needed for the scanning workstation. All other users can view the scanned documents without a DocAdmin installed on their computers.

FaxAdmin ($79)

FaxAdmin allows you to fax right from within ACT! 2005. FaxAdmin supports faxing via WinFax and MS Fax. Using this tool, you can easily write single personalized faxes; it will also allow you to perform a mass fax.

Crossroads Automation Solutions

http://www.crystalclearreports.com
tami@casmt.com
(877) 885-4ACT (4228)

Veteran ACT! add-on developers Tami Sauer and Stan Smith from Crossroads Automation Solutions have done it again with the latest versions of their ACT! reporting software. Everyone within the ACT! consultant community knows Tami Sauer as the "Crystal Goddess." She's the world expert on integrating ACT! and Crystal Reports. In fact, if you hire an ACT! Certified Consultant to write your Crystal Reports, chances are good that the job will actually get outsourced to Tami. So if you need to customize any of the reports included in Tami's product, Crystal Clear Reports, or if you have a special reporting need, you'd be wise to give her a ring.

Crystal Clear Reports ($199)

Crystal Clear Reports (CCR), an add-on product from Crossroads Automation Solutions, integrates ACT! and Crystal Reports. Though you can write Crystal Reports without CCR, the add-on product offers several compelling features.

With CCR, you can run a Crystal Report right from the Reports menu in ACT!. You can also build the record selection into your reports, so there's no need to perform a lookup of contacts before running a report. Reports can be exported to Excel, Word, PDF, and XML. The new version of CCR also offers a customizable menu structure.

CCR ships with over 50 reports that, quite frankly, will cover 95 percent of most people's reporting needs. You do not need a Crystal Reports license to run Crystal Clear Reports. Every user who wants comprehensive reports really should buy this product.

Crystal Clear Reports Auto Report ($299–499)

The Crystal Clear Reports Auto Report add-on product will schedule and run Crystal Reports with no user intervention. This is especially useful for situations where your reports take a long time to finish. When the reports finish running, you can have them automatically saved to a network drive or e-mailed to key staff. The basic version of the product costs $299, and the professional version is $499. The professional version includes the e-mailing options.

eGrabber

http://www.egrabber.com
info@asdscomputer.com
888-202-3573

For anyone who routinely transcribes information into an ACT! database, the eGrabber suite of products will be well worth the investment. Each of the eGrabber add-ons let you "grab" contacts from non-standard and non-importable sources and instantly import them into your ACT! database. The company behind these products is solid, and their products have been best sellers for many years.

AddressGrabber ($70–130)

AddressGrabber is the flagship product in the eGrabber suite. The concept behind AddressGrabber is simple: It lets you highlight a person's contact information, grab it, and import the parsed address into ACT!. The next time you receive an e-mail from a new contact, AddressGrabber would let you highlight the information in the person's e-mail signature and hit a hotkey to transfer the contact data into ACT!. When AddressGrabber sends the data into ACT!, it first prompts you to confirm that it has parsed the name, address, telephone, fax, and other fields correctly. It's surprisingly accurate.

AddressGrabber comes in a couple flavors. The standard version ($70) will "grab" information into ACT!. A higher priced ($130) business edition will transfer ACT! contacts to QuickBooks, Peachtree, UPS, FedEx, online forms, and other applications.

Web Response Grabber ($300–750)

If you have a form on your Web site that automatically sends an e-mail to someone in your office, Web Response Grabber can automatically import the contents of each e-mail into ACT!. You can set it to automatically scan for new form e-mails, and it can even schedule a follow-up activity for each newly created contact. Like AddressGrabber, Web Response Grabber comes in two editions, standard and business. The business edition works with other programs, like Goldmine, Outlook, Excel, and Access.

ListGrabber ($250)

If you ever get a text database that isn't in any sort of standard or delimited format, ListGrabber will quickly become your best friend. ListGrabber performs the same tasks as AddressGrabber, but it will do so with multiple contacts at once. If, for example, you have a 30-page Word document that contains labels for 900 contacts, ListGrabber will analyze the document, figure out how many contacts are contained in the document, parse them into individual contacts, and import them into ACT!.

Index

B

C

D

E

G

H

I

P

S

T

U

V

W